THE PLANTAGENET SOCIALITE

THE
PLANTAGENET
SOCIALITE

JAN-MARIE KNIGHTS

AMBERLEY

First published 2023

Amberley Publishing
The Hill, Stroud
Gloucestershire, GL5 4EP

www.amberley-books.com

British Library Cataloguing in Publication Data.
A catalogue record for this book is available from the British Library.

ISBN 978 1 3981 0892 9 (hardback)
ISBN 978 1 3981 0893 6 (ebook)

1 2 3 4 5 6 7 8 9 10

Typesetting by SJmagic DESIGN SERVICES, India.
Printed in the UK.

Contents

Introduction

Three hundred years of Plantagenet rule in England saw countless murders and bloody struggles against a backdrop of warring families, deeds of chivalry and complex romances.

Of Henry II it was said, 'Now in England, now in France, he must fly rather than travel by boat or horse'. His power struggle with one man, wanting to be more than king, ended in Thomas Becket's murder in Canterbury Cathedral. His son, Richard I, gained the respect of Saladin but the hatred of the French king, whose propaganda led to his trial and imprisonment by the Holy Roman Emperor, which ended only after England paid a huge ransom for his return. His brother John was labelled 'evil, cruel and tyrannical'; his disagreements with the Pope ended with England under interdict, and his disagreements with his barons led to the signing of *Magna Carta*. Then came the Edwards. To subdue the Welsh, Edward I built a chain of castles so strong we still visit them today. Edward II may or may not have been killed courtesy of a red-hot poker. Edward III lived through the Black Death, estimated to have killed three and a half million people in England alone, and turned Windsor into the Plantagenet Camelot.

In this book you can follow the Peasants' Revolt, glorious Agincourt, the War of the Roses and the deaths of the 'Princes in the Tower' and judge for yourself if the legends live up to the truths revealed in contemporary letters, accounts and chronicles. Let this book transport you back in time to give a socialite's view of the courts, scandals, tragedies and passions of those fourteen distant kings we call the Plantagenets.

Backdrop

A Sea Change

On Christmas Day 1066, William the Conqueror, Duke of Normandy walked down the nave of Westminster Abbey to be crowned King of England. Loud shouts and cheers greeted him, and the guards outside, fearing the clamour heralded an uprising, rushed in brandishing weapons. The terrified congregation fled, leaving only the alarmed clergymen anointing the new king.

The nobles may have cheered but the English people detested and resented their Norman overlords while they in turn were despised by the Normans. The comprehensive survey known as *Domesday Book* reveals that by 1086, apart from two lords, the Anglo-Saxon aristocracy had been completely replaced by French-speaking barons who lived in castles built to crush the natives, eating and sleeping alongside garrisons ready to issue forth to subdue any hint of rebellion.

William might have become king in England but in Normandy he was a duke who was required to give homage to the King of France for his duchy. The barons who had accompanied him on his conquest now held estates in England and Normandy. In a political sense, crossing the Channel became as inconsequential as crossing the River Thames. Normandy and its castles were eyed jealously, and not just by strangers.

William's eldest son, Robert Curthose, was first. After his younger brothers emptied a full chamber-pot over his head from a gallery above, Robert, in his mid-twenties and egged on by his friends, stormed after them. Hearing the commotion, William stepped in to stop him. Adding insult to injury, neither nine-year-old Henry nor the teenage William Rufus were scolded for 'casting water and their filth' over him. Fuming, Robert departed. Soon he was attempting to seize his father's capital of Rouen.

Like the rulers who followed him, William spent a lot of his reign campaigning overseas. He died in Normandy on 9 September 1087, confessing on his deathbed he had lied to the Pope and unjustly conquered England. He willed Normandy to Robert and England to red-haired William. His corpulent body was forced into an undersized coffin, and as it was carried into the Church of St Stephen in Caen it burst open, the stench of his corpse filling the church.

William 'Rufus' was duly elected King William II, but a year later Bishop Odo of Bayeux, backed by rebellious barons, tried to depose him in favour of Robert, who was threatening to invade. However, Robert failed to turn up. Instead, William invaded Normandy and defeated his older brother, who decided he would take 'the cross' and go on crusade to Jerusalem. Many believed he did it to solve his financial problems for it was rumoured he stayed in bed for lack of clothes. He pawned Normandy to William for 10,000 marks.

On the morning of 2 August 1100, William Rufus was joking with his attendants while they laced up his boots. A few hours later he was dead, killed by a stray arrow while out hunting in the New Forest. Among the party was his younger brother, thirty-two-year-old Henry, who raced to Winchester to take possession of the royal treasury before William's body was even lifted. He thereafter rode pell-mell to Westminster and was crowned three days later. In November, King Henry I married Matilda (baptised Edith), the daughter of King Malcolm III of Scotland, who was pleased with her tall, broad-chested, black-haired, blue-eyed bridegroom.

A year later Robert returned from the Crusades. In a bid to supplant his brother, he landed with an army at Portsmouth. Marching to Winchester, news came to him that Queen Matilda had given birth a few days before and Robert declared 'his heart' would not allow him to 'war by an attack upon a woman in childbed'. Henry and Robert pitched armed camps near to each other around Hampton. Envoys passed between them and brotherly affection resurfaced when they met face-to-face. Henry kept England while Robert kept Normandy with an annual pension of £2,000 from his brother. For months, Robert stayed at the English court enjoying the music, company and feasting. Once he returned overseas, Robert continually agitated against his younger brother and the duchy became a powerbase for discontented barons. In 1105, Henry went on the attack.

While her husband was overseas, Queen Matilda was undertaking her own campaign. Summoned to attend upon her, Matilda's brother David found her washing, wiping and kissing the feet of several lepers. Aghast he said, 'Surely, if the king knew of it, he would never again place his own lips in contact with yours.' His sister laughed and told him he should learn by her example. Chuckling, he left, replying never would he do as he saw her doing.

In 1106 at the Battle of Tinchebray, Henry captured Duke Robert. He would spend the next twenty-eight years in luxurious captivity, first at Devizes and then at Cardiff. It suited his preferred indolent lifestyle. Normandy belonged unconditionally to Henry I, but now his reign was spent in repelling invasions by the King of France, the counts of Anjou and Flanders, and, though he had treated them honourably and generously, his rebel barons. Continuous warfare and effective alliances required funding and he had to make constant requests for taxes and subsidies. He betrothed his six-year-old daughter Matilda in April 1110 to twenty-four-year-old Henry V of Germany and the two were married at Worms Cathedral in January 1114. Soon after, the two marched over the Alps to Rome and in St Peter's Basilica the Pope crowned Henry V as Holy Roman Emperor. Matilda thereafter styled herself Empress.

On May Day of 1118, Queen Matilda died. Under her royal mantle was found a haircloth. The people had always believed her a saint as for years she had nursed sick and suffering people and during Lent she walked the church floors in bare feet.

King Henry was overjoyed when his heir, Prince William Atheling, crossed the Channel to join his court in Normandy. A few months short of his seventeenth birthday he married the teenage Matilda, daughter of Fulk, Count of Anjou in June 1119. On 25 November 1120, just before twilight and in calm seas with a southerly wind blowing, King Henry set sail from Barfleur for England with his son's wife. Prince William, with his youthful retinue, elected to follow in the *White Ship* captained by Thomas FitzStephen. The young man, spoilt by an indulgent father, had been drinking with his friends and in rowdy bonhomie encouraged the crew and soldiers to drink too while they took possession of the rowing benches. William's cousin Stephen of Blois and a few others came ashore, observing the ship was 'overcrowded with riotous and headstrong youths'. Those youths, amid shouts of laughter, ordered their ship to race ahead of the king's. The oarsmen boasted that 'those ahead will soon be astern'. The ship flew out of the harbour into the open sea, and straight into a rock hidden by the high tide. Two planks on the starboard side were shattered by the crash. Seawater rushed in and the ship went down. Prince William might still have saved himself but his half-sister called to him, and in trying to rescue her they both drowned. The bodies were never recovered. Of three hundred passengers only one servant was rescued, having held on to a sail-arm all night; the captain, realising the enormity of the tragedy, deliberately allowed himself to drown.

So severe was the shock to King Henry that he fell to the ground on hearing the news. Carried to his chamber, he gave 'free course to the bitterness of his grief'. Henry's daughter Matilda was now his sole legitimate child.

In 1125 his daughter returned to England a childless widow after the emperor died of cancer. She arrived only with her personal collection of jewels, two of her husband's crowns and the Hand of St James the Apostle.

A year later, at Christmas, Henry decreed Matilda was his heir and made his barons swear their allegiance to her. He also arranged a second marriage for her, to Geoffrey, Count of Anjou and Maine, sometimes surnamed Plantagenet, which may or may not have referred to his tournament prowess and sturdy seat on his Spanish horse (*planta genet*) or, as some say, to his wearing a sprig of yellow broom in his cap.

Matilda argued bitterly with her father, incensed at being matched with a boy ten years her junior. She lost, and on 17 June 1128, in Le Mans, she married her fourteen-year-old bridegroom. The marriage was stormy. They quarrelled and split. They reconciled. On 5 March 1133, Matilda gave birth to a healthy son at Le Mans, named Henry after his grandfather. It was a difficult birth and she nearly died. Two more sons followed: Geoffrey on 1 June 1134 at Rouen and William on 21 July 1136 at Argentan. King Henry had no opportunity to delightedly dandle this third grandson as he had the others, for he died on 1 December 1135.

As soon as the news reached him Stephen of Blois quickly crossed into England and claimed the throne with a lie that Henry had made him his successor on his deathbed. His brother Henry, Bishop of Winchester backed him and the barons followed, reneging on their oath to Matilda, who was at that time pregnant. Stephen tried to move against her in Normandy but failed. Matilda had no intentions of giving up on her rightful inheritance. In this she was supported by her husband. She sailed to England to press her claim. This led to civil war in England and the period now called The Anarchy. For most of two decades the balance would tilt back and forth in attack and counterattack.

In 1141 Matilda's troops managed to capture King Stephen at Lincoln. Deposed, he was imprisoned at Bristol Castle. During preparations for her coronation, Empress Matilda was chased out of London by troops raised by Stephen's queen, also named Matilda.

They managed to capture Empress Matilda's chief supporter and half-brother, Robert, Earl of Gloucester. Earl and king were exchanged and freed. Empress Matilda herself evaded capture at least twice. Once she placed herself in grave clothes 'upon a hearse and being bound with cords like a corpse and borne upon horses' was safely carried to the safety of Gloucester. Another time she escaped to Wallingford from Oxford Castle by being lowered down the walls dressed in a white bedsheet as camouflage against thick snow.

Her son, Henry, now Duke of Normandy and Aquitaine, Count of Anjou, took up the fight. In November 1153, the forces of Henry and Stephen refused point-blank to fight each other. Stephen, almost in his sixties, agreed to Henry becoming his 'adoptive son' and inheriting the crown of England after his death. Rumours circulated that he would renege on the agreement and have Henry assassinated. On 25 October 1154 King Stephen suddenly died at Dover, apparently from a disease of the stomach. He was buried at Faversham Abbey, next to his wife Matilda and their eldest son, Eustace. Their surviving son, William, decided he was not remotely interested in the crown and would rather lead a quiet life. England had a new king: Henry II.

Henry II

1154–1189

Henry had learned lessons from The Anarchy. He had seen how the barons used weak leadership to augment their own power and the outright chaos and disorder which ensued. To combat lawlessness from the first he appointed strong and trusted men to a *Curia Regis*, a court of royal judges, and held regular councils with his nobles.

By the end of his first six months a chronicler wrote that Stephen's mercenaries 'sailed away, every man of them, bag and baggage; the castles all came down with a rush except the old towers and fortresses that served to keep the peace ... There was peace on every side, shields were no longer made at home but fetched from abroad, while the wares of England once more poured into the foreign mart.' Market fairs had goods for sale and fields were full of growing crops and 'pastures were full of oxen and folds of sheep'.

Having extensive lands on both sides of the Channel by inheritance and by right of his wife, Eleanor of Aquitaine, meant Henry had sufficient income to not overtax his subjects. In his own habits he was thrifty and frugal, to the misfortune of one prior and his monks who stopped him when he was riding and complained that their bishop had cut three dishes from their table.

The king asked, 'How many has he left you?'

'Ten,' they replied.

'I myself,' said the king, 'had never more than three and I enjoin your bishop to reduce you to the same number.'

He wore serviceable clothes and disliked ostentation. On Easter Day in 1158 he and Queen Eleanor laid their crowns upon the altar at the offering during Mass in Worcester Cathedral, solemnly vowing never to wear them again. As careful as he was with finances, so he was with words. Eloquent when necessary, he had the gift of knowing when to be silent. His temper, if suddenly provoked, could flare passionately but was over in a moment, and his humour was keen.

Once, after an angry summons, Bishop Hugh of Lincoln found the king sitting on the ground in a circle of his attendants. His greeting ignored, the bishop watched as the king with a borrowed needle mended a hole in his leather glove, then remarked, 'How like your cousins of Falaise you are!' The king roared with laughter. Chuckling, he explained to his perplexed courtiers that 'Falaise was famous for its leatherworkers' and that he was 'descended through William I from a girl of Falaise'.

The common people found Henry courteous, affable and approachable day or night. He had a prodigious memory, never forgetting a name, face or place. Although the price of goods stayed static while he was on the throne, when corn was extremely scarce in Anjou and Maine one year he maintained thousands of needy persons from April until harvest by opening up his storehouses of grain, meat and drink. A tenth of his household provisions were perpetually distributed to the poor.

If King Henry had one particular fault, if fault it could be called, it was that he was a doting father.

19 December 1154: Coronation

Joyful, cheering crowds lined the streets watching the long procession pass by bound for Westminster Abbey. Twenty-one-year-old King Henry, square-jawed, freckled and grey-eyed, his sandy, curly hair clipped square at his forehead, was crowned by Archbishop Theobald of Canterbury with the grander of the two imperial crowns his mother had brought from Germany. He was restless throughout the ceremony; it can be understood why courtiers already complain that he rarely sits or keeps still.

Queen Eleanor, though great with child, walked gracefully along the nave. From her youthful face, no one would know she is nine years older than her husband. An outer robe bordered with fur covered her gown. On her head was placed a circlet of gems over a headdress with a long gauze veil streaming down her back.

Eleanor is notorious for the pilgrimage she took to the Holy Land with her first husband, King Louis the Pious of France, with a band of noble ladies who dressed themselves like men and called themselves the queen's bodyguard. After ignoring the Pope by taking his forces to Jerusalem and not Damascus, Louis abducted Eleanor from Antioch to stop her sending her own vassals to assist her beloved uncle Raymond, later killed at Damascus. She never forgave him. Two months after she and Louis were divorced, Eleanor married Henry on 11 May 1152 at

Saint-Pierre Cathedral in Poitiers. Her title to Aquitaine and Poitou had made her an enticing prize. To reach Poitiers she first had to elude capture by Theobald, Count of Blois, disguising herself as a minstrel and escaping by boat in the night. She then evaded being seized by Henry's own brother, Geoffrey, who tried to waylay her on the River Loire. Rumourmongers in 1150 said a flirting Eleanor had fallen in love with Henry's father. Obviously, it was the son who caught her eye. Their keen wits match each other and both share a love of literature. The queen is also entertained by mystery and miracle plays and enjoys ballads; already troubadours flock from Anjou.

Their son, William, was born on 17 August 1153, the same day that King Stephen's son and heir, Eustace, died. The royal family intend to keep Christmas in great splendour at Bermondsey Abbey.

4–13 January 1155: 'Charms Everyone'
Thomas Becket, Archdeacon of Canterbury, was made Chancellor by King Henry. At six feet tall, the mild-faced thirty-seven-year-old Thomas is an imposing figure but his nature is amiable and he charms everyone he meets. His new role is to administer the revenue from vacant sees, abbacies and baronies. Working alongside Earl Robert of Leicester and Richard de Lucy, justices of the *Curia Regis*, they will act as the king's deputies while he is on progress enjoying some hunting and hawking.

28 February 1155: Prince Henry Born
Prince Henry was born today at the Palace of Bermondsey. A wet-nurse called Christina has been engaged by the queen.

28 March 1155: Westminster Repairs
Chancellor Thomas has so many carpenters and masons at work repairing the ruined Palace of Westminster ready for Whitsuntide that it is impossible to hear someone even if they are standing beside you.

4 June 1155: Royal Death
Two-year-old Prince William died of a seizure at Wallingford Castle. He is to be buried at Reading Abbey, at the feet of his great-grandfather Henry I.

December 1155: 'Great Charity'
A story doing the rounds in court is that while King Henry and Thomas Becket were riding through London, the king espied an old man coming towards them wearing a thin, ragged coat.

'Do you see that old man?' the king said to Thomas.

'Yes,' replied the chancellor.

'How poor and infirm he is,' said the king. 'Would it not be a great charity to give him a thick, warm cloak?'

'It would indeed and you as king ought to keep this matter in your eye.'

As the old man neared them, Henry playfully took hold of the chancellor's new scarlet and grey cape. 'No,' he said, 'you shall have the credit of such a great act of charity.'

As Henry tried to pull it away, the two tussled together. Winning it from Thomas' grasp, Henry laughingly bestowed it on the bemused fellow.

Much gossip follows the two who play together like young boys. They ride, hawk, play chess and hunt together. The king rides into Thomas's hall to say hello, or take a cup with him; other times he has vaulted over the table to sit and eat with him. Others think the king's overfamiliarity breeds pride in Thomas, who strews his hall floor every day with fresh straw and hay in winter, and with green branches in summer so if his benches overflow there is always a clean seat on the floor. Barons prefer to dine with him rather than the king for he provides them every day with good wine and richer dishes served on gold and silver.

4 January 1156: Homage

After spending Christmas at Westminster Palace, King Henry set off today to Dover, having already sent treasure, hawks and falcons to Shoreham. Leaving Eleanor as regent and quick with child, he travels to the French-Norman border to pay homage to King Louis VII on 5 February for Normandy, Aquitaine, Anjou, Maine and Touraine.

June 1156: Birth

The king and queen's first daughter was born in London, christened Matilda. After her churching the queen intends to cross the Channel to join the king in Anjou.

8 April 1157: Return

Landing at Southampton from Barfleur, King Henry rode straight to London to join the queen and their children who returned from Normandy two months ago.

8 September 1157: Birth

Prince Richard, the third son of Queen Eleanor and King Henry, was born at Beaumont Palace in Oxford, whence the king is hastening from his campaign in Wales to see his new son. Hodierna has been engaged by the queen as wet-nurse.

August 1158: State Visit

Starting on his journey to Paris to negotiate the marriage between three-year-old Prince Henry and Marguerite, the six-month-old daughter of King Louis, crowds gathered to watch, amused and bemused, as Thomas Becket's gay retinue passed by. First were 200 pairs of armoured knights, followed by their esquires in colourful liveries leading chargers or bearing hawks and falcons on their wrists, then clerks, butlers and huntsmen with greyhounds. Loud rumbling heralded eight carriages, with a fierce mastiff walking alongside each, drawn by five horses, large and strong as warhorses: two of which carried iron-hooped barrels of clear-coloured beer, much liked by the French; others housed chapel furniture, chamber carpets and hangings, boxes of money, food and drink and all the gold cups, platters, goblets, salvers and salt cellars the chancellor thinks he will use. The packhorses, each with a monkey riding on its back, carried his soft nightgowns and twenty-four changes of fine clothes and silk garments to give as gifts. Then came Thomas, in the midst of household officers and friends, the bridles of their horses shining silver. Once in France, he intends sending footboys ahead singing English songs to announce his entrance into towns and villages.

Meanwhile King Henry travels to Brittany as his brother Geoffrey died of fever on 26 July and he is his brother's heir.

23 September 1158: Another Prince

Queen Eleanor gave birth to her fourth son at Westminster. He has been called Geoffrey in honour of his grandfather and deceased uncle.

August–October 1159: Archdeacon Warrior

Claiming for Queen Eleanor the city of Toulouse, hers by inheritance, King Henry had set up his siege when, to his alarm, King Louis and a handful of French soldiers rode in through the gates. Ordering his soldiers to cease bombardment, Henry was pressed by Thomas Becket to fight on and capture Louis. The king replied that not only was it dishonourable, but it set a dangerous precedent for a vassal to fight his liege. Besieging rebellious Cahors instead, Henry left for Normandy after it surrendered, leaving the castle in charge of the Earl of Essex and Becket, the latter garrisoning it with his own contingent of 700 knights, 1,200 mercenary troops and 4,000 men-at-arms. Riding at the head of his men in helmet and cuirass, the chancellor stormed other rebel strongholds, the diplomat supplanted by the soldier ripe for glory. Many 'suffered death at his hands', and he attacked cities and towns, putting villages and farms 'to the greedy flames without one thought of pity', completely merciless to the king's enemies.

18 April 1161: Died Mourning

After a primacy spanning twenty-two years, Archbishop Theobald was buried at Canterbury today. He had sorrowed all through his illness that never had his beloved Thomas Becket, whom he had taken into his household, come to see him despite repeated requests. On his deathbed, the old man reproached Thomas for forgetting all the kindnesses he had received from his 'old and ailing father'.

September 1161: Birth

Queen Eleanor gave birth to a daughter at Domfront. She was baptised Alienor after the birth name of her mother by Cardinal Henry of Pisa.

Late April 1162: 'A pretty costume'

During Lent in Rouen, barons and bishops swore allegiance to Prince Henry 'saving the rights of his father'. Thomas Becket and his 'adopted son' sailed to England so that English barons and bishops could swear similarly to the prince.

Ignoring his mother's advice, King Henry has instructed Chancellor Thomas to be elected Archbishop of Canterbury. At first Thomas had demurred, smiling and pointing at his rich clothes and their gay colours: 'You have selected a pretty costume to figure at the head of the monks of Canterbury.' Though he said he would surely offend either God or the king if he took the office, his reluctance was soon overcome.

23 May 1162: Election

The assembly held at Canterbury debated long and hard whether Becket was a fit candidate. Called to London, the officers the king sent to oversee the election found monks and bishops still arguing. Finally, Cardinal Henry intervened and persuaded 'nays to become yeas', although the hearts of many 'went right another way'. Thomas, waiting outside the chamber, was brought in. At first he prayed they would spare him 'the responsibilities of such an exalted office' but he eventually accepted, resigning his fiefs and properties held of the crown to Prince Henry.

3 June 1162: Consecration

At an early hour, summer sunlight flooded Canterbury Cathedral. Prince Henry, barons, knights and commoners crowded into the nave. In the choir the gleaming rich vestments of the fourteen bishops were a bright contrast against the dark-robed monks. The tall figure of Thomas Becket emerged from the vestry doorway. Ordained the day before, he wore a simple black cassock and white surplice. He moved gracefully to the altar steps. Prostrating himself, he prayed for a while and upon rising resigned his position as chancellor to everyone's surprise. Consecrated by the Bishop of Winchester, he ascended to his throne. With tear-filled eyes, Thomas announced that henceforth this day would forever after be kept at Canterbury as the Feast of the Holy Trinity.

King's Tyranny?

Archbishop Thomas, as he had done previously, shaped his behaviour to his role, raptly and tearfully attending church services; his chaplain, FitzStephen, wrote, 'You would fancy he had before him our Lord's passion bodily in the flesh.' He dressed in a black habit and sat with the monks in cloister. Theobald had doubled alms to the poor; Thomas doubled them again. Herbert of Bosham wrote that Thomas, once on chariots and horses, now rode a packhorse with a halter for a bridle and the rags of the poor brothers for a saddle. He ate sparingly, often only bread with a little partridge, and drank hot water with herbs. Into hall every day he brought twenty-six poor men to eat. Yet his friend John of Salisbury wrote to him that the Pope 'throws in our teeth' that after everything Pope Adrian did for the see of Canterbury 'you are allowing his mother to starve in cold and hunger'.

He was obsessed with his rights, demanding that Henry return Rochester Castle and the manors of Saltwood and Hethe to Canterbury see and insisting that Roger, Earl of Clare should pay homage to him for Tonbridge despite it having been given to the earl's grandfather by William I. When William de Eynsford evicted a clerk Thomas had unrightfully placed in his manor church, he was excommunicated. William appealed to Henry that since Domesday no man could, without royal consent, be excommunicated. King Henry asked Becket to absolve Eynsford and was told he might be king but he could not 'inform him whom he should absolve and whom excommunicate'. Justices informed the king that, despite firm evidence, Becket had acquitted a Lincoln canon for murder and, despite it being customary, had refused to allow a Worcestershire clerk accused of rape and murder to be tried in a secular court.

At the Westminster Council on 1 October, King Henry proposed a resumption of the custom whereby clerics convicted of, or confessing to, murder or robbery should be degraded and sentenced in the king's court. Conferring in their own chamber, the bishops agreed his proposition was reasonable. Ignoring them, custom and reason, Becket marched up to the king and thundered that 'only a reoffender, once degraded, could be tried in the king's court' for 'God's law did not allow a man to be tried twice for the same offence'. Mildly, King Henry asked the prelates if they were willing to observe the 'customs of the crown and laws of the kingdom'.

Thomas instantly replied, 'We will, in all things, saving always our own order.'

Next morning, Prince Henry was removed from the archbishop's household. John of Salisbury wrote to Becket from Paris soon after that Count Philip would furnish ships when he required them and said that the Count of Soissons had told him all that had passed at the council 'as minutely as if he had been there himself'.

As arguments escalated, the Pope wrote to the archbishop ordering him to make peace with the king and promise, without exception, to obey his laws. At a meeting at Woodstock, Thomas gave his promise privately to King Henry. The king responded that as he had opposed him in public, in public he must give his promise.

At the council held at the king's hunting lodge of Clarendon on 25 January, King Henry proposed a debate to establish English laws of 'common practice' and 'usage immemorial'. When consensus was reached, Henry ordered them enrolled and read out in council, the main provisos being: serious crimes tried in church courts should be observed by a king's justice and if the accused confessed or was convicted he would lose church protection; great persons or prelates should not leave the realm without royal consent nor do ill to king or kingdom in leaving or returning; no tenant-in-chief could be excommunicated or his lands laid under interdict without royal leave; where criminals had intimidated accusers, the sheriff could swear twelve men to investigate the truth; and appeals for justice were to be hierarchical via archdeacon, bishop, archbishop and lastly the king.

When the king asked the bishops to make good their verbal consent by affixing their seals to the rolls, Archbishop Thomas at once refused to make good his avowal. After much remonstrance he muttered, 'It is God's will I perjure myself' and gave his assent 'honestly, legally and without reserve' and made the bishops swear after his example. Both archbishops of York and Canterbury received a copy; another was filed in the royal archives.

Six months later, Thomas tried to secretly flee England. On his first attempt the wind drove him back to shore; on the second sailors returned him to land having recognised him. Summoning him to his presence, King Henry, half-laughing and half-reproachful, asked if the kingdom was not big enough to hold them both. On 14 September 1164, the king summoned Thomas to attend a *curia* in front of him as his servant John Marshal claimed not to have received justice in the archbishop's court. Thomas did not appear. He sent the Sheriff of Kent who told justices that John had sworn on a troper (a book of liturgical music) and not on the Gospels, rendering his oath null and void. He was told such argument was unjust for such books of hymns have the Gospels at their beginning. King Henry, via the sheriff, sent a summons to the archbishop to attend the Northampton Council in October.

On the third day of council, King Henry charged Thomas for contempt of his royal authority. In full parliament Thomas was adjudged guilty; the sentence was to have his secular possessions and goods (his temporalities) confiscated and accounts rendered for monies spent while he was chancellor. After the archbishop absented himself through illness, earls sent to check on him found him lying on his bed with servants applying hot pillows to his side. He vowed he would attend court the next day, even if he had to be carried by litter.

The following day he dressed in the pall used for festivals, celebrated St Stephen's Mass – which included the words, 'The rulers took counsel together against the Lord and against his anointed' – and was stopped by wiser heads from marching barefoot from there all the way into council. Riding a palfrey to the castle's main gate, he dismounted and held up his cross in his right hand. He was denied entrance into the king's chamber by a Templar guard, and Bishop Gilbert Foliot tried to wrest the cross from him, remarking that for coming thus armed the king 'would draw a sharper sword' and rebuking him for the fool he had always been. When the prelates, bar Thomas, were summoned into council, King Henry asked them whether his request for a full accounting was unreasonable. Bishop Gilbert replied that 'debts were not remitted on promotion like sins in baptism' and then informed Henry that Thomas had forbidden them to be judges against him in any charge before he was made primate. Henry was furious. Allowed to return to the chamber where Thomas was sitting, the prelates entreated him to be reasonable or resign.

'In a strait place you have put us,' Bishop Hilary of Chichester said bitterly, 'by your prohibition you have set us between the hammer and the anvil.'

Rising to his full height, Archbishop Thomas bellowed that they were, on peril of their souls, to excommunicate anyone who dared lay hands on him. Bishop Hilary accused him of breaking his oath, being disloyal to the king and subverting the common law of the realm.

Meanwhile in council, prelates were replaced with sheriffs and lesser barons and unanimously judged Archbishop Thomas guilty of perjury and treason. The Earl of Leicester was sent to Thomas but before he could utter a word the archbishop shouted, 'I will be judged under God by the Pope alone' and stormed out. No one stopped him although jeers of 'traitor' and 'perjurer' were shouted after him. Hearing them, Henry ordered the archbishop was to depart unmolested. Nearing twilight, the great gate was already locked but the key hung nearby on the wall and a servant unlocked and opened it for him. As Thomas emerged, a cheering crowd accompanied him to his lodgings. In the morning, the archbishop was found to have vanished.

So, when King Henry's envoys left Sens after a stormy interview with Pope Alexander on 25 November 1164, they were astonished when Archbishop Thomas passed them by, riding gaily at the head of a retinue of 300 horsemen, on his way to the Pope. Their own audience had been stormy. When Bishop Gilbert complained that Thomas had fled into the night for no good reason as neither violence nor threat had been used against him and that only 'the wicked flee when no man pursues', the Pope scolded him. Into the silence, Archbishop Roger said he had known Thomas long and could vouch his obstinacy to the king was from vanity of his mind. The Bishop of Exeter, seeing the Pope had been beguiled by Thomas, suggested mildly perhaps the Pope could send legates with Thomas to England to try and heal the rift between prelate and king.

When Thomas entered the papal chamber on his first visit, he had thrown himself at Alexander's feet. He said having received his archbishopric from a secular power he relinquished it to him, to restore it or not as he willed. The Pope restored it; now he was archbishop by the Pope's will.

The night Thomas left Northampton, his departure was well planned. He had sent his retainers to procure horses 'not of his own stud'. He told the monks he intended to pray all night – alone. Then he left by an unguarded postern gate to ride to Lincoln where, at dawn, the novice Brother Dearman arrived. Eight days later, Brother Christian crossed the Channel in stormy weather in an open boat. He lodged incognito in a small hermitage outside St Omer awaiting Herbert of Bosham to bring him clothes, silver plate, valuables and money from Canterbury. Once suitably attired, he rode to the Monastery of St Bertin and asked the abbot for protection.

In June 1165 the Pope wrote to King Henry reproving him as a persecutor of the church, warning him 'heavy vengeance' would be visited upon him for conversing with excommunicates, forbidding appeals to Rome and exiling his archbishop; this was echoed by the letter from Thomas that came with it informing Henry he would feel the 'severity of God's vengeance'.

Bishop Gilbert wrote that King Henry had claimed only the customary right to hear civil causes before appeals were sent to the Pope, that he was unaware the Pope had excommunicated the emperor when envoys were sent to negotiate a marriage between his daughter Matilda and Henry, Duke of Saxony, and that the archbishop had left 'perversely and voluntarily'.

In April 1166 at Chinon Castle, King Henry told his court he had received menacing letters from Thomas since the Pope had created him Legate of All England, threatening to lay interdict on his lands and personally excommunicate him. The Archbishop of Rouen gently rebuked Henry when, dejected and tearful, he called his nobles traitors for neither having the zeal nor the courage 'to rid him from the molestation of one man'. On Whitsunday, without warning and with bell, book and candle, Thomas excommunicated the king's officers and, accusing the king of tyranny, threatened him with anathema.

20 December 1166: Papal Decision
The Pope has quashed Becket's sentences and forbidden Thomas to utter any fresh sentences or to molest the king. He intends to send arbiters, but their journey is likely to be slow and hazardous; all the roads in Italy are beset by imperial forces.

10 September 1167: Death
Having long been ill, Empress Matilda died at nine o'clock in the morning at Rouen. Archbishop Rotrou headed the procession of monks conveying her body, wrapped in a bull's hide, to be laid to rest before the high altar of the church of Bec-Hellouin. A crown of seven lights was placed above her grave. King Henry will distribute her treasures to churches, monasteries and leper-houses.

18 November 1167: Obdurate
Archbishop Thomas refused both the offer of the Pope's legates as arbiters and the king's suggestion of a compromise, saying he required proper respect for his dignity and restitution of all his property.

24 December 1167: Birth

Queen Eleanor gave birth today at Beaumont Palace in Oxford to a baby boy whom she has named John. The same evening there was a conjunction of Venus and Jupiter, both described as red in colour, one large and the other small. King Henry is spending Christmas at Argentan, where he has resided since November, intending to hold a great court in his newly built hall.

The queen had returned to England in September accompanied by eleven-year-old Princess Matilda who, next February, is to go to Brunswick to marry Henry, Duke of Saxony. He is nearly thirty years her senior.

February 1168: Unrest

With recent unrest in Aquitaine, King Henry requested that Queen Eleanor resume rule in her own lands. She sailed from England with seven ships carrying her retinue and belongings and will be setting up court in her favourite city of Poitiers.

'Wished to be more than king'

In early January 1169, at the signing of the Treaty of Montmirail, Prince Henry gave homage to King Louis for Normandy as did Richard for Aquitaine, the latter formally betrothed to Louis' daughter Alys. Geoffrey, betrothed to Duchess Constance, paid homage to Prince Henry for the lands of Brittany, Anjou and Maine. John was made Earl of Mortain. In a spirit of mediation, Louis had Thomas Becket brought in before Henry, and the archbishop promptly threw himself at his king's feet begging forgiveness. Henry asked Thomas to promise to 'observe the laws which were observed by his predecessors'. He agreed, paused, and added, 'Saving the honour of God.'

'This man,' Henry said to King Louis, 'deserted his church of his own will and tells you – and all men – that his cause is the cause of the church. He has governed his church with as much freedom as those who have gone before him, but now he stands on God's honour to oppose me when he pleases as if I cared for God's honour less than he.'

On Palm Sunday, 13 April, the archbishop excommunicated Bishop Josceline of Salisbury and Bishop Gilbert of London, accusing the latter of being a 'parricide, infidel and son of Belial'. All those previously excommunicated by him he threatened to excommunicate again at Whitsunday, which he did, adding others such as William de Eynsford and his brother.

Papal legates arrived at Domfront in August. Negotiations were stormy. Henry finally agreed he would receive the archbishop and allow his return to Canterbury, then insisted the written agreement should include, 'Saving the dignity of my realm.' A month later, Archbishop Thomas threatened to lay England under interdict.

In November, Henry came to the Shrine of St Denis and met Louis and his son, Philip. Louis again persuaded Henry to meet Thomas. The Archbishop of Rouen was sent to find out what the archbishop sought. The answer: everything he or Theobald had held with all the disputed estates and £20,000 owed, not one single penny of which he would remit. King Henry agreed to the first two requests but said he would recompense him after an impartial estimate for he believed the amount did not rise above £8,000. Scornfully, Thomas said that 'without restitution, there was no remission of sin' but that if the king would 'guarantee his promises' he would render all service to him, 'saving the honour of God and his order'. King Louis reproached him. Thomas demanded Henry give him the kiss of peace; he refused.

14–15 June 1170: Coronation

Crowds gathered to watch the unusual continental custom of King Henry's fifteen-year-old heir being crowned at Westminster Abbey. Before the ceremony he was knighted by his father. The young man stands taller than his father, with long red-gold hair down to broad shoulders. He has inherited his father's freckles but his eyes are blue rather than grey. Young Henry spoke the usual coronation oath and was crowned by Archbishop Roger and given a Seal of Regency for England. Bishops Gilbert and Josceline assisted and prelates from England and Normandy attended.

At the coronation banquet, the king served his son personally, bringing in a wild boar's head. The younger remarked, 'The son of an earl may well wait on the son of a king.' The king was delighted at his son's wit but everyone else was shocked. The king gave his son two new hawks as a gift.

The day after the coronation, the earls, barons and freeholders, including King William and David of Scotland, swore fealty to him, saving their allegiance to King Henry the elder.

22 July 1170: Blackmailed

When Henry met Louis at Freteval to explain why his daughter, Margaret, had stayed at Caen with Queen Eleanor instead of being crowned with her husband, Louis arranged for Archbishop Thomas to meet with King Henry, this time meeting on horseback in the open within a ring of nobles. King Henry doffed his cap and stayed bareheaded while the two spoke privately. Archbishop Thomas complained only he had the right to crown Prince Henry. The king protested that no offence was meant and the Pope had given authority for Archbishop Roger of York to crown his son.

Not so, said the archbishop, he had got the papal bull revoked but with the see of Canterbury being vacant the letter remained undelivered. The king immediately realised the implication: the Pope would presume he had been disobedient. Becket again asked for reparation, 'for the sake of your son and his crown'.

In front of the nobles, the archbishop loudly asked for peace and favour, restoration of all and amends for the injury recently done to him in regard to young Henry's coronation. Mutely, the king gave a curt nod.

1–2 December 1170: His Throne

To the delight of a waiting crowd, when Archbishop Thomas sailed into Sandwich he stood tall, his crozier raised conspicuously above the ship's figurehead. Awaiting him after having ridden from Dover were Sir Reginald de Warenne, Ranulf de Broc and Gervase, Sheriff of Kent. The day before, to catch them before they sailed to see the king, Thomas had sent a small boy or nun disguised as a boy to Dover to secretly slip letters of excommunication to Bishops Gilbert and Hilary and one of censure to Archbishop Roger. When they asked him to lift his sentences and not reduce English law to his edicts, Thomas boldly asserted they were issued with the king's permission and knowledge. After the French clergy in the train with no passports were asked to take the usual oath, Thomas scornfully said that no clerk with him would take any oath.

Riding to Canterbury the following day was a long, triumphal procession for Thomas. Men, women and children lined the roads, some on their knees, waiting to be blessed. Arriving early evening, garlanded by clergy and their parishioners, his face shining 'like Moses when descending from the mount', Thomas entered his cathedral and sat on his throne.

18 December 1170: Armed Escort

At the London palace of the Bishop of Winchester where Thomas had lodged, Sir Jocelyn Arundel arrived with an order from King Henry the younger for him to return to Canterbury and desist from moving about the realm with his armed escort of 100 knights. The archbishop retorted he had the right to visit his diocese and had it not been for Christmas being so near he would refuse to go at any man's bidding. Arundel replied he came to deliver the king's commands, not to dispute them.

'Carry back then my commands to your king.'

'Your commands! Address your commands to those of your own order.' Turning sternly to the young knights in the archbishop's suite, Arundel bade them remember their duties and rode off.

25 December 1170: 'Peace to men'

The Christmas Day sermon at Canterbury was on the text 'Peace to men' but near the end, Archbishop Thomas lit candles and, his face twisted in anger, vehemently cursed several of the king's most intimate councillors. A candle was violently dashed to the ground at each name he excommunicated. At the festival afterwards he was in exceptionally good spirits, eating and drinking more than usual.

Overseas, King Henry, Queen Eleanor and their younger children enjoyed a family Christmas at Bure, near Bayeux.

29 December 1170: Murder at the Cathedral

Just after five o'clock, in the first darkness of the winter evening, Archbishop Thomas was murdered in Canterbury Cathedral by four barons of the king's household: Sir Reginald FitzUrse, Hugh de Morville, William de Tracy and Richard le Breton.

They had arrived at the palace gate two hours earlier. Dismounting, they unbuckled their swords and left them at the lodge. As they entered the antechamber the steward recognised them. He directed them into the chamber where the archbishop, sitting on his bed, was conversing with John of Salisbury, FitzStephen, Edward Grim from Cambridge and his monks, all seated around him on the floor. Slipping into the room, the knights too sat down, the archbishop ignoring them. After a while, FitzUrse quietly asked whether the archbishop would speak publicly or privately with them. Saying he cared not, the room was at first cleared. Monks and visitors waiting outside heard raised voices. Called back in they witnessed FitzUrse accusing the archbishop of breaking the peace and his promises and allowing his pride to tempt him to defiance. When he asked Thomas to remove his sentences of excommunication, the archbishop told him to go to the Pope, saying the affair was none of his, adding King Henry had given him permission to obtain from the Pope any satisfaction he liked to ask.

'Ay, ay, will you make the king out to be a traitor then?' asked FitzUrse. 'The king gave you leave to excommunicate the bishops when they were acting by his own order? It is more than we can bear to listen to such monstrous accusations.'

When they said he should leave England, Thomas told them only death would part him from his church. Launching into a tirade of complaints, Morville told the archbishop he should take any just cause to the *curia* but the archbishop replied, 'Neither one king nor the other will do me right. I will endure it no more.'

'You will lay the realm under interdict then and excommunicate the whole of us?' asked FitzUrse.

'So God help me,' said one of the others, 'he has excommunicated over-many already.'

Knights and archbishop sprang to their feet in anger. As the knights left the room, one ordered, 'In the king's name, see that this man does not escape.' The archbishop shouted after them, 'Do you think I shall fly, then? Neither for the king nor for any living man will I fly. You cannot be more ready to kill me than I am to die.'

John of Salisbury restrained him, saying quietly, 'Why won't you be advised, why exasperate these men with your bitter speeches … you would do better giving them a milder answer.'

As the knights returned to the lodge, the vesper bell sounded. While they buckled on their swords, frightened monks barred the door behind them but, even in the dark, Richard le Breton knew the palace well and he led them to an oriel window with exterior stairs from the orchard into the antechamber. Then they were inside, swords drawn and axes in their left hands. All this time, Thomas refused to stir from his chamber until his cross was brought to him. When the monks tried to hustle him along the corridors, he resisted them. They tried to persuade him to take the little-used passage through the cloister into the cathedral but he pulled them with him through the door into the south transept. They barred the door but Thomas, cursing them for cowards, unbarred and opened the door, telling them 'it was not meet to make a fortress of the house of prayer'. His clergy scurried to hide, shouting, 'Armed men in the cathedral!' Singing ceased.

In the middle of the transept rose a single pillar; to its east was the Chapel of St Benedict, to its west a lady chapel with steps behind it leading up into the choir. The archbishop was on the fourth step when he heard, 'Where is the traitor? Where is Thomas Becket?'

'I am here,' he said, descending the steps. 'I am no traitor to the king but a priest. Why do you seek me? Be it far from me to flee from your swords or to depart from justice.'

While Morville stopped people from entering the area, the other three tried to take the archbishop prisoner but as FitzUrse touched him, the archbishop exclaimed, 'You pander, touch me not.'

FitzUrse, furious at the insult, swept his sword around. Though Edward Grim intercepted the blow, which broke his arm, it still had force enough to wound Thomas in his forehead. Blood trickled down his face as a second blow fell on his head, but still he stood firm, hands clasped. A third blow by Tracy felled him. On his knees and elbows he bent his head as if for a death-stroke, saying in a low voice, 'I am prepared to die for Christ and for his church.' Le Breton dealt a blow which severed crown from head, breaking his sword on the stone floor beneath. A cleric who had entered with the knights placed his foot on the archbishop's neck and scattered his brains and blood across the floor, proclaiming, 'Let us away, the traitor is dead; he will trouble us no more.'

As they left, Grim heard one of the monks say, 'He was justly served.' Another said, 'He wished to be king and more than king.'

Saint and Sinners

Clearing the cathedral and shutting its gates, the monks turned the archbishop's body face upwards and found he was almost smiling. Underneath the body there lay an axe, a small iron hammer, two fragments of broken sword and his cap. Carrying the body on a bier, they placed it in front of the high altar and placed vessels underneath to catch his blood; into other vessels they scraped up the blood and brains from the floor where he had died. By morning, people who had dipped their handkerchiefs or scraps of cloth in the archbishop's blood were claiming miracles of healing. The monks quickly erected a wooden altar over the bloodstains. The corpse was carried into the crypt to be washed and beneath his vestments, surplice and Benedictine habit they found he wore a knee-length hair shirt and 'hair drawers' with vermin 'boiling over like water in a simmering cauldron'.

'What a true monk he was,' they murmured, and left him unwashed, covering the haircloth garments with his pontifical robes before placing him in a stone sarcophagus. Within days pilgrims were visiting Canterbury to touch his sarcophagus. The monks mixed his blood and brains with water and sold tiny clay bottles, claiming a tiny drop was in each. When these at first cracked or exploded, the monks told pilgrims they had left some sin unconfessed. No further problems ensued when they began using tin bottles with neck-cords. Soon, miracles by St Thomas were recorded all over Europe. The common people canonised Thomas Becket; the Pope followed on 21 February 1173.

King Henry received news of Becket's murder on New Year's Day. One moment he wept loudly, the next he appeared dazed before bursting out crying again. Wearing sackcloth, he repeated over and over he neither wished nor ordered his death. Shutting himself up in his chambers and refusing food, his courtiers feared his excessive grief would kill him.

Henry sailed on papal-sanctioned crusade to Ireland in the autumn of 1171 to show his remorse outwardly. Nominally Christian, Ireland had no confirmed bishops and paid no tithes, Peter's pence nor first fruits to Rome. Children were baptised by being dipped three times in water or milk. Irish chiefs either did not marry or took as many wives as they pleased. The expedition was peaceable. On Christmas Day the king held a feast in Dublin, his new nobles suspiciously eyeing the dishes of delicacies on the table, including crane.

Young Henry held his Christmas court in Normandy, decorating his hall with mistletoe, ivy and holly, and thought it fun to invite only those knights and barons called William.

In May 1172, King Henry swore on the Gospels at Avranches Cathedral he had neither ordered nor wished Archbishop Thomas to be murdered. He claimed that upon hearing Thomas had asked Pope Alexander for 'all persons' concerned in the prince's coronation to be excommunicated he had said, 'By God's eyes, I am excommunicated also' and admitted crying out in perplexity, 'How many useless drones have I about me who will let their lord be treated with such shameful contempt by a low-born clerk!'. He feared his grief and fury had instigated the act, and wholly repented uttering the words that led four of his knights to murder the archbishop. Those listening to him were moved to tears by his humility. Led to the door, he meekly knelt on a stone block to receive absolution.

King Louis, hearing that the king was in Normandy and no longer in Ireland, exclaimed, 'He may rather be said to fly than go by horse or boat!'

On 27 August 1172, Young Henry and Margaret were crowned at Winchester Cathedral by Archbishop Rotrou of Rouen. Few nobles attended and the banquet cost £55. Six months later Young Henry, refused joint rule or absolute rule of either England or Normandy by his father, and complaining he had only £1,000 a year to call his own, travelled to Paris. When King Henry sent messengers to his son, they were told by King Louis, 'The king of England is here, he sends no message to me ... but if you so call his father who once was king, know ye that he as king is dead.'

Queen Eleanor travelled to Paris, taking with her princes Richard and Geoffrey, needling her elder son that a crown without power was worthless. Attempting to return to Aquitaine, she was arrested after being caught travelling in male disguise.

In July 1173, the Scots poured over the Tweed but were driven back by Richard de Lucy and Humphrey de Bohun who, apprised of a landing by the Earl of Leicester with mercenary Flemings, raced back to defeat him. In the spring of 1174, William of Scotland once again broke truce and it was said his army in Northumberland 'ripped apart pregnant women, dragged out embryos on points of lances, slaying without mercy ... children, men and women, highest to lowest'. In Aquitaine, Richard declared war on his father. Geoffrey fomented revolt in Maine and Anjou. King Louis mustered his troops to invade Normandy and news came that Young Henry was ready to sail from Gravelines with a fleet to invade England. Knowing he was the only person who could fight his son, King Henry boarded ship at Barfleur with the wind favourable in direction but fitful and squally, uttering a public prayer that 'if his arrival in England would be for good, it might be accomplished; if for evil, never'. He reached Southampton safely before night fell on 8 July.

At this time King Henry was forty-one years old, red hair greying around a tonsure of baldness, with an ingrowing toenail on one foot which gave him much pain. His legs were bowed, he had horseman's shins, he wore boots without a fold and caps without decoration and only wore gloves when using bow, sword or arrow; otherwise his hands always held books, particularly history. He was still strong, agile and broad-chested with boxer's arms.

As the three towers of Canterbury Cathedral came into view, King Henry dismounted to continue on foot to St Dunstan's church. There removing his boots, he walked barefoot through the mud and puddles to the cathedral porch. Underneath his long woollen shirt he wore a haircloth and his feet left bloodstains on the rough stones of the streets.

Taken to the north transept, he kissed the stone where Becket had fallen and made confession. In the crypt he kissed the martyr's tomb, remaining long in prayer. As penance, the king patiently bore five strokes from each bishop and abbot and three from each of the eighty monks and passed the whole night fasting. Next morning, after Mass, he drank water from St Thomas' Well and, gifted a bottle with Becket's blood, continued to Westminster where he fell ill.

At midnight on 18 July violent knocking roused the guards. A messenger told the recovering King Henry, 'Ranulf de Glanville has taken the King of Scots prisoner. He is in chains at Richmond Castle,' On the same day news came that Young Henry's invasion fleet had been dispersed in a storm and it was openly said St Thomas had forgiven the king. On 30 September 1174, King Henry for love of his sons freely forgave them.

6 August 1178: Knighthood
At Woodstock, King Henry knighted Geoffrey, off overseas to attend tournaments and win feats of arms in emulation of his brothers Henry and Richard, both adroit in handling lance and sword. So fond of them is Young Henry that he has spent most of the last three years courting knights and the applause of the populace while Richard fights insurrections in his duchy.

22–25 August 1179: Canterbury
After his fourteen-year-old son, Philip, fell gravely ill, King Louis was granted safe conduct by the king to visit the shrine of St Thomas, meeting him on the seashore at Dover and escorting him to Canterbury.

1 November 1179: Coronation
King Philip Augustus was today crowned at Reims, after his father was struck by paralysis when he reached St Denis on his return from Canterbury. He has lost use of the right side of his body. Young Henry bore the golden crown and afterwards assisted Philip to keep it on his head and at the banquet he served the new king the first dish.

25 December 1182: Christmas
King Henry kept his Christmas at Caen with his exiled son-in-law Henry, Duke of Saxony and his daughter Matilda, together with his sons bar John, who remains under the tutelage of Ranulf de Glanville. In the New Year, the king, with Duchess Matilda and her husband, will be joining Queen Eleanor at Windsor, recently released from her strict custody.

17 April 1183: King Nearly Killed
After a call for aid from Prince Richard, King Henry crossed the sea to prevent his sons Henry and Geoffrey from driving their brother out of Aquitaine. Burning and plundering villages and churches, the two with rebel insurgents had taken the castle of Limoges. When King Henry

arrived at Limoges he was shot at, arrows piercing his coat armour and wounding one of his own knights, but he eventually gained the city and besieged the castle. Young Henry, asking for a twenty-hour truce, came out of the castle and sat with his father, eating out of the same dish. Meanwhile Geoffrey left the castle, using the lull to bring in new troops.

On 17 April the king again acquiesced to allow his sons to converse with him and was shot at by an archer while they talked. He would have been killed had not his horse tossed its head at that moment and received the arrow meant for the king's breast. The king retired to await reinforcements.

11 June 1183: 'Flux of the bowels'
After Young Henry had slipped out of Limoges Castle to stir up more rebellion, the people refused to let him back into the city and he vowed to plunder the religious houses of the duchy. Shortly after, he fell ill with a severe fever and a 'flux of the bowels' and had to be carried to a village blacksmith's cottage.

Believing God was punishing him for stripping the shrine of Roquemadour and realising he was dying, he sent for his father. Fearing further treachery, the king sent him a message of love with a sapphire ring. Given the ring, Henry undressed and put on a hair shirt and placed a noose around his neck. He then asked attendants to drag him from his bed onto a bed of ashes and place large square stones under his head and feet. He made his confession, kissed his father's ring and died.

Learning his twenty-eight-year-old heir had died, the king sobbed, totally grief-stricken, saying, 'He cost me much but I would he lived to cost me more.'

31 March 1185: Knighthood
Being sent to rule Ireland, Prince John, now seventeen years old, was knighted by his father at Windsor. The prince had thrown himself at his father's feet begging to be allowed to go on crusade. Instead he will sail from Milford Haven for Waterford on 24 April.

17 December 1185: Recalled
Prince John and his band of young nobles were recalled from Dublin. Irish colonists had complained the prince cared only about wine, women and giving lands to his friends. Ranulf de Glanville agreed the prince had ignored advice given by wiser men of the country.

August 1186: Tournament Death

In a tourney, Prince Geoffrey, a month short of his twenty-eighth birthday, was unhorsed and trodden underfoot. Bruised and cut badly, he became ill with fever and died on 19 August. King Philip insisted he was buried in the choir of Notre Dame in Paris and had bystanders not held the French king back he would have flung himself into the grave. Geoffrey leaves behind one daughter, Eleanor, taken into ward by King Philip along with the duchy of Brittany. Rumour had it Philip and Geoffrey were plotting together to invade Normandy.

29 March 1187: Posthumous Birth

Duchess Constance, widow of Prince Geoffrey, bore him a posthumous son at Nantes and called him Arthur.

September 1187: Betrayal

At the peace treaty agreed in June between France and England, King Philip had private conference with Prince Richard, inviting him to Paris. During his stay, Prince Richard was so honoured by King Philip that 'by day they ate at one table, off one dish, and at night they slept in one bed'. Messengers sent to summon the prince back to his duties were ignored. When his father refused to have him crowned as he had his brother, Richard left Paris and seized the treasury at Chinon to use it for raising troops to make war on his father.

18 November 1188: Bonmoulins

Prince Richard rode openly with King Philip to meet with King Henry at the peace conference arranged at Bonmoulins. King Philip proposed King Henry should have Richard recognised as his heir to all his dominions but the king replied he would not give his consent under constraint. Prince Richard, hot tempered and hasty, threw off his sword and fell at the French king's feet and paid him homage for his father's Continental lands. Philip and Richard departed together.

19 May 1189: Ferte-Bernard

Having just recovered from his recent illness, King Henry agreed to meet again with King Philip and Prince Richard. The new demands were for Alys to immediately marry Richard, the barons of England and Normandy to give fealty to Richard as his heir and Prince John to be sent on crusade. King Henry refused. Prince Richard, threatened with interdict on his lands by Cardinal Anagni, furiously drew his sword on the papal legate but was stopped before he could follow through. King Philip sneered he feared not, for the church had no power to pass judgement on him if he thought it fit 'to punish rebellious subjects', and accused the legate of 'smelling the King of England's pounds sterling'.

12 June 1189: Surprise Attack

Faced with a surprise attack by Prince Richard on Le Mans, where his father lodged, Stephen de Turnham, Seneschal of Anjou, passed through the troops desperately holding the stone bridge and fired the suburbs to deter Richard's advance but the wind changed. Flames swept towards the city. Caught between flames and Frenchmen, King Henry evacuated the city. Reining in his mount on the spur of a hill a few miles away, he watched in bitterness as the city of his birth and burial place of his father was burned.

At first he headed for Normandy but, changing his mind, he sent John on with troops, commanding that if anything should happen to him Norman castles were to be delivered to his youngest son. He backtracked to Chinon but was spotted. He managed to outrun Richard and Philip, who chased him along narrow lanes and broken roads in the scorching sun. Richard almost came up alongside the king and his retinue, and William the Marshal turned and raised his lance to defend the king.

'God's feet, Marshal, do not kill me,' Richard cried out.

William struck the other's horse. 'I will not kill you. Let the devil kill you.'

3–4 July 1189: Indomitable Will

Though King Henry was ill with fever, he summoned enough strength to attend the conference set up by Prince Richard and King Philip at Colombieres but on his arrival he was seized with such intolerable agony he had to lean for support against a wall. Pitying bystanders laid him on a bed. Though Richard was told his father was ill, he relayed to Philip that his father was feigning illness and sent a message he should appear the next day.

With indomitable will, the king rose the next day, riding through the sultry heat to the meeting place. The great many people who had assembled to see his defeat were shocked at the marks of suffering on his face, even Philip, who called for a cloak to be spread on the ground. Henry refused it, saying he would hear their demands sat on horseback. The air was still, the sky cloudless. As the two kings advanced towards each other, there was a sudden clap of thunder. Each drew back. Again they advanced and there came another thunderclap, louder, startling Henry's horse. The ailing king was only kept on his horse by his attendants.

To each unreasonable demand the beaten king assented: full homage to the French king; Richard to receive the fealty of barons on both sides of the sea; restitution to be paid; Richard to go on pilgrimage to Jerusalem and on his return to marry Alys. King Henry made only one request: a list of the conspirators who joined with Richard to betray him.

Philip laughed when Richard jested that his father, as he gave the kiss of peace to his faithless son, whispered, 'May God not let me die until I have worthily avenged myself on thee!'

6 July 1189: Death of King Henry

From the conference, King Henry was carried by litter to Chinon Castle. His fever raged for the next few days, growing worse after Geoffrey, his chancellor and natural son, returned with the list of conspirators: the top name written on it was 'John'.

The king started up from his pillow, 'Is it true, that John, my very heart, whom I have loved beyond all my sons, has forsaken me?' Lying down again, he turned his face to the wall.

'You have said enough,' he said, 'Let all the rest go as it will, I care no more for myself nor for the world.' Growing more and more delirious, he called down heaven's vengeance on his sons.

On 6 July, seized with a violent haemorrhage, he died almost immediately.

His face was left uncovered. He was crowned and dressed in his coronation robes with gold ring, gold shoes and spurs, his sceptre in hand and girded with his sword to be carried to Fontevraud Abbey.

Richard I

1189–1199

Richard was praised by friend and foe for his personal courage and regarded as an able commander so long as his hot temper did not make him reckless and high-handed. Those who knew him considered him of excitable temperament, often ill with attacks of 'ague'. In Aquitaine, Richard ruled with hard justice. Despite a charm of manner and his love of poetry and music, his barons never warmed to him, nor he to them. Most of his life before becoming king was spent in fierce warfare against them, or his brothers and father. Now he ruled lands three times larger than those held by King Philip of France. His first action as king was to imprison Stephen, Seneschal of Anjou, forcing him to deliver over castles and treasury; his second was to forgive those who had taken his father's part and dismiss those who had taken his.

Henry's natural son, Geoffrey, had walked by his father's corpse from Chinon to Fontevraud Abbey. Richard, when he arrived at the abbey, stood looking down into his father's uncovered face, his own devoid of emotion. He knelt in silent prayer and left. Legend soon arose that blood had dripped from Henry's nostrils to signify his indignation at the son who caused his death.

After the burial, Richard, John and Geoffrey travelled together. On 20 July Richard was invested with the ducal sword and standard of Normandy in Rouen, having the day before received absolution from the archbishops of Canterbury, Rouen and Treves for having carried arms against his father after he had taken the cross, he being the first man in Europe to take it.

Meanwhile, in England, Queen Eleanor as Richard's regent made a country-wide progress accepting oaths of fealty in Richard's name from all freemen, pardoning criminals and releasing captives.

Sailing in different ships, on 13 August Richard landed at Portsmouth while John and Geoffrey landed at Dover and the three met the queen at Winchester Castle. Richard had his father's treasury inventoried and weighed. The total, without all the precious stones, came to £900,000 in gold and silver.

The office of Chancellor of the realm Richard gave to a man who despised the English and was more than willing to show it: the plain, short and lame William Longchamp. Richard honoured his father's bestowals: John was re-granted Marlborough Castle and the counties of Nottinghamshire and Mortain; Geoffrey was reaffirmed as Archbishop of York.

At Marlborough Castle on 29 August, at Richard's insistence, John was married to Hawisa, heiress of the Earl of Gloucester, gaining the earldom in right of his wife, along with Ludgershall Castle and the honours of Wallingford, Tickhill, Bolsover and The Peak. Archbishop Baldwin immediately put the lands under interdict in protest at the marriage (later lifted by the papal legate in November, at which time Richard gave John the counties of Cornwall, Devon, Somerset and Dorset).

As soon as Queen Eleanor had completed the coronation preparations, King Richard travelled to London. On his arrival, a proclamation was made: no Jew, man or woman, should enter either abbey or palace on the day of his coronation.

3 September 1189: Coronation

Emerging from his private chamber into Westminster Hall, Richard began the walk on the rich purple cloth laid all the way to the abbey, preceded by cross, clergy and four barons each carrying a tall wax candle. William, Earl Marshall carried the gold sceptre, William, Earl of Salisbury the rod and dove while John Marshal carried the weighty gold spurs. The three royal swords in golden sheaths were carried by Earl David of Scotland, Earl Robert of Leicester and Prince John, walking between them. Six earls and barons followed carrying a chequerboard on which were laid the royal regalia and robes. William, Earl of Essex carried the great gold crown, adorned on all sides with precious stones, and placed it on the high altar. The clamour of the watching crowds penetrated into the abbey as cheers rose even louder as the king passed.

Richard had a silk awning held high over him. Over six feet tall, graceful of limb and supple of form, his auburn hair shone in the candlelight and his blue eyes were solemn. A neatly trimmed beard and moustache framed a small, delicate mouth. A bishop on each side took hold of a hand to lead him to the high altar where, on Gospels and saints' relics, he swore to observe peace, honour and reverence all his life

God and the holy church, exercise true justice, abrogate all bad laws and unjust customs and observe those which were good. Stripped to hose and shirt, the latter ripped apart over his shoulders, he was anointed on head, breast and shoulders. After a coif and hat was placed on his head and buskins on his feet, he was dressed in a royal tunic, gown and mantle. At the last a sword was placed in his hand with which to crush all enemies of the church.

'In the name of God,' intoned the archbishop, 'do not presume to accept these honours unless your mind is steadily purposed to observe the oaths you have just made.'

Richard answered, 'With God's assistance, I will faithfully observe everything which I have promised.' He then took the crown from the altar and gave it to the archbishop, who placed it on his head, two earls either side supporting it on account of its weight. He sat on his throne holding sceptre and rod where, though the day was bright and candles made the abbey lighter, bats wheeled around him and fluttered through the abbey.

After Mass and the offertory, the king was escorted in procession to the choir where he removed his royal robes for rich clothes of lesser weight, and exchanged the crown for one lighter. He then returned to the hall for a splendid breakfast feast. The citizens of London served wine from the butlery and those of Winchester served from the kitchen the 1,900 chickens bought at a cost of slightly more than 1*d* each with many other dishes, while wine flowed along the pavement and walls of the palace for those celebrating outside.

3–4 September 1189: Unbridled Fury

Around the palace gates and doors, crowds of people had squeezed in to watch the king at table. Some Jewish people mingling in the crowds had been caught in the crush and swept inside. Caught looking in at the king, they were sworn at for their insolence. Ill language turned to blows. As the violence escalated, a rumour ran through the crowd that the king had ordered all Jews to be killed. Many Jews trying to run away were caught and beaten to death. Mobs roamed the streets, setting fire to Jewish houses and causing fires across the city. Trapped families were burnt inside their houses and any who escaped the flames were stabbed to death by the raging multitude.

Hearing sounds of tumult outside, King Richard sent Ranulf de Glanville to deal with the situation. Though he took a troop of soldiers, they were forced to retreat before such unbridled fury. Rioting continued all night. The next morning the king issued a proclamation that Jews were under his protection and all commotion must cease. Several ringleaders were arrested and hanged.

15–16 September 1189: Sold!

In council at Pipewell Abbey in Northamptonshire, Queen Eleanor was entitled queen regent. The king appointed two justiciars: William, Earl of Essex and Bishop Hugh of Durham. The latter was given charge of Windsor Castle and, for a price, the earldom of Northumberland. The four vacant sees were filled: the Bishopric of Ely was given to Chancellor William Longchamp, as was control of Westminster Palace and the Tower of London; Richard FitzNigel, the treasurer, became Bishop of London; Godfrey de Lucy became Bishop of Winchester; and Hubert Walter was now Bishop of Salisbury.

On the second day offices of ministers, royal officers and sheriffs were, in effect, auctioned, the king selling anything which might raise money including releases from offices, crown rights and crown property. Councillors remonstrated. Did he not think to return to England? Did he mean to diminish the power of the crown and its revenue? Offending many, the king retorted that he would 'sell London itself if a purchaser could be found'. The bruit is as the king is so often ill, with swelling in his limbs, he believes he will not return from crusade and cares nothing for his kingdom.

Prince John was absent from council, being sent to subdue Rhys of South Wales who had broken the king's peace. John had persuaded Rhys to surrender. With John taking homage on his brother's behalf from all other Welsh princes at Worcester, Rhys said he would only submit personally to Richard, whereupon John coaxed him as far as Oxford. There, word came that Richard had no intention of travelling to Oxford and he should send Rhys home.

11 December 1189: Released

King Richard, leaving without ceremony, crossed from Dover to Gravelines, accompanied by Archbishop Baldwin, Ranulf de Glanville and Hubert Walter, Bishop of Salisbury, who intend to accompany him on crusade. Before he left, King William of Scotland attended the council held at Canterbury on 5 December and for ten thousand marks King Richard restored to him the castles of Roxburgh and Berwick and released him and his heirs forever from giving homage for Scotland.

6 January 1190: Flexing his Muscles

At the Court of Exchequer today, newly enthroned William, Bishop of Ely maliciously forbade entrance to Bishop Hugh, audaciously seizing his sword of investiture and revoking all the grants given to him by King Richard. Not content with this injury, the chancellor deprived

Bishop Godfrey of Winchester of his sheriffdom of Hampshire, his castles and even his own inheritance.

14 March 1190: Normandy Council

Returned from his Gascon court at La Reole, King Richard summoned his mother, brothers, chief ministers and his betrothed Alys, the French king's sister, to Nonancourt. The chancellor arrived first ready to defend his actions. Rather than berate him, King Richard told him he had asked the Pope to create him papal legate of England, and made him Chief Justiciar with full royal authority. At first, Richard sought oaths from John and Geoffrey not to set foot in England for three years, but at Queen Eleanor's request he released John from his vow.

16 March 1190: Massacre

A wave of riots and killings had erupted against the Jews in the major towns of Lynn, Norwich and Stamford and other places. Young crusaders 'without any scruple of Christian conscience' murdered Jews in the streets, their own houses and at fairs.

At York, sheriff John Marshal allowed Jewish families – over five hundred men, women and children – to take refuge in the castle. Rioters sacked their houses, killing anyone found hiding, and destroyed bonds and all records of debt, including those held by the king in the Minster. Called away on business, the sheriff returned to find the Jews had barricaded the keep, fearing treachery by him. Losing all sense, John called knights out to attack the castle who came with bands of armed men. Having no weapons, Jewish men pulled stones from the walls to throw at their attackers. One stone accidentally killed a hermit who had been inciting the mob to more violence. Seeing the rabid, fanatical hatred, on 16 March, the head of each family using sharp razors cut the throats of wives, children and other family members and set the wooden keep alight for a funeral pyre to kill themselves.

3 May 1190: Investigation

King Richard ordered Chancellor Longchamp to investigate the recent unlawful acts and treasonous injury to his revenues at York. The chancellor listened as important citizens stoutly denied their involvement, affirming stranger ringleaders had fled into Scotland, but he fined each man according to his fortune.

26 June 1190: Pilgrim

To formally enter crusade, King Richard laid on the ground. Rising, in tears, he was passed the two gold-crossed banners he will carry with him and the pilgrim's staff and wallet. Today the royal family left Tours. Geoffrey travels to Vézelay with King Richard to meet up with King Philip; Queen Eleanor, though in her late sixties, is travelling to Navarre; John, accompanied by his friend Bishop Hugh of Durham, is returning to England.

Mid/late August 1190: Fortifications

By letter sent from Marseilles, King Richard instructed Chancellor Longchamp to return the earldom of Northumberland and the manor of Sedbergh to Bishop Hugh of Durham or incur the anger and curse of both king and God. Ignoring his king and using his own seal, Longchamp seized Bishop Hugh at Southwell and imprisoned him in his own manor house at Howden and took charge of Windsor Castle. Since his return in March the chancellor has paid out over £2,881 fortifying the Tower of London, which he has surrounded with a very deep moat. He has also spent £1,058 on Dover Castle, held by Matthew de Cleres, who is married to his sister Richenda.

13 October 1190: Papal Legate

Since June, when King Richard's letter from Bayonne was read instructing all his subjects to obey Longchamp without question, he has travelled the shires like a 'flash of lightning', leaving 'no man even his belt, a woman her necklace or a nobleman his ring'. Nobles have been married to his female relatives or subdued by intimidation, bribery or fines. He rides around the country like a pompous eastern prince, 'bearing a sneer in his nostrils', ruling everything to his own impulse, keeping guards around his chamber and riding with a thousand horse and more. Now he says the king requires each city to provide two palfreys and two sumpter horses and one of each from every abbey and manor. At council today, he showed the instrument creating him papal legate as if it made any difference. He has also appropriated the revenues of Canterbury and York sees while archbishops Baldwin and Geoffrey are overseas.

18 November 1190: Secret Whispers

Hugh Bardolf arrived with letters from King Richard who has been at Messina since 23 September. 'Secret whispers' say that Richard has made his three-year-old nephew, Arthur, his heir and arranged a marriage between him and one of the King of Sicily's daughters.

The open news is that when Richard arrived at Messina to trumpets and clarions, crowds rushed to the waterside to see his galleys enter the harbour. Adorned with shining pennons and standards, each vessel had shields glittering along their sides in the sun. King Richard, magnificently dressed, stood proudly on an elevated ornamental prow. His entrance completely overshadowed that of King Philip seven days earlier.

Camped in the vineyards outside the city, Richard, in his usual custom, caused gibbets to be erected to hang any thief or robber, no matter the sex, age or nationality. After the two kings met and talked, King Philip boarded his ship but the wind shifted, forcing him to return to harbour.

Initial hostility between King Richard and King Tancred of Sicily was smoothed after royal messengers secured the immediate release of the king's widowed sister, Queen Joanna. Although he demanded her dowry and legacy – a golden seat and table 12 feet long, golden cups and dishes, a silk tent, galleys and two years' worth of wheat, barley and wine – she arrived on 28 September with her bedchamber furniture and barely enough money to cover her expenses. The king has lodged her in the Castle of La Bagnara, after expelling the Griffones (as the English call the natives) from it. It was at La Bagnara that the king had seen a fine hawk in a house as he rode by and carried it off. The peasants chased after him throwing stones, but one man drew a knife and the king broke his sword using the flat of it on him. For a provisions store, the king expelled monks from a monastery, exhibiting as 'gazing-stock' those who resisted. Citizens, discontented at such high-handedness, barred King Richard from entering the city but in one short attack he gained possession of the city, placing his banners along the walls. When King Philip indignantly demanded his banners should fly alongside, Richard replaced his banners with those of the Templars. Because King Philip 'winked at wrongs', Richard is called a 'lion' and the other a 'lamb'.

24 March 1191: Refused
At Winchester, Earl John asked Longchamp to release to him his own castles and provide money from the Exchequer given to him by King Richard. Refused, John was much displeased, evidenced as he left by the angry white that displaced his usual rosy complexion.

25 April 1191: Arbitration
Gerard Camville, with his wife Nicholaa, refused to surrender Lincoln Castle to Longchamp after he peremptorily removed the offices of

Sheriff of Lincolnshire and Constable of the Castle from Gerard, held by right of his wife. When Longchamp besieged the castle, husband and wife fought, 'she like a man', and sent for aid from Earl John. He sent word to the chancellor to raise the siege or he would come to his liegeman's aid and immediately garrisoned his castles of Tickhill and Nottingham.

A council was called at Winchester. Earl John contended it was improper to take offices from the loyal men of the kingdom and commit them to strangers unknown. With arbiters agreed between the two, judgement was given in favour of John. The chancellor was instructed not to seek to disinherit John from the succession and Gerard and Nicholaa retained their castle in 'peace and safety'.

27 April 1191: Messina Dispute

Walter Coutances, Archbishop of Rouen, who left Messina on 2 April, landed today at Shoreham, and brought news that on a visit to King Tancred at Catania on 3 March, King Richard was told by the Sicilian king that King Philip had told him not to trust Richard's word. In gratitude, King Richard gave King Tancred Excalibur, the sword found at Glastonbury. When Richard returned to Messina, he charged Philip with being base. The French king countered Richard was using a lie to break his oath to marry Alys. Richard bluntly replied he would never marry her for being 'improperly intimate' with his father. King Philip angrily released Richard from his betrothal, vowing he would 'be the enemy of him and his so long as I live'. The moment King Philip left for Jerusalem on 28 March, Queen Eleanor arrived with Princess Berenguela of Navarre, Richard's future bride and sister of his friend Sancho the Strong. The two women were lodged with Joanna but Queen Eleanor stayed only for a few days before setting out again to Rome, on her son's behalf, to see the Pope regarding Geoffrey's consecration to the see of York.

23 June 1191: Eclipse

An eclipse of the sun took place at six o'clock. The stars were 'visible for three hours'.

28 July 1191: Second Arbitration

Boasting that either he or John would be 'ousted from the kingdom', Longchamp brought in foreign troops to besiege Lincoln Castle. To prevent full-scale bloodshed, Archbishop Walter arranged a second arbitration. Set for today at Winchester, the arbiters set the original agreement with the addition that the chancellor's case against Gerard was to be put before the *curia*. John agreed to this, saying that as it is lawful custom that freeholders cannot be disseised of their lands except by judgment of the king's court he would abide by the court's decision.

14–26 September 1191: 'Wings of the wind'

Newly consecrated Geoffrey, Archbishop of York, was stopped from sailing in a Flemish ship though they happily took his baggage across to Dover. Alerted, he arrived in an English boat on Saturday 14 September about nine in the morning where, expecting soldiers, he disguised himself and mounted a horse on the beach. As he galloped towards the Priory of St Martin, one of the soldiers spotted him and managed to catch Geoffrey's horse by its bridle, but kicking his adversary's horse in its side with his steel heel, Geoffrey nearly unseated its rider.

Arriving as Mass was starting, soldiers surrounded the priory and Geoffrey asked who had authorised his capture. He was told it was by order of William Longchamp via his sister, Lady Richenda, and if her brother told her to burn down Dover Castle and London Town she would obey. He was asked to take the oath of fealty to Richard. He replied he had already done so and would not upon compulsion do it again.

The following day, soldiers came into the church. Geoffrey excommunicated them and Richenda. On 18 September, losing patience, Richenda ordered soldiers to seize him. Hauled from the altar while assisting at Mass, he was dragged by hands and feet, still holding his cross, to the castle and thrown into prison.

'Flying as it were upon the wings of the wind', the news of such an outrage on the king's half-brother and an archbishop raged around the country. After an imprisonment of eight days, Geoffrey was released by order of the chancellor who had received a vehement remonstrance from John, who had sent a summons for a council to Archbishop Walter, justices, bishops and nobles. Longchamp issued letters in rebuttal and accused John of being a traitor. Travelling to Windsor, a counter-summons arrived asking him to answer for his conduct at a council arranged for Saturday 5 October at Lodden Bridge between Reading and Windsor.

5–12 October 1191: Accusations

On the first day of the assembly at Lodden Bridge, in the absence of the chancellor, who sent to say he was too sick to attend, Archbishop

Geoffrey showed his letter of authority from Richard permitting his return to England. Archbishop Walter showed Richard's letters of instructions which the chancellor had ignored and that he had been warned if he crossed London Bridge it would be to his peril. Justiciars and councillors agreed all their counsels had been ignored.

On Monday, the chancellor still absent, the barons crossed Lodden Bridge to take the highway towards Windsor, sending their baggage separately to London under strong guard. Seeing the train, one of the chancellor's men rode to Windsor to tell him John was on his way to seize the capital. Longchamp, thinking to intercept his enemy at Hounslow, immediately set out across the Thames to take the shorter road to London. At the crossroads, a skirmish took place and John's justiciar, Roger de Plasnes, was killed. Longchamp continued to London where he ordered the gates shut. Calling the citizens to Guildhall, he entreated them to defend the king against Prince John and shut himself in the Tower. City officials, far from shutting the gates, welcomed John with lanterns and torches when he arrived that night.

As church bells rang on Tuesday, Prince John, Archbishop Walter, clergy and nobles assembled in St Paul's where the archbishop was welcomed by John as Chief Justiciar of England, 'supreme over affairs'. Both of them agreed a grant of commune to London citizens, giving them the right to keep and maintain their own peace and to see right done in all things without fear or favour.

On Wednesday, four bishops went to the Tower to tell William he had been replaced by Archbishop Walter. He fainted, coming round only after cold water was sprinkled on his face. So angry he foamed at the mouth, William shouted that they were disloyal to King Richard and had given the kingdom to John. Near nightfall, he yielded the Great Seal and agreed to appear before council early the next morning in the fields to the east of the Tower.

Ringed by the barons and prelates, themselves ringed by a circle of citizens 'and an attentive populace', William stood face-to-face with his accusers. As the charges were pronounced, he declared he was innocent and could justify his every action and account for every farthing. The council decreed they would no longer have him rule over them and took charge of all his castles except his own of Dover, Cambridge and Hereford. At sunset, he finally relinquished the keys to the Tower: 'I, chancellor and justiciar of the kingdom, sentenced contrary to the form of all law, yield to the stronger.' Promising not to leave England until the castles were handed over, he gave as surety his brothers as hostages.

Sat alone on a rock by the seaside, a sailor noticed a hooded woman dressed in green gown and cape and holding linen. Wishing some sport, he shouted aloud in astonishment at what he found and stumbled away. A number of idle women crowded round to ask if her linen was for sale. Receiving no reply, they ripped away the hood and veil to find a man 'dark and lately shaved'. Shouting that Longchamp was a disgrace to both sexes, they dragged him over sand and stones, through the streets and into a cellar where orders soon came for his release.

22 October 1191: Hawk's Pike

One of the young men of the Bishop of London's household taught a hawk to hunt teals but once, when a teal was startled into flight at the sound of a tabor, the hawk 'baffled of his booty' intercepted a pike swimming in the water and carried it forty feet to dry land. The bishop, astonished at the singular circumstance, sent hawk and pike to Prince John as a gift.

January 1192: Acre

After leaving the Holy Land on 1 August 1191 with King Philip, Roger of Howden, King Richard's chronicler and secretary, returned safely to England after spending Christmas Day at Fontevraud Abbey. He reported to council that King Philip was boasting that he intended to lay waste to all Richard's territories and castles and, in audience with the Pope, had said King Richard had treacherously forced him into leaving Jerusalem, failing to mention his illness and the gift from the English king of his two best galleys. The king's councillors said that no one will believe talk resulting from jealousy and envy.

Roger brought news that on Good Friday the king's fleet had been scattered in fearful storms, being driven to Crete, Rhodes and Cyprus. Isaac, self-styled Emperor of Cyprus, had refused aid to the shipwrecked, killing those who reached land and seizing their goods. Seeing the danger, the ship with the king's betrothed and sister stayed outside of the harbour at Limassol where Richard found them the sport of wind and waves. Messengers sent to Isaac to complain were told, 'Pruht', he was 'more than a king' and could act as he pleased. Richard called, 'To arms!' As his boats rowed rapidly towards shore, his archers released arrows to darken the sky like rain. Men hidden behind doors, shutters, casks and crosswise benches fled, while Isaac in costly armour on a warhorse champing at the bit shouted at them to return and then retreated himself as King Richard, first out of a landing boat, vaulted onto a horse by the aid of a lance and gave chase.

In the night, noiselessly entering the emperor's camp where all were 'buried in sleep', King Richard and his soldiers set upon the emperor's force like 'ravening wolves'. Escaping in the nude, the emperor left behind treasures, steeds, arms, beautiful tents and his imperial standard, wrought with gold, which Richard immediately dedicated to St Edmund and had sent to England.

On 12 May, in the presence of Guy, King of Jerusalem and Raymond, Prince of Antioch and other nobles, a merry and affable Richard and, as she became known, Berengaria were married just after dawn in St George's Chapel by the Archbishop of Bordeaux. Immediately afterwards, Richard's bride was crowned and consecrated Queen of England and Cyprus. Twenty-one years old, the queen's beautiful, bright countenance was framed by her hair, parted in the middle and swept over her shoulders to hang down her back in long tresses covered by a veil.

Isaac sued for peace that morning, arranging a meeting on the plains. In his festive dress, King Richard was an arresting figure. His rose satin tunic was belted at the waist and girded with a gold-hilted sword. His striped mantle was adorned with silver half-moons and his scarlet bonnet was embroidered with gold birds and beasts which shone in the sun. Richard's spirited Spanish charger champed on its golden bit as he vaulted onto the gold-spangled saddle, its crupper decorated with two fierce gold lions poised in attack. Exchanging terms, emperor and king kissed the peace and entered Limassol together. While guards took their midday sleep, however, the emperor sneaked away and decamped to his castle at Nicosia where he declared war. His daughter threw herself on Richard's mercy and was sent to the queen.

On 1 June, all his castles taken, the emperor cast himself at Richard's feet and begged for mercy, asking not to be put into irons. Richard was merciful: he put him into silver chains.

Reaching Acre seven days later, King Richard was welcomed by war-worn and starving pilgrims. They cheered even harder at news of the new supply base in Cyprus and the taking on the way of Saladin's ship full of provisions, trying to emulate a previous occasion when he had successfully smuggled grain, cheese, onions and sheep into the city by dressing his men as clean-shaven Franks and attaching crosses to the masts and showing pigs on deck.

The triangular city, washed on one side by the ocean and defended on the other two by a ditch, has been besieged for four years. Every time Christians attack the city, hordes of Saracens sweep down from surrounding mountains and hills to attack them, their colourful tents dotting the slopes like flowers. When darkness fell, so many fires were lit and waxen lights gleamed that night 'usurped the brightness of day'. Soldiers sang, drank and danced to horns, tambourine and harp, all for Richard's arrival.

Philip, who had arrived at Acre at Easter, had attempted one assault and seen his siege engines destroyed by Greek fire. Richard immediately oversaw the building of new engines and towers but soon fell ill of a wasting fever the physicians called *Arnaldia*. Patients lose their hair, fingernails and toenails. While Richard lay powerless in his tent, Philip ordered heralds to proclaim another attack. Defenders poured Greek fire over the walls, killing and wounding thousands, and then King Philip fell ill of the same disease and it was feared both kings might die.

With attacks continuing on the city walls night and day, King Richard, though ill, had himself carried out on a silken bed under cover of a *circleia* and used his crossbow with deadly skill, protecting miners while they tunnelled and burned logs under the walls, cheering his men when they toppled a tower. Wide breaches in the walls appeared caused by his English sappers. On 12 July, Acre surrendered.

20 January 1192: Forgery

King Philip showed forged documents to the Seneschal of Normandy declaring King Richard had given him the castles of Gisors, Eu and Aumale and instructed his sister was to be brought from Rouen and sent to him. Having received no instructions from King Richard, the seneschal refused.

11 Feb 1192: 'Kicked it off his head'

After spending Christmas in Normandy, Queen Eleanor landed today at Portsmouth, where she found John at the port and tearfully requested him not to leave the kingdom.

The queen, in Rome on 14 April when Pope Celestine III was consecrated, was present the following day to watch King Henry of Germany and his wife, Constance, give their oaths to the Pope on the steps of St Peter's before being crowned Emperor and Empress. Sitting on his throne, the Pope sat with the gold imperial crown at his feet. Henry, head inclined, received the crown and the Pope immediately kicked it off his head, signifying papal power to cut him down if he should so deserve. The cardinals picked it up and replaced it on his head.

March 1192: Rain or Tears

Crusaders coming home brought news that on 17 August 1191, Saladin broke his agreement to give up the Holy Cross and 1,500 captive Christians; however, King Richard kept his word and executed the 2,600 Saracens he held in his hands, retaining only a few nobles. Five days later, King Richard left Acre, walls repaired and a stronger garrison in place. His aim was to reach Jaffa, eighty miles distant, and travel inland once he was almost opposite Jerusalem. Dividing the army into twelve companies of five divisions, they crossed the river and marched south along the seashore, supply ships sailing alongside.

In stifling heat, Saladin's troops constantly poured down on the men from the mountains like 'rushing water' and each day's encampment was built only through struggle and butchery. The day they reached the outskirts of Arsuf and tried to make camp before the day's heat intensified, Saladin sent his army of ten thousand to make a violent attack on the rear-guard. Dark-skinned Sudanese thundered down on them, their dust blackening the air, their fierce battle cries drowning all other noise. Four squadrons wheeled about to the attack. King Richard, on his bay Cyprian, protected by metal shielding and his own coat of mail to his knees, aimed for the thickest fighting. He cleared a pathway either side of him, a reaper with his sickle, sparks flying from his double-edged sword, dagger with jewelled hilt flashing in the sun. Saladin in the heights could only watch as an entire wing of his army was driven into the sea and slaughtered.

At Jaffa, there was a respite as soldiers gorged themselves on figs, grapes, pomegranates and citrons brought in from the surrounding countryside and on the provisions brought by sea.

Hearing Saladin had levelled Ascalon, King Richard wanted to force-march on; the other commanders wanted first to repair Jaffa's walls and towers, clean the moat and dig trenches. Saladin saw their delay as his opportunity to destroy all the crusader castles between Jaffa and Jerusalem. When they finally moved, winter had set in. In heavy rain, hail and freezing cold, despondent and drenched men marched, their provisions soaked and spoiled. It took two months to reach Beit Nuba, twelve miles from Jerusalem, only for morale to be completely shattered as supply lines were deemed too precarious to carry on and manpower insufficient to recover Jerusalem.

On 13 January 1192 came the order to march to Ascalon, which they reached in seven days, so weary no one knew if it was rain or tears on their faces when they found walls so demolished there was no shelter. Many discouraged Christians left the Holy Land while Saladin disbanded his army for the winter. Nobles, knights and esquires dug foundations and tossed stones hand-to-hand to build the walls. King Richard, setting an example, worked with his own hands alongside his men. When Leopold, Archduke of Austria refused to help, claiming

The Plantagenet Socialite

that as neither son of a carpenter nor mason he should not 'work like a labourer', King Richard told him he and his followers should camp outside the walls for he would not allow them to share protection of walls they refused to help build.

2 April 1192: Failed Reconciliation

Queen Eleanor, visiting her dower houses in the diocese of Ely, found Archbishop Walter had put it under interdict. Barefoot men, women and little children flocked from the hamlets, hair uncut, clothes unwashed and in tears, asking for her help as their loved ones lay unburied. Moved by pity, she entreated the archbishop to lift it and absolve the Bishop of Ely. She then sent word to William that if he returned to England she would speak for him at council. But when he came, the council ignored her intercession and told him if he did not depart the kingdom he would be taken prisoner.

1 July 1192: Assassination

News arrived of the assassination in Tyre of Conrad, king-elect of Jerusalem, on 28 April. King Philip is telling everyone that King Richard had 'employed murderers to kill' his friend and 'is alarmed for his own safety' in case he sends emissaries from the Old Man of the Mountain to 'thrust their daggers' into him too. King Richard's nephew, Henry of Champagne, has been asked to take the throne. The king was pleased but apparently distracted as he had received mixed letters, some saying all was well in England and others that John had usurped his kingdom.

December 1192: Where Is King Richard?

Crusaders arriving home were surprised that King Richard had not reached England before them, his ship having left Acre on 9 October, sighted last near Brindisi. They brought news that the army reached Beit Nuba again on 10 June. Soldiers were in high spirits, despite being attacked by small swarms of insects with stings like sparks of fire that left them with 'leper-skin'. Provisions had been plentiful, shared out by the king after he attacked a Muslim caravan. Travel was easy. Then scouts found Saladin had poisoned all the cisterns and wells around Jerusalem. No water, no attack. It meant retreat.

When Saladin launched a lightning strike on Jaffa, the king had immediately left Acre to go to its defence, arriving at dawn on 5 August unsure whether or not the citadel had fallen. A defender dived from its walls into the sea and swam to the king's boat to say they were still fighting. King Richard jumped into the sea, armed but with legs and feet bare, and threw himself like a raging lion into Saladin's troops, hewing them down right and left. Saladin fled, and the king pitched his tent where Saladin's had been.

When Saladin realised Richard had only fifty-four knights with him, he sent troops to surround the English camp. Guards spotted them and Richard, arming himself and 'laying aside all fear of death', mounted his horse and flew, dealing thunderous blows on helms and freeing Arab horses for his unmounted men. Fighting dawn to dusk, the enemy were dispersed. For their bravery, the king singled out Robert, Earl of Leicester, Andrew de Chauvigny, Hubert Walter and Hugh de Neville. Then King Richard fell ill, the air tainted with the miasma of thousands of rotting corpses and horse carcases. Messengers were sent to Saladin to propose a truce. Saladin agreed: three years, three months, three weeks, three days and three hours and they would battle again. He agreed the Christians could keep Jaffa if they razed Ascalon and would be permitted free access to the Holy Sepulchre. King Richard never visited Jerusalem; deeming himself unworthy, he sailed away.

January 1193: Captive

A copy of a letter dated 26 December between Emperor Henry VI and King Philip was read out at the Oxford Council. King Richard had been 'shipwrecked at a place lying between Aquileia and Venice' and on 20 December Leopold, Archduke of Austria captured the king 'in a humble house in a village in the vicinity of Vienna and he is now in our power'. Two abbots have been sent out into the German territories to ascertain where King Richard is imprisoned.

After receiving assurances from King Philip that Richard would never escape from the emperor, Earl John, 'despairing' that Richard would return to England, travelled to Paris.

4 March 1193: Heaviness of Sorrow

After riding in heavy rain without his usual quilted gambeson, fifty-five-year-old Saladin fell ill with fever. Worsening every day, he was buried on the day he died, sword beside him, in the garden house of Damascus's citadel. Every man went home after the simple funeral, and the empty, silent streets reflected the heaviness of sorrow lying on the city.

20 April 1193: King's Ransom

Hubert Walter, archbishop-elect of Canterbury, sent news that King Richard had been put on trial before Emperor Henry on Palm Sunday as if he was a criminal. He was charged with insulting Archduke Leopold, treachery, murdering Conrad, causing the crusade to fail and basely treating with Saladin. He defended himself so well he was deemed innocent, but the emperor demands a ransom of 150,000 marks for his release.

10 February 1194: John Excommunicated
Archbishop Hubert excommunicated John and judged his castles forfeit although Queen Eleanor had persuaded her son to keep peace until All Saints' Day. The garrisons of John's castles have refused to surrender except to King Richard or John. Fleeing overseas, John gave custody of Windsor, Wallingford and The Peak to his mother.

13 March 1194: King Richard Returns
After captivity of one year, six weeks and three days, King Richard, met at Antwerp by his sea captain Alan, landed today at Sandwich. England had made a titanic effort to raise the ransom. Chalices and church treasures, major portions of incomes of clergy and laity and personal treasures poured in from all sides.

Two days before the king's release on 4 February, Emperor Henry produced letters from King Philip offering him a large sum of money for every month he detained the king. His own nobles revolted and boldly urged him not to so dishonour himself.

1–2 April 1194: Nottingham Council
Once assured that King Richard had really returned, the castles of Lancaster, Tickhill and St Michael's Mount surrendered to him. Nottingham Castle followed suit upon seeing the king in the flesh. The rising, if such it could be called, was over.

Summoning a council to Nottingham the following day, King Richard stated he intended to cross to Normandy to defend it against King Philip, who had attempted and failed to take Rouen. He asked for a grant of 2s out of every carucate of land and every man the third part of a knight's service. Further, all that he had bestowed or sold for a weighty price before setting out on crusade he demanded back as if he had only lent it. No one dared plead against the crown.

17 April 1194: Benediction
In his royal robes, holding sceptre and rod and wearing his gold crown, King Richard walked down the nave of Winchester Cathedral watched by a great crowd of common people. A restored Chancellor Longchamp

was at his right hand, the Bishop of London on his left. The sword of estate was carried by King William. Richard knelt before the archbishop and received benediction and was led to his seat opposite Queen Eleanor, surrounded by her maids of honour. Mass over, a banquet was held in the refectory, the citizens of London serving in the cellars, those of Winchester serving in the kitchen until a late hour.

12 May 1194: Forgiven
Waiting tediously at Portsmouth for the bad weather to clear, King Richard and his mother sailed to Normandy with a fleet of 100 large ships, laden with warriors, horses and arms intended to stop King Philip besieging Verneuil Castle. Within a few miles of the port, Queen Eleanor as mediator arranged for John to meet with his brother. Richard told him though he had acted foolishly: 'Those who have led him on have already had their reward, or will soon have it.' At dinner, for a gift, Richard had a fine salmon cooked for John.

22 August 1194: Tournaments
With a truce in place and all castles recaptured from King Philip, King Richard sent a letter to Archbishop Hubert that he wished to hone the skills of his knights by holding tournaments. To enter they would have to buy a licence – 20 marks for an earl, 10 for a baron, 4 for a landed knight and 2 for the landless – and take oaths to keep peace, pay reasonable market prices for food and necessities, and take nothing by force.

31 December 1194: Death
Leopold, Duke of Austria fell from his horse during a tournament held on St Stephen's Day. His foot was so crushed his physicians thought it needed to be amputated. With the surgeons reluctant to do it, the archduke got a servant to chop it off with an axe. People consider it a 'just judgement of God' that he died in great suffering.

Christmastide 1195: Poitiers
Recovering from a severe illness and criticised by the Pope for consorting with other women, King Richard spent Christmas with his queen at Poitiers.

28 August 1198: 'Kiss me then'
At the December council in Oxford, Archbishop Hubert proposed for all barons, including the clergy, to assist King Richard and Prince

John in their overseas campaign against King Philip by providing 300 knights, paid at 3s a day, for a year's service abroad. Bishop Hugh of Lincoln disputed whether the church was bound to give overseas military service to the king. Richard was so angry at this that he summoned the bishop, an instruction that was ignored for nearly eight months until, fearing he would get other officials in trouble, the bishop crossed the Channel to face the music.

Finding the king at Mass at his castle of Roche d'Andeley, Hugh saluted but the king ignored him after one fierce glance.

'Kiss me, O lord my king.'

Richard ignored him.

As if he was a schoolboy, Hugh seized the king's mantle in both hands and drew it tightly around the royal chest and shook him. 'Thou owest me a kiss as I come from afar.'

'Thou deserves it not,' muttered Richard.

The bishop just shook him again. 'Kiss me then.'

Richard, unable to hold out any longer, laughed outright and kissed him. Later he sent him a large pike as a gift.

13 January–2 February 1199: Sower of Discord

While suing for a truce, King Philip informed King Richard that Prince John had placed himself in his hands and that he could prove it by signed document. Indignant at John, King Richard dispossessed him of all his lands. Finding the cause of his brother's hatred, John sent two knights to the French court demanding to prove his innocence of the charge. When not one person challenged his defence, King Richard swore he would give less credence to the French king and received John into greater favour.

6 April 1199: Death of King Richard

Fighting fire and sword against his own rebel Poitevin barons, King Richard laid siege to the castle of Chalus. Although the garrison had offered to surrender when Richard arrived on 24 March, he swore he would rather hang them all. Having eaten, the king was watching operations without armour except an iron helm. Not quite under cover, he stopped to watch a man parrying arrows with a frying pan. Amused, Richard applauded him. Suddenly a crossbow bolt struck him between his left shoulder and base of his neck, penetrating downwards deep into his side. Making light of his wound, he rode to his tent as if nothing was amiss. When he rashly tried to pull the quarrel out, the wooden shaft broke off, leaving the iron barb inside. A surgeon tried to cut it out.

Despite his wound, the swelling and terrible pain, the king insisted on fighting but day-by-day the wound blackened. Aware he was dying, King Richard sent for his mother. He declared John his heir and left three-quarters of his jewels to his nephew Emperor Otto, the rest to be divided between his servants and the poor. He ordered his body to be buried at Fontevraud at the feet of his father to show his repentance, bequeathing his heart to Rouen for its fidelity to him and his entrails to the castle chapel in memory of Poitevin treachery. His life drew to a close as the day faded.

John

1199–1216

Asked about King John, many would immediately label him 'evil, cruel and tyrannical' and, moulded by childhood tales of Robin Hood and school lessons, make mention of *Magna Carta,* papal interdict and the 'softsword' king who lost his overseas dominions and his treasure in the Wash.

When Richard died, John was in Normandy and he rode to Fontevraud to visit the tombs of his father and brother. He then spent Easter at Beaufort with his mother, Queen Eleanor, and Richard's widow, Queen Berengaria. All during Holy Week, John humbly thanked poor men and women who stood by the roadside and wished him good fortune.

Contemporaries write he was affable and cordial, that his 'hospitality was wholehearted and generous, and at mealtimes the doors to his hall always stood open. Anyone at all wishing to eat at his court could do so.' Courtiers received gifts of fine clothes and cloaks on feast days or grants to hunt hares, wildcats, foxes and deer. John enjoyed hawking and hunting, riding his much-loved dapple horse with his favourite hunting dogs, and reading, carrying a library with him wherever he travelled. Although considered irreligious, he read religious works.

He paid penance for hunting or eating on fast days by giving alms or food to paupers. He fed 350 poor men one day after a good day's hunting netted him seven cranes. Large churches and abbeys did not particularly receive rich gifts and endowments but smaller houses received grants of land and money, and practical gifts such as cartloads of wood. During 1211 and 1212 records show he purchased nearly half a million salted herrings to supply nunneries all over England.

As a result of King Philip's warring in France, John's own revenue diminished and forced him into raising feudal and fiscal dues, alienating his nobles. Their disaffection eventually led them to compel him by force to sign their Charter of Liberties – later called *Magna Carta* – in which, not content in naming John's wrongs as they perceived them, they added his father's and brother's too. Grumbling that he distrusted them, they accused him of relying on 'wicked counsellors', actually the men most loyal to him. John reposed his trust in those who earned it, whether man or woman. Nicholaa la Haye was confirmed as constable of Lincoln Castle and sheriff of Lincolnshire in 1216; Joan, who kept his hounds in Norfolk, held a serjeantry; and Savaric de Mauleon, captured by John in 1202, became a trusted official and trustee of his will.

John could be hot-tempered but soon calmed. Servants happily took his money as they beat him regularly at backgammon. Queen Isabella, his wife, was never afraid to make sharp retorts. On one occasion, he said, 'Listen, my lady, I have lost everything for you.'

She snapped back, 'Sire, I lost the best knight in the world for you.'

Once, telling her he would keep her safe from the King of France, she replied that his deviousness would end up in him getting 'cornered and checkmated'. Contemporary consensus agrees theirs was an affectionate relationship. Even when fighting his barons in 1215, John was solicitous of her safety and welfare, sending orders for her to be supplied with foodstuffs or 'silks and furs for her wardrobe'. Entries reveal the Scottish and Breton princesses, with their maids, were honourably kept well-clothed and supplied with outdoor cloaks, furred capes, saddles and harnesses. Chambers were adorned with cloth-of-silk and arras and John dressed well in fine, clean clothes – his washerwoman received regular wages. He also bathed regularly, his bath attendant William receiving 5*d* each time. To relax after a bath John designed a night-time 'supertunic'.

John had at least nine illegitimate children, seemingly all born before he married Isabella, though there is an intriguing reference in 1212–13 to a chaplet of roses being carried to the king's mistress. A point in his favour to consider: all his natural sons stayed completely loyal to him.

18 April 1199: Pointed Lesson

At Mass on Easter Sunday, when John came to the altar to offer, he softly jingled twelve gold coins in his palm. Bishop Hugh of Lincoln asked what he was doing. John replied he was looking at them, for a few days ago he would have put them back in his purse. Bishop Hugh, assuming John was grudging their surrender, refused to touch them when they were proffered, indignantly ordering, 'Throw down what you are holding and withdraw.' John put the coins into the silver offertory dish and returned to his place. Hugh then gave a pointed sermon comparing the habits between bad and good princes which went on so long that John sent a message asking if the bishop would kindly bring it to an end so that his audience might to go dinner. Ignoring it, the bishop raised his voice and increased his fervour. He was applauded when he finally ceased.

25 April 1199: Ducal Crown

Queen Eleanor was absent at the ceremony in Rouen Cathedral where Archbishop Walter, after girding the sword of Normandy around John, placed the coronet of golden roses on his head.

On 19 April she and John had received a message that Maine, Anjou, Touraine and Brittany had declared Arthur, John's twelve-year-old nephew, their rightful ruler. Gathering troops, the castle and all stone-built houses of Le Mans were levelled. While John travelled on to Rouen, Queen Eleanor, though in her seventies, led the army to ravage Anjou.

27 May 1199: Coronation

Two thousand yards of linen was laid between Westminster Palace and Westminster Abbey along the nave to the high altar for King John to walk upon. He gave the honour of bearing the royal canopy to the Barons of the Cinque Ports.

The king, thirty-three years old, has finely arched eyebrows in a face with high cheekbones. In build he resembles his father, is five feet seven inches tall, has thick curly hair and wears a trim beard, with his moustache turned neatly downwards. As customary, King John took the triple oath and when Archbishop Hubert Walter declared he should only accept the crown if he 'purposed to fulfil in deed what he had sworn in words', King John replied with the formulaic, 'With God's help, I will keep the oath in all good faith.' The archbishop declared that John, brother of King Richard, being 'prudent, active, and indubitably noble, we have, under God's Holy Spirit, unanimously elected him because of his merits and his royal blood'. Cheers resounded around the abbey as John was crowned.

A banquet followed. Twenty-one fat oxen had been sent from Worcester at a cost of £6 10s 6d to be served alongside many delicacies. Geoffrey FitzPeter, Earl of Essex, who remains Chief Justiciar, served at the king's table with William Marshal, Earl of Pembroke. Archbishop Hubert was appointed Chancellor. After the king takes homage and fealty of his nobles tomorrow, he intends visiting the shrines of Saints Edmund, Alban and Thomas.

August 1199: Divorce
The marriage between Hawisa and King John was pronounced invalid by the Archbishop of Bordeaux. Part of her dowry was granted to Aumary de Montfort, son of Hawisa's older sister, Mabel, who has received the earldom of Gloucester.

December 1199: Wine Regulation
King John has fixed the maximum price of red wine at 4*d* per gallon and white wine at 6*d* per gallon and decreed in every town twelve inspectors will oversee wine prices and measures.

22 June 1200: Marriage
Honouring the agreement reached between Philip and Richard, Queen Eleanor had journeyed to Castile to fetch her granddaughter Blanche to marry thirteen-year-old Prince Louis, heir of the French king. In compliance with the treaty made on 18 May, King John gave homage to King Philip for his continental lands while Duke Arthur paid homage to his uncle John for Brittany.

26 August 1200: Royal Wedding
At Angouleme, the Archbishop of Bordeaux married King John and fifteen-year-old Isabella, daughter of Aymar, Count of Angouleme and Alice de Courtenay. Rumour is that her parents summarily broke off her betrothal to Hugh 'le Brun' Lusignan, Comte de la Marche because King John was entirely enamoured of her. By marrying Isabella, the king will acquire a key land route between Poitou and Gascony and, as King Richard had given away various key castles, strengthen Aquitaine.

10 October 1200: Coronation
A few days after King John and his young bride landed at Portsmouth, they were both crowned by Archbishop Hubert in the presence of all the nobles and bishops of England. The queen is rightfully celebrated for her beauty, with her blue eyes and long, glossy blonde hair falling in ringlets around her face. The king's clerks, Eustace and Ambrose, for chanting *Christus vincit* during Isabella's anointing, received 25*s* from the king.

22–24 November 1200: Honouring Hugh
Before leaving for the hill outside the city of Lincoln to accept the oath of fealty from King William of Scotland, early in the morning of 22 November King John offered a gold cup on the altar of the newly

erected chapel of St John the Baptist, built by the recently deceased Bishop Hugh with his own hands, carrying stones and mortar on his shoulders. King John had visited the dying bishop at his London residence of the Old Temple. He sat alone with him for a long time saying many kind words.

The cortege bearing his body from Holborn to Lincoln, through driving wind and rain, arrived on the following day and was met by the king. In pouring rain as the city bells tolled, King John was one of the pall bearers, walking through the muddy streets crowded with grief-stricken and weeping mourners to the cathedral porch. The body was received by the clergy, who took it into the choir for Masses and vigil. The bishop laid in state with his face uncovered and a mitre on his head, wearing his pontifical vestments, gloves on his hands and the ring on his finger. At first daylight of 24 November, King John attended the Requiem Mass and burial.

10 April 1201: *Charter*

The king has granted to all the Jews of England and Normandy free and honourable residence and to 'reasonably hold in land and fees and mortgages and goods', to have all liberties and customs as in the time of Henry I. Where any dispute arises between a Christian and a Jew, the complainant must have as witnesses a lawful Christian and a lawful Jew.

Overseas

In response to the Lusignan family stirring up open revolt in Poitou, King John sent out a summons on May Day to his barons owing military service to muster at Portsmouth for 13 May. After meeting at Leicester beforehand, they sent a message refusing to serve unless he redressed 'certain wrongs'. He replied that if they 'continued disobedient' he would deprive them of their castles, showing he was in earnest by seizing William d'Albini's castle of Belvoir. Capitulating, they assembled as ordered. Taking their expense money and giving no reason for his decision, John ordered them to return home, although he had already sent William Marshal and Roger de Lacy overseas with detachments of knights. He and Queen Isabella embarked for Normandy two days later. Before leaving the king gifted 50 marks to his nephew Philip, bastard son of King Richard.

At the end of the month, after conference on the Isle of Andely, King Philip invited the royal couple to Paris. They arrived on 1 July and were lodged in the French king's palace, provided with the best wine and food and given gifts of gold, silver, palfreys and Spanish warhorses. At the end of July, John and Isabella moved to Chinon. Queen Berengaria visited them there in September where John settled her dowry by giving her the city of Bayeux, two castles in Anjou and an annual income of 1,000 marks. In November, they were at Mortain when John rewarded the finder of his favourite necklace of stones and jewels with 20s worth of rent in his birthplace of Berkhamsted. Christmas was spent at Argentan where the king was indulged by a gift of his favourite dish of lampreys. They spent New Year at Domfront.

Viewing the stone bridges built with townhouses at Saintes and Rochelle, the king wrote from Molineux on 18 April 1202 to the Mayor of London requesting they grant his desire for Isenbert to build such a bridge in London.

During Lent, King Philip suddenly renewed hostilities by demanding King John 'restore' Normandy, Touraine, Anjou and Poitou to Arthur of Brittany. John declared he was Arthur's liege lord. In response Philip said John, as his liege subject, should answer Poitevin baronial complaints at his court. Refused a safe conduct, John declined to appear. King Philip decreed John was in default and his lands belonged to Arthur, whom he knighted. Bestowing a troop of 200 knights upon him, Philip gave Arthur leave to foment trouble while he went to besiege the castle of Butavant.

On 29 July, Arthur heard his grandmother Queen Eleanor was at Mirebeau Castle and marched there with a substantial army of soldiers. Although the castle surrendered, Queen Eleanor and her small troop held out alone in the Tower, attacked relentlessly by Hugh de Lusignan. Riding day and night in forced march from Le Mans, King John arrived on 1 August, quicker than anyone thought possible. Geoffrey de Lusignan was so confident it could not be King John that he refused to arm and insisted on finishing his breakfast of pigeon pie. As King John met Arthur's scouts he attacked them so fiercely they fled to the castle for shelter but, fast as they were, the king and his knights were faster. All swept through the gates and into the castle at the same time, where King John, in the thick of the violent fighting, with his first sword stroke severed the hand of a fully armoured knight.

When the battle was over, upwards of 200 Poitevin and French knights were captured including Arthur, Hugh and Geoffrey de Lusignan, Raymond de Thouars and Savaric de Mauleon. As rebellious vassals, John ordered them to be put into irons and conveyed by carts to various prisons on both sides of the Channel. Many murmured the king was cruel to visit such indignity on noble prisoners, yet their servants were allowed to visit. Some prisoners pledging their word, like Andrew de Chauvigny, were released. Finding Arthur's sister Eleanor at the siege, John sent her to Corfe Castle to be lodged honourably in the Gloriette Tower with her meals to be taken in the Long Hall.

Christmastide was kept at Caen and the court were scandalised that the king and queen stayed in bed until noon every day, rising only for dinner. In January, staying with the Count of Seez at Alencon, King John was informed that enemy forces had trapped Queen Isabella at Chinon. He abruptly left to rescue her. As soon as he was gone, the count handed over Alencon Castle to King Philip; this treachery left the king particularly bitter.

1–2 February 1203: 'Never enjoy peace'

As 'some lapse of time' had passed since the fighting at Mirebeau, King John visited Arthur at Falaise and tried to persuade him to return to his allegiance. Swearing vehemently, Arthur demanded his uncle restore to him his continental lands and hand over England to him as the rightful king. He vowed that until he was given all his lands he would ensure his uncle would 'never enjoy peace for any length of time'. King John gave orders for Robert de Vieuxpont, his director of military works, to transport his nephew to Rouen and keep him under close guard in the new tower, removing him from the influence of Geoffrey de Lusignan. William des Roches, denied custody of Arthur by the king, stormed off renouncing his service and fealty. French prisoners in England were ordered moved to Corfe Castle. To the king's unhappiness, some prisoners released after pledging loyal service have revealed their promises to be hollow.

April 1203: Rumours

There is gossip that Arthur, attempting to escape from the tower at Rouen, either fell into the River Seine and drowned or died of his wounds sustained in a fall. King Philip is spreading his own rumours. King John had spent Easter Sunday, 6 April, at Rouen and the French king says he killed Arthur with his own bare hands in a drunken rage and threw the body into the Seine weighted by a stone; another tale is that the king took Arthur out in a boat alone and rowed three miles before plunging a sword into his stomach and dumping the corpse overboard.

Whatever the truth, King Philip has roused William des Roches into leading a Breton army into Angers and the Loire, blocking movement between Le Mans and Chinon. King Philip on a second front attacks castles and uses his 'malignant fables' to turn John's nobles from their allegiance.

5 July 1203: Vaudreuil Castle

Vaudreuil Castle, chief bulwark guarding access to Rouen, was surrendered to King Philip without a fight by Saer de Quincy and Robert FitzWalter, despite being newly provisioned and the garrison strengthened by King John.

29 July 1203: 'Protection to a dog'

From Montfort Castle, King John wrote to the Mayor of London, 'astonished and concerned' that Jews, despite being under his special protection, were being injured. He insisted on their defence, stating that had he even granted protection to a dog he would expect it to be 'inviolably observed'.

20 August 1203: Breakout

In Corfe Castle, where some of the prisoners from Mirebeau remain, Savaric de Mauleon encouraged his gaolers to drink so much they fell into a stupor whereupon he picked up a cudgel and killed them. Breaking free from his shackles, he barricaded himself in the tower.

In France at the same time, while King John attempted to regain the castle at Alencon, King Philip began besieging Chateau Gaillard, sited on a dramatic crag overlooking the rivers Gambon and Seine.

31 August 1203: Joint Attack

In a bid to relieve Chateau Gaillard, King John devised a plan for a nocturnal land and naval attack: land troops should engage soldiers on the riverbank while troopships sailed downriver to demolish the bridge the French had built to isolate the castle and prevent supplies reaching it. Though William Marshal was successful in his attack, leaving many dead and others with shattered bones, loss of limbs or eyes, owing to a mistake in the tide the navy arrived late. Having lost the element of surprise, they attempted dismantling the bridge through a deluge of arrows, bolts, stones and tar. The French, able to regroup, took back town and island, harrying townspeople toward the castle to further drain its resources.

December 1203: Defensive Line

Arriving back in England on 6 December, a furious King John confronted his earls and barons five days later accusing them of deserting him in the midst of his enemies. Before his return, the king had attempted to draw enemy forces by ravaging Brittany. In Normandy all the castles, including Rouen, had been provisioned, setting up a defensive line to the west of Chateau Gaillard. In a letter to de Lacy, the king asked him to persevere but if 'in such straits you cannot hold out longer' he was to act as instructed by Peter de Preaux, his castellan of Rouen. Meanwhile, King Philip is telling Norman barons that their king has deserted them and they should receive him as their rightful overlord or be hanged or flayed alive.

2 January 1204: Oxford Council

After spending Christmas at Canterbury with Archbishop Hubert, King John attended his Oxford Council and was granted subsidies, levies and taxes from his nobles and the Church to continue his fight against King Philip. In lieu of providing an actual military presence, many barons offered to pay 'shield-money'.

6 March 1204: Chateau Gaillard

After digging large trenches and building equidistant forts complete with their own moats and drawbridges, the French blockaded Chateau Gaillard all winter. Commander Roger de Lacy, being realistic, expelled 'all useless mouths'. At first the French allowed these refugees to pass through their lines, but King Philip ordered the next party to be stopped by arrows and crossbow quarrels. Refused re-entry into the castle, they were stuck in no-man's-land facing either starvation or death by exposure. De Lacy's harsh but pragmatic measures kept those inside the castle alive while they awaited assistance. A blind eye was turned to those outside fighting over a chicken carcase, a newly delivered baby or dogs kicked out of the castle.

King Philip returned in February with a new plan. He allowed the few survivors to leave and gave them food. One ragged man refused to part with a dog tail until bread was placed in his hands. After surviving so long, many died from overeating. These impediments removed, the French king ordered the moat filled in and the area flattened and widened to create a platform for his newly built ballistae, mangonels and trebuchets. Although the walls were hammered until they breached, de Lacy and his men continued to fight, disdaining surrender even though they had been reduced to eating their horses. Making a last stand on 6 March, they were overwhelmed by numbers. He, forty knights and 120 of his garrison were ordered shackled in irons and transported as prisoners to Compiegne. The same day, King Philip began repairs to make the walls 'more solid than they had ever been'.

14 April 1204: Pardon

Queen Eleanor, after slipping into a coma, died in her eighty-second year at Poitiers on 1 April and was buried beside her husband at Fontevraud Abbey. Today, for the 'safety and soul of his very dear mother', King John has sent to all sheriffs of England a general pardon to release all prisoners except those taken in the late war.

7–19 May 1204: No Resistance

After Chateau Gaillard fell, one by one towns surrendered the moment King Philip's army was seen approaching. Argentan was followed by Falaise. Mont-Saint-Michel and Avranches were destroyed. Caen opened wide its gates, as did Bayeux, Domfront, Lisieux, Barfleur, Cherbourg and Coutances.

24–30 June 1204: Rouen

All Norman resistance having collapsed, King Philip turned his gaze upon the strong-walled, triple-ditched capital of Rouen. He relayed his usual persuasion: John has abandoned you; pay homage to me or be hanged or flayed alive. Peter de Preaux surrendered. King Philip, in the hearing of everyone, instructed his clerks to draw up a charter for £2,000 promised to Peter for surrendering his liege lord's city. Refusing to accept it, Peter crossed to England to beg King John for mercy. He was permitted to retire to his English estates.

17 July 1204: Knighthood

Wanting to knight his valet, Thomas Esturmy, King John purchased for him two robes – one scarlet and one green – and a fine linen cloak, a saddle, reins, a rain cloak, a pair of linen sheets and a couch for him.

8 August 1204: Pledge

Young Savaric de Mauleon, famous for his love songs and of whom it is said 'sweetly could he say and sing of love that me hath vanquished', was freed after pledging loyalty to King John. Word came that he, Hubert de Burgh, Gerard d'Athee and Robert Turnham have devised a treaty offering those who had joined King Philip a way to return to John's allegiance.

Christmas 1204: Bejewelled

Spending Christmastide at Tewkesbury, King John appeared for the festival wearing a red satin robe and mantle patterned with sapphires and pearls, a tunic of white damask and red satin shoes edged with gold. His sword belt was set with gems and his white embroidered gloves were adorned with an emerald on one and a topaz on the other. His sceptre was studded all over with diamonds and rubies. As is the king's custom at the four major festivals, knights at court received rich gifts of fine clothes.

25 January 1205: King's Beaulieu

For the souls of his ancestors, his father, mother, brothers, himself and his heirs, King John has built and founded the Abbey of the Blessed Virgin Mary at King's Beaulieu, a beautiful place in the New Forest.

27 March 1205: Sapphires

The Prior of Jerusalem gave to King John at Oxford this Passion Sunday seventy rings set with sapphires as a gift.

2 April 1205: 'The nearest privy'

After King Philip proclaimed that he had confiscated English lands in France, several leading magnates pleaded with King John to allow them to pay homage to Philip for their overseas estates, pledging that though their bodies were Philip's their hearts were John's. Baldwin de Bethune, Earl of Aumale, so crippled with arthritis and gout that he had to be carried into the council chamber, told his friend, 'Of course the decision is yours, but in your shoes, if I saw them acting against my interests though their hearts were for me, if only I could get my hands on these dissidents' hearts, I would chuck them all down the nearest privy.' This made the king laugh. Sceptical that any subject would assist him to recover any lost lands once they had paid homage to the French king, King John made one exception: William Marshal, whom he considered his most loyal knight.

Writs were sent out for sheriffs to divide knights into groups of ten, one to serve and muster at Portchester at Whitsun while the other nine provide horses and arms at 2s a day.

1 May 1205: Niort

Hidden by branches of flowers as if they were townspeople returning from collecting May in the woods, Savaric de Mauleon and his men passed through the gates of Niort and took over the castle. The returning townspeople were imprisoned but released as soon as they swore allegiance to King John.

2 May 1205: Pottage
By order of the king: because of the severe frost and frozen land of last winter, loaves and pottage are to be made, either from 'flour, beans or pease', to feed paupers throughout London, Oxford and all the western and southern counties so they 'may be sustained and perish not'.

1–5 June 1205: Wrangles
At Portchester, where King John had mustered a great fleet and army, his barons told him they would not serve him overseas. As the king sat on the shore moodily looking out to sea, William Marshal, recently returned from France, came to him and said he could no longer serve him overseas after paying homage to King Philip for his lands. Angrily, King John accused Marshal of allying himself with his enemy, saying, 'You shall come with me to Poitou to fight.' William replied, 'It would be an evil thing, since I am his man.'

In bitter silence, the king went to dinner after demanding William's eldest son be given as a hostage. The stores and munitions already embarked, the king sent them to the relief of La Rochelle with his natural son, Geoffrey, and half-brother, William Longsword, Earl of Salisbury.

23 June 1205: Valiant Defence
Besieged for many months, Chinon Castle fell. Hubert de Burgh was injured and taken prisoner. Girard d'Athee at Loches had also fallen a few days earlier after a valiant six-month defence against a formidable army of archers and siege machines.

13–15 July 1205: Archbishop Hubert
Archbishop Hubert died of fever in his forty-sixth year at Teynham Manor in Kent on 13 July, having been ill for three days. The archbishop was much admired for the purity of his life and King John considered him his ablest minister and most tactful diplomat. He stayed for the funeral at Canterbury, held in Trinity Chapel on 15 June, and asked the prior and monks to wait until after Michaelmas before electing a new archbishop.

20 December 1205: Archbishop Elected
Today, King John sent an embassy, including six monks, with letters to the Pope affirming bishops and monks had elected John Gray, Bishop of Norwich in his presence, with his consent, to be England's

new Archbishop of Canterbury on 11 December. Archbishop John, a close adviser and friend of the king, is known for being a man of great learning and has a pleasant and agreeable disposition.

8–26 May 1206: Papal Letters
Letters came from Pope Innocent III who informed King John he has received three delegations from England. Clearly surprised, the king has found out that the young monks of Canterbury had clandestinely elected and enthroned their sub-prior Reginald as archbishop in the night, whispered a *Te Deum* and sent him to secretly travel to the Pope for ratification before John found out. This was the first delegation.

The second was the king's delegation informing the Pope that Archbishop John had been elected and enthroned. Told about Reginald, they affirmed he had neither been elected nor enthroned and should not receive the pallium.

A third delegation had arrived from bishops not part of Canterbury province who said, having previously participated in Canterbury elections, that the monks had no right to hold one without them.

Pope Innocent requests the king to send a new delegation of bishops and monks, with power to hold a valid election, to Rome by 1 October, when he will announce his ruling. King John has sent two envoys, with sixteen Canterbury monks, with a request the Pope respect his royal prerogatives and uphold the election of John Gray.

9 June–26 October 1206: Success
Since arriving at La Rochelle on 9 June where he was welcomed by crowds delighted to see him, King John has successfully defeated King Philip. Among other achievements he has taken the castle of Montauban in fifteen days; it took Charlemagne seven years to subdue the same castle. Triumphant in Anjou and Brittany, and now with Angers won, King John has forced King Philip into agreeing a two-year truce to begin on 1 November.

4 November 1206: Angouleme
Saving fealty to himself while he lives, King John required the freemen of Angouleme to swear fealty to Queen Isabella as Countess of Angouleme and their liege lady.

25 December 1206: Festival
After landing at Portsmouth on 12 December, King John and Queen Isabella elected to hold their Christmas season at Winchester. At the

Christmas feast, twenty oxen, 100 pigs, 100 sheep, 1,500 chickens and 5,000 eggs were consumed at a cost of £11 16s 5d, with 500 yards of linen making up the table napery.

20 February 1207: Papal Decision

King John, incandescent with rage, was informed by letters arrived today that the Pope, threatening them with excommunication, had forced the Canterbury monks to elect Cardinal Stephen Langton, the intimate advisor and friend of King Philip, as Archbishop. Condemning Reginald's election for its irregularity and secrecy, he then quashed John Gray's election for having occurred while Reginald's election was pending papal confirmation. In his flowery *fait accompli*, the Pope praised the cardinal for his learning and piety. The king said the Pope had not only deprived the English crown of its just and customary rights but had shown contempt towards king and realm.

11–14 July 1207: Open Enemy

Against the express wishes and concerns of King John, who is beyond angry, news came today that on 17 June at Viterbo, Pope Innocent had consecrated Cardinal Stephen Langton, a man who has been the king's open enemy. King John has taken it as a direct personal insult for the position of Archbishop of Canterbury means Langton is entitled to be included in the most confidential counsels. Riding to Canterbury, the king shouted at the monks that had they behaved like grown men worthy of his trust the affairs of the kingdom would have been in capable hands. Furiously cursing them for their childish and irresponsible behaviour in secretly electing Reginald without his knowledge, he ordered them to be expelled from the kingdom and their property seized.

1 October 1207: Prince Henry

A prince was born to King John and Queen Isabella at Winchester Castle today. The baby has been christened Henry after his grandfather. His nurse is called Helen and is paid 2d per day.

20 November 1207: Intercession

After intercession by his friends at Gloucester, King John granted permission for William de Braose to meet with him at Hereford. William owes great sums to the exchequer. Accounts show he has only paid 700 marks for the honour of Limerick granted in 1201. The contract was for 5,000 marks paid at the rate of 500 marks per year.

Either as surety for his debts or as part repayment, he was asked to surrender three of his castles to the king.

18 March 1208: 'Eyes plucked out'
Bishops advising King John of the Pope intending to lay interdict on England for his refusal to allow Archbishop Stephen into England were told that 'by God's Teeth' if any priest was presumptuous enough to lay his realm under an interdict he would send all priests and clerks to Rome, and anyone from Rome would be sent back with their 'eyes plucked out', further warning that if they 'wished to keep their bodies free from harm' they would stay out of his sight. He then ruled that any clergy who refuse to celebrate divine service after today will be imprisoned and their goods seized.

23 March 1208: Interdict
Today, Passion Sunday, the Bishops of London, Ely and Worcester, as commanded by Pope Innocent, have announced and published interdict on England. From today, no churches will be open, bells will be removed from steeples or made silent and crosses, relics and images stored away or covered. No Masses will take place although prayers and sermons will be allowed in churchyards. Taking of confessions, churching of women and weddings can be performed in church porches. Baptisms and use of the chrism are allowed in private houses. Burials are forbidden in churchyards but may be carried out silently elsewhere and although priests are forbidden to attend funerals, they may say the offices of the dead in private houses and give the viaticum to the dying.

5–11 April 1208: The Clergy
Since ordering all priests to leave the kingdom, King John has calmed down. Peter des Roches, Bishop of Winchester and John Gray, Bishop of Norwich were restored. With regard to bishops who have fled overseas, the king has ordered their houses to be 'overturned, the woods cut down and the fish destroyed'. For clergy who have stayed, despite his displeasure, and especially any who are poor, he has ordered a small allowance of food and clothing to be doled out by royal officers. He has locked up concubines (or wives) and housekeepers of priests although as soon as a ransom is paid they have regained their liberty.

On 11 April, the king issued a proclamation that 'if any one injures religious persons or clerks, they shall be hung on the nearest oak'.

23 May 1208: Braose Flees
Using Welsh troops and unsuccessfully attempting to reclaim his castles by force, William de Braose sacked and burnt the town, priory and church of Leominster to the ground and ill-treated the inhabitants. While Gerard d'Athee, Sheriff of Gloucester was engaged fighting his grandsons, sons of Gruffydd, William fled with his family into Ireland.

5 January 1209: Second Prince
A prince and second son was born to King John and Queen Isabella at Winchester Castle. They have named him Richard after his uncle. His nurse is called Eva, and she will receive 4d a day.

24–25 April 1209: Mired
King John, after being mired in a pool, arrived at Alnwick wet and muddy. The following day he decreed that henceforth on St Mark's Day, before a freeman be first admitted to the common, he must subject himself to the same 'filthy ablution' by walking through a mire as a punishment and reminder to maintain their roads.

25 July 1209: Scottish Peace
Drawn up in battle array, King John awaited the elderly King William at Norham. The Scottish king sued for peace, agreed to pay a fine of 12,000 marks and asked King John to arrange marriages for his daughters, Margaret and Isabella. They will join the queen's household.

Christmas 1209: Anathema
With King John not submitting, Pope Innocent personally excommunicated him, making it unlawful for any Christian to associate with him, or give him food, drink or shelter. English bishops have refused to publish the order.

6 June–29 August 1210: Ireland
Sailing into Dublin on 6 June, King John was met by Irish magnates who paid homage and swore fealty to him. Meanwhile, fleeing the king and his troops, William de Braose sailed to Wales to join Llywelyn. Walter and Hugh de Lacy, who had been harbouring the family, fled into Scotland and with them William's wife, his eldest son and his wife, but the three were captured and brought to John at Carrickfergus Castle at the end of July. Before leaving Ireland at the end of August, King John received the oath that the Irish would in future observe

English laws and customs, the text of which was sealed and deposited at the Irish Exchequer. He has also issued coinage, minted with the image of a harp, and appointed John Gray as Justiciar of Ireland.

22 July 1210: Birth
Queen Isabella gave birth to a daughter today at Havering-atte-Bower. The baby has been named Joanna.

8 July–15 August 1211: Submission
Responding to the Welsh ravaging Earl Ranulph's lands in retaliation for the campaign against them last year, King John assembled an army at Whitchurch. Marching into north Wales, he penetrated as far as Snowdon. Routing the Welsh, he burned down Bangor and seized its bishop for disloyalty. The king's natural daughter, Joan, was sent by her husband Prince Llywelyn to sue for peace. King John agreed but deprived Llywelyn of some of his lands in Conwy and required a tribute in cattle and horses and twenty-eight young men of noble birth as hostages, including his natural son Gruffydd.

9–10 August 1211: Death
William de Braose died at Corbeuil. Although expressing his wish to be buried in Brecon, he was buried the next day at St Victor's Abbey in Paris. To the fury of the king, Archbishop Stephen conducted the funeral. William and his wife Matilda had last met King John on 20 September when they reached agreement to pay their arrears. Instead, William fled disguised as a beggar and reached France that October. Many say he fell ill after hearing rumours that his wife and eldest son had starved to death either at Corfe or Windsor.

Christmas 1211: Fishy Feast
Despite Pope Innocent extending his sentence of excommunication to include all who associate with King John 'at table, in council or in conversation', at the Christmas festival the court were served 10,000 herrings, 1,800 whitings, 900 haddock and 3,000 lampreys. The kitchens got through 60 lbs of pepper, 18 lbs of cumin, half a pound of sedge root, 3 lbs of cinnamon, a pound of cloves, half a pound of nutmeg, 2 lbs of ginger and used 1,500 cups, 1,200 pitchers and 4,000 plates.

25 March 1212: Knighthood
Holding a feast at London at St Bridget's in Clerkenwell, King John at table knighted Alexander, the fourteen-year-old son and heir of King William.

10 July 1212: Great Fire

Much of London today burnt to the ground after a fire, beginning near St Mary's Church in Southwark, crossed the river by leaping along the wooden houses standing on New London Bridge. Many men, women and children were killed by fire and smoke. King John has decreed bakers are forbidden to work at night.

14–22 August 1212: Axel the White

On their way towards Nottingham from Wales, the king's party was met at Gunthorpe on 14 August by falconers from King William bringing the king a gift of three falcons. Lodged at Nottingham Castle, King John feasted and hunted with Axel the White, Earl of Sjaelland and son of Esbern Snare, erstwhile chancellor and close adviser to King Valdemar of Denmark, ordering the earl's retinue of sixteen Danes left lodged in London to be provided with all necessaries at his expense. To assist Robert de Vieuxpont and Earl Ranulph fighting the Welsh, who had destroyed the castles built by the king last year and beheaded their garrisons, King John sent eighteen galleys to destroy Welsh ships and boats.

24–26 December 1212: 'Another more worthy'

Pope Innocent has decreed, in the face of John's obstinacy, he should be deposed and he will choose 'another more worthy' to have his crown, promising King Philip perpetual possession of England. Letters have been sent by Innocent to all of John's nobles and others releasing them from their allegiance to him.

January 1213: Holy War

The King of France has ordered all his nobility, knights, their attendants and others to equip themselves with horses and arms to assemble in force at Rouen by the Octave of Easter to fight the Pope's Holy War against England under penalty of being branded with cowardice and charged with treason. His ships, being provisioned with an abundance of corn, wine, meat and other stores and necessaries for a large army, are ordered to assemble at Boulogne.

4–6 May 1213: Waits in Strength

At Barham Down near Canterbury, 60,000 men – all conditions and ages – poured in from every part of England to support King John, with more following. Bishop Gray and William Marshal arrived from Ireland with practically its whole knight service of five hundred knights and a large army. Forces have already been despatched to various ports including Ipswich, Dover and Faversham. So many soldiers have now arrived that the king sent inexperienced men home. King John, in full strength with a superior navy, awaits Philip's strike at England.

Submission

On 15 May, the papal legate, Pandulf, was given permission to visit Dover to hold private talks with King John. Two days later, at the Templar house on Bredenstone Hill, King John publicly placed his crown at the legate's feet, submitting England into the hands of Pope Innocent. Pandulf returned the crown to him, held from the Pope 'as from a supreme king'. John agreed to pay the Pope a thousand marks per annum in two instalments (seven hundred for England and three hundred for Ireland), 'saving to us and our heirs all our rights, privileges and royal customs'. He agreed to make peace with Archbishop Stephen and the bishops of London, Ely, Hereford and Bath, paying out £8,000 to defray their immediate expenses.

On 22 May Pandulf sailed to France to tell King Philip to stand down his troops and dismiss his ships. In blazing anger Philip refused, saying it had cost him £60,000 and even if excommunicated he would continue his venture. When Count Ferrand said it would be an unjust war and he for one would not follow him as he had no claim whatsoever to the English crown, he was declared an enemy and fled. Philip ordered his fleet to sail to the mouth of the River Seine. The count sent a message to King John asking for help; in response, he sent his fleet of 500 ships, 700 knights and an army of foot. Three hundred of Philip's ships were captured and burnt, as were 100 ships drawn on shore. An onlooker remarked it looked like 'the sea was on fire'. Undeterred, King Philip moved land troops to Flanders but was opposed by a coalition army led by John's nephew Emperor Otto.

On 20 July, Archbishop Stephen and the bishops landed at Dover. As they approached Winchester, King John met them and, tearfully throwing himself at their feet, begged them to have compassion on him and his realm. Raising him up, they led the king to the cathedral door and absolved him. His nobles wept with joy as he renewed his coronation oath. On 25 August, a chronicler wrote that the archbishop met with a few barons at St Paul's Cathedral and, showing them a copy of Henry I's coronation charter, suggested they used it to recall their 'long-lost' rights.

At the end of September, Cardinal Nicholas, Bishop of Tusculum, sent by the Pope as arbiter, was accused of taking 'the king's side more than was right' after he showed his indignation at the demands being made by the prelates. King John had offered to pay 100,000 marks immediately and pledge to pay any insufficiency by Easter but the archbishop and bishops demanded that the exact sum they had calculated for their demolished castles, houses, orchards and woods should be paid. At a council in Reading held between 8 and 14 December, when the clerics brought in their lists of property with the amounts of restitution they required, Pandulf sided with the king, saying the sums they asked were unreasonable and far beyond his ability to pay. They refused to compromise and Pandulf wrote to the Pope that he had never seen such a 'humble and moderate king' with clergy 'too grasping and covetous and oppressing him'.

On 9 February 1214, with papal approval, King John embarked at Yarmouth to join with his allies, the counts of Holland, Boulogne and Flanders, dukes of Lorraine and Brabant and Emperor Otto, in defeating King Philip once and for all, the coalition attacking him via Flanders and King John attacking him from Poitou, where his half-brother William had already made some inroads.

29 June 1214: Interdict Lifted

Amid chanting of the *Te Deum* and the ringing of the bells of St Paul's, Cardinal Nicholas lifted the interdict from the realm of England which had lain on it for six years, three months and six days.

27 July 1214: Battle of Bouvines

The day was scorching hot. King Philip allowed his men to refresh themselves by a bridge on the River Marque while he removed his chainmail and sat in the shade of an ash tree with some bread and wine. Suddenly, peace was shattered by trumpets warning of a fast-approaching enemy. Otto and his troops rode at breakneck speed towards the French, who hastily armed and assembled on the plain on the eastern bank. As the two armies faced each other, Otto's right wing charged first and broke through French ranks. Count Reginald of Boulogne struck King Philip with a lance and nearly killed him. But then the French rallied. Swords were lightning flashes as they thundered on helms and daggers pierced into eyes as men and horses were slaughtered. Otto fought with such ferocity that three horses were killed under him. As the fighting concentrated around him, he fended off attackers using his single-edged sword held in both hands like a billhook. When at last he was alone, all his knights around him dead, his foes opened a way for his retreat instead of taking him prisoner as they had so many.

8 September 1214: Quandary

The king's son, Oliver, brought a letter to the council from his father written at St Maixent. In it he asked for advice on King Philip's dishonourable proposal to free 'our beloved brother William now held in chains' if the son of Robert, Count of Dreux was freed 'whom we hold captive', but if he is freed Count Reginald of Boulogne 'will be put to death' which is not 'conducive to our honour'.

Robert has been kept in honourable captivity and has even gone out hunting with King John. In contrast, King Philip keeps Count Reginald in interlaced chains so short he cannot move more than half a step, attached to a tree trunk so large it can barely be moved by two men when the count needs to relieve himself.

13 October 1214: Triumph

The royal family landed at Dartmouth today. Even though English barons refused to serve overseas or pay scutage, King John has returned triumphant from his campaign in Poitou and has forced King Philip into agreeing a five-year truce.

4–6 December 1214: King Alexander

Alexander was enthroned at Scone two days after King William died at Stirling Palace, aged seventy-two years.

14–17 December 1214: Birth

The royal household, moving from Corfe, lodged at Gloucester Castle where Queen Isabella has given birth to a second daughter, named Isabella after her mother. King John, staying with her, has ensured a supply of almonds for his wife who has craved them throughout her pregnancy.

7–14 January 1215: Good Laws

At the council held at New Temple, certain disaffected barons attended in full armour. Denouncing King John for trusting overmuch to foreigners in government, they complained that grants of lands and offices and charge of his castles should truly be given to them. They declared that unless he restored the 'good laws of King Edward' and the coronation charter of Henry I they would renounce their allegiance and make war on him. King John replied that such serious matters needed deliberation with his council and asked to be given until Low Sunday, 26 April.

4 March 1215: Crusades
Today, Ash Wednesday, King John took the cross from William, Bishop of London, for he wishes to go on crusade to 'succour the Holy Land' and has been preparing for the journey and equipping a ship since New Year. The earls of Chester, Ferrers and Winchester also took the cross to go with him and all have sewn white crosses onto their garments.

19–27 April 1215: War
Rebel barons assembled at Stamford on 19 April, bringing with them two thousand knights and additional foot soldiers. King John sent Archbishop Stephen to hear their demands. On his return, King John listened to the laws and customs his barons demanded and their threats to force his compliance by seizing his castles. Angrily exclaiming, 'Why, did the barons not ask for my kingdom as well?' he declared their demands foolish and vain and insisted he would not become their slave. On Low Sunday, the rebels travelled to Brackley and asked a canon of Durham to release them from their oaths of allegiance before travelling on to besiege Northampton Castle. Robert FitzWalter named himself leader, calling himself Marshal of the Army of God and of Holy Church. His second-in-command is Saer de Quincy, Earl of Winchester.

17 May 1215: Occupation
Repelled at Northampton Castle, the rebel barons arrived at dawn at the gates of London. Some cut through beams that secured the gates; at Aldgate a ladder left by workmen was used to clamber over and open the gates from the inside. While oblivious citizens attended Mass, guards were stationed at all the gates. The royal garrison at the Tower of London made a brave but futile defence against the 'army of God', alerted by their breaking into the houses of Jews and rifling their goods to fill their empty purses. Holding London, the barons wrote to all nobles faithful to the king warning them either to join their cause and fight for their rights or have their castles destroyed, goods burnt and lands laid waste.

27 May 1215: Fish
King John sent word to the constable of Marlborough Castle to ensure he provides a good supply of fish for Queen Isabella, in particular roach and small pike for Saturdays and Sundays.

10 June 1215: Articles

At Windsor, after negotiations between King John, Archbishop Stephen and rebel barons, agreement has nearly finalised the clauses to be signed and sealed by charter and the setting up and election of a committee of twenty-five barons through whom, with their approval, the king will conduct royal business and appoint royal officials.

15–19 June 1215: Runnymede

In the meadow called Runnymede between Windsor and Staines, King John came accompanied by men from Normandy, Gascony and Flanders as well as his barons and bishops to witness the signing and sealing of the Charter of Liberties, or *Magna Carta*. The kiss of peace was given to the barons who gave fealty anew, and then all ate and drank together.

27 June 1215: Royal Letters

Rebel barons, using the royal seal, have sent letters to all sheriffs, foresters and other local officials ordering the Charter of Liberties to be publicly read, a French translation having been made available to ensure all knights of the counties understand it. King John has ordered all his sieges to be raised, and surrendered the manors and castles held by him. The mercenaries ordered to go home jest that he has been reduced to 'the twenty-sixth king in England'.

6 July 1215: Defiance and Compliance

In defiance of the agreement to lay down arms, rebel barons staged a tournament at Hounslow while attacks continue on the king's manors and forests, especially in the north, with felling and selling of timber and wholesale butchery of the king's game.

In compliance with the charter, King John was advised to order the release of Everard de Mildeston in Wiltshire who had been appealed by Seina Chevel for the murder of her son, Richard; the charter only allows appeals by women in cases where their husbands have been murdered; the men of Dunwich were advised to prevent anyone being granted custody of sons and daughters save with permission of their own kinsmen and friends, nor are those daughters or heirs to be married without consent or to someone of a lower social class.

16–20 August 1215: Papal Commissioners

At the Oxford council summoned by Archbishop Stephen, Pandulf rose. He read out letters from the Pope to all assembled, including armed rebel barons, stating that he, Peter, Bishop of Winchester and Simon, Abbot of Reading were created papal commissioners and they and the bishops are commanded to excommunicate all disturbers of the peace.

5 September 1215: Sentenced

Pandulf accused Archbishop Stephen of being a disturber of the peace, if not an instigator, and suspended him from office. All the rebel barons were excommunicated for making war on the king and overturning the customs of the realm. Save for baptism and viaticum, London has been placed under interdict. The Pope personally wrote to King John that in degrading his rights and dignity, the Barons' Charter is not legally binding.

The King's Travails

Ignoring the Pope's edict, rebel barons continued their attacks on King John. With approval of his restored council, John besieged Rochester Castle to block access to London with an army made up of his loyal Normans and southern Frenchmen.

Robert of Bethune, riding with the king, said, 'Sire, you have a low opinion of your enemies attacking with such a small number of troops.'

'Ah, Robert,' replied the king, 'I know my adversaries well. They are neither to be admired nor feared. Even with fewer men, we could undoubtedly make a fight of it. What I find very sad is that our troops from abroad are going to see just how perfidious my fellow countrymen can be. This causes me even more grief than the damage they are already doing to me.'

As they approached, townspeople laid down arms and fled. The rebel barons barricaded themselves into the castle. During the eight-week siege that followed, the king's troops held off rebel attacks at Oxford and Northampton. Tonbridge Castle fell and Bedford Castle surrendered.

On 25 November, the starving Rochester garrison, having eaten their own warhorses, surrendered after the walls were toppled by the king's miners. Forty of the fattest bacon pigs 'least worth eating' were burned, sent at the request of the king by Hubert de Burgh at Dover. Savaric de Mauleon, following the custom of royal clemency, knelt to ask King John to spare their lives and that of their leader, William d'Albini. William was sent to Corfe. The king hanged the crossbowmen who had killed royalist soldiers, but the others he gave to his own soldiers for ransom. Having regained all his castles in the Midlands and with some barons, such as John de Lacy, returning to their allegiance, King John spent his Christmas at Nottingham Castle and his New Year at Doncaster.

Peace was not on the horizon. Unbeknownst to the king, Saer de Quincy and Robert FitzWalter had journeyed to France and offered the English crown to Prince Louis. Towards the end of February Londoners enthusiastically welcomed an advance party of French soldiers who had sailed up the Thames and organised a tournament in their honour. As soon as news of Louis' proposed invasion of England reached the Pope he promptly sent Legate Gualo to King Philip to forbid it. The French king and his son declared to the legate that King John, having been found guilty in Philip's court of murdering Arthur, was not the true king of England, his kingdom being forfeit. Prince Louis added that, by right of his wife, Blanche, he had right to the crown and would fight to the death for her inheritance. The legate told them they were talking a farrago of nonsense.

While John's southern troops kept the barons pinned in London, King John journeyed north to fight King Alexander, who had invaded England, seized and levelled Berwick and captured rebel castles in Yorkshire and Lincolnshire. Northern and eastern counties under control, King John visited his castles around London, ensuring they were well provisioned before travelling to Dover where he arrived on 26 April ready to meet the French. In May, a heavy storm dispersed his fleet and Louis and his forces, in 680 vessels, were able to land near Sandwich on 21 May 1216.

28 May 1216: Dragon Standard

Arriving at Winchester Castle, King John raised the White Dragon Standard, the call for the English to defend their homeland without quarter. News came that in London Prince Louis was named king, with barons and citizens swearing fealty to him; only the monks of Westminster refused. Appointing as chancellor Simon Langton, brother to Stephen, Louis wrote to all the barons faithful to John demanding that they either come to London to pay him homage or leave the kingdom. The Pope has told Louis' messengers he is excommunicated and that when Arthur was captured at Mirebeau it was not as an innocent man but one guilty and a traitor to his lord, and that he could 'by law be condemned to even the vilest death without a trial'.

June–October 1216: Brave Defiance

Prince Louis managed to capture Winchester Castle and moved to besiege Odiham. On the third day the garrison sallied forth, capturing thirteen of the enemy. When they were forced to surrender a week later, the French were amazed to find the heroic defence had been made by only three knights and ten soldiers. French troops moved to lay siege to Dover Castle, held by Hubert de Burgh and Oliver FitzRegis.

In Kent and Sussex, French forces are being harassed by a guerrilla force of archers living in the forests led by William of Cassingham, nicknamed Willikin of the Weald. They have slain many thousands of French. During July and August, while King John fought in the Welsh marches around Hereford and Shrewsbury, rebel barons crept out of London in frequent raids, took Cambridge, Colchester and Norwich, then attacked King's Lynn. At the same time, elated by their successes, they sent troops to besiege Windsor Castle, held by Engelard d'Athee.

On 17 September King John marched across the Midlands. After regaining Cambridge, he turned his attention to Lincolnshire. At Lincoln Castle, Gilbert de Gant fled at his approach. On 9 October, King John was enthusiastically greeted by citizens at King's Lynn for their deliverance from the barons. Next day, before he left, King John made a grant to Margaret de Braose, married to Walter de Lacy, for 'three carucates of land to be assarted and cultivated in our forest of Aconbury' to establish a religious house to pray for the souls of her parents, William and Maud, and her brother William.

11–12 October 1216: Calamity

Intending to cross the flooded marshes of the Wash between Norfolk and Lincoln, King John was unexpectedly delayed and was overtaken by the tide swirling up the River Wellstream. To his great distress, some of his household and packhorses were submerged by the waters of the sea and sucked into the quicksand. He himself narrowly escaped drowning but lost people he cared for, plus his chapel and relics, household items and some cherished items. The party continued on to Swineshead Abbey. Arriving worn out and wet, with a high fever, King John was given some of the abbey's peaches in cider for refreshment. Leaving the next day, the king was still feverish and seized with dysentery. In great pain he left on horseback but, unable to continue riding, he was carried on a litter to Sleaford.

16–20 October 1216: Begged Allegiance

Only pure grit kept King John in the saddle. Arriving at Newark Castle on 16 October, he realised he was dying. The next few days saw him making confession and writing his will in which he stated he was 'hindered by grave infirmity' and trusted his faithful men would support his sons and defend their inheritance, reward those who had served him faithfully and assist poor and religious houses for the sake of his soul. Those names were: the bishops of Winchester, Chichester and Worcester; Brother Aimery de St-Maur; Earl William Marshal; Earl Ranulf of Chester; William, Earl Ferrers; William Brewer; Walter de Lacy; John of Monmouth; Savaric de Mauleon and Falkes de Breaute. He sent out letters under personal seal to all sheriffs to receive his son Henry as their king.

Messengers had been arriving. Letters from more than forty of his rebel nobles begged to make peace, asking to return to his allegiance. By then he was too ill to attend to them.

Asked where he wished to be buried, John told the Abbot of Croxton, 'To God and Saint Wulfstan I commend my body and soul.' He died during the night of 18–19 October, aged forty-eight. His body was dressed in his royal robes: a red wide-sleeved, open-sided samite tunic bordered with jewels over cloth-of-gold, a gold mantle over his right arm. On his head they placed his coronation coif and his crown; his sword was placed at his side. His right hand grasped the sceptre, and gold spurs were placed on his feet. His hands were gloved and a ring placed on his middle finger. His body was borne to Worcester where it was buried before the high altar between the shrines of Saints Wulfstan and Oswald. His trust in his loyal men was well placed: nine-year-old Henry was immediately crowned.

Henry III

1216–1272

During the first part of his reign King Henry was described as pious, well mannered, benign and generous. He fed anywhere from 100 to 500 paupers every day with bread and herrings and thousands of poor were fed by him on the anniversary of his father's death and other family 'death anniversaries'. At Easter, Whitsun and Christmas, he gave the poor tunics, cloaks, shoes and sometimes pieces of cloth. Richer men received gifts of rings, brooches, cups and cloth of gold.

In 1245 King Henry began rebuilding Westminster Abbey and created the shrine for Edward the Confessor, taking him as his personal patron saint. Henry slept in the room in which the Confessor reputedly died and had murals painted of the saint's life: at his bedhead was Edward's coronation framed with green-painted hangings, the bedposts painted green with gold stars to match, and at the bed's foot St Edward offering his ring of St John in alms to a pilgrim. Despite thick curtains around the bed, he often complained about being cold from draughts.

King Henry spent a lot of his revenue on refurbishing royal residences and decorating them with painted murals: the story of Alexander the Great at Clarendon and Nottingham Castle; at Westminster Palace, the Tower and Clarendon he commissioned his uncle Richard's battles with Saladin and in 1256 he sardonically ordered Master William to paint in his lavatory the King of Garamontes being rescued from seditious subjects by his faithful hounds.

An idea of Henry's humour is also revealed in the records: in the Fine Rolls, cancelled immediately, those in the know must have smirked as an incredulous Peter the Poitevin read that he owed the king 'five dozen capons for a trespass on board ship' and '34 tuns of wine for the arrears of wines bought to the king's use at Mussak where he dreamt he had seen the Emperor Otto'; the Patent Rolls record a letter granting William de Peretot full power to cut the hair of long-haired clerks and tonsure their curls, to be diligently pursued so the king did not have 'to apply the scissors to your own locks'.

Slapstick also appealed to him. He found it funny when a jester was thrown into the Roman Baths at Bath and another into the Thames. At St Albans, in sight of a disapproving Matthew Paris, a fool pelted the king with turf, stones and green apples and squirted apple juice in his face.

He enjoyed wearing rich clothes and paid out generously to see his wife, Eleanor of Provence, in beautiful attire. As a leader of fashion she brought in parti-coloured tunics, gold and silver belts and pillbox hats. They were staunchly devoted to each other. His sister-in-law, Margaret, in October 1265 joked with him saying she was making haste to send Eleanor back from France lest he should take it in mind to marry someone else. And they were loving parents. When their eldest son fell ill at Beaulieu Abbey, his mother upset the monks by staying at his bedside for three weeks. When their two-year-old son Edmund was fretful the king paid for a harper to soothe him, and when their little Catherine died both parents made themselves ill with grief. In 1256, when Margaret, their daughter and her husband came from Scotland to visit, King Henry met and stopped them on the road at Woodstock so he could embrace them sooner and had colourful pavilions set up in the fields around.

Those chroniclers who at the start of his reign talked of a good man doing pious and generous deeds wrote at the end of it decrying those same actions, calling him simple, a fool and an inept tyrant.

28 October 1216: Coronation

A small figure stood before the great altar of Gloucester Abbey. Knighted the day before by William Marshal, Earl of Pembroke, nine-year-old King Henry swore the customary oath on the Gospels and relics. In front of the multitude of people gathered, he turned towards Gualo, the papal legate, and promised to pay Rome the thousand marks. The legate accepted his homage on behalf of the Pope. Using a gold circlet sourced for the occasion by his mother, Queen Isabella, he was crowned by Peter des Roches, Bishop of Winchester. After prayers and Mass he was clothed in royal robes and led into a dinner attended by his father's most loyal men. The rebel barons sent word they will 'accept no heir of King John as their king'.

19 May 1217: 'The Fair of Lincoln'

Prince Louis, unsuccessful in his siege of Dover Castle, where Hubert de Burgh shouted defiance at him every time he was threatened with hanging, returned to London and sent his army to raise the siege at Mountsorrel Castle. The 600 knights, led by Count Thomas of Perche, Saer de Quincy and Robert FitzWalter, looted every dwelling place and took prisoners, high or low. Warned of their approach, Earl Ranulf retreated to Nottingham Castle. The count decided to take the army to aid Gilbert de Gant, unsuccessfully besieging Lincoln Castle, defended staunchly by the elderly Nicholaa de Haye.

Royalists were on the march too. After a rest-stop at Newark, they circled around to Stowe to approach the city from the north-west, arriving on 18 May. As the sun rose the next day, standards and bucklers glittering in the sun, they marched out in seven dense and orderly battalions. A mile in front of them was a company of crossbowmen led by Falkes de Breaute. Passing through a secret postern gate, he and his men slipped unseen onto Lincoln Castle's ramparts.

Scorning the advice given by Quincy and FitzWalter to take the men to fight in open country, Count Thomas filled the streets between castle and cathedral with mounted men and posted guards at the gates. While a battalion of the king's army forced the gates, the crossbowmen rose and discharged their deadly bolts into enemy horses and riders. 'In the twinkling of an eye they became foot soldiers', crammed in the streets unable to either advance or retreat. Elsewhere, at a breach in the wall, Marshal spurred his horse, crying, 'Charge! They are beaten already!' With a sound of thunder, swords hit helmeted heads and sparks flew. Horses were killed, their riders taken prisoner. Surrounded, the count refused to surrender but a knight rushed him and pierced his eye with his sword. After he dropped dead, the French lost the stomach to fight and fled; any who managed to get through the southern gate were allowed to escape. All enemy English were imprisoned.

The king's army, informed all clergy were excommunicates, broke open churches and storerooms and seized chests of money, clothes, women's ornaments and jewellery together with the French wagons and sumpter horses already loaded with silver vessels, furniture and utensils. The Count of Perche was buried outside the city in the hospital orchard. Also buried were the women, children and servants who, having climbed into small boats on the river for safety, had drowned either through mishandling the boats or overloading them.

24 August 1217: *Intercepted*

By pawning her jewels, Blanche, wife of Prince Louis, raised enough money to send him 300 knights, foot soldiers and supplies, and on a bright, sunny day they sailed on a 'swelling fair wind'. Mid-Channel the French fleet, commanded by the turncoat Eustace the Monk, spied eighty small ships coming at them fast on an intercepting course.

Commanded by Hubert de Burgh, English galleys sunk French ships, piercing some with their iron javelins or by divers boring holes in their bottoms. Sailors threw hot-lime dust in French eyes while Philip d'Albini's crossbowmen and archers killed them. French nobles were taken prisoner and the captured vessels were towed into Dover. Richard, natural son of King John, searched for Eustace; finding him, he told the turncoat that never again would he deceive any with false promises and beheaded him with his sword.

11–13 September 1217: *Blockaded*

The royal army having blockaded London by land and water, Prince Louis was forced to talk peace. King Henry, Queen Isabella, Legate Gualo and William Marshal signed the Treaty of Kingston, granting Prince Louis and his men freedom to leave England, aiding his departure with a gift of money.

14 May 1219: *Guardian*

Asking his devoted wife to kiss him one last time, Earl William Marshal had himself dressed in the silk Templar robes he had brought back from crusade thirty years earlier. In his seventy-fourth year, he died peacefully in his bed at Caversham Manor, having been ill since Candlemas. His eldest son, William, inherits the earldom and Richard, his second son, inherits his father's lands in Normandy.

Aware he was dying, William had asked King Henry to come to his bedside and in mid-April barons and bishops had squashed themselves into his bedchamber. William told the king he had served him loyally but now someone else had to guard him. Bishop Peter des Roches of Winchester placed a hand on the boy's head, saying as his tutor he would keep him. Too weak to sit, the earl, leaning on his side, took the king's hand and placed it in one of Pandulf's, saying, 'I wish here in the presence of all to give the king to God, to the Pope and to you who represent him.'

17–18 May 1220: *Second Coronation*

In front of people arrived from every part of the kingdom, Archbishop Stephen crowned King Henry at Westminster Abbey. Dressed in royal robes of red with jewelled gold border, holding gold sceptre and silver rod, he renewed his coronation oath. Fair-haired, graceful in movement, he looks set to grow tall and straight and is handsome although one eyelid droops slightly.

On the eve of the ceremony the king laid the foundation stone for a new chapel at Westminster dedicated to St Mary.

22 May 1220: Council Scandalised
A letter came from Queen Isabella telling the king she has married her daughter's betrothed, Hugh de Lusignan, son of the man to whom she had been betrothed before marrying King John. She said she married him to stop Hugh allying with the French king but rumour is Hugh is smitten by her beauty. For Joanna, she has negotiated a marriage instead with King Alexander of Scotland.

Barons holding the king's castle agreed to resign them instead of holding them until he comes of age and render faithful accounts to the Exchequer.

26–28 June 1220: Suspicions
While returning from York, rumours came to Henry that Rockingham Castle was being provisioned and garrisoned by William de Fortibus, Earl of Aumale. Suspicious, he stopped at the castle but was refused entrance. Distrustful, he commanded the castle be surrendered to him. After the earl, who had been away on the king's business, submitted to the king on 28 June, King Henry found few men and not three loaves.

7 July 1220: St Thomas
King Henry, with nobles from home and abroad, assembled at Canterbury Cathedral to view the body of St Thomas being removed from its marble tomb and placed into a gold-plated, bejewelled shrine built behind the high altar of Trinity Chapel. Supported on three pairs of pillars, it is accessed by three steps. Archbishop Stephen gave sumptuous hospitality to rich and poor in the large guesthouse he had built.

18–19 June 1221: Marriage
Eleven-year-old Princess Joanna, half the age of her bridegroom, was married to King Alexander in York Minster by Archbishop Walter in the presence of her brother, King Henry. On the journey northwards, King Henry filled the castles of Oxford, Northampton and Nottingham with men of his choosing.

1–13 August 1222: Harsh Justice

The Abbot of Westminster's steward proclaimed a rematch, with a ram as the prize, for 1 August after London youths had beat the abbot's wrestlers. On the day, however, the youths were beaten and wounded by the abbot's men. Led by one Constantine, hot-headed Londoners stole twelve of the abbot's horses and demolished many of his buildings. On another day they threw stones at the abbot, who had to escape them in a boat.

Justiciar Hubert had Constantine arrested and brought before him, and the man declared he regretted nothing and what was done was less than it should have been. He was sentenced and hanged immediately. Hubert rode into the city and arrested other troublemakers; he allowed them to depart after some had their feet cut off and others their hands.

13 January 1223: Liberties

Archbishop Stephen asked King Henry in council to confirm those liberties obtained by the barons in the war against his father. The judge William Brewer replied, 'The liberties which you demand, since they were extorted by force, ought not by right to be observed.' When the archbishop angrily rebuked him with, 'William, if you loved the king you would not disturb the peace of the kingdom', the king intervened to say he was already bound by oath to preserve those liberties and 'what was sworn he would observe'.

14 July 1223: Death

Laid low with the wasting sickness he had contracted last September, King Philip's death was presaged by a fiery-tailed comet. His son succeeds him as King Louis VIII.

16 June–26 October 1224: Siege of Bedford Castle

After Falkes de Breaute refused to give up his castles of Plympton and Bedford to Hubert de Burgh, saying they were part of his wife's dower, a royal writ was sent to him to attend the next shire court and answer for the breach of peace he committed eight years previously or be outlawed. On 16 June, while Falkes was absent, an eyre was held at Dunstable at which he was accused, without warrant, of sixteen counts of forcible disseisin by Henry Braybrooke and was found guilty. William, Falkes' brother, hearing what had happened, kidnapped Braybrooke and threw him into Bedford Castle dungeon. His wife raced to the king, who was at Northampton, to complain.

Four days later, royal troops and siege engines surrounded the castle. King Henry ordered a high wooden tower to be built and filled it with crossbowmen. Bishops excommunicated the garrison and the king swore, by the soul of his father, that if he had to imprison them by force he would hang them all.

The king ignored the letter he received from Earl Ranulf a few days after 4 August which assured him that Falkes, in Wales, had persuaded Llywelyn to stop his incursions, concluding a truce of one month for common cause to be made.

On 14 August, with the walls nearly breached, a few soldiers of the garrison asked the king for mercy. Allowed to come out, they were immediately imprisoned. The following day, defences gone, the rest of the bruised and wounded garrison emerged. Refused pardon by the king, William, his eighty knights and all the prisoners were hanged.

Four days after the death of his brother, Falkes came in submission before the king. His wife, Margaret de Redvers, complaining she had been forced into marriage, asked for a divorce which the king refused. For two months, nobles interceded for Falkes, reminding the king of his long and faithful service not only to him but to his father. Finally, he decided to exile him forever rather than deprive him of 'life or limb'. William, Earl Warenne, charged with keeping Falkes' wife, was ordered to conduct her husband to the coast. As he embarked on 26 October, tears running down his face, Falkes begged the earl to carry his greetings to 'his lord the king'.

2–11 February 1225: Gascony
By reissuing the Charter of Liberties, King Henry gained the tax he required to pay for his sixteen-year-old brother's expedition to Gascony. Knighted and made Earl of Cornwall and Poitou, Richard will sail to loyal Bordeaux on 23 March to subdue the king's rebellious subjects. Meanwhile, King Henry has dismissed Savaric de Mauleon as Seneschal of Poitou, blaming him for losing towns to the larger hosts of the French although his request for more men and arms had been ignored.

30 November 1226: Death
Twelve-year-old Louis IX was crowned after his father died of dysentery while on the Albigensian Crusade.

5 February 1227: Full Age
At his council in Oxford, King Henry declared himself of full age to rule and, to great murmuring, cancelled the charters of liberties

and forests 'as made and signed when he was not his own master', not being 'bound to keep what he was forced to promise'. He made Hubert de Burgh Earl of Kent.

26–31 December 1227: Short Measures
Having spent Christmas at York, King Henry set out by direct road for London, checking measures on his way. Finding in places corn, wine and beer deficient, he broke some measures and burnt others, substituting larger ones, and ordered bread to be made of heavier weight. Anyone found breaking the law will be heavily fined.

9 July 1228: Death
Stephen, Archbishop of Canterbury, in his late seventies, died at his manor of Slindon, near Chichester.

29 September 1229: Accusations
Ready to embark at Portsmouth to make war on France, King Henry was informed by his chiefs and marshals there were too few provisions, and arms on board too few ships, meaning the expedition would need to be delayed until after next Easter. Calling Chief Justiciar Hubert, Earl of Kent a traitor, the king accused him of thwarting his commands and taking bribes from Queen Blanche to frustrate his plans. As the king raised his sword, Earl Ranulf stepped between them before Henry could kill Hubert. Rumour says that the casks that should have held money for funds held only stones and sand.

30 April 1230: King Embarks
King Henry with his army embarked from Portsmouth, sailing to St Malo to meet with the Count of Brittany, while the fleet anchored at St Gildas.

14 May 1230: Eclipse
An unusual eclipse of the sun took place immediately after sunrise. It became so dark that labourers, who had already commenced their morning's work, left to return to their beds to sleep; after an hour, the sun regained its usual brightness.

29 September 1230: King Returns
Having been ill since his triumphant entry into Bordeaux after capturing Gironde Castle, the king has returned to England.

March 1231: Marriage
Richard, Earl of Cornwall, much to his brother's displeasure, married Isabel Marshal, the widow of Earl Gilbert of Gloucester and sister of William Marshal, Earl of Pembroke. Along with Wallingford Castle he acquires six stepchildren.

6 April 1231: Death
The sudden death of Earl William Marshal of Pembroke in his forty-second year has surprised many. He will be buried in New Temple near his father. Being childless, his heir is his younger brother Richard.

Christmastide 1231: Charitable Plunder
Bishop Peter's tales of his five-year pilgrimage hugely entertained King Henry and those members of the court spending Christmas at Winchester with him.

A tale has come that a small body of armed, hooded men plundered the well-stocked barns of a Roman priest at Wingham. When soldiers investigated, the granaries were nearly empty and the grain had been given to the poor. The hooded men had been challenged but allowed to depart after showing royal warrants forbidding anyone to obstruct them; they are believed now to have been forged by Justiciar Hubert.

13 August 1232: Magic Stone
Having sacked Hubert de Burgh on the advice of Bishop Peter and asked him to provide an accounting since William Marshal's death in 1219, Hubert's personal possessions, including his own castle of Hadleigh, built on land given to him by King John, were seized today. Rumour is rife: Hubert has looted the treasury, poisoned magnates, mismanaged military operations, seduced Princess Margaret to marry her to gain the Scottish throne and given Prince Llywelyn a magic stone which protects anyone holding it in battle. Although the king appointed Hubert Chief Justiciar for life, Stephen de Segrave replaces him. The bishop's son, Peter de Rivaux, is appointed chamberlain and treasurer of the royal household, keeper of the privy seal and custodian of the mint.

27 September 1232: Persecution
Today, after the Bishop of London rebuked King Henry for persecuting Hubert de Burgh, the king ordered him removed from the Tower and returned to the sanctuary from which he was snatched, but blockaded so he could receive no food.

At first King Henry had allowed Hubert to go to Merton Priory. Inconstant, he sent the Mayor of London orders to bring him back dead or alive, but these orders were recalled on the persuasion of Earl Ranulf, and a safe conduct was sent allowing Hubert to join his wife at Bury St Edmunds. On his way, Hubert stopped for the night to lodge with his nephew, the Bishop of Norwich. Changing his mind, King Henry sent Geoffrey Crowcombe with 300 soldiers to arrest him. Awakened by their violent entrance, and believing they came to kill him, Hubert fled naked from his bed to the church for sanctuary. They dragged him out and then woke the blacksmith, ordering him to forge fetters. The blacksmith refused when he saw they were for the hero of Chinon, Dover and Sandwich. Hubert was placed on a horse, his feet tied under the animal's belly, and taken to the Tower.

26 October 1232: Death

Since his return from campaign, Earl Ranulf had never quite recovered. Aged sixty-two, he died at Wallingford. His body will be buried at Chester, his heart at Dieulacres Abbey. His eldest sister's son, John the Scot, inherits the earldom of Chester; the earldom of Lincoln he willed, via his youngest sister, Hawise, to her son-in-law John de Lacy.

25 December 1232: Mass Redundancies

During his Christmas court in Worcester, as advised by Bishop Peter, King Henry replaced all his native-born household officers and custodians of his castles with alien Poitevins.

11 July 1233: Refusal

Earls and barons refused to attend the king's council today, as they did his Oxford council on 24 June. Bishop Peter has advised the king to seize their castles and give them to Poitevin nobles who would defend him against traitors.

9–30 October 1233: One Voice

For condemning his magnates without trial, burning their manors, cutting down their woods and orchards and destroying their parks and lakes, several bishops present at Westminster council criticised the king and humbly begged him to make peace with his barons. He replied his nobles were traitors. Then they, as if of one voice, threatened Bishop Peter with excommunication. Contemptuously he told them the Pope had consecrated him and they had not the authority. Ignoring him, they excommunicated all those who had 'estranged the king's affection from his natural English subjects'. Enraged, the king ordered them to excommunicate Richard Marshal, Earl of Pembroke for seizing Hereford Castle but they refused, saying he had only retaken his own castle.

Determined to take it from Richard, King Henry mustered an army of English and foreign soldiers at Gloucester. Reaching Hereford, he found all cattle and provisions removed. On 30 October he was forced to retreat and make camp at Grosmont Castle.

A little after dusk, an attack signal roused sleeping soldiers. Hundreds of nearly naked men fled in all directions until they realised there was no pursuit. Returning, they found all the wagons, their equipment and baggage and 500 horses had been spirited away. Those who had lost their property returned home while a dispirited king returned to Gloucester, where he received news that Hubert de Burgh, though chained to a wall in the dungeon in Devizes Castle, had been rescued.

9–16 April 1234: Ambuscade

On 9 April at the Westminster council, Archbishop Edmund bluntly told King Henry to make peace with his subjects or be excommunicated. Three days later, King Henry ordered Bishop Peter to Winchester to attend to the 'cure of souls' and dismissed Peter de Rivaux with an order to render an account of royal money, telling him that only right of clergy allowed him to keep his eyes. All Poitevins were ordered to leave court and royal castles, and the king sought peace with his barons, especially Earl Richard – quite an about-turn considering the king had previously said they would never come to terms unless the earl put a halter around his neck and begged for mercy.

Believing the king's peace, Earl Richard sailed to Ireland. On 16 April, they buried his corpse at Kilkenny. He had been ambushed. Six knights he had slain quickly; the seventh, bearing the arms of the king's justiciar, Richard de Burgh, tried to lift off the earl's helm and had his hands sliced off, the sword piercing his gauntlets. Another assailant was cut in two at his middle by the earl. Finally surrounded, he and his horse were stabbed on all sides until he was thrown off after his horse's feet were cut away with axes.

29 May 1234: 'Examine your conscience'

In council at Gloucester, Archbishop Edmund read out letters which revealed Earl Richard's death had been ordered. King Henry denied all knowledge of them, saying he had set his seal to some letters placed before him but was unaware of their purport. The archbishop said,

'Examine your conscience, my king, for all those who caused those letters to be sent were aware of the treachery intended, and are just as guilty as those who slayed him with their own hands.'

10–11 May 1235: Empress Isabella

Starting her journey to Worms for her coronation and marriage to Emperor Frederick, arranged for 20 July, twenty-year-old Princess Isabella shone with such a profusion of jewellery and jewels on garments embroidered in shimmering gold and silver silk that the cheering London crowds could not take their eyes off her as she and her colourfully attired ladies passed by on slow horses, remarkable themselves for their trappings and saddles of gilt and gold.

The king's wedding gifts to his sister included a beautiful pure-gold crown decorated with jewels and images of the four martyrs of England, silk and wool garments, gold cups and dishes, silver cooking pots and a bed with coverlets, fine linen sheets and pillows so soft they invite slumber.

Accompanied by the Archbishop of Cologne and the Duke of Louvain, both delighted with her grace, manners and beauty, the colourful train proceeded through Rochester, overnighting at the Abbey of Faversham before visiting Canterbury to pray at the Shrine of St Thomas, thence to the Port of Sandwich. Embarking on 11 May, brother and sister wept as they said their goodbyes, the king continuing to wave as the fleet put to sea under full sail.

14 January 1236: Royal Wedding

King Henry and twelve-year-old Eleanor, second daughter of Count Raymond and known as La Belle of Provence, were married at Canterbury Cathedral today by Archbishop Edmund. The bride, dark-haired and dark-eyed, wore a long-sleeved shimmering golden dress which cinched in at the waist and flared out to her feet in wide pleats. The new queen loves reading classical and Arthurian romances and the king has said he will take his bride to Glastonbury.

20 January 1236: Coronation

Riding with the king and queen from the Tower to Westminster were three hundred citizens, in their best silk clothes and gold-worked mantles, carrying gold and silver cups for their butler duties. The streets, cleansed of mud, dirt, sticks 'and all things offensive', were decorated with flags, silk banners and leafy boughs.

From the palace, King Henry, crowned and wearing full regalia, walked beneath a purple silk canopy with silver gilt bells. The stone chalice, plate of St Edward and his sword Curtana were borne before him into the abbey. Queen Eleanor walked behind him under a similar canopy, bells softly tinkling. The constable used his wand several times to stop people pressing forward. Reaching the steps of the high altar, Eleanor knelt and was anointed by Archbishop Edmund who placed the diadem on her head.

The banquet served afterwards was overseen by Simon de Montfort, Earl of Leicester and steward for the day. Earl Warenne served as butler, replacing the excommunicated Earl of Arundel who had seized the archbishop's hunting hounds despite the prelate insisting he had the right to hunt in any forest he pleased. The great chamberlain, Earl Hugh of Oxford, served the water at breakfast and guarded the king's chamber door while Earl Gilbert Marshal of Pembroke guarded the doors of the king's hall, receiving a palfrey and saddle from every man knighted by the king. Gilbert de Sandford claimed the right to be the queen's chamberlain and to guard her door, receiving her whole bed and basins for his troubles.

While the London citizens served wine in their costly cups, an abundance of venison and other meat and fish dishes were placed on the table by Winchester citizens. The sounds of the gleemen and the gaiety of the waiters made it a joyous affair despite the heavy rain outside, and when darkness fell the city was beautifully illuminated with lamps, cressets and candles.

10 February 1236: Floods
With rain persisting since the start of January, swollen rivers have rendered fords impassable, bridges have disappeared, and mills and dams have been carried away over flooded fields, meadows and marshes. Today, the Thames overflowed its usual banks and entered the Palace of Westminster so that people ride on horseback to their apartments and others get around in small boats.

7 January 1238: Marriage
At Westminster, the king gave his widowed sister, Eleanor, in marriage to Simon de Montfort, Earl of Leicester. The nuptials were performed in the king's small chapel in a corner of his chamber.

9 September 1238: Screaming Murder
In the middle of the night at Woodstock Palace, unable to sleep, one of the queen's maids was softly singing psalms to herself by candlelight when she heard an intruder. Her screams woke the

king's attendants who rushed in and found the 'madman' the king had allowed to stay in the palace. He had gone to stab the king but on finding his bed empty – the king had chosen that night to sleep with his queen – had begun searching other rooms. The king ordered him to be torn limb from limb by horses at Coventry and his body parts dragged through all the largest cities and afterwards hung on a robber's gibbet.

17–18 June 1239: Royal Birth

At Westminster, a son was born to King Henry and Queen Eleanor during the night. To celebrate, the citizens of London danced through lantern-lit streets playing drums and tambourines.

The baby boy was christened Edward after the Confessor. Gifts flooded in but those the king considered not good enough he returned, making a courtier quip, 'God has given us this child but the king is selling him to us.' A nursery has already been set up at Windsor Castle, staffed with two nurses called Alice and Sarah. Since his wedding the king has refurbished the castle with large glazed windows, painted walls and a brand-new chamber for the queen.

9 August 1239: Defiled

Crowds thronging around Westminster Abbey to see the churching of Queen Eleanor were agog when King Henry stopped Simon and Eleanor de Montfort from entering the abbey. The king openly accused the earl of seducing and defiling his sister, saying he only allowed them to marry against his own wishes to avoid scandal. Now he accused the earl that, 'so the vow she made to remain celibate in front of the archbishop might not impede your marriage, you went to Rome, gained papal sanction by bribery, [was] excommunicated for non-payment only to falsely name me as guarantor'.

Fleeing the king's rage, they returned by water to their lodgings at Winchester House in Southwark, only to find he had sent soldiers to forcibly eject them. Back at Westminster, they begged tearfully for his pardon. Towards the end of the day, he gave them leave to depart from the palace. The earl, his wife and a small retinue embarked in a small boat on the Thames, sailing to the coast and out of England.

2 October 1240: Birth

Queen Eleanor bore the king a baby daughter. She has been named Margaret after her aunt the French queen and because, during the pains of childbirth, the queen had called upon St Margaret.

1 December 1241: Death

Empress Isabella died in childbirth, at Foggia near Naples. In her dying moments her thoughts turned to her brother, for her last words to her husband were for love of her, to keep friendly relations with him.

May–June 1242: Overseas Campaign

Sailing to France to aid his mother, King Henry rushed to defend Taillebourg but upon arriving at nightfall found the citizens had made peace with King Louis. Believing the Comte de Marche was bringing troops to augment his own force, King Henry made camp opposite the French but morning light revealed the formidable size of the French host. Turning to his stepfather, he asked the whereabouts of the promised troops and was told no promise had been made. When Earl Richard backed up his brother, the count said, 'Blame your mother, by God's throat, she has contrived all this without my knowledge.'

Earl Richard, disarming, took his crusader staff in hand and asked for an interview with the French king. He was honourably received – for while in the Holy Land he had negotiated for the release of French prisoners. King Louis agreed a truce of one day but when the earl returned he whispered into his brother's ear, 'Quick, quick, let us go for we are in imminent danger of being taken prisoner.' They retreated quickly, making for Bordeaux. Nobles left behind half-cooked food as they mounted swift horses. The foot soldiers were left behind and many died of hunger or illness; others sustained themselves by eating berries.

Staying in a tent pitched in pleasant fields near Bordeaux, Queen Eleanor gave birth to a daughter on 25 June who was called Beatrice in honour of the queen's mother, who attended her.

23 April 1243: Truce

A truce was concluded between the kings of England and France to last for five years.

27 September 1243: Entry Orders

Returning from his prolonged stay in Bordeaux, King Henry when he landed at Portsmouth immediately sent his heralds to Winchester to announce his arrival with orders for his nobles and the most important citizens to meet him wearing rich garments and mounted on costly chargers, with the city's church bells ringing and streets adorned with hangings, curtains, garlands and lighted tapers, and thronged with citizens dressed in their best holiday clothes.

His baby daughter, with her nurse Agnes and her husband, were sent on to the nursery at Windsor.

16 January 1245: Royal Birth

In London, Queen Eleanor gave birth to a son, who was by the king's order named Edmund after Saint Edmund. The queen had felt ill throughout much of her pregnancy and the king gave large amounts of money to the church to help safeguard her.

13 August–3 November 1245: Welsh Campaign

To subdue David, Prince of Wales, King Henry and Queen Eleanor first travelled to Chester with an army supported by his nobles. After building a strong fortification at Gannock they rode out, burning towns and laying cornfields to waste. One of the nobles wrote of the campaign, 'We lie in our tents, watching, fasting, praying and freezing. We watch, for fear of the Welshmen who are wont to invade us in the night; we fast for want of meat, for the halfpenny loaf is worth 5*d*; we pray to God to send us home speedily, and we freeze for want of winter garments, having nothing but thin linen between us and the wind.'

31 May 1246: Death

On hearing the news of the death of his mother, Queen Isabella, Countess of Marche and Angouleme on 31 May, King Henry invited his half-siblings Alice, Geoffrey, William, Aymer and Guy de Lusignan to England.

13 October 1247: Blood of Christ

As ordered by the king, prelates were dressed in festival surplices and hoods, holding lighted tapers. In stark contrast, King Henry, dressed as a pilgrim, held up the crystal vessel in which the Patriarch of Jerusalem had sent him the Blood of Christ. He walked the mile between St Paul's and Westminster Abbey holding it above his head, using two hands where the road was rugged or uneven, two attendants supporting his arms. All the way he kept his eyes fixed on heaven – or his canopy roof.

Met at the abbey by monks singing, tears running down their faces, King Henry led the procession round the abbey, his own palace chambers and finally to the shrine of St Edward.

While the solemnity continued in the church, the king changed from his hermit garb to a soft garment embroidered with gold and put on a gold crown. Sitting on his newly built throne of white marble with Plantagenet leopards on either side of the seat, he knighted his half-brother William.

13 May 1250: Archbishop Terror

The queen's uncle Boniface, created Archbishop of Canterbury by King Henry, came to London where without consent he lodged in the Bishop of Chichester's house rather than his own dwelling at Lambeth. Although visitation was the right of the Bishop of London, the archbishop went to the Priory of St Bartholomew. They honourably met him with lighted tapers and ringing bells in solemn procession, and the sub-prior welcomed him but told him that only their own bishop had the right of visitation. Punching him several times in the chest, the archbishop shouted, 'Thus it becomes me to deal with you English traitors.' As canons tried to rescue the aged prior, the archbishop tore off his cloak, breaking its bejewelled golden clasp, shouting for a sword to be brought to him. Horrified crowds saw he had armour under his robes. His retinue attacked the canons, leaving many bruised and bloody. After the attack the canons complained to their bishop. He sent them to see the king at Westminster but they were refused an audience although they waited for hours. Meanwhile, in the city, there were many who wanted to ring the common bell and cut the archbishop to pieces.

1–7 October 1250: Red Moon

The new moon appeared swollen and red. Violent winds tore away trees, and the sea roared in twice without any ebb and in the night appeared to burn like fire. Strong vessels, large and small, were sunk and tidal rivers flooded houses, meadows and fields. At Winchelsea more than 300 fishermen's houses, salt-houses, bridges, mills and churches were destroyed.

Christmastide 1251: Marriage

The royal court travelled to York for the marriage of eleven-year-old Princess Margaret to nine-year-old Alexander III, King of Scotland. An immense multitude were crowded into the city and to keep the peace different national retinues were lodged separately, although the Scots decided to fight each other.

On Christmas Day, King Henry knighted Alexander who paid homage for Lothian but politely said he would take proper counsel regarding giving homage for Scotland. At the feast 450 rabbits raised in cony-garths were set before the court as a new delicacy.

Before any were risen next morning, the couple were married in a quiet ceremony to stop their being pressed in an unruly manner by crowds. King Henry had ordered for his wife (besides seven robes to his two) a beautiful bejewelled violet brocade robe with three small leopards decorating the front and three in the back. At the banquet, English, French and Scots nobles were dressed in colourful silk garments, their colours as diverse as the dishes and jokes from jesters. More than sixty pasture cattle formed the first course at table.

8–16 September 1252: Round Table Murder

Knights from all over England and even the continent flocked to Wallenden Abbey for a new sport called a 'Round Table' which replaces the charge-and-turn as knights showcase their skill, with crowds cheering on their favourites.

Two well-known knights who had fought before entered the lists. Mounted on handsome horses, Sir Arnold and Sir Roger rushed to meet one another with lances. Roger's lance entered under Arnold's helmet and pierced his throat, severing his windpipe and arteries. He fell from his horse already dead. No one cried more than the sorrowful Roger, who vowed he would take the cross. Knights carried Arnold's body into the abbey. The Earl of Gloucester withdrew the fragment of lance and cut out the iron head. When he found a sharp point instead of the customary blunt end, he looked hard at Roger and accused him of murder.

6 August 1253: Aquitaine

After King Henry gave oath to faithfully observe the Great Charter in May, Parliament granted him money for his expedition to Aquitaine to deal with rebellious barons who have complained that Simon de Montfort, Earl of Leicester governed the duchy tyrannically. Appointing Queen Eleanor and Earl Richard guardians of the kingdom, the king today sailed from Portsmouth. Prince Edward, after his father had many times embraced and kissed him, stood crying and sobbing on the shore, refusing to leave until he could no longer see the sails of the ships.

25 November 1253: Birth

Queen Eleanor, in London, gave birth to a 'beautiful daughter'. She was baptised Catherine as she drew her first breath on St Catherine's Day.

27 January 1254: Council

At the council held by Queen Eleanor and Earl Richard, letters from King Henry were read out in which he asked for more money to assist him in his war against the King of Castile, sending crossbow bolts of a wondrous size as proof of his need.

Richard, Earl of Gloucester promised assistance to the best of his ability; the Earl of Cornwall immediately promised 300 soldiers at his own expense to fight for a year, adding the proviso, 'If what is told us is true.' He was not the only one to wonder as the bruit is Edward is promised in marriage to Eleanor of Castile and is about to cross the sea with his mother. Thus, the king 'rendered himself unworthy of belief and the council was dissolved' for 'the nets which are too clear to the view the bird avoids'.

1 November 1254: Marriage
Prince Edward was married at Burgos to Eleanor, the younger sister of Alphonso X, King of Castile.

February 1255: Elephant
People flocked to see the elephant, gift of King Louis. It is ten years old and ten feet high, with a greyish-black rough hide, and walks with a ponderous but robust gait. Transporting it from Wissant via Dover to London cost £9 6s and to house it the sheriffs of London have erected a building forty feet by twenty feet in the Tower of London, costing just over £22.

It joins the polar bear gifted by the King of Norway which crowds of Londoners over the last two years have watched while its keeper takes it for a swim in the Thames to play and catch fish.

Queen Margaret's gift to King Henry is also curious: a washing basin shaped like a peacock, its body in gold and silver, with a tail that when opened out into a circle is decorated with sapphires to resemble a real bird.

23 June 1255: Entry
Citizens dressed in their holiday clothes welcomed Eleanor, wife of Prince Edward, with bells and songs as she rode through the streets tapestried and decorated with flowers. Her lodgings, walls and floors have been covered in Spanish fashion with cloth of silk and tapestry.

16–25 March 1257: Promises
In council, King Henry brought in Prince Edmund wearing royal robes of Sicilian fashion. He told them he had bound himself, under penalty of losing his kingdom, to pay the Pope 140,000 marks plus interest and asked their aid to help his son obtain Sicily. The 'ears of all tingled' and tearfully they begged the king for a respite but eventually swore that if the king would inviolably observe the *Magna Carta*, as

so often promised, he would be granted 52,000 marks to meet his pressing necessities.

Earl Richard took leave of the council. He and Lady Sanchia, his wife and the queen's sister, are going to Aachen to be crowned King and Queen of Germany in May. He had previously declined the crown of Sicily, telling the Pope he might as well say, 'I make you a present of the moon, step up to the sky and take it.'

3 May 1257: Death
Catherine, the beautiful three-year-old daughter of King Henry and Queen Eleanor, died at Windsor Castle. The queen has shed so many tears she has made herself ill and the king is feverish from grief. The little girl, who was dumb, was often ill in winter months. She is to be buried at Westminster and King Henry has ordered a gilded silver effigy to 'recall more worthily to his mind the features of his little girl'.

August–September 1257: Wales
When soldiers working in the marches for Prince Edward were wiped out by Llywelyn ap Gruffudd, King Henry with his son mustered troops at Chester and marched into Wales laying waste the rich and abundant crops. When Llewellyn sent messengers to beg the king for peace and ask that the Welsh be allowed to 'retain their ancestral laws and liberties in peace', the king's reply was to unfurl his royal standard and threaten to exterminate them all. Less than a month later, when supply ships failed to arrive from Ireland, King Henry and Prince Edward were forced to retreat, attacked all the way by guerrilla forces.

March 1258: Famine Alleviated
After the crops failed, people who had begun eating the bark of trees to survive cheered as fifty large ships arrived from King Richard of Germany laden with corn, wheat and bread.

11 June 1258: Provisions of Oxford
After a month of council sessions during which Simon, Earl of Leicester and Richard, Earl of Gloucester opposed him, King Henry, fearing deposition and swearing once again to faithfully observe *Magna Carta*, agreed to be advised by a council of fifteen persons, elected solely by the barons and headed by Simon and Richard, monitored by parliaments held in October, February and June. Hugh Bigod, brother of Earl Roger of Norfolk, appointed Chief Justiciar, swore he would do justice 'uninfluenced by hate or love, prayer or

price'. Provision was made to appoint a chancellor and treasurer and for all aliens, especially the king's half-brothers, to be expelled and offices given to faithful Englishmen. In every local court, four honest knights are to enquire into grievances and oppressions and, upon oath, make a report bearing their own seals to be delivered by the sheriffs at the next parliament. The Provisions of Oxford and *Magna Carta* are to be issued in every county – in Latin, French *and* English.

The Road to Civil War

Towards the end of 1259, King Henry and Queen Eleanor, accompanied by the Earl and Countess of Leicester, left for Paris to confer with King Louis about reclaiming his inheritance and rights unjustly taken from him and his father; however, in the peace treaty negotiated, Henry was confirmed as ruler of Gascony but gave up his family lands in the north of France.

Early in February 1260, Earl Simon left France and once in England requested a council be summoned immediately in accordance with the Provisions of Oxford. He was thwarted in that aim as King Henry had written from St Omer asking for it to be delayed as he was ill. He also relayed concerns that Prince Edward had allied with Simon and intended to seize his throne.

On 30 April, King Henry returned from France. Distrustful of his son, he refused to see him in case his love made him reckless but forgave him in May when Prince Edward made a public avowal in St Paul's that he had done nothing to injure his parents. At Westminster on 13 October, amid hilarity and rejoicing, the king knighted his son, his brother's son Henry of Germany, John of Brittany and Henry and Simon, the sons of Earl Simon, before they all left to attend a tournament in Paris. King Henry spent Christmas quietly with Queen Eleanor in the Tower of London.

At the parliament held at Winchester on 12 June 1261, King Henry exhibited the dispensation received from the Pope absolving him and Prince Edward from the oaths forced upon them at Oxford and annulling the laws made there. The barons begged him to preserve the oath, saying they would amend anything that displeased him. He said he would rule his kingdom, and without council, as he saw fit. He replaced sheriffs and governors of his castles with his own men. When the barons backed down from civil war, Earl Simon left England.

By 1263 Henry's authority had disintegrated. The barons refused to work with the king unless he observed the Provisions of Oxford. Prince Edward remained aloof from court, living at Bristol. In a bid for resolution, King Henry suggested King Louis be asked to mediate. To this the barons agreed. They also invited Earl Simon to return to England. In July 1263, Earl Simon, supported by London citizens, took King Henry prisoner and put him under guard in the Tower. Prince Edward raised troops to support his father but was forced to disband his knights when his father was threatened. On 13 July, Queen Eleanor, thinking to sail from the Tower for Windsor to join her son's wife, was pelted with stones and mud, rotten eggs and vegetables as she tried to pass under London Bridge. After Prince Edward submitted, the king and queen with their son were allowed to lodge at Westminster and soon after she escaped with Edmund to the continent. Early one morning before Christmas, King Henry went to Windsor Castle to see his son, who had been given permission to visit his wife in mid-October.

On 2 February 1264 in council the Mise of Amiens was read out. King Louis had found for King Henry and in his view the Provisions of Oxford were invalidated except those of the ancient charter of King John. On 30 March, Earl Simon, styling himself Steward of England, refuted both the papal bull and the French king's judgement, contending the Provisions of Oxford were founded wholly on *Magna Carta*, which he would defend to the death.

3 April–6 May 1264: Civil War

Mustering troops and royalist barons at Oxford on 3 April, King Henry secured Northampton first, then Leicester, Salisbury and Nottingham while Prince Edward raced to secure the loyalty of the Cinque Ports.

Like de Montfort supporters in other towns, Gilbert de Clare, newly created Earl of Gloucester, massacred Jews at Canterbury. He journeyed to Rochester and took the castle, but not the keep, on 19 April. King Henry successfully raised the siege after taking Gilbert's castle at Kingston and two weeks later his castle of Tonbridge. Because his cook was killed by an arrow at Flimwell on 2 May, King Henry ordered all 315 surrendered archers executed. They were beheaded in his presence.

Planning to blockade London, the king was thwarted by Earl Simon marching out of the city on 6 May, having first plundered and destroyed all Jewish property and stripped naked and murdered all those he had taken prisoner. Only those who gained the safety of the Tower were saved.

13–17 May 1264: Battle of Lewes

Aware King Henry had encamped his army at Lewes, Simon de Montfort set up camp at his manor of Fletching, a village just to the north surrounded by dense forest. Before dawn on 14 May, the earl positioned his troops above the town on the high downs, overlooking the king's army, so that his flanks were defended by steep ground and at his front the slope gradually stretched down over half a mile. He deployed his soldiers into three divisions, mirroring the king's.

On his right he placed a division of Londoners, zealous but undisciplined, led by Nicholas de Segrave opposite Prince Edward; the centre was led by Earl Gilbert of Gloucester opposite Richard, King of Germany and his son Prince Henry. Montfort's sons, Henry and Guy, commanded the left opposite King Henry displaying the royal standard of a golden sapphire-eyed dragon on red silk. A fourth division was retained as strategic reserve under his command.

As the trumpets blew, Prince Edward and his men, well armoured, well armed and mounted, erupted furiously into the Londoners for the prince seethed with rage at their insulting his mother the previous July. Londoners, foot and horse, fled and were pursued by the prince for a few miles, being slaughtered by unsparing swords, but his vengeful chase gave Earl Simon a vital opening. The earl threw his forces towards the king, who had two horses killed under him. No matter his personal bravery, severely wounded by sword and mace, seeing several of his most faithful friends killed, he was forced to withdraw into Lewes Priory. Prince Edward returned to find no one fighting, only the dead and dying of both sides, and forced a way into the priory to his father.

Earl Simon suggested an immediate truce and the king surrendered his sword to Earl Gilbert.

On the Friday, Prince Edward became a hostage for his father and was sent immediately to Dover Castle with his cousin, Prince Henry, kept under the charge of their cousin, Henry de Montfort. On the following day, all royal court and other officers were dismissed and Earl Simon conducted King Henry to London.

24 June 1264: Agree or Be Deposed
Along with baron and prelates, Earl Simon summoned four knights to be elected from each shire to attend Parliament at Westminster. King Henry was presented with a Schedule of Grievances and informed he would govern with a council of nine who would appoint all officers as required including a justiciar, chancellor and treasurer. Three councillors would attend him at all times. He could agree or he could be deposed.

28 May 1265: Prince Escapes
In custody in Hereford Castle, Prince Edward was given permission by his guards to exercise his horse in the fields outside the city. One day,

chatting and joking with the guards about the speed of their horses, he tried them out and in so doing tired them. Mounting his own, fresh horse, he waved a farewell to his guards and crossed the river. Although outpaced, they pursued him until they saw the banners of Roger Mortimer and Roger de Clifford coming with men to escort him to the safety of Wigmore Castle. Outmanoeuvred, his guards returned to Hereford.

4 August 1265: Battle of Evesham

After managing to box Simon, the son of Earl Simon, into the fortress of Kenilworth, capturing many valuable prisoners in the process, Prince Edward sent spies out to shadow and watch the earl, who had marched from Hereford, crossed the Severn at Kempsey and was marching towards Evesham intending to unite with his son.

At daybreak, Earl Simon's troops were cheered when they saw the banners of a large army of orderly squadrons coming from the direction of Kenilworth. Simon's barber, Nicholas, hoping for a good view, climbed the abbey's clock tower. Suddenly he shouted, 'We are all dead!' He could see the triple lions of Prince Edward in one place, the banner of the turncoat Earl of Gloucester in another direction and from a third line the banner of Roger Mortimer.

A premonition seized Simon as he said, 'Let us commend our souls to God, because our bodies are theirs ... they are approaching wisely, they learned this from me.' He gave permission for friends to take flight. His son, Henry, offered to take full brunt of the battle to give his father the opportunity to escape. He refused. Henry and his younger brother, Guy, refused to leave, as did Hugh Despenser and Ralph Basset, saying they did not wish to survive their earl.

Forming his cavalry into a wedge to try and break through the royalist lines and lead his foot soldiers out, the fighting for the next two hours was desperate for Prince Edward had given the order: 'No quarter!'

Earl Simon fought with all the vigour and courage of a young soldier. His horse trampled many under its hooves. One by one his friends 'dropped in death'. Weakened by wounds, his horse killed under him, wielding his sword in both hands against twelve knights, he continued dealing out vigorous blows, fighting to the last. Felled by a blow from behind, he was 'overwhelmed by numbers rather than conquered'. His son, Henry, goaded to madness by seeing his father's death, fought for a similar fate, while Guy fell nearly lifeless among the heaps of dead and dying.

William de Mandeville and John de Beauchamp, though only youths of tender age, were butchered in cold blood after being taken prisoner. Sir Guy Balliol, who had borne the earl's standard, was mangled with wounds.

King Henry, put in a suit of Montfort's armour, was wounded in the neck, and was only recognised when he shouted, 'By the head of God, I am the king.'

Though the battle was over, Montfort's corpse was mutilated. His hands, feet and limbs were cut off and his torso was divided into fragments among other atrocities. His head was fixed on a spear-point and sent to Matilda de Mortimer at Wigmore. Prince Edward, sincerely mourning the death of Henry de Montfort, insisted on and attended an honourable burial for his boyish playmate and comrade.

8–13 September 1265: Winchester Parliament

In his parliament at Winchester, King Henry imprisoned the Mayor of London and his chief officers for the unusual oath of loyalty he received in March: 'Lord, as long as you will be a good king and lord to us, we will be your faithful and devoted men.' He further deprived the city of its ancient liberties and privileges for the sacking of Westminster Palace and other actions.

All those who had stood with Simon de Montfort were disinherited, chief among them his nephews, Simon and Guy. Their mother, whom the king refuses to call sister, was permitted to depart England. The king declared the lands he has seized will never be returned to their former owners or any part of their family and they will be perpetually disinherited.

The king's brother, Richard, openly remonstrated with him that such a policy will only lead to further conflict; if the barons have no hope, why would they lay down arms? The king was adamant. The earl has withdrawn from court.

13 July 1266: Birth

Eleanor of Castile bore a son during the night at Windsor Castle, a first son and heir for Prince Edward. He has been named John after his great-grandfather King John.

August–December 1266: Kenilworth

As vigorously as King Henry has besieged Kenilworth Castle, it has been no less vigorously defended from within, both sides having a great number of siege engines, similar in size and number so that sometimes stones hurled clashed in the air. Even when their siege engines were finally broken, the defenders refused to surrender until December, worn out by famine and misery.

Summer 1267: New Terms

Although most of the disinherited laid down their arms when the king ameliorated his harshness by agreeing fines – assessed on the degree of support given to Earl Simon, to be paid and the land returned at the end of term – a hardcore band lived as outlaws on the Isle of Ely, saying it was too bitter to see others living in their ancestral estates. Earl Richard, who had condemned the harsh treatment from the first, mediated a new agreement with Cardinal Otto whereby rebels who agree to redeem their lands at the fines judged would obtain immediate possession and pay the fines to the Exchequer.

5 May 1268: Birth

An addition was made to the nursery: a second son has been born to Prince Edward and his consort, Eleanor. They have named him Henry, after his grandfather.

16 June 1269: Third Marriage

Richard of Germany married today as his third wife the beautiful fifteen-year-old Beatrice of Falkenburg. Now sixty years old, the earl is besotted with her.

18 June 1269: Birth

Eleanor, consort of Prince Edward, has given birth to a baby girl, who has been named Eleanora.

13 October 1269: St Edward

The body of St Edward the Confessor was solemnly transferred to a shrine of gold which King Henry had prepared for it in Westminster Abbey. The saint was carried by the king, his brother Richard and his sons, Edward and Edmund.

20 August 1270: Crusade

Prince Edward and Princess Eleanor, with four earls and four barons and a thousand men, have set out on pilgrimage to the Holy Land with the blessing of King Henry.

2 April 1272: Death

Richard, King of Germany died at his Castle of Berkhamsted. After suffering a stroke in December he had been paralysed and unable to speak. He will be buried at Hailes Abbey next to his second wife,

Sanchia, and his son, Henry, murdered in the church at Viterbo in spring 1271 by Simon and Guy de Montfort as revenge for Evesham. He is succeeded by his son, Edmund.

16 November 1272: Death of King Henry

Highly enraged by the citizens burning Norwich Cathedral and carrying off books, jewels, vases and the gold chalice, King Henry set out for Norwich attended by the Bishop of Rochester and Gilbert, Earl of Gloucester. When he saw the entire building had been destroyed, Henry wept. The bishop excommunicated all those who had taken part and the king fined them three thousand marks of silver to be put towards rebuilding the cathedral and replacing what had been stolen.

On his way back to London, the sixty-five-year-old king, who has been in frail health for much of the last two years, fell ill while lodged at the abbey of St Edmund's and was transported to Westminster where Queen Eleanor stayed by his bedside. In his dying moments, on the evening of 16 November, in the presence of barons and prelates, King Henry remitted ill-will to all. He desired his body to be buried in front of the high altar of Westminster Abbey where once St Edward's body had lain, with his royal rod and dove but no sword; his heart was to be interred at Fontevraud. He had reigned for fifty-six years.

Edward I

1272–1307

Though he was overseas, Edward's accession was peaceful. The moment King Henry was interred on 20 November 1272 the nobles swore fealty to their new king. Government continued: a new seal was made, ministers were appointed and accounts paid such as the decoration of the King's Great Hall by Stephen the painter.

Edward, recuperating from an assassin's poisoned dagger, left the Holy Land and was at Sicily when news of the deaths of his father and five-year-old son John arrived. Rather than return home, Edward and Eleanor decided to see the 'changes and variations of the world'. They travelled to Rome to meet the Pope, to Savoy to attend a parliament and from Paris they journeyed to Gascony where a pregnant Eleanor met her brother, King Alfonso. When King Edward and Queen Eleanor finally landed in England in August 1274, the people enthusiastically cheered them all the way from Dover to London.

Coronation robes packed away, Edward reverted to good, plain, comfortable clothes made from fine English wool, telling critics they were absurd if they thought 'he could be more estimable in fine than in simple clothing'. Queen Eleanor liked to wear loose-fitting under-gowns with sleeves that buttoned from elbow to wrist and plain outer gowns in red, deep blue or green; mention is made in the accounts of robes being repaired.

Edward seems to have admired his grandfather King John. He emulated his encouragement of trade through new towns and boroughs, markets and fairs, which stimulated wealth (and increased tax revenues). He was constantly on the move and kept precise records.

He was regarded as lucky for he survived many mishaps. Once, playing chess, he arose to stretch his legs just as a stone fell where he had been sitting. He and Eleanor, chatting by an open window, had a lightning bolt pass between them and kill two of Eleanor's maids.

In religion the royal couple were conventional. They ate only herring, eels, trout, minnows, lampreys, oysters, whelks and saltfish during Lent. Every Easter, Edward paid a ransom to Eleanor's giggling ladies before he could 'sleep' in his wife's bed. When Eleanor bought Leeds Castle in 1278, she widened the moat, isolating the gloriette to make it their romantic hideaway. They enjoyed being together and shared the same pursuits: chess (Edward gave her a jasper and ivory chessboard with crystal chessmen), hunting, hawking and gardening.

In 1276, when Edward built a new mews for his hawks he incorporated a courtyard garden in the middle with an elaborate ornamental birdbath. At King's Langley, their favourite residence, Eleanor and two Spanish gardeners created water gardens in which she planted vines and grafted fruit trees, particularly apple. Wherever they lodged, a garden would soon follow boasting lawns, ponds with seating, arbours and orchard, even at the building sites that were Edward's ring of castles in Wales built to subdue the local populace.

They loved each other the whole of their thirty-six-year marriage. In seclusion two months after her funeral, he wrote to the abbot of Cluny to tell him Eleanor had been summoned to God, 'who we loved dearly in life and whom we cannot cease to love now she is dead'.

Two months after marrying his second wife, Marguerite, Edward made a payment on 30 November 1299 for the ringing of a knell for his Eleanor. He was fortunate in his second marriage for Marguerite came to love him and his children. After Prince Edward angered his father in August 1305, she interceded for him and succeeded in getting two of his valets, Gilbert de Clare and Piers de Gaveston, restored 'to his great comfort'. A loving soul, she even agreed to name their daughter after his first wife. When Edward died, Queen Marguerite wrote that 'all men died' for her.

18–19 August 1274: Coronation

Excitement boiled over as King Edward and Queen Eleanor rode through the London streets adorned with silks and cloth of gold. Laughing and shouting crowds of magnates and citizens disrupted pageant speeches with raucous cheer.

After the feasting, King Edward went to his father's chamber and held vigil until daybreak.

In bright, sunny weather, under individual purple silk canopies, King Edward and Queen Eleanor walked on the blue ray cloth decorated with roses and flowers laid from Westminster Palace to the aisle crossing in Westminster Abbey, transepts crammed with people in apparel of various vibrant colours. Climbing the stairs onto the giant stage, high enough for officials to ride beneath, the two took their seats. Led to the high altar, King Edward made his coronation oath, adding that he would 'protect the rights of the crown'. Anointed, he was an all-gold figure in gold tunic and mantle, gold spurs on his heels and gold coronation ring on his finger. After being girded with his sword, rod and sceptre, the heavy gold crown of St Edward, shining with rubies and emeralds, was placed on his head. Immediately he removed it, setting it on the altar, saying he would not wear it again until he had recovered that given away by his father. For his motto he has taken '*pactum serva*', 'keep faith'.

Queen Eleanor, in a simple but flowing robe, made her coronation oath and had placed upon her head a glittering circlet of golden lilies, a shining contrast against her long dark hair.

Though the palace had been refurbished, over £1,000 was spent on temporary lodgings, covered walkways and kitchens to house and feed the thousands of guests. Hugh Malvern, the king's cook, had six oaks and six beeches turned into tables for the preparation and cooking of the many dishes of peacocks, cranes and swans, a thousand pigs and boar, 540 oxen, 27,800 chickens, 250 sheep as well as rabbits, kids, eels, pikes, salmons and lampreys. Outside, London citizens partied in the streets drinking the red and white wine freely running from water conduits.

Queen Margaret, the king's sister, and her husband, Alexander, came from Scotland to attend, arranging for 100 mounted knights to ride into the hall and release their horses, to be taken by anyone who could catch them.

Within a few days the royal couple will move to the lavish residence at Kempton, with the statue of a crowned king on its roof, and then move on to Windsor Castle to lodge for some weeks.

16 October 1274: 'Looked forward to riding'

Six-year-old Prince Henry died at Guildford and is to be buried at Westminster Abbey next to his brother John. He was already ailing when, along with his five-year-old sister Eleanora, he met their parents and baby Alfonso in Canterbury in August, although not two-year-old Joan of Acre who stayed with her grandmother in Seville. Queen Eleanor, four months pregnant, had not been allowed to visit her son but sent sheepskins to keep him warm and, just before he died, a white palfrey which he had looked forward to riding; his father had sent him a toy trumpet and arrows.

15 March 1275: Birth

At Windsor, Queen Eleanor bore a daughter. She has been named Margaret, after the king's sister.

24 March 1275: Deaths

Edward, reeling from his sister Margaret's death in childbirth three weeks ago at Cupar Castle, was further grieved when his sister Beatrice died in London. She had been in delicate health since giving birth to her youngest daughter, Eleanora. She is to be buried at Greyfriars but her sorrowing husband, John of Brittany, Earl of Richmond, is taking her heart to Fontevraud. Their children are joining the royal nursery. The only sibling left to King Edward is his brother, Edmund, Earl of Lancaster and Leicester, whose own wife, fifteen-year-old Aveline de Forz, recently died in childbirth.

26 April 1275: First Parliament

Burgesses and knights were called to the largest parliament yet held. After the special commissions sent out last October to compile the Hundred Rolls, new laws were enacted to maintain order and relieve the oppressed. King Edward has ordered they are to be read out in local courts and marketplaces. He wants it known that he wishes his people to make their complaints and petitions known; further, he wants Parliament to be a regular assembly for king and people to come together to their mutual benefit. With this he has 'bound the hearts of his people' to him.

18–24 October 1275: Statute of Jewry

By royal decree 'all usuries of the Jews' which times past had caused 'disinheritances of good men' are to cease; that Jews may gain their 'living by lawful merchandise and their labour' including trading with Christians and, as if in chief of the king, are to live and buy houses in the king's cities and boroughs but have no Christian living among them. Each Jew above seven years old is to wear a yellow felt badge on his outer garment, and after twelve years old each shall pay an annual tax of 3*d*. In Parliament, and in response to the statute, King Edward was granted the tax he sought to pay off his debts.

21–27 November 1275: Tower

King Edward rode to the Tower of London to see his new works for he has extended the site on the south side to the River Thames and had a wider trench dug for the new moat. To the west, new gatehouses and a main entrance have been built and also under construction are a new tower to be called St Thomas and royal apartments for the queen, to be decorated in her favourite colours of red and green, with a garden boasting lawns, pear trees, roses and lilies.

December 1275: Secret Voyage
A ship intercepted crossing the Channel without licence was carrying Eleanor de Montfort from France to Wales for her marriage to Llywelyn. Found hidden beneath its boards were the de Montfort arms and banner. An angry King Edward has sent her to Windsor Castle to be kept in close captivity and her brother, the cleric Amaury, is to be imprisoned at Corfe Castle for escorting her.

25 March 1276: Horse Sense
In Castle Barnard Ward Henry de Flegge was found dead on the quay of the Thames. He had used his spurs to encourage his horse into the river to drink, whereupon it carried him out into deep water and he drowned.

1 May 1276: Princess
At Kempton Manor, Queen Eleanor bore a baby girl who has been called Berengaria.

29 October 1276: Marriage
In Paris, Prince Edmund was married to Queen Eleanor's cousin, Blanche of Artois, the twenty-eight-year-old widow of King Henry of Navarre, whose only son had died when a nurse carelessly dropped him from the battlements.

12 November 1276: Declared 'rebel'
At the end of the autumn parliament, Llywelyn of Wales was declared 'a rebel and disturber of the peace'. King Edward sent out a summons for horses and arms to be mustered at Worcester next July.

Welsh Campaign

Parliament was abuzz with the news in April 1277 that during his Worcester court in January, King Edward, his Welsh border lords and Dafydd of Wales had undertaken a campaign that had resulted in everything Llywelyn had seized in the marches being retaken, with central and south Wales capitulating and the king establishing bases in preparation for the next stage: to tackle Prince Llywelyn in Gwynedd.

As part of a two-pronged strategy, Edward's brother Edmund moved from Worcester to Carmarthen, thence to Aberystwyth. By 25 July he started building a new castle with materials shipped from Bristol, and the Welsh he fought along the way fled into Snowdonia to join their prince. Meanwhile, King Edward made for Chester with the main strike force: an army of magnates, a thousand horsemen and thousands of foot along with legions of masons, carpenters, diggers and woodsmen. He began his campaign by building a castle on a spur of rock called 'the Flint' on the Dee estuary, with supplies coming by raft from Chester. At the same time he started to create a wide road by chopping and burning the dense forest, intending to march his army north into Wales, supplied by ships from the Cinque Ports and Gascony.

At the beginning of August, King Edward and Queen Eleanor toured around the Wirral and Cheshire. On the banks of the River Weaver he found a lovely spot to build an abbey which he named Vale Royal. On 9 August he laid the foundation stone where the high altar would be placed. Queen Eleanor laid the second and third stones for herself and their son, Alfonso.

On the first day of his march on his new road on 23 August, Edward reached Rhuddlan. He ordered a new castle to be built beside the river, instructing engineers to straighten it by canal to enable supplies to be brought in by sea. By the end of the month King Edward reached Deganwy, where he and his father had been forced to retreat twenty years earlier.

In the first days of September, Edward sent two thousand soldiers into Anglesey with 360 men with scythes to gather in the harvest; the island bore the richest grain in Wales and was called its storehouse. On 11 September Llywelyn sent his surrender. On Christmas Day, in the presence of the whole court, the prince placed his hands within the king's and promised his obedience. He gifted four hunting dogs to the king and two greyhounds to the queen.

20 January 1278: Inquest

The inquest held respecting the pelterer William le Pannere, who dropped dead near Cheap Conduit on his way home, determined that after being 'blooded' by his physician he had had too much blood taken from him.

Easter 1278: Arthur and Guinevere

At Glastonbury Abbey, King Edward showed Queen Eleanor the tombs of Arthur and Guinevere, discovered by his great-grandfather Henry II.

Caskets inside contained their bones: King Arthur's of wondrous size; Queen Guinevere's delicate and petite. King Edward wrapped Arthur's bones in silk, the queen doing the same for Guinevere's, to be stored in the abbey's treasury while a new tomb of black marble, a lion at each end, is constructed for them.

10–15 July 1278: Great Tournament

Thirty-eight knights, foreign and native, took part in King Edward's great tournament held in Windsor Park. Necklets with little bells on the horses harmonised with minstrels' music. Horses and knights sported the same crests on their heads. Behind the scenes, the shields were wooden and cost 5*d* each before being emblazoned with heraldic emblems. The swords were made of whalebone and parchment, costing 7*d* each and if silvered 25*s* plus 3*s* 6*d* for 'gilting the hilts'.

13 October 1278: Marriage

The royal family travelled to Worcester to attend the marriage of the king's cousin Eleanor de Montfort to Prince Llywelyn. Prince Edmund gave away the bride at the cathedral door and King Edward paid for the wedding feast.

11 March 1279: Nursery

At Woodstock Palace, Queen Eleanor gave birth to a princess who was christened Mary. She will soon join the nursery at the Tower of London, which now includes Joan who arrived last year in England with her governess, Lady Edeline, but not Berengaria, who died a few months ago.

21 December 1281: Drowned

Hartman, the eighteen-year-old Prince of Hapsburg and son of King Rudolf of Germany, betrothed to Princess Joan, was rumoured to have carelessly skated on shallow ice at Rheinau and drowned. The official account is that he set out to visit his father in a terrible fog and his boat smashed into a rock.

25 December 1281: Wolves

Frost and snow have blanketed London and the Thames has frozen so hard people walk on it from Westminster to Lambeth. The ice has brought down five arches of London Bridge. In the marches winter is so hard that wolves are coming down from the mountains and an order has been sent for them to be killed.

Wales Subdued

Distressing news reached King Edward that on 21 March Dafydd made a surprise nocturnal attack on Hawarden Castle, burning it down, killing several of the household and taking the king's friend Roger Clifford prisoner. Attacks on Flint, Rhuddlan and Aberystwyth followed with houses looted and burnt and townsfolk killed. The king sent out his household knights to the Marches while he made preparations to bring an army to join them.

By summer they were at Rhuddlan where, on 7 August 1282, Queen Eleanor gave birth to Princess Elizabeth. To ease her pregnancy, Edward built a lawned garden with fishpond and decorative seating, paying Peacock and his boy 20*d* for laying 600 turves. Whether the queen received much peace was debateable for the castle, still being built, was the base for mustering troops, crafting weapons and amassing provisions including venison, rabbits, figs, raisins, prunes and spices. Messengers and spies – £1 was given to a 'certain female spy' to purchase her house – came and went.

Llywelyn, after his wife Eleanor had died in childbirth on 19 June, joined his brother's rebellion. They laid low at the prince's coastal hall of Garth Celyn, not far from Bangor. As before, Edward sent men to occupy Anglesey to take in the harvest. Thinking to link isle to mainland, he ordered a bridge of boats be created to cross the Menai Strait to access Snowdonia from the rear. On 6 November, one Luke de Tany led an attack. Men poured across the bridge to the shore opposite. Suddenly an unexpectedly large Welsh force swept down from the mountains. As Luke's soldiers fought and retreated, they found the incoming tide had blocked their way to the bridge. Many of the soldiers braved the water rather than be hacked to death, but heavy armour caused most to drown. A few survived as their brave horses swam them through the waves to safety.

On 11 December, Llywelyn left Dafydd in charge of Snowdonia while he marched to Powys with a host of men, informed that Roger Mortimer was dead and his tenants hostile to the king. It was a trap and he was slain by the river near Builth Cilmert by a Shropshire soldier unaware of the identity of the man he had killed. Once his corpse was identified, Roger Lestrange sent his head to the king, writing, 'Know, Sire, Llywelyn is dead, his army broken and the flower of his men killed.' Sent first to Anglesey to raise English morale, the head was sent on to London where on 22 December, to trumpets and cornets, it was carried through the streets and stuck in the pillory all day. In the evening, carried on a spear, it was placed on an iron spike on the Tower of London with a crown of ivy.

For the next six months Daffyd was chased from stronghold to stronghold through the mountains, fleeing just ahead of Edward's forces. Starving, he was captured near Llanberis on 21 June 1283. Because he held estates in England he was tried at Shrewsbury on 30 September for treason. Found guilty, he was forthwith drawn through the streets at 'the horse's tail' to a scaffold where he was hanged for murder, cut down alive and beheaded and quartered for treason. His head was bound with iron and carried off to be placed next to his brother's in London.

On 19 March 1284, King Edward, still at Rhuddlan, decreed Wales would be divided into shires with sheriffs. English common law would be used in cases of murder, larceny and robbery while civil law would remain under Welsh custom, with additions: daughters could inherit their father's land if he had no son, widows were entitled to dower and bastards were excluded from inheriting.

On 25 April 1284, in luxurious new royal apartments at Caernarfon Castle, Queen Eleanor gave birth to a prince. He was baptised Edward. Many who saw the castles built by Edward praised them. Caernarfon was described as a slice of Constantinople come to Wales with its seven polygonal towers made up of different coloured bands, Conwy was likened to Leeds Castle and Harlech was made of fairy-tale towers and turrets. Near Caernarfon, Edward proclaimed he had found the grave of Maximus, grandfather of King Arthur. The remains were exhumed and reburied in the local church. He sent out Snowdon Herald to proclaim a Round Table event for 2 August 1284 at Nefyn, where legend said the Prophecies of Merlin were found. Open to all comers, the dancing celebrating the finale of the event was so enthusiastic that the floor of the hall collapsed.

19 August 1284: *Great Mourning*

Eleven-year-old Prince Alfonso suddenly died. Queen Eleanor has instructed his heart to be preserved to be buried with her. He will be buried with his siblings. The prince had recently received the model of a castle with knights and a siege engine from his father. Only a few months ago he made his first public appearance, presenting King Arthur's crown to the shrine of St Edward.

4 May 1285: Croes Naid

Walking on foot from the Tower to Westminster, King Edward and Queen Eleanor followed Archbishop John carrying the *Croes Naid*, a portion of the True Cross brought to Wales by Helena, mother of Constantine. It is adorned with gold and silver and precious stones and like Arthur's crown was found in the Gwynned Treasury. Placed on the high altar, it will be sent into the keeping of the nuns of St Helen at Bishopsgate.

15 August 1285: Taking the Veil
Six-year-old Princess Mary, accompanied by her parents, left Leeds Castle for Amesbury Abbey to be veiled as a nun, to the unhappiness of her mother. King Edward's mother is delighted for she has been requesting the little girl to join her for three years. Thirteen high-born girls took their vows with the princess, who was awarded an annual income of £100.

8 September 1285: Round Table
At Winchester, King Edward created forty-four knights and hosted a Round Table tournament with an Arthurian theme for the queen's forty-fourth year. To that end, a beautiful new table was created for the feast, eighteen feet across and three-quarters of a ton in weight.

8 October 1285: Statutes of Winchester
With robberies and murders growing day by day, armed gangs roaming streets after curfew and wrongdoers escaping punishment, King Edward at Winchester Castle decreed that cities – especially London with its rapidly growing population of around 80,000 – and large towns and boroughs must shut their gates from sunset to sunrise. No stranger is to be allowed lodgings unless his host be willing to answer for him; anyone passing is to be detained until morning and, if their journey is untoward, to be set free. Hue and cry is to be raised for anyone resisting arrest. Highways are to be widened by chopping back hedges and woods, excepting large or oak trees with no growth under them. Men between the ages of fifteen and sixty are to have appropriate arms for keeping the peace. Fairs and markets are no longer to be held in churchyards.

26 February 1286: Excursions
In two well-fitted barges, each with a master and seventy-four oarsmen, Princesses Eleanora, Joan and Margaret sailed with King Edward and Queen Eleanor up the Thames to Brentford. The three sisters, who travelled in one barge while their parents used the other, have only just returned from Glastonbury Abbey after the king gave them comfortable chariots for the journey.

19 March 1286: Shocking Death

Though the night was dark and tempestuous, King Alexander insisted on travelling to Kinghorn to be with his pregnant wife, Yolande, for her birthday. Ignoring advice to turn back, first from the ferryman and then a baillie after he had crossed the Forth at midnight, he ridiculed the offered caution and rode off along the coast road. Next morning they found his body on the shore, his neck broken from the steep fall. Until his unborn child lives, the heir presumptive is his seven-year-old granddaughter, Margaret of Norway, all his sons and daughters having predeceased him.

August 1286: Summer Wedding

Having forbidden their attendance, the Bishop of Hereford was furious to find Christians had attended a Jewish wedding and eaten, drunk, played and jested with Jews as well as indulging in 'horsemanship, stage-playing, sports and minstrelsy'.

6 April 1287: King's Luck

News arrived from Bordeaux that on Easter Sunday while King Edward was standing talking to his nobles in the topmost room of the castle, the floor beneath their feet fell away. Three knights were killed and many were crushed. King Edward, found under a knight with a broken leg, survived the fall with just a broken collarbone. To thank God, the king is expelling all Jews out of Gascony.

6 November 1289: Betrothal

After Queen Yolande suffered a stillbirth, Margaret of Norway, now Queen of Scotland, was betrothed to Prince Edward at Salisbury Castle. King Edward, King Eric and the six Guardians of Scotland (two bishops, two earls and two barons) agreed the marriage will take place within the year; she alone will be inaugurated at Scone and Scotland to preserve its independent identity, laws and customs.

30 April–7 May 1290: Royal Wedding One

The pear trees planted by King Henry at Westminster Abbey were in full blossom and made a beautiful backdrop to the private marriage between the high-spirited eighteen-year-old Princess Joan and the forty-six-year-old divorcee Gilbert de Clare, Earl of Gloucester. So enamoured is the earl he has indulged his bride with expensive gifts and silk clothing and resigned nearly all his lands to the king, who has settled them upon his daughter and heirs of her body.

Insiders say there have been tantrums from bridal nerves soothed away by her parents' wedding gift of a gold belt with emeralds and rubies with matching headdress purchased from a French jeweller. In the few days since her marriage she has complained that her sister, Margaret, will have more attendants at her wedding and sulked she would not attend. The earl has since given in to her wishes and they are honeymooning at his manor of Tonbridge. For leaving court Joan's parents have reproved her by taking back seven dresses they had made for her and given them to Margaret.

11 May 1290: King Henry III
At Westminster, King Edward has caused his father's body, which was intact and his beard luxuriant, to be moved from its current resting place to a new grave alongside the Shrine of St Edward.

8 July 1290: Royal Wedding Two
Today, fifteen-year-old Princess Margaret married John, the twenty-year-old son and heir of the Duke of Brabant, at Westminster Abbey. John has lived in England for the last five years, spending most of his time hunting and hawking and attending tournaments. The king pays his expenses for robes and losses at chess and gives him two falcons every year.

With cheerful face, the bride wore a magnificent dress with a gold belt studded with pearls, rubies and royal leopards in sapphires. Her gold headdress had 300 emeralds and an eagle clasp. Her sister, Eleanora, wore a dress ornamented with 636 silver buttons. The bridegroom was dressed in a close tunic, loose overtunic with sleeves to the elbows and capes of squirrel fur. During the course of the day he changed his dress three times, each outfit finer and more costly than the last.

The lavish affair saw all the men in full armour, including King Edward and Duke John. Prince Edward attended with a train of eighty knights, Earl Gilbert attended with 103 knights and six ladies and the bride's uncle Edmund with 100 knights and six ladies, all in rich attire. Not to be outdone, the bridegroom was attended by eighty knights and escorted by sixty ladies, all dressed elegantly.

The king paid for 426 minstrels with harpists, violinists and trumpeters at the wedding feast, joining the procession that formed to traverse the streets so that thousands of Londoners cheered at the seven hundred armoured knights and the richly dressed ladies. Afterwards the citizens partied into the night, and as darkness closed in an illumination of thousands of candles, built by four boys over fourteen days, lit up the palace.

18 July 1290: Proclamation

All Jews are to leave the realm of England forever before 1 November upon pain of losing their heads if any are found within the realm afterward. It is ordered that nobody should 'injure, harm, damage or grieve' the Jews in their leaving with their personal property.

August 1290: Entertained

Citizens of London were entertained by the procession of sumpter horses belonging to Joan, Countess of Gloucester travelling to the earl's manor in Clerkenwell. Chosen by her for their residence near court, she says the air is wholesome and streams run clear. The first carried her chapel ornaments, another her bed, a third her jewels, a fourth her chamber furniture, a fifth her candles, a sixth her pantry stores and table linen and a seventh her kitchen equipment. To grace her new home, her father has given her 100 silver dishes and 100 saltcellars, four wine and four water containers, two small dishes for spices and two for fruit, sixty silver spoons, silver bowls and one of pure gold while for her chapel she has a flagon, censer, a ship alms-dish and two gold phials for wine. In addition, before she left court, the king added forty-six gold cups, twenty golden clasps and cloth of silk trapped with silver, four beds (one for Lady Edeline), a canopy and cushions and napery. Joan and Gilbert gave a splendid feast at their new home to honour Margaret and John.

23 September–7 October 1290: Scotland

Seven-year-old Margaret, Queen of Scotland, falling ill on her journey, was carried ashore in Orkney on 23 September but a few days later she died in the arms of Bishop Narve of Bergen. Within a few days of her death, William Fraser, Bishop of St Andrews and Guardian of Scotland, has written to King Edward asking for his impartial mediation to prevent civil war and place a lawful claimant upon the Stone of Scone.

9 October 1290: Ask Moses

Jews embarking on a boat belonging to Captain Henry Adrian were invited by him to stretch their legs when he grounded his ship on a sandbank at Queenborough. Aware the tide was already coming in he cast off and when they asked for mercy he told them they should cry unto Moses who parted the Red Sea. He watched as many drowned and shared out their goods with his sailors, but they were not to be enjoyed for long as sheriffs were on hand to arrest them and all will soon hang for murder.

28 November 1290: Queen Eleanor Dies

This evening, forty-nine-year-old Queen Eleanor died. She had first fallen ill at the king's Nottinghamshire palace of Clipstone on 11 October and although the king sent to Lincoln for medicines, none gave her relief nor improved her condition. Deciding to travel to Lincoln and visit the shrine of St Hugh, the couple had to stop because the pain was too much for her even in short bursts of travel. On 20 November, unable to go further, they rested at Harby in the house of local knight Richard Weston. As much as humanly possible, King Edward has remained by her bedside. All her family were with her when she died.

17 December 1290: Funeral

Setting out from Lincoln Cathedral on 3 December, the long, slow funeral cortege of Queen Eleanor reached London and today she was buried near the high altar at Westminster Abbey. The king has ordered twelve monuments in stone and marble to mark each place her body rested on its final journey. Besides the tomb at the abbey, two others are to be built at Lincoln and Blackfriars.

King Edward will today set out to stay at Ashridge – the first time he has left his dead wife's side – to mourn in seclusion the death of the woman he had loved for thirty-six years, hardly ever being parted from her.

8 September 1291: King's Mother

Having died peacefully in her sleep at Amesbury Abbey on 24 June, Queen Eleanor, the king's mother, was committed to the earth in the presence of her sons with many noble lords and ladies. Enshrined in gold, the king handed his mother's heart to the Minister General of the Minorite Friars for burial at Greyfriars on her birthday of 30 November.

Her death occurred while King Edward was at Norham meeting Scottish delegates regarding the rightful claim to the Scottish throne, mainly contended by Robert de Bruce, Lord of Annandale, and John Balliol, Lord of Galloway (whose brother-in-law, John 'the Black' Comyn, Lord of Badenoch, has left his own claim aside).

2–25 June 1292: Scottish Succession

Earl David, brother of King William I, had six children. His three sons died. From his three surviving daughters, John Balliol claims the superior right being the grandson of the eldest daughter Margaret;

Robert de Bruce is the son of the middle daughter, Isobel. Robert contended that if Scotland is an estate like any other then the inheritance should be divided equally between the daughters and he would hold his third part *in capite* of the King of England, as would Henry de Hastings, Lord of Abergavenny, descended from the youngest daughter, Ada. The issue was debated and decided: kingdoms are not estates like any other and should remain intact. Bruce said then that nearness of blood should count and he was a son while his rival was a grandson. The convention agreed to adjourn proceedings for three months and allow the lawyers at the University of Paris to make a ruling.

30 November 1292: King John
Today, in the churchyard of Scone Abbey, John Balliol was enthroned King John of Scotland after judgement in his favour by Scottish nobles. On 19 November he paid homage to King Edward, who handed over the kingdom to him.

15 May 1293: War to the Knife
News that Norman ships, flying red streamers signalling 'war to the knife, killing without quarter', had attacked English and Gascon ships near Brittany interrupted Parliament. In retaliation for the unwarranted attack, Gascons sacked La Rochelle. King Edward is sending an embassy to the French king to ask whether he wants complaints decided by Anglo-French commission according to the 'Law of the Sea' or the whole matter laid before the Pope for arbitration.

20 September 1293: Marriage
Princess Eleanora, who has fallen in love with Henry, Count of Bar, married him today at Bristol. He has been staying with the royal family since spring.

28 October 1293: Rejected
Edward's suggestion of arbitration has been rejected by King Philip IV, who declares the dispute not to be a matter of two equals but one between a superior lord, the King of France, and his vassal, Edward, Duke of Gascony, offensively summoning King Edward to appear at Paris or forfeit his lands.

19 May–21 June 1294: Diabolical Plot
In a bid to reknit relations between England and France, Prince Edmund, his wife and stepdaughter had gone to Paris in the New Year. He was told

that King Philip would be satisfied if King Edward submitted to a public dressing-down and surrendered Gascony to him on the understanding it would be immediately returned. The prince sealed the deal by agreeing Edward would marry the king's sister, Blanche. Without consulting his council, the king gave the order to dismayed officials who began packing their bags to leave. John St John, Seneschal of Gascony, came to see King Edward and told him that on 19 May King Louis had announced in Paris that Gascony now belonged to France, Edward having forfeited the duchy. Further, the name of Blanche had been replaced in the treaty by that of her younger sister, twelve-year-old Marguerite.

King Edward 'went red' at the news that he had been duped and at the news that King Philip's new fleet was not destined for war against Sicily but against England. Parliament granted funds for an army to go to France. Orders have gone to the ports to seize French ships and goods.

3 May 1295: Death

Aged eighty, Robert Bruce died at Lochamaben Castle, remembered as a 'handsome and gifted speaker' who kept an open door and liberally feasted the poor outside his gates. He will be buried at Guisborough Priory in Cleveland. His lordship of Annandale and claim to the Scottish throne passed to his eldest son, Robert, whose own earldom of Carrick devolves to his eldest son, also called Robert.

6 October 1295: Traitor

Thomas Turbeville, the French spy seized on 29 September, was brought from the Tower to Westminster Hall. Hooded and mounted on a poor hack with his feet tied beneath its belly, he was led in by the hangman holding a noose. Wearing striped coat and white shoes, he was sentenced to be drawn from Westminster on a fresh ox hide at the tails of six mounted constables, surrounded by four masked executioners, to the Conduit to be hung on the gallows by iron chains and to hang until nothing of him remains. He has rewarded Edward's sympathy with his fable of escaping from a French prison by encouraging rebellion in Wales and sending King Philip details of provisions and arms sent to Gascony and informing him the south coasts were little watched.

7 December 1295: Death

At Monmouth, Earl Gilbert died after a short illness. He will be buried at Tewkesbury on the left hand of his father's tomb. Besides his four-year-old son and heir, Gilbert, he leaves three daughters by his young wife, Princess Joan: Eleanor, Margaret and Elizabeth.

Scotland

After Parliament was shown by King Edward the proof that King John of Scotland had joined with King Philip to provide aid by sea and land, and invade England when Edward travelled overseas, summons were sent out for a muster of men, horse and arms at Newcastle for 1 March next.

Philip's threatened invasion received a setback: gales had sunk and dispersed his ships. He ordered rescued sailors hanged and told the rest of his fleet not to return unless they brought him the relics of St Thomas. At Dover a French galley tried to land and all the French were killed once the element of surprise had faded. At Hythe the men of the Cinque Ports killed nine-score men with steel caps, putting them 'all to death in less time than it would take to bake a single biscuit'.

While Prince Edward with troops safeguarded the coasts in the south, King Edward rode to the Scottish border town of Berwick where on 30 March he suggested to the defenders they surrendered. In answer, they bared their buttocks at him. Described as being as 'angry like a boar pursued by wolves', King Edward led the assault, leaping over ditches and palisades, riding his great warhorse Bayard, as his soldiers poured into the town to torch buildings and 'slew all the men by sword they found there ... bodies falling like autumn leaves'.

A few days later John Balliol sent a message to Edward that he renounced his homage for Scotland. Loudly calling him a foolish knave, King Edward said, 'If he will not come to us we will go to him.' Then news came that a Scottish force had slain men, women and children at Corbridge and Hexham and were now lying at Dunbar Castle. On 27 April Edward sent John de Warenne, Earl of Surrey (and John Balliol's father-in-law) to Dunbar Castle. At the same time King John had sent a large part of his army commanded by John Comyn to Dunbar. The two forces espied each other at Spottmuir. The Scots were on high ground, below them a stream and gully. As Surrey's cavalry crossed the stream, their ranks parted to negotiate the gully; the Scots thought they were leaving the field in disarray and abandoned their strong position and charged... straight into the reformed cavalry advancing in perfect disciplined order. The Scots fled, many into the safety of Ettrick Forest, while the earls of Buchan, Athol, Ross and others were captured. When King Edward appeared the next day, the garrison surrendered. Roxburgh and Jedburgh followed.

Reaching Edinburgh Castle by 6 June, Edward set up three siege engines bombarding the walls day and night. After five days the garrison asked to surrender. He carried on the siege another three days before accepting. Visiting Stirling Castle on 14 June, he found it empty but for the 'porter who rendered the keys'. A week later he followed Balliol to Perth, Clunie and up to Forfar, 'panting to drag the King of Scotland out of his caverns'.

On 8 July, at Montrose Abbey, John Balliol submitted to King Edward. The royal red and gold arms were ripped off his tabard.

Tidings came to Edward that his brother, 'always devoted and faithful' Edmund, and his uncle William de Valence, Earl of Pembroke had died at Bayonne in June. Henry de Lacy, Earl of Lincoln was left in sole charge of Gascon forces.

Requesting money to continue defending Gascony and England in the November parliament, King Edward was told the country was groaning from the two heavy taxes it had already paid and goods were being seized without payment by royal officials. Although the laity finally granted a subsidy, Archbishop Robert Winchelsey told the king bluntly that the church was forbidden by the Pope to grant taxes to secular rulers. King Edward said then his only choice would be to call in the thousands of pounds owed by the church to the crown and gave him time to reconsider.

1 January 1297: *Gifts*
Spending Christmastide at Ipswich, King Edward gave his children, Margaret, Elizabeth and Edward, New Year gifts of gold clasps studded with gems; Margaret's was in the shape of an eagle. He also gave her a silver coronal adorned with rubies and emeralds, a gold crown with emeralds and pearls, twenty-eight silver chaplets with pearls and gold ornamental birds and leopards to wear with them, four brooches for her mantle, ten golden rings, a gold belt and a seal of gold for her rank of duchess. She gave her father a pair of knives of ebony and ivory with ferrules of enamelled silver.

8 January 1297: *Marriage*
Princess Elizabeth, fourteen years old, was married to thirteen-year-old John, Count of Holland at St Peter's Church in Ipswich in the presence of her father and her sister.

20 January 1297: 'Unfailing love'

Princess Margaret, with her new brother-in-law, John, embarked at Harwich on one of the largest ships of the royal fleet, the *Swan of Yarmouth*. Sailing within a fleet of six ships and galleys for the three-day voyage to Brabant, they have ample provisions with thirty-nine oxen, four pigs, fifty-seven sheep, over ten thousand herring, 293 cod, four barrels of sturgeon, 489 fowls, 700 eggs and eleven cheeses as well as provender for 300 horses.

King Edward has inundated his daughter with gifts of plate and chandeliers; dishes, silver cups and plates for her table; copper pans, silver dishes and plate for her kitchen; chalices, a ship censer, alms dish and silver cross for her chapel; and silver basins for her personal chamber, not to mention for her luggage an abundance of sumpter horses, six saddle-horses for riding and a new chariot, richly painted, trimmed with silk and with gilded chains with six horses; the chariot made for her maids will be drawn by five. His parting gift was a golden pyx containing a ring as a pledge of his unfailing love for her, which he placed in her hands with his blessing as they made their farewells.

The newly married Elizabeth has refused to sail with them and it is said the king lost his temper with his daughter and threw her coronet into the fire, losing the great ruby and emerald that adorned it.

30 January 1297: Outlawed!

Archbishop Robert has consistently refused to grant King Edward any aid to defend the country and he has outlawed the whole clergy. Royal officers are seizing church estates, food and livestock. The king has said if the church pays the same amount as the tax they have denied him they can buy back his protection.

24 February 1297: 'Go, or you will hang'

Magnates asked by King Edward to fight in Gascony point-blank refused. Even the Earl of Norfolk, who has served and paid out of his own pocket more than once, complained of his grain being seized without payment and his wool unsold. He declared he was obligated to fight with his king but not to be sent elsewhere: 'I am not bound, nor is it my will, to march without you.'

'By God, Earl, either you will go, or you will hang,' came the response.

'By the same oath, I will neither go, nor hang,' he replied, and he walked out of the court, the other earls following in his footsteps.

14 July 1297: 'Castle for you'

Outside Westminster Hall, standing on a raised wooden dais, King Edward addressed the crowds that had assembled to hear him speak. With him stood his son. Tears running down his face, he humbly entreated their pardon for governing them 'with less propriety and tranquillity than a king ought' and insisted that whatever had been extorted by his ministers was to help him defeat his enemies and keep them safe, for he was 'castle for you, and wall, and house'. About to go into danger for their sakes, he begged if he returned that his people 'receive me as you have now received me and I will restore to you all that I have taken from you. And if I do not return, then I beg of you to crown my son as your king.' Vowing to observe his promises faithfully, the people stretched out their hands and promised fidelity to him.

2 August 1297: Forgiven

After sending his grandchildren to soften him, a tactic which had not worked, and confessing her secret marriage to squire Ralph de Monthermer, the pregnant Princess Joan has been forgiven by King Edward who has returned his daughter's goods, lands and honours. Ralph, released from rigorous confinement at Bristol Castle, was today at Eltham created Earl of Gloucester by the king.

22 August 1297: Leaving

As King Edward embarked with his fleet of 500 ships for Flanders 'with a fair wind over the dark waters', the barons, led by the earls of Norfolk and Hereford, burst into the exchequer at Westminster and ordered the collectors and assessors to stop seizing wools or collecting taxes, saying it was illegal without their consent and they refused to be 'tallaged like serfs'.

That same day in London, Archbishop Robert declared no clerical tax would be granted to the king and he would excommunicate any royal officer who laid hands on church property.

11 September 1297: Stirling Bridge

Late in rising and deaf to cautious voices, Earl Warenne, after gathering an army to counter the Scots continually raiding England, ordered English soldiers to cross the narrow Stirling Bridge and array on the northern shore. The bridge, wide enough only for two soldiers at a time, led into narrow, boggy ground on the other side. When half the division had crossed, Scots led by William Wallace and Andrew Moray came out of nowhere and attacked, cleaving the force in two and slaughtering everyone who had crossed while those stranded on the southern shore watched in horror. The earl ordered the bridge destroyed before riding away, leaving the Scots victorious over a mass of English bodies.

9 November 1297: Charters
Prince Edward has reissued the Great Charter of Liberties and the Forest Charter to pacify the magnates. King Edward, staying at Ghent, confirmed them with his own seal.

Christmastide 1297: Family Celebration
Princess Elizabeth joined her husband and father, King Edward, in Ghent to spend Christmas with Eleanora whose husband was a prisoner of the French king. Margaret was also there and the king knighted her husband on Christmas Day. For a New Year gift, Eleanora gave her father a portable leather dressing box with comb, mirror and silver bodkin.

When Robert the Purveyor found he was unable, through insufficient cash, to buy good enough bread to feed the knights at board, they sent into the city to purchase their own. They entered the king's hall, each with a valet bearing 'his mess'. Angry at such contempt shown to him, the king was furious when Robert explained his lack of money in front of them and was fined one month's wages for his indiscretion.

22 July 1298: Falkirk
Responding to depredations made by William Wallace, King Edward led 26,000 infantry and 3,000 cavalry into Scotland along with Gascon veterans commanded by the Earl of Lincoln. They crossed the border on 3 July but for three weeks no intelligence had been forthcoming as to Wallace's whereabouts. When they were about to retire to Edinburgh, a spy entered camp and told the king he would be harried and ambushed if he turned his army. Taking note, Edward made camp at Linlithgow and ordered his men to sleep on the ground next to their standing horse, using shields for pillows and armour as bedclothes. The king had had a particularly restless night as his horse trod on him in the night, breaking two of his ribs.

At dawn, King Edward spotted spears glinting in the sunrise on high ground near Falkirk. Wallace had arrayed for battle on the side of a small hill, massing his unarmoured pikemen shoulder to shoulder in four circular schiltrons. They looked like giant hedgehogs with their three-metre pikes turned outwards at oblique angles.

The first line of English cavalry thundered forward, led by the earls of Norfolk, Hereford and Lincoln, veering to the left to avoid the boggy marsh formed by the stream at the foot of the hill. The second line, led by the Bishop of Durham, veered right, creating a pincer movement. Welsh archers, as ordered by the king, concentrated on the pikemen and the barrage of arrows broke their ranks and allowed the English cavalry to ride into the thinning ranks and slaughter them. The Scottish cavalry had already left the battlefield 'without a sword's blow', seeing the overwhelming odds and inevitable defeat. William Wallace escaped into the woods around Falkirk.

29 August 1298: Death

Princess Eleanora, Countess of Bar died suddenly at Ghent. Her subjects said she was worn out with sorrow, her health broken by months of worry after the French king refused to release her husband. King Edward said he would not allow his twenty-nine-year-old daughter to be consigned to an 'unmourned grave' abroad and is bringing her to England to be buried in Westminster Abbey.

10–18 September 1299: Royal Wedding

King Edward, now sixty years old, married seventeen-year-old Marguerite at the door of Canterbury Cathedral. After young men of the court finish feasting and fighting tournaments, the couple will honeymoon at Leeds Castle.

10 November 1299: Murder?

John, Count of Holland, husband of Princess Elizabeth, has died. Dysentery is said to be the cause but many suspect murder. The seventeen-year-old widow will be returning to England to join her stepmother.

1 June 1300: Royal Birth

Queen Marguerite, travelling on expedition with the king, was delivered of a son at Brotherton Manor. He has been called Thomas, after the saint to whom she prayed for ease. Her confinement was due to take place at Cawood but her labour pains started while she was out hunting.

10–15 July 1300: Caerlaverock

To fight his 'foemen of the north', eighty-seven English barons and several knights from Brittany and Lorraine rode out of Carlisle on a fair day led by King Edward to besiege Caerlaverock Castle. Well-armoured nobles carried richly embroidered and colourful pennons of silk or satin. The neighs of their horses and the jingle of the harnesses of the four squadrons sounded far over hills and vales, wagons and sumpter horses following carrying stores and tents.

An eyewitness recorded the arms wending by: gallant Humphrey de Bohun, Earl of Hereford with six lions rampant against blue, led the first squadron; John, Earl Warenne the second, his blue and yellow check banner contrasting with the blue lion on gold of his nephew Henry Percy and Aymer 'the Valiant' de Valence's banner of six red swallows over silver and blue stripes. King Edward commanded the third squadron, his banner showing the three English gold leopards 'malign and fierce like the king', whose foes will find 'his fangs will deeply pierce whosoever incurs his anger'. With him were John of Brittany, amiable and handsome, with yellow leopards, and John de Bar with his two blue fishes. The fourth squadron was commanded by Prince Edward, 'handsome, sensible and debonair', sitting well on his charger and with him his sister Joan's husband, Ralph, bearing the Gloucester banner and that of his own arms, a green eagle against gold.

The corner-towered, shield-shaped castle set pleasantly within a moat, having a strong gate, drawbridge and barbican, was approached from the east. To the west the Irish Sea protects it, to the north some beautiful countryside embraced by the sea and to the south sea-girt marsh and wood. Tents, all rich of colour, were pitched, strewn inside with leaves, herbs and flowers. Siege engines were set up and archers discharged their arrows, bolts and stones. Fiercely, the defenders sent them back again. On both sides many were maimed and wounded. The noise and mayhem continued night and day until finally a pennon was held aloft to signal peace, but before word was given to cease an archer pierced the man's hand into his face. When the garrison submitted and delivered up the castle it was found only sixty men had held it. Flying his banners and those of Saints Edmund, George and Edward from the battlements, the king spared the garrison and gave them new garments.

7 February 1301: Prince of Wales

At parliament in Lincoln today, Prince Edward was solemnly created Prince of Wales and Earl of Chester.

5 August 1301: Birth

Queen Marguerite gave birth to a son at Woodstock who has been named Edmund. After her churching she will join King Edward, who is again in Scotland on his sixth campaign. The king has ordered dimity from his stores to make his wife a feather bed and cushions for her carriage.

14 November 1302: Marriage

At Westminster Abbey today, Princess Elizabeth married twenty-six-year-old Humphrey de Bohun, Earl of Hereford and Essex, Constable of England. The earl is known to be well educated, a book collector and scholar, and is said to be much in love with his new bride. The two pre-empted the marriage as the princess has given birth to a little girl they have named Margaret.

10 January 1303: Treaty

At the council at Odiham, the peace treaty between England and France was concluded; Scotland was not included. Gascony has been restored to King Edward.

Warwolf

At Whitsuntide, King Edward determined he would finally conquer Scotland. As on his sixth campaign he split the army into two. One he led to fight Comyn in the east, the other led by Prince Edward to fight Wallace in the west. The prince took with him on the campaign his lion. It travelled in a cart costing 10*d* a day and its food cost 4*d* a day. Its keeper, Adam de Lichfield, received wages of 2*d* a day. The prince also carried a tent for his carthorses to keep them covered when resting.

From Roxburgh, King Edward travelled via Linlithgow to Stirling and then stayed at Perth all June. In July he travelled to Arbroath, then Montrose, joining his son to besiege Brechin. While Prince Edward took Inverness, Urquhart, Cromarty and Lochindorb castles, thence to Dundee in October 1303, King Edward travelled to Aberdeen, returning south via Badenoch to Dunfermline where he was joined by the prince for winter.

In the New Year negotiations for submission began. At a two-day parliament held at St Andrews on 14–15 March 1304, all the leading Scottish nobles paid homage to King Edward as their liege lord.

Only one pocket of resistance remained: Stirling Castle, held by Sir William Oliphant.

Reaching the castle on 22 April, the king set up twelve siege engines to bombard the castle day and night with Greek fire, a gunpowder mix of sulphur and saltpetre, stone balls and heavier lead balls taken from the lead roofs of Scottish churches and brought by several cartloads from towns under command of Prince Edward. The castle withstood everything. Resolute that it would fall, King Edward ordered his engineer, Master James, to devise a new engine. Five master carpenters and fifty workmen tirelessly assembled winches, massive wooden beams and an enormous counterweight. Edward named this massive trebuchet Warwolf. When William Oliphant saw it in its final stages he sent his surrender to Edward, but Edward declined. He wanted to see his new weapon in action, and had a gallery constructed so that he might show it off to the ladies present. The first stone shattered the castle's curtain wall. Sir William was allowed to surrender on 22 July 1304. Despite Edward's threats, the garrison were spared; their commander he sent to the Tower.

Just over a year later, on 23 August, William Wallace was executed on a high gallows specially made for him. He was hanged, cut down half dead, had his genitals cut off and was disembowelled and beheaded, his head put on a stake on London Bridge.

Peace at last. Then on 24 February 1306 there was an argument at the altar in Dumfries Church. One man drew a dagger and stabbed the other. While he lay injured on the altar steps he was finished off by sword. John 'the Red' Comyn, Lord of Badenoch and Guardian of Scotland, was thus murdered by thirty-two-year-old Robert the Bruce, Earl of Carrick. Immediately after the deed he rode straight to the Bishop of Glasgow, who absolved him and produced regalia and a banner with Scottish arms to enthrone King Robert I at Scone Abbey. The raiding started all over again.

6 May 1306: Birth

Queen Marguerite gave birth to a baby girl at Winchester who was named Eleanor by request of the king, who had sent an ermine-covered cradle with a counterpane of cloth of gold for his newest child.

22 May 1306: Feast of Swans

Edward of Caernarfon, given charge of the expedition to Scotland, was knighted by his father in the king's chamber. Going then to the abbey, the prince knighted the 267 men who came to Westminster to swear they would march with him against the Scots. Among those knighted were Piers Gaveston; Hugh le Despenser; Roger Mortimer, 1st Earl of March; John de Warenne, Earl of Surrey; and Roger Mortimer of Chirk.

So great was the pressure of people in front of the altar that two knights died and many fainted, the prince then tasking mounted guards with dispersing the crowds. The youths that came, sons of earls, barons and knights, were given purple and fine linen cloth and mantles embroidered in gold by the king. At the feast that followed the ceremony, King Edward had two gold swans brought in with golden trappings.

24 June 1306: Round Table
For the delight of Queen Marguerite, King Edward held a Round Table and gave her as a gift a rich circlet of gold for which he paid £22 10s.

October 1306: Caged Women
The bishops of St Andrew and Glasgow, wearing armour beneath their priestly robes, were captured by Aymer de Valence. He nearly captured Bruce but the latter managed to escape into the mountains after throwing a linen shirt over his armour to hide it. His womenfolk – along with Isabella MacDuff, Countess of Buchan said to have 'crowned' Bruce – were captured. His youngest sister, Mary, has been imprisoned in Roxburgh Castle on the king's orders, as has Isabella at Berwick in one of the turret rooms. They are both to be kept in 'a cage of stout lattice of timberwork, barred and strengthened with iron'. Bruce's other sister, Christina, was sent for confinement at a nunnery in Lincolnshire; his ten-year-old daughter, Marjorie, is at Walton Abbey. Robert's wife, Elizabeth de Burgh, was placed under house arrest at Burstwick Manor in Yorkshire, already complaining she has only two women servants, few clothes and no headgear nor bedlinen.

26 February 1307: 'Quit the realm'
At Lanercost, where King Edward has lodged since he arrived by litter on 29 September, the barons told the king there was undue familiarity between Prince Edward and Piers de Gaveston, a young man of similar age. Piers has been ordered by the king to quit the realm at Dover three weeks after the jousting finishes on 26 March and not return without his leave. He has given him 100 marks per annum to ease his expenses while overseas. Before he left, Prince Edward gave him gifts of two fine sets of clothes, five horses, swans and herons, and travelled with him to Dover, taking with them two minstrels.

14 June 1307: Last Strength

Hearing rumours that many thought he had died, King Edward, although he has been ill and weak for many months, found the strength to rise from his sickbed, mount his horse and order an immediate advance.

7 July 1307: Death of King Edward

In the thirty-fifth year of his reign, at Burgh-upon-Sands, King Edward died within sight of Scotland having managed only ten miles since setting out from Carlisle. The queen had journeyed with him all expedition, the two being very loving of each other. At three in the afternoon, his attendants came to help him eat. Upon being lifted from his bed, he died in their arms.

Edward II

1307–1327

Mention Edward II and most people think of an effeminate, homosexual king hated by his wife, deposed by her lover and killed with a red-hot spit pushed up his 'fundament'. His contemporaries said he was elegant, tall, handsome, 'well-formed' and 'physically one of the strongest men in the realm'.

Next most likely mention will be of Piers Gaveston, Edward's friend, his 'adoptive brother' placed in his household by his father. At the Siege of Caerlaverock, Piers was Edward's squire. Three years older, he was witty, clever in all knightly arts and skilled with a lance, defeating many a jouster. The temporary exile of January 1307 may have come about when he and other knights of the prince's household, Gilbert de Clare and John Chandos, deserted the army in Scotland to attend tournaments in France. The magnates hated him, yet no chronicler wrote of Piers that he was cruel or oppressive; instead, they record that he was irreverent and sharp in his witticisms, and probably made Edward laugh.

Edward had a fine sense of humour, some of it slapstick, paying out money to those who made him laugh: a dance on a table, his cook falling off his horse or an acrobatic tumbler. To Louis d'Evreux he wrote in jest, 'We are sending you a big trotting palfrey which can hardly carry its own weight, and stands still when it is laden.' In another Edward says he is sending him some 'misshapen greyhounds from Wales, which can well catch a hare if they find it asleep, and running dogs which can follow at an amble, for well we know how you love the joy of lazy dogs'.

He enjoyed hunting with sparrowhawk and spaniel, and bred his own horses and dogs and cared for them. Letters show he asked his sister Elizabeth to send her white greyhound to him as he had a beautiful white and had 'a great desire to have puppies from them.' His sister Mary was given a greyhound as a gift. Letters flowed from him to various people regarding stallions he could purchase to breed. His stepmother sent him a gift of foals while to his sister Elizabeth he sent 'two beautiful mares along with foals they are carrying'.

He was deemed a good fighter and commander and fond of the joust. At King's Langley, Edward commissioned a painting of four knights on their way to a tournament and in 1304 arranged for wine to be made available for his household going to Reading for tilting and jousts. More strangely, he commissioned a painting in 1302 for Chester Castle which was of the four knights who killed Thomas Becket.

When Edward II received the homage of his lords on 20 July 1307, he immediately dismayed them by recalling Piers from exile and creating him Earl of Cornwall, upsetting them even further when he left Piers in charge of the kingdom while he sailed to France to marry Isabella. The self-important earls soon ganged up to show how their twenty-three-year-old king should govern – of course, with their assistance. The coronation oath signified their intent to constrain and confine him to their rule and expectations. Piers was the shuttlecock in their struggle which finally led to his death and a rift between magnates and king which would never heal; Edward's distrust of them led to his bitterest actions.

They distrusted him in turn because they considered him 'unkingly'. He enjoyed athletic sports such as rowing and swimming, and manual labour like digging ditches, thatching and blacksmithing. He liked to mix with the lower classes, playing dice and cross with his barber and chatting to fishermen while boating up and down the Thames. It was thought he preferred the commons to his own nobility; in response, they said of him he gave himself to 'improper works and occupations' and neglected the business of governing.

His letters show a loving nature and a closeness with his stepmother and sisters – and in Joan's case, her husband Ralph, with regular visits between the two men. One of his wet nurses, Alice de Laygrave, whom he called 'our mother who suckled us', was maintained in his household until he married, when she entered Queen Isabella's household.

When Edward married Isabella she was half his age at twelve; no wonder he preferred the company of his male friends. His bride was fond of reading and had her own library with more than forty books and particularly loved tales of chivalry. Edward may have given her a lovely wedding present of an illuminated psalter.

During her first pregnancy he brought jewels costing £40, and when pregnant in 1316 he paid for comfortable cushions for her travelling carriage. He may not have been a faithful husband; he had an illegitimate son, Adam, whom he took on campaign with him in 1322, and he may possibly have set up a trysting place in Southwark around the time he is criticised in the *Flores Historiarum* for scorning his wife's 'loving embraces'.

Or was it the Despensers who came between the king and his wife? It was his unwise support of them that ultimately led to his deposition and imprisonment, yet during his captivity Isabella sent loving letters and gifts to him.

After Edward had taken revenge on his magnates for Piers' death it could be said they finally changed him. The author of the *Vita Edwardi Secundi* wrote: 'The harshness of the king has today increased so much that no one however great and wise dares to cross his will. Thus parliaments, colloquies, and councils decide nothing these days. For the nobles of the realm, terrified by threats and the penalties inflicted on others, let the king's will have free play. Thus today will conquers reason. For whatever pleases the king, though lacking in reason, has the force of law.'

20 July 1307: Proclaimed

King Edward II was proclaimed king at Carlisle. At six feet tall, he towers above those around him. His wavy hair is fair and long, parted so that it falls either side of his face to his shoulders and curls at the end. His forehead is wide, and a long, straight nose complements a strong face. Led by the Bishop of Coventry, his father's funeral cortege began its slow journey south moving through crowds of mourning subjects to Waltham where it will lie in state until 18 October.

27 October 1307: Funeral

King Edward I was buried today at Westminster Abbey, witnessed by the nobles of England and other lands. It is said that he had 'no equal as a knight in armour', was an 'outstanding warrior since he was a teenager, in tournaments most mighty, in war most pugnacious and ruled prudently'. The ceremony was conducted by Antony Bek, Patriarch of Jerusalem and Bishop of Durham. Dressed in his coronation robes, the king was entombed near the altar in his unadorned and simple tomb made of black Purbeck marble.

30 October 1307: Templars

King Philip IV has accused the Knights Templar of denying Christ's divinity, spitting on the cross, worshipping idols and engaging in obscene acts. Every knight in France was arrested at dawn on 13 October. To justify his charges, King Philip sent his clerk to King Edward with letters detailing the evidence of their 'abominable heresy', which were read in council. King Edward's response was that 'he is unable to credit the horrible charges brought against the Knights Templar who everywhere bear a good name in England'.

1 November 1307: Marriage

At Berkhamsted, Earl Piers of Cornwall married Margaret de Clare, King Edward's niece and sister of sixteen-year-old Earl Gilbert. The match is well liked by the bride, who admires her handsome husband. To honour the couple, the king spent in excess of £100 on jewels, horses and other gifts. For the ceremony he spent £20 on minstrels and over £7 worth of little coins were tossed over their heads at the door of the church. The new countesses' ladies and chamber-women were given silk cloth worked with gold from Paris for their headdresses and tunics worked with gold and pearls in silk and velvet of various colours costing £36 17s 7d.

In the rumbustious merrymaking accompanying the wedding, the adjoining property of Richard le Kroc was damaged and the king reimbursed him 5s for the damage.

To celebrate his marriage, Earl Piers proclaimed a tournament to be held at his castle of Wallingford on 2 December, sixty knights against sixty.

15 December 1307: Papal Bull

On 4 December, King Edward had written from Reading to the kings of Portugal, Castile, Sicily and Aragon urging them not to give credence to reports against the Knights Templar, believing it to be 'excited by cupidity and a spirit of envy', but today he received Pope Clement V's papal bull which orders the king to arrest all the Knights Templar within his realm on the same day. The king has relayed orders to all his sheriffs for their arrest on the morrow of Epiphany.

26 December 1307: Custos

Earl Piers, who has been celebrating Christmas with King Edward at the Manor of Wye with the Abbot of Battle, was created Custodian of England while the king 'is absent in parts beyond the sea' to marry his betrothed, Isabella of France, daughter of King Philip IV.

5 January 1308: Consecration

Sir Walter Reynolds, treasurer to the king, was consecrated at Canterbury as Bishop of Worcester. An embroidered cope has been presented to him by the City of London.

25 January 1308: Royal Wedding

At St Mary's in Boulogne, King Edward II, in presence of all the royals and nobles of Europe, married twelve-year-old Isabella, half the age of her tall and handsome bridegroom, who wore a jewel-studded and embroidered satin surcoat with jewelled mantle.

The bride, called 'the Fair', wore a shiny blue and gold mantle over a gown of blue, her hair flowing down her back to her knees. Both bride and bridegroom wore sparkling crowns with precious stones.

The French king has given his son-in-law a ring, a beautiful bed, warhorses and many other extravagant gifts which will be sent forthwith to England. As for the bride's trousseau, Queen Isabella will bring with her to England chests of clothes with gowns of gold, embroidered velvet and more of silk, and hats decorated with rubies and emeralds as well as many jewels including three crowns, two gold circlets, a chaplet and two gold cloak fasteners, one of two lions with precious stones; the other a *fleur-de-lis*. Her father has given her everything she needs for her oratory with cushions and carpets for comfort, luxurious bedcurtains, mattresses, pillows and blankets, a bolster with a sparrowhawk embroidered in gold, tapestries for her bedchamber and linen for her bed and table, along with gold and silver cups, spoons, plates and dishes. For furniture she brings chairs, four of which fold, a dressing cabinet and a table. Being sent to England with the king's gifts are six horses for her carriage with counterpanes, one for sleeping, five palfreys for riding, saddles, saddlecloths and harness. Her father has spent well in excess of £4,000.

To bring his queen home to England, the king had outfitted the ship *Margaret of Westminster*, by his own devising equipped with pantries, butleries and wardrobes for her ease. At the same time works have been carried out at Westminster Palace to repair and restore all the areas burnt with especial regard to the Queen's Hall, wardrobes and chambers. All the 'herbaries, vineries and gardens' within the Palace and the Tower have been fully refreshed with trellises and turf.

25 February 1308: Coronation

To reach Westminster Abbey, King Edward had to leave his palace by a back door to avoid being crushed by the pressure of the crowd. Within the abbey a stout wall was broken and one of the prominent citizens was squashed to death as the area reserved for the ceremony was invaded for a while. Order restored, the barons of the Cinque Ports carried a square canopy of purple silk on four silver spears with four little turrets of silver gilt over the king as he walked on the carpet laid in the abbey to the foot of the throne housing the Stone of Scone. A similar canopy was carried over the queen.

Four earls supported the king. The king's right boot and spur was carried by the queen's uncle, Charles of Valois, the left by William Marshal, Earl of Pembroke, and St Edward's crown was carried by Earl Piers. Thomas, Earl of Lancaster and son of the king's uncle Edmund, carried Curtana, the sword of Justice, unsheathed and pointing upwards.

Archbishop Robert Winchelsey being ill in France, where he has been living in exile, the ceremony was conducted in French by Henry, Bishop of Winchester. The coronation oath has been changed, with an addition for the king to promise to hold and observe the 'just laws and customs that the community of our realm shall determine'. At the altar, the king offered a pound of gold.

The wedding feast was served on marble tables. Forty ovens had been built to cook all the dishes and to the surprise of all present the Earl of Cornwall appeared dressed in royal purple trimmed with pearls and the earl and king spent more time conversing and laughing together than the king did with his new bride.

For people outside, three conduits ran continually with wine, red and white and wine mixed with spice and honey known as piment.

The coronation, originally appointed for 18 February, was delayed by a week to give the Archbishop of Canterbury time to recover and return to England, though some say it was delayed because the king had argued with his earls over the form of his coronation oath; others that the queen's brother Charles and her uncles Charles of Valois and Louis of Evreux had at first refused to let the coronation proceed, displeased by the king running to Sir Piers and hugging and kissing him on their arrival in England on 7 February.

28 April 1308: Parliament

In Parliament today, the earls of Lincoln, Gloucester, Hereford, Surrey, Arundel, Warwick and Pembroke turned up fully armed although King Edward stayed in Westminster Palace. When he gave them audience, the Earl of Lincoln invoked the coronation oath and demanded the king exile Piers Gaveston and confiscate his lands. When the king said he could neither exile his 'adoptive brother' nor sustain the diminution of his honour they made it clear allegiance was given to the crown, not the king.

18 May 1308: Caved

King Edward yesterday gave in to pressure from his earls and agreed to send his friend into perpetual exile on 24 June and restore the earldom to the crown. The Archbishop of Canterbury has passed sentence of excommunication on 'Sir Peter de Gaveston knight' should he ever return to England.

28 June 1308: Lord Lieutenant

After staying with King Edward in Bristol for five days, Piers Gaveston and his wife sailed for Ireland where he takes up his appointment as Lord Lieutenant.

2 August 1308: The Green Grove

To effect a reconciliation between himself and his discontented nobles, King Edward went to vast expense to provide sport for them at Kennington, calling the tournament the Green Grove, 'but the Green Grove was made a Barren Grove for earls and barons' did not attend.

11 November 1308: House Specification

Carpenter Simon de Canterbury presented specifications at Guildhall of the house he is building for William de Hanigtone, skinner. From the ground to the hall door is a step and porch, then a hall with a recessed bay window and larder, with a solar above. Beneath the hall are two cellars, one with two pipes leading to the sewer. There is also a stable with a solar above and a garret above the solar. At one end of the solar is a kitchen with chimney and an oriole between the hall and the old chamber. Cost: £9 5s 4d and 500 marten skins, fur for a woman's hood to the value 5s and fur for a robe for him.

30 April 1309: Proclamation

It is forbidden for those collecting ordure in their houses to place it on the king's highways, streets and lanes and it should be taken to the Thames or elsewhere out of town. Any person having any dung raked or removed to the front of others' houses and so discovered will be fined and made to carry such dung into his own house and kept there a day and night.

24 June 1309: Piers Recalled

King Edward left Windsor to ride to Chester when news came that Piers Gaveston had sailed from Ireland. He takes with him the Pope's absolution for his return. Sir Piers has served well in Ireland and the Irish admire the way he has driven insurgents out of their retreats, built castles and roads and brought them the king's peace.

4–5 August 1309: Restored
With the full consent of council, Piers has had both lands and earldom of Cornwall restored to him, the grant now including his wife and heirs.

Christmastide 1309: Fire and Ice
The Thames has so iced over a fire was lit in the middle of the river around which people danced and played games.

King Edward has spent Christmas at Langley enjoying 'daily and intimate conversation' with Sir Piers and rumour is Piers has upset certain people by playfully giving out nicknames: the Earl of Lincoln is Burst Belly, Earl Thomas of Lancaster the Buffoon, and Earl Guy of Warwick the Black Dog. The latter said that as soon as he had opportunity he would bite Piers.

7 February 1310: Refusal
Although the earls have come in answer to the king's summon to Parliament as far as London, they refused to present themselves before the king while 'their chief enemy was lurking in the king's chamber', adding that if they did attend they would be armed.

27 February–20 March 1310: Reform
At Parliament, the discontented earls now including Thomas, Earl of Lancaster and Leicester, calling themselves the 'community of the realm', presented the king with a petition. In it they say he shames the realm by unsuitable and evil counsel and that the state of king and kingdom has deteriorated. They have demanded the election of a council of discreet and powerful men to have full power to reform the kingdom and the king's household. When the king at first refused he was accused of breaking his coronation oath and threatened with deposition.

15 August 1310–30 July 1311: Scottish Campaign
Leaving Westminster, the king went north to defend England against the attacks made by Robert the Bruce. The earls of Cornwall, Gloucester and Warenne accompanied him but the dissenting earls refused to march with him, sending men instead. Enclosing the town

with a strong, high wall and ditch, King Edward made Berwick his base. Earl Piers guarded Roxburgh and its district and Earl Gilbert of Gloucester guarded Norham and its district until, after Henry, Earl of Lincoln died in London in February, he was appointed guardian of the country while King Edward stayed in the north.

12 March 1311: Fraudster and Rioter
Elmer de Multone was found guilty of enticing strangers to a tavern in Cheap and using false dice to deceive them, and in Tower Ward for being a bruiser, nightwalker and common roarer. He was committed to prison.

29 September 1311: Lords Ordainers
The self-elected commission of six bishops and eight earls headed by the Archbishop of Canterbury now calling themselves the 'Lords Ordainers' proclaimed two days before Parliament in St Paul's Churchyard, without the king's consent, their decisions on how king and kingdom could be better regulated.

The first ordinances dealt with the king's revenue being used improperly and demanded the king cease living on money raised by purveyance and pay all revenue into the Exchequer to be paid out under their supervision. Only by their advice and consent were great offices of state to be filled or the king allowed to go to war or quit the realm. They directed certain officers and servants, except those they deemed suitable, be dismissed from the king's and queen's households and devoted four articles to permanently exiling Piers Gaveston, accusing him of turning the king's heart away from his people. They insist he must be gone before All Saints' Day. When the king protested that some were inconvenient to him and some dictated by malice, he was told they were acting as his faithful counsellors and threatened peace would be banished from the land if they did not get their way.

3 November 1311: Exiled
Earl Piers sailed from London, rather than Dover as had been instructed, and it is thought will stay in Brabant as he has been denied refuge in any of the king's lands on this side of the sea or beyond. He was told if he returns he will be treated as an enemy.

29 January–3 April 1312: 'Good and loyal'
At York, King Edward had proclamation made that, being put under duress, he refuses to observe the Ordinances. A letter has been sent to

all sheriffs informing them he is recalling Piers for being always 'good and loyal' to his king.

Six days earlier, in York, Countess Margaret had given birth and Piers had arrived on the eve of his daughter's birth at Knaresborough.

Earl Thomas of Lancaster, made spokesman and leader for the earls, demanded that the king command Piers to leave the kingdom immediately or forfeit his life.

On 3 April, the king reinstated Piers in the office of justice of the forest north of the Trent, removing Henry Percy.

5–19 May 1312: The Chase

The Earl of Lancaster arrived at Newcastle upon Tyne only to find his quarry gone: Piers, Queen Isabella and King Edward had left for Tynemouth on 5 June. Arrival and departure must have nearly overlapped for the king and earl left behind many valuables, a large stock of arms and nearly a hundred horses which Lancaster seized. He also imprisoned the king's servants.

The king and Piers first went to Scarborough Castle by sea. Leaving the earl at the castle, Edward went to catch up to the queen at Ripon or Knaresborough for, being three months pregnant, she had gone overland via Darlington. They entered York on 14 May.

Surrounded at Scarborough Castle, on 19 May Piers surrendered to Aymer, Earl of Pembroke. Two armies had chased after him, one force blocking the way to the king and the other led by Henry Percy who had besieged the castle.

10 June 1312: Deddington

Wishing, he said, to see his wife staying at his Manor of Bramthorne, the Earl of Pembroke left Earl Piers under guard at the house of the rector of Deddington. Guy, Earl of Warwick, given news of Piers' whereabouts, took forty armed men at sunrise on Sunday morning and surrounded the rector's house, summoning Piers to come forth. With his guard putting up no resistance, Piers dressed and came down. Rather than being treated as an earl, he was treated like a thief, the populace made to follow blowing horns and shouting the hue and cry. After a short distance, Piers was given a horse for greater speed and was escorted to Warwick Castle and thrown into a dungeon.

19 June 1312: Execution

Removed from the dungeon but put in chains, Earl Piers was delivered to Thomas, Earl of Lancaster, in company with Humphrey, Earl of

Hereford and Edmund FitzAlan, Earl of Arundel. While the Earl of Warwick stayed in his castle, the other earls took their prisoner to a place called Blakelowe, between Warwick and Kenilworth. At midday they stabbed him and cut his head off. Many had gathered to see his unlawful execution. His body was left where it had fallen.

28 June 1312: Vigil

News of his friend's execution brought to him, King Edward sent a group of Dominican friars to find Gaveston's body and head and asked them to take both to Oxford, embalm the body and sew his head back on, then dress him in cloth of gold. Unable to bury him in consecrated ground while Archbishop Robert Winchelsey refused to lift his excommunication, the king gave the friars a large allowance for two of them to watch over the corpse and for others to pray over his body.

13 November 1312: Royal Birth

Queen Isabella was delivered of a son at Windsor, named Edward after his father. By vespers, the news had been announced at the Guildhall and the citizens of London carolled and danced through the city to trumpets with 'great glare of torches'. Tomorrow is a day off work for people to dress in their best clothes and make praise and offerings at St Paul's.

4 February 1313: Fishmongers' Escort

The fishmongers of London, richly costumed, fitted out a boat in the guise of a great ship and sailed it through Cheap as far as Westminster and presented it to Queen Isabella for her pilgrimage to Canterbury, escorting her all through the city. Baby Edward has his own household and he and his nurse have travelled to Bisham.

10–30 June 1313: Pointoise Fire

News has come from France that King Edward saved the life of his wife. The nights being warm, they had been sleeping in a silk pavilion when a fire broke out in their bedchamber. Though they were both naked, he scooped her up, stopping her trying to rescue her things and burning her arms, and rushed outside with her before going back in to help save others of their retinue from the flames.

There has been gossip that Edward arrived late for one meeting with the queen's father because they had both 'overslept'.

On the anniversary of Piers' death, King Edward paid Bernard the Fool for fifty-four naked dancers to perform before him.

16 July 1313: Returned
At sunset, King Edward and Queen Isabella landed at Dover and are returned safely to the realm.

15–16 October 1313: Pardon
At Westminster Hall, after the earls of Lancaster, Warwick and Hereford had knelt before him King Edward raised them and kissed them one by one and pardoned them and their adherents for all causes of rancour, anger, distress, actions, quarrels and accusations from the time of his marriage to his very dear lady the queen. To cement the peace he held a banquet in their honour.

17 January 1314: Enthronement
After the death of Archbishop Robert last May, King Edward's friend Walter Reynolds was enthroned today as Archbishop of Canterbury in his presence.

23–24 June 1314: Battle of Bannockburn
King Edward set off for Scotland with 2,000 cavalry and numerous infantry, accompanied by the earls of Gloucester, Hereford and Pembroke. He allowed only short time for sleep, and shorter for meals, and marched them inward to Edinburgh, past Falkirk, arriving close to Stirling on the scorching hot Sunday afternoon of 23 June.

Awaiting him, Bruce had moved his army, mainly infantry, to an area bordered on one side by upland, woody New Park and on the other by wet marshland sloping downhill to the River Bannock. He had the rearguard while his vanguard was commanded by his nephew Thomas, Earl of Moray; a third battalion was under command of his brother, Edward.

Twenty-three-year-old Earl Gilbert had command of the English van. Emerging from Torwood, he saw Scots apparently in retreat and ordered pursuit, charging without discipline into Bruce's division. Sir Henry de Bohun, seeing Robert Bruce on a grey palfrey, charged him but had his head broken open by Bruce's axe. Earl Gilbert was unhorsed and killed. At the same time, under St Ninian's kirk, Sir Robert Clifford and his cavalry detachment of 800 fought the Earl of Moray. The fighting was fierce, not finishing until dark, when a heap of English men and horses lay wounded and dying.

The English encamped that night after crossing the Bannock, breaking down house doors to make bridges over marshy pools of the Carse and passed the night uneasily without sleep, under arms with their horses bridled, expecting a night attack. At sunrise, the

Scots emerged on foot from the woods in three battalions marching upon the English. Scottish schiltrons in close order speared English horses through the bowels and then their riders, a horrible din rising from their screams. For a time the two sides were locked together fighting on the 'evil, deep and wet marsh'. Rearmost soldiers could not advance and soldiers tried to retreat and fell into the Bannock burn, dead piling on dead, blood flowing in every direction.

As Scots neared King Edward's charger, he struck out vigorously with his mace, felling every man he touched, but the Earl of Pembroke and Sir Giles d'Argentan, despite him resisting and having one horse killed under him, compelled Edward to leave the field. The king's withdrawal caused widespread panic and flight. Denied entrance to Stirling Castle, the king fled fast to Linlithgow and on to Berwick.

9 September 1314: York Parliament

Thomas of Lancaster has bound King Edward to observe the 1311 Ordinances. Strong-armed by his magnates, 'the king granted their execution and denied the earls nothing'. They have removed many of his officials, replacing them with Lancaster's 'nominees'.

3–4 January 1315: Funeral

The funeral of Piers Gaveston took place in the royal chapel at King's Langley after his body was transported from Oxford, dressed in cloth of gold costing the king £300. Those attending with the king included Queen Isabella, his half-brother Thomas, Earl of Norfolk, his brother-in-law Humphrey, Earl of Hereford, Aymer, Earl of Pembroke, father and son Despenser, Archbishop Walter, Bartholomew Badlesmere and the Mayor of London alongside four bishops, fourteen abbots and fifty knights. The king provided a dinner costing £15 and spent £64 on twenty-three tuns of wine (purchased by Walter Waldeshef on Edward's order on Christmas Day and sent onto Langley, with three pavilions after they had been dried so they could be used).

Two days after Christmas Day the chancellor and scholars of Oxford University received £20 to pray for Piers' soul, expected to be a regular occurrence.

12 August 1315: Poisoned?

Guy de Beauchamp, Earl of Warwick died at his Castle of Warwick, having withdrawn from government because of illness. Some murmur that King Edward had him poisoned. He will be buried at Bordesley Abbey and many say he will be missed for 'in wisdom and council he had no peer'.

Summer and Autumn 1315: Supplication
With the failure of the harvest, and cattle and sheep dying owing to torrential rain that never stops, Archbishop Walter has sent out orders for every parish to ring the bells and perform solemn processions with the clergy walking barefoot to implore mercy from God. Scarcity is keeping prices rising and people are starving.

15–20 August 1316: Birth
A prince was born to Queen Isabella at Eltham Palace on 15 August. For his christening, John de Fouteneye, clerk of the queen's chapel, lined the font with a piece of Turkey cloth and a piece of cloth of gold. The Bishop of Norwich and the Earl of Lancaster stood as godfathers for the baby who was named John. The queen's tailor also received five pieces of white velvet to make the queen's churching robe.

Summer 1317: Famine
There being a great dearth of corn and other victuals for the third year, poor people are eating cats, dogs and horses to keep body and soul together. There is rumour that some poor and starving have stolen and eaten children. Prices continue to rise despite Parliament limiting the price of goods and food.

18 June 1318: First Princess
The queen has given birth to a daughter at Woodstock. She has been christened Eleanor.

22 July 1320: Overseas Visit
Leaving the Earl of Pembroke as keeper of the realm, King Edward and Queen Isabella returned to England after sailing to France on 19 June where, in the cathedral at Amiens, the king paid homage for Aquitaine and Ponthieu owed to King Philip V since his accession in 1316.

6–26 October 1320: Prudence
It was remarked that during Parliament King Edward, bringing Prince Edward with him, had attended unusually early and showed prudence in answering the petitions of the poor, and was as merciful as he was severe in judicial matters. Hugh Despenser the younger, the king's chamberlain, was granted, at his request, the lordship of Gower on the last day.

5 July 1321: Second Princess

Today, in the Tower of London, the queen was delivered of a baby girl named Joan. While the queen lay on her childbed she was rained upon. The Constable of the Tower has been dismissed for not maintaining the building properly.

28 July 1321: Earldom

Edmund of Woodstock, a week before his twentieth birthday, was created Earl of Kent by his half-brother; the king also gave him additional revenues.

1 August 1321: Demands

Marcher lords dressed in green bearing his royal arms and their own came, with armed retinues, into King Edward's presence to demand he exile the Hugh Despensers, father and son. They accuse them of encroaching upon royal power, perverting the law, using false jurors, illegally seizing lands and not allowing anyone to have access to him without one or other of them being present.

There have been murmurings all spring and summer that the earls, barons and clergy have wanted to remove the Despensers, who have illegally gained possession of lands and castles, especially in and around Wales, particularly Hugh the younger who, to extend his own lands by right of his wife Eleanor de Clare, has laid false charges to either confiscate land or to assault those who resist him. They have also persuaded the king to grant them lands to which they had no right, disinheriting many.

14 August 1321: King Yields

The Earl of Pembroke, after meeting with the marcher lords at Clerkenwell, told King Edward the earls had issued an ultimatum: remove the Despensers or be deposed. The king gave the order for the Despensers to leave the country by 29 August.

13–31 October 1321: Siege of Leeds Castle

Queen Isabella was refused entrance and lodging at her royal castle of Leeds by Lady Badlesmere, wife of Bartholomew, appointed the king's steward in 1318. He has sided with the marcher earls against the Despensers. King Edward, angry at the insult to his wife, immediately besieged the castle, which surrendered on 31 October. The leader of the garrison, Walter Culpepper, was executed on the spot. Lady Badlesmere and her children were sent to the Tower.

8 December 1321–9 March 1322: Civil War

After the Archbishop Walter declared the sentence of exile on the Despensers to be null and void, King Edward and his army left London and set off for Cirencester. After making surprise attacks and taking the castles of the marcher lords, King Edward moved to Shrewsbury where he received news of other castles taken by loyal Welsh forces.

On 22 January, Roger Mortimer of Wigmore and his uncle Roger Mortimer of Chirk surrendered and were sent to the Tower.

On 6 February the king reached Gloucester where Maurice of Berkeley and Hugh Audley the elder surrendered. The Earl of Hereford fled to join the Earl of Lancaster who had fled from Tutbury by the time the king arrived on 9 March.

16 March 1322: Boroughbridge

Andrew Harclay, fighting for King Edward who was at Doncaster, came down from Westmoreland and took up position at Boroughbridge on the River Ure to hold it against the earls of Lancaster and Hereford and force them to battle. Dismounting his horsemen in Scots fashion, Harclay defended the bridge and ford with solid bodies of spears and arrayed archers on each flank. Earl Humphrey was killed by a spear thrust from underneath the bridge and Earl Thomas was repulsed at the ford and surrendered.

22 March 1322: Lancaster Executed

At the trial held in his own great hall of Pontefract Castle, Earl Thomas was charged with many things, including heckling and jeering as the king passed and blocking Yorkshire roads but most seriously of all for treason and bearing arms against the king. He was sentenced to be beheaded, remitted the punishment of drawing and hanged for reverence of his royal blood. He was led from the castle, mounted on a mule and taken to a hillock outside the castle and executed. Nor is this the only execution; the king has ordered twenty-five executions of nobles by hanging and for them to be left in their chains with no prospect of burial. He has shown himself merciless; wives and children of rebels are arrested, and lands seized are kept in his hands. The sons of Roger Mortimer and the Earl of Hereford have been imprisoned at Windsor Castle.

2 May 1322: Statute of York

King Edward formally revoked all of the Ordinances in the York Parliament, decreeing such ordinances in future would be null and void unless agreed in full parliament. He reissued six 'good points'. Hugh Despenser the elder was made the Earl of Winchester and the young Despenser was given many of the estates taken in forfeit from the rebels. Much revenue has also gone into the exchequer.

12 August–18 October 1322: Second Scottish Campaign

Crossing the border on 12 August, King Edward found Robert Bruce had ordered his troops to destroy any food the English could use and has paid Flemish ships to prevent Edward's supply ships arriving to provision his army. By the time the king reached Edinburgh in late August his men were already starving and sick. He was forced to retreat to Newcastle, arriving on 10 September, intending it to be his base.

Informed Edward was at Byland, Robert Bruce invaded Yorkshire on 30 September in a bid to capture him, defeating English troops at Blackhowmoor and leaving the Scots free to chase after the king as he fled to Rievaulx. So close were they that he fled to Bridlington, leaving baggage and state papers behind. Nearly caught, he managed to reach York on 18 October still pursued by his enemy.

Queen Isabella, left in security at Tynemouth Priory, found herself cut off behind enemy lines. Sir Henry de Sully and his troops, sent to protect her by Edward, were captured by the Scots. Managing to commandeer a ship, Queen Isabella escaped but one of her ladies-in-waiting was killed and another went into premature labour.

At York, the king was forced into signing a temporary truce with the Scots.

He is also in mourning for the death on 18 September of his natural son Adam, who was buried at Tynemouth Priory on 30 September. His father paid for a silk cloth with gold thread to be placed over his body.

30 May 1323: Truce

A thirteen-year truce with Scotland was confirmed at York.

1 August 1323: Escaped!

Drugging his gaoler, Roger Mortimer of Wigmore made a successful bid for freedom from the Tower of London and has escaped into France.

29 March 1324: Investiture

Henry of Lancaster was invested with his brother's title of Earl of Leicester by King Edward but not the earldom of Lancaster.

15 August 1324: Dispute

Since the death of King Philip V in January 1322, the dispute over Gascony and the date for the king to pay homage to King Charles IV has so escalated that the French king, younger brother of Philip, has invaded the Duchy of Aquitaine. Today, the city of Agen surrendered. La Reole is next to be put under siege, where Edmund, Earl of Kent is awaiting reinforcements of men and money.

18 September 1324: Queen Treated as Enemy

As if his wife is an enemy, King Edward has taken into his own hands all of Queen Isabella's castles, lands and the county of Cornwall. All her French attendants and servants have been arrested and all her ingoing and outgoing correspondence is to be screened.

9 March 1325: Mediation

King Edward, instead of taking an army to France, has decided to see if Queen Isabella can mediate terms with her brother, Charles IV; she has previously been successful as an ambassadress in France in March 1314. Orders have been given by the king that no messenger from the queen is to see anybody without first being sent to him.

13 June 1325: Treaty

The draft treaty Queen Isabella had negotiated with her brother for her 'very sweet heart' Edward received royal approval today. A date of 29 August is agreed for him to pay homage at Beauvais to the French king for his continental lands.

After Henry of Lancaster gave moral support to the Bishop of Hereford seeking the king's favour and set up a cross outside the town of Leicester in memory of his brother Thomas, King Edward has accused him of treason, ordering him to appear at the next parliament.

24 September 1325: Homage

Charles IV agreed that twelve-year-old Prince Edward could pay him homage in King Edward's place, with the latter ill, on condition that he transferred the lands to his son. Prince Edward was therefore granted the title of Duke of Aquitaine at Bois-de-Vincennes near Paris.

1–2 December 1325: King's Disquietude

The King of England has urged Queen Isabella, for 'grief of heart at her long absence', to return home and begged his son, for 'uneasiness of heart' that his mother has not allowed him to travel, to return without her. He asked them to avoid the company of certain English traitors and not consort with 'The Mortimer', the king's enemy and rebel.

Queen Isabella, in front of her brother, refused to return, declaring that 'marriage is a joining together of a man and woman ... and that someone has come between my husband and myself trying to break this bond; I protest that I will not return until this intruder is removed' and would wear 'robes of widowhood and mourning' until such time as that happens.

24 September 1326: Queen Lands

Queen Isabella, sailing with a fleet, landed somewhere near the mouth of the River Orwell in Suffolk, near the lands of Thomas Brotherton, Earl of Norfolk, who joined her. Despite orders sent by the king, the coast had been left unguarded. Accompanying her from overseas among many were Roger Mortimer, William Trussell and Edmund, Earl of Kent.

6 October 1326: London Letters

The news of Queen Isabella's landing only spread when one of the fleet, after she unloaded her men and arms, sailed round and up the Thames to London but today, affixed to the cross at Cheapside at dawn and to the windows of many houses, were letters from the queen requesting the Despensers be arrested.

11 October 1326: Resistance

A substantial force of Edward's followers mustered in Yorkshire led by Earl Warenne. Isabella to date has met no opposition and has moved across the country following in the tracks of her husband. Basing her force in Hereford, she intends to besiege Hugh the elder in Bristol Castle.

27 October 1326: Death of Elder Hugh

The garrison having surrendered the previous day, Hugh Despenser, Earl of Winchester was arrested and today placed on trial before a court presided over by the earls of Leicester, Norfolk and Kent and Roger Mortimer. Thomas Wake read the indictment. Judgement was death for encouraging evil government and enriching himself illegally from other people's lands. He was immediately drawn, hanged and beheaded outside Bristol Castle, his head sent to be displayed at Winchester.

16 November 1326: *Caught*

The king was found at Neath, near Llantrissant. He was placed in the custody of Henry of Lancaster, Earl of Leicester and taken first to Monmouth Castle to rest, and will thereafter be taken to lodge honourably at Kenilworth Castle. Taken with him were Hugh Despenser the younger, Robert Baldock, Hugh's marshal Simon Reading and what remained of the king's household.

17 November 1326: *Arundel Executed*

Edmund, Earl of Arundel was arrested in Shropshire by John Charlton, whose son is married to one of Roger Mortimer's daughters. Brought to Hereford, he was executed in an act many consider to be illegal, and which only took place as Arundel's lands are close to Mortimer and Charlton lands in the marches.

24 November 1326: *Hugh the Younger*

William Trussell presided over Hugh the younger's trial, in which a long and detailed indictment was read accusing him of bringing about many deaths, seizing and appropriating lands and crown lands, trying to separate the king from the queen, bribery to prevent her returning and encouraging the king to keep away from her and attempting to bring about her destruction.

Convicted of treason, he was sentenced to hanging for robbery, beheaded for his unlawful return and disembowelled for being a sower of discord. Immediately horns and trumpets blew and he was drawn through the streets to a fifty-foot-high gallows. Patiently he watched his entrails burned. After he was beheaded, his head was sent to London Bridge and his four quarters displayed at York, Bristol, Carlisle and Dover.

20 January 1327: *'Edward put adown'*

In the absence of King Edward, who had refused to attend, Parliament resolved that he should be deposed and his son put in his place. He met the deputation dressed all in black. Told that he was to be deposed, he looked stricken with grief, tears running down his face, saying he felt 'much pain that his people thought he deserved thus'.

Edward III

1327–1377

Renowned for creating the Order of the Garter, King Edward III enjoyed tournaments, which he used to sharpen his own martial skills and those of his men. His predecessors had aspired to emulate legendary figures and perhaps this helped crystallise his own ideas of forming a court of chivalry based on a fellowship of knights: a band of elite companions bound together in one ideal, based on service not birth, who surrounded the king as a personal honour. As a commander, he inspired those he led. He fired them with a common vision of military glory and chivalrous deeds, and his comrades-in-arms ran extraordinary risks for him in France and Scotland. Providing this outlet for the warlike energy of young men reduced the risk of domestic strife, and he ensured good relations with his magnates by regularly consulting both houses of Parliament.

Edward was an excellent promoter of image, using heraldic crests, mottos, motifs and colours to stimulate the imaginations of his subjects. He was also fluent in English and French, and conversant with Latin and other European tongues. His tournaments grew into lavish, boisterous affairs of pageantry and colour, sometimes causing offence. The chronicler Knighton wrote disdainfully that women turned up at them 'dressed like men, sometimes forty or fifty of them, wearing parti-coloured tunics with small hoods, across their stomachs in pouches knives they call daggers. They ride in on excellent chargers, spending and wasting their riches … and vexed their bodies with scurrilous wantonness [but] God brought about a marvellous remedy for this vanity, putting their frivolity to rout, defeating them with heavy rainstorms, thunder and lightning.'

Men came in for criticism too. Malmesbury wrote they had gone 'stark mad', wearing 'wide surcoats to the hips; others clear down to the heels, not open in front as becomes a man but spread out at the sides to arm's length' so from the back they looked like women, calling the garment a 'goun', and also wore 'small hoods fastened right up under the chin ... embroidered all about with gold, silver and jewels' or embroidered figures of animals or dancing men and 'tight two-piece hose' fastened with latchets, costly gold and silver girdles and long-pointed shoes fastened to the knees with gold or silver chain. They were, he wrote, 'lions in the hall and hares in the field'.

Edward was fortunate in having a loving wife, soon nicknamed Queen Philippa the Good for her kindness, good humour, charm and skill in calming her husband's quick temper. They both enjoyed hunting with hounds and falcons, and shared ideals in encouraging learning at Cambridge and Oxford.

After Philippa died in 1369, and throughout the 1370s, Edward may have suffered a series of strokes. He found comfort in his mistress, Alice Perrers, who shocked society in 1375 by appearing as Lady of the Sun at the Smithfield Tournament, taking precedent over noble-born ladies. When Edward was in good health, they hunted and hawked together, hardly ever being apart. Murmured criticism said the king was giving her too many clothes, jewels, bed hangings and tapestries. Many chroniclers who wrote that early in his reign he was 'gracious and worthy' stripped him of all virtue because of this lapse into sin as they saw it – but then perhaps a warrior is only as good as his last campaign.

1 February 1327: Coronation

Crowds cheered and waved as fourteen-year-old King Edward walked barefoot along the striped Candlewick-street cloth that lay from palace to abbey and along the nave to the stage erected before the high altar, covered in quilted silk and coloured gold. Over his head four knights held a gold canopy with cords of gold and purple, bells softly tinkling.

Seated on a gold throne on gold cloth with gold cushions beneath his feet, Edward's red silk attire was in striking contrast, his fair hair gleaming in the light. He swore the same coronation oath written for his father in 1308. Handing the king his gold sceptre and the gold orb, Archbishop Walter placed on his head the heavy gold crown of St Edward. His mother wept throughout the ceremony.

Now wearing his own, lighter crown sporting sprays of sapphires and rubies, emeralds and four great pearls, the king returned to Westminster Hall, to his seat at the upper end covered with Turkish cloth of gold. He was joined at the banquet by the men he had dubbed as knights the day before, after his own knighting by Roger Mortimer. These had included Mortimer's sons, dressed in clothes suitable for earls with cloth of gold and furred mantles. The other men made knights were resplendent in scarlet, green and brown bordered with squirrel fur.

3 April 1327: Transfer

Today, Lord Edward of Caernarfon, king-that-was, has been moved under armed guard from Kenilworth to Berkeley Castle and closer confinement. The king's exchequer is paying for wine, wax, capons, kids, eggs, cheese and cows, and the king has granted an allowance of £5 a day 'for the expenses of the household' to the custodians who are Thomas Berkeley, married to Mortimer's daughter, and John Maltravers, married to Berkeley's sister.

May-July 1327: Rescue Attempts

Rumours of attempts to rescue and free Lord Edward have abounded all summer with many secretly apprehended and indicted while the deposed king has been moved, either to Corfe or other castles unknown.

1 July–7 August 1327: Scots Campaign

Mid-May Robert the Bruce, ignoring peace overtures, sent an army across the Tyne to lay waste fields and burn towns. On 1 July, King Edward with an army set off from Durham, trumpets sounding, pennons of St George fluttering, hoping to waylay the Scots on their return. Camping on the north bank of the Tyne, the English waited, ill-sheltered from drenching rain, the only available victuals poor bread and pear wine. The whereabouts of the Scots remained undiscovered; they move fast on their hardy little horses. As they only drink river water and each man carries a bag of oatmeal and an iron plate to bake a biscuit, they have no baggage.

Edward told his bedraggled men that whoever located the Scottish force would receive a knighthood and annual income of £100 for life. On 30 July, Thomas Rokeby came into camp. Confessing he had been captured but released, Edward, true to his word, knighted him (as much for his honesty). The English marched, taking up position directly across the river from the Scottish army encamped on the bank of the River Wear near Stanhope Park. Next dawn, the two armies drew into battle array and, to Edward's chagrin, Mortimer called a halt. Neither side advanced. It was stalemate as they stared at each other in silence.

On the night of 4 August, Sir James Douglas, captain of the Scottish army, using an English password, thundered into camp with a band of men. Killing many in their beds, Sir James 'struck his horse with his spurs and galloped up to the king's tent and cut two or three of its cords' before being repelled. Another day of stalemate followed, the English keeping closer guard day and night. The morning after, they found burning campfires and no Scots. The king wept on finding they had left unscathed.

21 September 1327: Death

Lord Edward died at Berkeley Castle although apparently healthy the evening before. Knights and others of Bristol and Gloucester came to view the body and found no 'outward mark'. Secret whispers say he was murdered, probably by suffocation, but others say it was a natural death from grief, although he was only forty-three years old and had always been vigorous in health. He will be embalmed and dressed in his coronation undergarments and his heart placed in a silver vessel for burial with his wife.

20 December 1327: Funeral

At Lord Edward's funeral, large oak barricades were erected in Gloucester Abbey to hold back the crowds of several hundred mourners, which included the king and his mother, from pressing near the hearse surrounded by hundreds of candles and gold incense burners shaped like angels and leopards. On the gold-leafed coffin, covered by a cloth with a gold leopard, rested his carved wooden effigy with a gilt crown but without rod or sceptre. Four great lions draped with the royal arms adorned the four corners of the hearse. After Mass the coffin was lowered into a tomb on the north side of the nave.

24–25 January 1328: Royal Wedding

Waiting at the gates of York, King Edward met his fourteen-year-old bride, Philippa of Hainault and Holland. She has dark brown hair, almost black, with brown eyes. She is tall and comely though not slender, with a cheerful, open face betokening a generous nature. Side by side they rode into the city through a joyfully celebrating crowd.

The day after, the two were married in York Minster by Archbishop William Melton. Philippa brought wedding gifts of books on rulers and governments and one of music with an illuminated picture of Edward holding a falcon.

Three weeks of jousts and tourneys have been arranged. King Edward intends to show off his prowess and his armour decorated with flowers and animals. Dancing and feasts at night will allow the ladies to show off their dresses and jewels.

1 February 1328: French Crown

News came that thirty-three-year-old Charles IV died on 1 February. The Estates have elected to give the French crown to Philip of Valois as eldest grandson of Philip II; King Edward has sent envoys to Paris to claim the French throne as he is the grandson of Philip IV.

Above: 1. The tombs of Queen Eleanor of Aquitaine and King Henry II at Fontevraud Abbey. (Courtesy of Adam Bishop)

Left: 2. The martyrdom of Thomas Becket, depicted on a leaf from the Carrow Psalter, *circa* 1275. (Courtesy of Walters Art Museum, acquired by Henry Walters)

Above: 3. Canterbury Cathedral. (Courtesy of Greg Waskovic from Pixabay)

Below: 4. Chateau de Chinon. (Courtesy of Skeeze from Pixabay)

Above: 5. The effigy of King Richard I on his tomb at Fontevraud Abbey. (Courtesy of Adam Bishop)

Right: 6. King John, drawn from his tomb at Worcester Cathedral. (*Old England: A Pictorial Museum of National Antiquities*, 1844)

7. Newark Castle. (Courtesy of Mariusz Matuszewski from Pixabay)

Above left: 8. King Henry III. (*A Short View of the Long Life and Raigne of Henry the Third*, 1627)

Above right: 9. King Edward I sitting on his throne. (*The Regal and Ecclesiastical Antiquities of England from ancient illuminated manuscripts*, 1842)

Below: 10. Snowdonia seen from Beaumaris Castle, Isle of Anglesey. (Author)

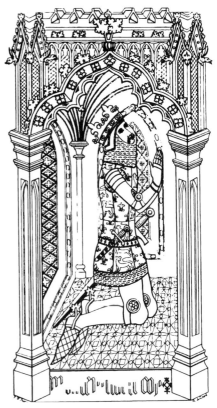

Above left: 11. King Edward II. (*A Continuation of the Complete History of England*, 1700)

Above right: 12. King Edward III, drawn from a painting in St Stephen's at Westminster Abbey. (*The History of The Life and Times of Edward the Third*, 1869)

Below: 13. Windsor Castle. (Courtesy of Andreas H from Pixabay)

Left: 14. King Richard II. (*Vetusta Monumenta*, 1746)

Below: 15. King Henry IV and court. (*The Regal and Ecclesiastical Antiquities of England from ancient illuminated manuscripts*, 1842)

Above left: 16. King Henry V. (*Henry of Monmouth: or Memoirs of the Life and Character of Henry the Fifth*, 1838)

Above right: 17. King Henry VI drawn from a contemporary sketch made between 1460 and 1470. (*Original Letters written during the Reigns of Henry VI, Edward IV and Richard III*, 1787)

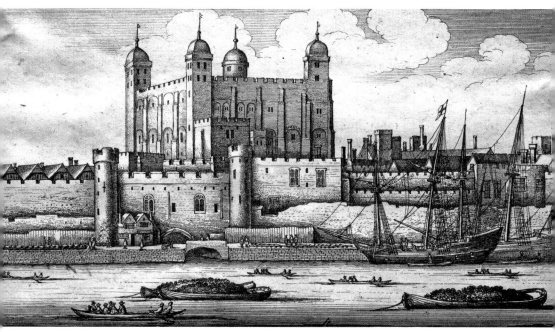

18. An etching of the Tower of London by Wenceslaus Hollar. (Courtesy of The Cleveland Museum of Art, Gift of the Print Club of Cleveland in memory of Mrs Ralph King)

Above: 19. Earl Rivers presenting his book and Caxton to King Edward IV, Queen Elizabeth and Prince Edward. Etching and line engraving by Charles Grignon based on a manuscript in Lambeth Library. (Courtesy of Yale Center for British Art, Paul Mellon Collection)

Left: 20. King Richard III. (*History of the Life and Reign of Richard III*, 1898)

1 March 1328: Permanent Peace

To cement peace, Roger Mortimer and Queen Isabella issued sealed letters, against Edward's fervent protests, in the king's name renouncing all English claims to Scotland. His seven-year-old sister, Joan, was betrothed to four-year-old David, son of Robert Bruce; the marriage is arranged for 17 July at Berwick. They sent back the 'Ragmans Roll of Homage' and the Black Rood, the piece of the True Cross, but London citizens adamantly refused to release and return the Stone of Scone.

6 January 1329: Conflict

Convincing King Edward that his cousin Henry of Lancaster meant to make war on him, Mortimer summoned a host to attack Lancaster's castle of Leicester, destroying the park and woodlands, draining the fishponds and driving off his game and cattle. Earl Henry marched from Bedford ready to give battle but the king's uncles, Edmund, Earl of Kent and Thomas, Earl of Norfolk, mediated before blood could be spilled. Earl Henry was fined £11,000 and forced to give up some of his lands to Mortimer.

6 June 1329: Homage

Philip of Valois, crowned King of France in May, insisted King Edward pay homage to him for Aquitaine. On the day appointed, King Edward walked towards the French king in the cathedral at Amiens accompanied by two of his uncles, four earls, three bishops and forty knights. Crowned, with his royal sword by his side and gold spurs on his heels, he wore a long robe of crimson velvet embroidered with gold leopards. The French king, crowned and sitting on his throne with sceptre in hand, wore a blue velvet robe covered with gold *fleurs-de-lis*.

Asked if he was the King of France's man in respect of the duchy, King Edward bowed, placed his hands between those of Philip and answered, 'Truly.' When Philip remarked that Edward's predecessors laid aside their crown, sword and spurs and made homage kneeling, he responded it was unfitting one king should kneel to another but agreed to consult the records to see if remedy was required.

7 June 1329: Robert the Bruce

At the Manor of Cardross, Robert the Bruce died a month short of his fifty-fifth birthday. Although the reason for his death is unknown, his Milanese physician believes eels are dangerous eating for those in advancing years.

27 August–6 September 1329: Camelot

Emulating his grandfather's 1279 event at Kenilworth, Roger Mortimer, created Earl of March last October, put on a Round Table, inviting every nobleman in England to Wigmore Castle. Combatants took the names of Arthur's knights. Around the high castle walls, a kaleidoscope of colours spiralled from the mingling throngs of people in rich or 'best' clothes clustered around the bright splashes of pavilions and tents.

On the first day, Mortimer entered dressed as King Arthur while King Edward, in armour covered in white muslin and red velvet, entered the lists as Sir Lionel, perhaps to humour his mother's nickname for him of 'little lion'. Taken by his own playacting, Mortimer walked 'with the king equally, step-by-step and cheek-by-cheek' and interrupted the king as he was speaking. He conducted himself with such vanity and insolence his own son called him the 'King of Folly'.

17–18 February 1330: Queen Crowned

The days being cold, Queen Philippa rode from the Tower of London to Westminster Palace on the eve of her coronation wearing a tunic of green velvet with a squirrel-furred red cape.

For her coronation the next day, she wore a robe of green cloth-of-gold and a fur hood and rode to the abbey between the earls of Kent and Norfolk dressed as pages. After her anointment at the high altar, she was dressed in a red-and-grey striped silk tunic and mantle. Her crown was decorated with ten *fleurs-de-lis* with rubies and emeralds, and groups of emeralds and six pearls. Leaving the abbey, she wore a furred purple tunic and mantle.

19 March 1330: Execution

Edmund, Earl of Kent was led from prison, hands bound, to be beheaded on Mortimer's order. The Captain of the Guard declared that neither he nor his men would carry out the sentence. In the evening a convicted murderer, in return for a pardon, beheaded the earl. Rumourmongers say Mortimer intended to cause Edmund's death laying a trap for him. At his trial for treason on 11 March, Edmund begged the king, his nephew, for his life, saying he had firmly believed his brother, Edward, was imprisoned at Corfe Castle and had only endeavoured to find out if it was true.

15 June 1330: Prince

At Woodstock Palace, Queen Philippa gave birth to a son, named Edward after his father. His nurse is called Joan and his rocker

Matilda. The baby's cradle coverlet is of cloth of scarlet lined with squirrel fur. For her uprising, the king gave Philippa a robe of red velvet faced with squirrel fur and for her churching a coverlet, coat and hood of cloth of gold.

18–19 October 1330: *Clandestine Plotting*
After moving the court to Nottingham, Earl Roger summoned a Great Council to meet on 19 October and placed Welsh archers on the castle battlements to keep watch over city and river. Other than the guard, Mortimer allowed no one to lodge in the castle except himself, his family and trusted councillors, King Edward and his mother.

On the eve of council, Edward's closest friends, William Montagu (who had once bluntly told him it would be better to eat dog than be eaten by it), Edward de Bohun, Ralph Stafford, Robert de Ufford, William de Clinton and John Neville were apprehended. Brought before Mortimer, they were interrogated as to their presence in the city. Unable to find evidence of any wrongdoing, Mortimer allowed them to depart. Just before dusk they left the city.

When it was dark, they secretly returned to meet the governor of the castle, Sir William Elland. He told them the gates had been fitted with new locks, the keys of which Queen Isabella kept under her pillow while she slept, but he knew a secret way into the castle. Ascending rough-hewn steps that took them directly into the castle keep, the men drew their swords and stealthily approached a door that was unlocked by King Edward, who had pleaded ill-health to be alone in his chamber so as to be able to lead Sir William and his comrades to Mortimer's chamber. Bursting in, they cut down two of the guards and although Mortimer had time to grab his sword he was quickly disarmed and seized. The queen, woken by the fracas, called out, 'Good son, good son, have mercy on gentle Mortimer.'

Mortimer, alive and unharmed, was arrested, as were his sons Geoffrey and Edmund. Chancellor Burghersh, Bishop of Lincoln was captured attempting to escape down a privy chute.

The next morning Edward proclaimed the arrests to startled citizens, telling them he intended in future to govern for himself with the advice of the great men of his kingdom. Henry, Earl of Lancaster and Leicester, though nearly blind, turned out at the cheers of the crowd and, hearing the news, flung his cap into the air for joy.

29 November 1330: *Condemned*
Doors and windows of his cell unblocked, Roger Mortimer was brought from the Tower to stand before his peers. He was

charged with usurping royal power, causing the death of the king's father and uncle, obtaining grants of castles and lands which decreased crown revenue, damaging the king's heritage in respect of Scotland, and giving evil counsel to the king and his mother. Found guilty, he was condemned to be drawn and hanged upon a common thief's gallows. The execution was carried out that evening at Tyburn.

3 May 1331: Horses
Three new chargers have been purchased by King Edward: a grey with a black head called Pomers for £120, a dapple with grey spots called Labryt for £70 and Bayard, a bright brown bay with two white hind feet, for £50. The king intends to hold a four-day tournament at Stepney to celebrate his son's first birthday.

21–25 September 1331: Cheapside Tournament
Between the Great Cross and Great Conduit in Cheapside, the market stalls were removed and the street well sanded for the king's tournament. In brilliant sunshine, music blaring, King Edward, William Montagu and eleven other knights came in dressed and masked as Tatars in the colours of St George, leading women by silver chains attached to their right hands through the madly cheering crowds. The king led in his sister, Eleanor.

As Queen Philippa and her ladies stood watching in the gaily decorated wooden tower built across the top of Soper Lane, it collapsed beneath them, the loud splintering frightening the horses. The ladies were bruised and cut but otherwise unhurt, and to save the carpenters from punishment the queen, on her knees, 'pacified the king, whereby she purchased great love of the people' and the tournament was continued.

30 November 1331: Scotland
David Bruce was anointed and enthroned King David II of Scotland at Scone.

Christmastide 1331: Gift
The royal family spent Christmas and New Year at Wells. Queen Philippa gave King Edward a silver ewer decorated with Arthurian figures and a goblet enamelled with castles, ships and beasts; inside was an image of a great castle with unfurled banners, the king seated in the middle.

16 June 1332: Princess
Queen Philippa gave birth at Woodstock to a daughter who has been named Isabella after her grandmother. Her gilded cradle is lined with taffeta and has a fur coverlet.

12 July 1332: Churching
At Queen Philippa's churching, the altar of the church was embellished with a purple silk cloth embroidered with birds and beasts. In celebration, King Edward put on a lavish tournament.

24 September 1332: Scottish King
Edward Balliol was crowned King of Scots at Scone Abbey today. Landing on the Fife coast, he beat a superior force of Scots at Dupplin Moor.

9 May–19 July 1333: Halidon Hill
By breaking through a partition wall and riding bareback towards Carlisle, Edward Balliol escaped a nocturnal attack though his men were killed in their nightshirts defending him. On receiving the request for aid, King Edward sent men to besiege Berwick who arrived on St George's Day. When he himself arrived on 9 May, he gave immediate orders for the aqueducts to be broken to stop the water supply. Bringing with him two siege engines with a range of three-quarters of a mile, he brought these to bear on the town, blasting it day after day, destroying houses and churches.

The king's ships arrived on 27 June and he ordered them to make a direct attack at high tide. The Scots threw flaming tar-soaked faggots at them but the wind blew them back. While quenching the fires, the townspeople begged a fifteen-day truce.

On the last day of truce, Sir Archibald Douglas with a troop of horsemen forded the Tweed, razed English Tweedmouth and on their return hurled meat and bread over Berwick's walls, shouting they intended to attack Bamburgh Castle and Queen Philippa. Leaving part of the army to continue the siege, King Edward took the rest to engage the Scots. They met two miles outside Berwick at Halidon Hill, the English on high ground, the Scots lower in marshy ground. Douglas called out, 'No prisoners.'

English horsemen dismounted while their archers guarded the flanks of each brigade. The Scots' leading brigade attacked Balliol, the second attacked the centre led by King Edward, the third the brigade led by the Earl of Norfolk. The Scots tried to send a fourth brigade around the foot of the hill to relieve Berwick but the king had a picked body of horse ready for such a tactic and they were driven into the sea. The fighting was fierce, with so much slaughter that the Scots' three brigades became one and men began fleeing. King Edward and his men mounted their horses and pursued their enemy. They had given the cry for no quarter; King Edward obliged.

20–23 January 1334: Victory

To commemorate his victory at Halidon, King Edward held a tournament at Dunstable. Every time the king entered the lists flying his lioness banners, the crowd cheered wildly. He had two jousting suits of gold-fringed Tatar cloth, one bearing a lioness and gold leaves, the other a lioness with silver rosettes. On his armour were baboons and other animals and he wore gold-encrusted pearl garters. Studded with gold and jasper, a silk bed decorated with foliage and baboons with hangings to match was brought in.

His knightly band wore green surcoats embroidered with a knight and damsel within gold foliage, the squires wore blue with knight and damsel encircled by silver foliage, and Edward's fur-lined russet surcoat had gold-leaved branches. Other suits included a set in black decorated with red roses with hoods lined in red scarlet and five squirrel-trimmed brown and scarlet surcoats embroidered with the letter 'M' above the arms showing two silk figures holding a roll with silken letters.

28 January 1334: Birth

Lodged in the Tower of London, Queen Philippa gave birth to a baby girl who was named Joan.

May–September 1336: Prevention

Leaving London on 15 May, King Edward arrived in Perth on 19 June with the intention of stopping the French landing an invading army and supplies in Scotland. Abbeys and houses were emptied of stores, cattle slaughtered, cornfields burned and towns destroyed as far north as Aberdeen.

22 December 1336: Birth

At Hatfield, Queen Philippa gave birth to a baby boy named William. To ease her confinement, the king ordered a bed in green velvet embroidered in gold with sirens bearing a shield with the arms of

England and Hainault (costing over £3,000), a gold-embroidered velvet robe and a white robe worked with pearls.

15 January 1337: Funeral
Prince John, Earl of Cornwall, was buried today in St Edmund's Chapel in Westminster Abbey. Aged only twenty years old, he died of fever on 13 September. He had marched to Perth in August, bringing reinforcements to his brother. King Edward had escorted the body from Perth to the Tower, and finally from the Tower to St Paul's for his lying-in-state. Devastated by his brother's death, he has ordered nine hundred Masses to be said for his soul and an alabaster carved tomb.

9 February–5 March 1337: New Creations
Henry, son of Henry of Lancaster, was made Earl of Derby; Sir Hugh de Audley, Earl of Gloucester; Sir William de Bohun, Earl of Northampton; Sir William Montagu, Earl of Salisbury; Sir William Clinton, Earl of Huntingdon; and Sir Robert de Ufford, Earl of Suffolk. Prince Edward was promoted from earl to Duke of Cornwall.

10 February 1337: Burial
William of Hatfield was sadly buried at York Minster today.

Michaelmas 1337: Parliament
In the face of fresh Scottish incursions and a belligerent Philip VI, who with 'great brags' and 'great cruelty' is slaying and imprisoning Englishmen, attacking English coasts and seizing towns and castles in Aquitaine, Parliament agreed taxation for three years to fund two armies.

Christmas 1337: Baboon Forest
During the Christmas festival King Edward had a gold and silver forest created. Baboon head masks and some heads with long beards were made.

13 January–10 June 1338: Black Agnes
William, Earl of Salisbury began – and ended – his campaign in Scotland besieging Dunbar Castle. It was held by 'Black' Agnes, wife of the absent Earl Patrick, who for months yelled defiance at her attackers from the battlements. And if any boulder smashed near to where she was standing she took out a cloth and ostentatiously dusted the walls.

The only time supplies got past the two Genoese galleys guarding the sea approach, she sent a freshly baked loaf and fine wine to Salisbury. A Scottish archer, managing to strike an English soldier next to Salisbury, called out, 'Agnes' love shafts go straight to the heart.'

13 April 1338: Siege Engines
Mock siege engines were built at Havering-atte-Bower for an entertainment. King Edward wore a hooded costume decorated on one side with tigers created from pearls, silver and gold with a pearl pear tree between each animal; on the other side created all in pearls was a castle with a horseman riding towards it.

12 July 1338: To War
To join his allies, King Edward, with Queen Philippa, sailed from Orwell for Antwerp with some of his fleet. His ship, *The Christopher*, carried the banners of Saints Edward, Edmund and George as well as the royal arms on 40-foot streamers. The rest of the fleet will sail from Great Yarmouth.

Princesses Isabella and Joan with most of the royal household including musicians, clerks, cooks and butlers assembled to see them depart. To each of his daughters the king gave a pair of decorative silver basins. Prince Edward has been left regent with John Stratford, Archbishop of Canterbury as his chief officer.

29 November 1338: Birth
Queen Philippa gave birth to a son at Antwerp nine days after her husband returned to the city. The royal couple have given him the name of Lionel.

6 March 1340: Birth
Queen Philippa, still in Ghent while King Edward is in England debating subsidies and reform with the Commons in Parliament, has given birth to a third son and named him John.

23 June 1340: Blockade
Masts of French, Genoese and Spanish ships rose, like a forest of trees, around the mouth of the River Swine. Prows lined up and armoured with wooden castles, they totally blocked the estuary. At dusk, King Edward ordered his fleet to drop anchor and await the dawn. At sunrise neither fleet moved, but as soon as the sun was behind his ships and wind and tide with him, King Edward

sounded the advance. The first of three lines sailed forward, the great ship *The Thomas* in the centre. The English loosed arrows from their longbows and they tore through men on the enemy ships. As English ships sailed into the French line, men threw grappling hooks to draw the ships together, causing the French first line to block their second and third lines. Fighting was then hand-to-hand with pikes, pole-axes and swords. From the tops of enemy ships stones were thrown 'wherewith many were brained'. Though struck by a spear through his thigh, the king continued fighting encouraging his men to greater ferocity. By the end of the day the English had captured 166 ships and the rest disappeared into the night.

30 November 1340–3 May 1341: Shades of Becket

After a terrible three-day crossing, on 30 November, King Edward landed unannounced at the Tower at one in the morning where he found both the Tower and his children unguarded. The Constable, Nicholas de la Beche, was arrested and thrown into one of his own dungeons.

The king was in a foul humour. Anticipated funds not arriving, he had been unable to pay his army or allies, mainly owing to the high-handedness of his own officials. Blaming and arresting his faultless exchequer officers, he sent guards for Archbishop Robert who took sanctuary in Canterbury Cathedral, waiting for the flare of royal temper to subside.

On 21 December, the Festival of St Thomas, the archbishop excommunicated anyone, except the king and his family, who had violated *Magna Carta*. The king retaliated. Calling the archbishop 'a mouse in the bag, a fire in the bosom, a serpent in the lap', he publicly accused him of plunging the crown into the 'devouring gulf of usury' either by mishandling or misappropriating funds.

On Ash Wednesday, 12 February the archbishop declared from his pulpit that 'God expects from man no more than he can' and revealed he had received precisely £300 from the exchequer and challenged Edward to let him answer before his peers in Parliament. King Edward held out from summoning Parliament until 24 April and then denied the archbishop entrance, repeating the act four days later. Rebuked by councillors, on 1 May the king ceded and admitted the archbishop, who immediately demanded right of trial by his peers. The dispute ended in compromise. On 3 May, the archbishop knelt and asked for pardon whereupon King Edward declared him free of all charges.

5 June 1341: Birth
Queen Philippa bore her seventh child and fifth son at Langley, a boy who has been christened Edmund.

23 July 1341: Traders
The Earl of Gloucester, ordered to supply 300 sheaves of arrows and 1,000 bows (250 painted at 18*d* each, the rest white) to the Tower of London for France, is ordered to redeploy them for Scotland because in April Scotsmen seized Edinburgh Castle, held by the English since 1335, by infiltrating it shaved like Englishmen and dressed like coal and corn traders.

11–12 February 1342: Love Joust
To mark Prince Lionel's betrothal to eight-year-old Elizabeth de Burgh, heiress of the Earl of Ulster, King Edward held a great tournament at Dunstable. The king entered as a simple knight, wearing a green tunic with a white hood bordered with Catherine wheels and the motto 'It is as it is' spelled out in jewels and pearls. Both king and prince had state beds; Lionel's was decorated with love knots with silk roses and leaves, the king's covered in green cloth with silk dragons.

March 1342: Sorrow
Queen Philippa gave birth to a daughter named Blanche at the Tower of London. She died soon after her christening and was buried in Westminster Abbey.

12 May 1343: Prince of Wales
During Parliament, Prince Edward was created Prince of Wales, invested with the circlet, ring and silver rod. At the three-day joust to be held in June at Smithfield, King Edward and his band will fight the Pope and twelve cardinals.

19–22 January 1344: Arthurian Tournament
Excited London merchants, bringing their wives, were invited to participate at Windsor tournament along with the nobility. Commemorating King Arthur, King Edward challenged that he and nineteen knights would hold the field against all comers.

At the end of the first day, Queen Philippa with Queen Isabella hosted a banquet for three hundred ladies, wives of nobles and burgesses, who were served in the castle's great hall in front of blazing fires with minstrels playing in the gallery. The men ate in pavilions erected outside in the courtyard but entered the castle for the dancing and singing.

At the end of three days of tilting, running at the ring and other displays of skill, the king rose early. Dressed in fine velvet clothes and crowned, he escorted red-gowned Queens Philippa and Isabella to Mass in the chapel. Afterwards, holding a Bible, King Edward swore to the assembly he would, like King Arthur, build a Round Table and hold a great tournament and feast every year.

30 January 1344: Death
King Edward's closest friend, William Montagu, Earl of Salisbury, badly injured at the Windsor tournament, died of his wounds and is to be buried at Bisham Priory. Only forty-two years old, he leaves his wife Catherine and six children; his eldest son, William, is sixteen years old and still a minor.

26 February 1344: Round Table
To build his Round Table at Windsor, King Edward appointed his carpenter William de Horle with leave to press as many carpenters into service as he required; ditto William de Ramseye, head bricklayer. The diameter of the tiled-roof building will be 200 feet with the table placed in a wooden gallery within the tower wall, with a passage under it for the servants and an open space in the centre.

10 October 1344: Birth
At Bishop's Waltham Palace, near Winchester, Queen Philippa gave birth to her fourth daughter, named Mary.

22 September 1345: Death
Henry, 3rd Earl of Lancaster died in his sixty-fifth year at Leicester Castle where he has spent the last fifteen years. His only son, Henry, is away 'doing chivalrous acts' as the king's lieutenant in Gascony. His funeral will be attended by the king and queen.

11 July 1346: Normandy
After weeks of bad weather, King Edward boarded his flagship on a bright, sunny morning. Trumpets signalled the navy to set sail from Portsmouth for Normandy beaches. The king plans to march 8,000 men, half of them archers, and burn a twenty-mile-wide swathe through the richest lands in France, looting and razing towns and villages up to the suburbs of Paris before turning north to Calais to join with the Flemish. The Prince of Wales, knighted on the seashore, goes with him. Prince Lionel has been appointed Guardian of the Kingdom.

20 July 1346: Birth
Queen Philippa gave birth to her fifth daughter at Windsor Castle who has been called Margaret.

25–26 August 1346: Crecy
Philip VI marched rapidly across the plain of the Somme in a bid to block and attack King Edward. Marching to the beat of 'kill, kill', the French had a hard day's march from Abbeville to the little village of Crecy and at four in the afternoon the two armies faced each other, thousands of Genoese crossbowmen forming the French king's front line.

King Edward had taken up station on the upper part of sloping ground, near a windmill. Causing his men-at-arms to dismount, he placed horses and baggage at his rear enclosed in a park. He formed a solid line of spearmen, his archers flanking them. As the armies engaged, a tremendous storm began, turning daylight into night. Noise of thunder, rain and hail intermingled with the cries of crows. Just as suddenly, the sun broke through the clouds. Genoese crossbowmen firing into the sunlight found their bolts falling short. The King of France ordered his mounted men-at-arms to trample the Genoese and charge the English front. English archers let loose their arrows, so fast and furious that those who saw it said it was like sleet falling. Men and horses were killed in droves.

Sixteen-year-old Prince Edward, on his first campaign, waded into the thickest of the fighting. Asked to send his son aid, the king, watching from higher ground, saw that although the prince was wounded there was little need: 'Let him win his spurs and let the day be his.' Fighting continued through evening and into the night. Against the odds, the English won. In the light of a blazing fire, the king was seen embracing his son.

4 September 1346–4 August 1347: Calais
Outside Calais, as well as erecting elaborate siege defences around the town, King Edward constructed a marketplace with stone houses and shops for his men and a palace for himself. When Jean de Vienne, governor of Calais, expelled 1,700 poor women and children thinking they would be trapped between the walls and English defences, they were allowed through the English lines and given food.

Four months into the siege, Edward sent for the queen to join him for Christmas. Another five months on, a French messenger was intercepted. He thrust an axe through the letter he carried and threw it into the sea but it was retrieved at low tide. Addressed to King Philip, it revealed the town was in 'sore need of corn, wine and meat ... nothing herein which has not been eaten, both dogs and cats and horses ... we cannot find any more food ... unless we eat human flesh ... we are at that point that we have nothing on which to live ... if we do not receive help soon, we shall all march out of the town into the open field to fight for life or death for better to die with honour in the field than to eat each other.' Edward affixed his seal to it and sent it on to the French king.

The besieged were overjoyed when they saw the French army arrive on 27 July, lighting bonfires and raising flags. Five days later, the French left and de Vienne sent for terms. At first refused, he told Edward's envoy, 'We are just a few knights and squires who have loyally served our master, as you would have done, and have suffered much as a result ... I entreat you, out of compassion, to return to the king of England and beg of him to have pity on us.'

Edward again told his envoy he refused and was told, 'My lord, you set a very bad example. If you order us to go to any of your castles we will not obey you so cheerfully if you put these people to death; for they will treat us likewise if we find ourselves in a similar situation.' Considering this, Edward said if six of the principal citizens of Calais marched barefoot and bareheaded out of the town with ropes around their necks and the keys of the town and castle, he would pardon the remainder and send in food and drink.

On 4 August, Eustace de St-Pierre, Jean d'Aire, brothers Jacques and Pierre Wissand, Andrieu d'Andres and Jean de Vienne himself came out, the latter so weak he could hardly walk. Lord Manny led them before the king and they prostrated themselves before him. Edward ordered them to be beheaded. When Philippa knelt before him and implored him to show mercy, he relented. The castle was strongly garrisoned with English soldiers, and before he leaves Edward intends to establish a mint and a trading staple.

14–17 October 1346: Neville's Cross

At the request of King Philip, King David crossed the English border to lay siege to the fortress of Liddell, held by Sir William Selby. His forces took two days to fight their way inside where they butchered Sir William's two sons in front of him before beheading him. Meanwhile, 4,000 English troops mustered at Barnard Castle. The Scots king headed towards Durham and his force was looting a village within sight of its cathedral when a thick fog descended. While David's breakfast was being prepared, some Scotsmen, hearing noises about them, were told by their king to stop panicking: 'There are no men in England but wretched monks, lewd priests, swineherds, cobblers and skinners. They dare not face me.'

The fog lifted and confronting him was an army as large as his own. English archers devastated the Scots who broke rank. King David was captured found hiding under a bridge. The yeoman who captured him had two front teeth knocked out by the king. The Earl of Moray was killed on the battlefield. King David received two head wounds from arrows and will be allowed to recover before being sent to the Tower of London.

December 1347: Pageantry?
For Christmas at Guildford, King Edward ordered tunics in all colours, three sets in plain white, cloaks painted with peacocks' eyes and gold and silver stars and masks of women's faces, bearded men and silver angels, as well as reversed legs with shoes, hills and rabbits, dragons' heads, peacocks' heads and wings and swans' heads and wings.

23 April 1348: Order of St George
Having rededicated the chapel of St Edward at Windsor to St George, King Edward has determined his Order of St George shall comprise twenty-six knights, distinguished by wearing blue garters embroidered in gold silk with the motto *Honi soit qui mal y pense*, 'Evil to him who evil thinks'; twelve will be led by himself and twelve by the Prince of Wales. Edward chose as his first knight his cousin, friend and most trusted captain, Henry, Earl of Lancaster.

24 June 1348: Birth
Queen Philippa gave birth at Windsor to her eleventh child, William. King Edward ordered a tunic embroidered with gold birds encircled by pearls for the queen, and for her chamber to be arrayed in red with two beds, one with scarlet covers and hangings and the other green taffeta with red roses. Her churching will be celebrated with a joust and tilt at Windsor in August.

5 September 1348: Funeral
Baby William died of the plague at Windsor. In a full royal funeral, gold cloth covered his body, with sixty pennons around the bier, and six lamps and 170 wax candles burning around him.

The Great Pestilence

The chronicler Knighton wrote that a 'general mortality of men throughout the world' began first in India, spread among the Saracens and then reached Christians and Jews. In Europe it showed first in Cyprus and Sicily in November 1347. In December it had reached Genoa, then Marseilles and Avignon.

Agnolo di Tura of Sienna, who had buried his five children with his own hands, wrote, 'I do not know where to begin to tell of the cruelty and the pitiless ways ... victims died almost immediately. They would swell beneath the armpits and in their groins, and collapse while talking ... none could be found to bury the dead for money or friendship ... in many places great pits were dug and piled deep with the multitude of dead. And they died by the hundreds, both day and night.'

King Edward had left Normandy just before it reached the duchy in the spring of 1348. Tales arrived across the sea of whole families dying and houses left empty. Thousands were killed in Paris. In England the dying started but the jousting continued. Besides the Windsor tournament, a joust was held at Bury St Edmunds where Edward had an eagle costume; in early May he held a great tournament at Lichfield, he and eleven knights wearing blue and white robes; later in the month another was held at Eltham, followed later in the year by jousts at Canterbury and Westminster.

The ports remained open. Princess Joan, now fourteen years old, departed for Castile to marry Prince Pedro. Arriving at Bordeaux, she died of the plague on 1 July. First she would have felt a chilly stiffness and tingling. Painful boils, burning like cinders, would have erupted in her groin, armpit and throat, followed by nausea, fever, severe headache and aching limbs. Symptoms could also include vomiting up blood and diarrhoea. Boccaccio wrote that many dropped dead in the open streets day and night or lay in houses, the smell alerting neighbours.

King Edward wrote to King Alfonso XI on the death of his daughter, 'See (with what intense bitterness of heart we have to tell you this) destructive death (who seizes young and old alike, sparing no one, and reducing rich and poor to the same level) has lamentably snatched away from both of us our dearest daughter ... no human being could be surprised if we were inwardly desolated by the sting of this bitter grief, for we are human too.'

Continuing with Knighton, in August 1348 'the dreadful pestilence penetrated the sea coast by Southampton and came to Bristol where almost the whole population perished by sudden death', and throughout England 'in every parish died a great multitude' and 'a great murrain of sheep everywhere in the kingdom ... in a single pasture more than 5,000 sheep died; and they putrefied so that neither bird nor beast would touch them'. Prices dropped for in fearing death people took little care for riches or property. 'Sheep and cattle ran at large through the fields and among the crops, there was none to drive them off or herd them and for lack of care they perished in ditches and hedges in incalculable numbers.' None knew what to do. In the autumn crops wasted in the fields.

The Scots when they heard of the 'dreadful plague' assembled in Selkirk Forest to invade the kingdom, mocking and swearing it was the Sword of God's wrath, but then it slew and consumed the Scots in no less numbers and they themselves were overtaken by the 'fierce mortality'.

The Black Death first appeared in London at the end of October. During the first five months of 1349 over 200 bodies were buried every day in the new cemetery near Smithfield until it was recorded in 1350 that so great was the death from the pestilence that above 50,000 persons were buried there.

Christmastide 1348: 'Hay, Hay'

The royal family spent their Christmas at Otford where King Edward ordered silver-spangled armour for himself and his horse, tunic and shield worked with the motto, 'Hay, hay, the white swan by god's soul I am thy man.' In sets of twelve he ordered masks of men with crests of lion and elephant heads, heads of men with bats' wings, girls and wild men, as well as two sets of worsted tunics, one green and the other red.

23 April 1349: St George's Knights

After ending the chapter meeting with prayer, King Edward ordained that the Knights of St George will meet, pray and joust every year on St George's Day. Taking Arthur for the theme of the joust, one band was led by Thomas Holland, the other by William Montagu, both of whom believe they are married to Joan the Fair Maid of Kent, who was also present.

18 June 1349: Proclamation

Every man or woman, free or bond, able in body, under sixty and required to serve is ordered to take only their ordinary wages or salary; if they refuse, they will be imprisoned. As also will any workman, servant or craftsman leaving service without reasonable cause. Nor is any man to pay, or promise to pay, wages or salary higher than before accustomed. Any who live by begging and refuse to work shall neither receive food nor alms for pity and will therefore be compelled to labour for their necessary living.

23 April 1350: Installation
At his castle of Windsor, after Mass, King Edward held a solemn feast and installation for the Knights of the Garter. All, including the king, wore russet gowns decorated with blue garters, blue mantles with escutcheons of St George and blue garters on their right legs.

13 July 1350: Proclamation
By the king, it is strictly forbidden for any person, on pain of forfeiture of life and limb, to bathe in the Fosses of our Tower of London, or in the water of the Thames opposite the Tower, by day or by night.

22 August 1350: Death
Fifty-six-year-old King Philip VI has died, succeeded as King of France by his eldest son, Duke John of Normandy.

29 August 1350: Victory Report
After a Spanish fleet sank ten English ships sailing from Gascony to England, King Edward assembled a navy of fifty ships. The fleets met off the coast at Winchelsea. A sailor reported that the forty-four Spanish vessels 'surmounted our ships and foists like as castles to cottages sharply assailed our men with stones and quarrels flying from their tops and cruelly wounding men' but English archers pierced their crossbowmen before they could strike again and entered the Spanish vessels with swords and halberds until the ships were full of Englishmen and the Spanish were dead or thrown overboard, at which point, to cheers, the ships were found to be loaded with treasure. Henry of Lancaster, seeing Prince Edward's ship had been holed, moved his own ship to his other side; between them they captured one of the ships. Beset by dark, untaken ships could no longer be discerned, so anchor was cast, the wounded dressed and others refreshed with sleep though watch was kept. At daybreak, the English prepared for a new battle but the rising sun revealed the Spanish had sailed away in the night.

8 March 1351: Duke
Henry, Earl of Lancaster was made Duke of Lancaster with palatinate power over Lancashire.

23 April 1351: Eagles

For the St George feast King Edward wore a red velvet surcoat and a cloak with silver clouds, under each cloud alternately a pearl or gold eagle, each holding in its beak a garter. He also ordered a streamer with golden eagles, twenty-four robes embroidered with garters and three blue taffeta garters with silver-gilt buckles with the motto picked out in pearls.

Christmas 1352: Devils and Friars

The entertainment laid on by King Edward at court this Christmas was between thirteen devils, thirteen friars in black habits and thirteen merchants in white robes. The king's costume was embroidered with gold falcons.

7 January 1355: Seventh Son

Queen Philippa gave birth to a son at Woodstock who was christened Thomas.

10 July 1355: Gascony

Edward, Prince of Wales was appointed the King's Lieutenant in Gascony and will sail in August and set up court in Bordeaux.

27 January 1356: Cession

After French troops landed in Scotland, King Edward, forced to move against the Scots, burned Edinburgh, Haddington and much of Southern Scotland. Tired of the fighting, Edward Balliol gave up his claim on the Scottish throne to King Edward at Roxburgh and requested leave to live in England. The king granted him a pension of £2,000.

19 September 1356: Poitiers

In the face of continued French hostility, Prince Edward embarked on a systematic plundering expedition in France chased by King John, who caught up with him on the high upland fields south of the city of Poitiers where two ridges of rising ground are parted by a gentle hollow. Prince Edward took up his position on the higher ridge, behind which was a large copse with a narrow lane leading up to it from a hollow overhung by trees and fringed by hedges with vines behind.

King John adamantly insisting on absolute surrender the previous day, battle began the following morning at nine o'clock. As the French charged up the lane, they were caught between showers of arrows coming from behind the hedges on each side, aimed at their horses. In an instant the lane was full of dead and dying men and horses, driving the rest of the first line back in confusion. English and Gascon forces reformed, awaiting the next wave, and English archers removed arrows from the dead and wounded to resupply their stock. After hours of fighting, the prince sent a party of men to circle around the French flank and attack them in the rear, bearing the flag of St George high. At sight of the flag, Prince Edward and his division of men attacked fiercely. A panic seized the French, who fled pell-mell, leaving a defenceless King John to be taken prisoner.

That night Prince Edward gave supper in his lodgings to his noble prisoners, seating King John and his son at one table and serving them himself, saying he was not qualified to sit at the table with so great a prince as the king.

5–24 May 1357: Robin Hood

Arriving at Plymouth on 5 May, people rushed to see Prince Edward and the French king. The prince rode on a black palfrey beside King John, who rode on a magnificent cream-coloured charger. They stopped first to visit the Shrine of St Thomas before taking easy stages to London. On the highway, 500 men dressed in green tunics, holding longbows and arrows, emerged from the trees in ambush. Prince Edward told King John they were English foresters who lived in the forest and waylaid travellers. Then the French king realised it was an amusement from popular tales.

Reaching London, the prince's procession was met by the mayor and aldermen in bright colours. The city conduits flowed with wine, arches thrown across the streets were decorated with tapestries, shops and houses displayed armour, bows and arrows in their windows and balconies while girls sat in birdcages scattered gold and silver leaves over the cavalcade and the throngs crowding the streets. At noon, King John entered Westminster Hall, greeted by King Edward, who rose and embraced him.

23 April 1358: Windsor

Knights, foreign and native, crowded into Windsor for the St George feast and tournament attended by King Edward and Queens Philippa and Isabella. Common people, wearing their best clothing, flocked to see the colourful clothes and cheer their favourite jousters and prancing steeds, all against a backdrop of music by Hankin FitzLibbin and his twenty-three minstrels.

22 August 1358: Death of Queen Isabella

At Hertford Castle, in her sixty-third year, Queen Isabella died. She had been in much pain and had accidentally taken an overdose of her medicine. Her grandchildren visited frequently and will miss her. She willed her library to the king and his sister, Joan, who was living with her. She will be dressed in her wedding mantle and buried, with her husband's heart, at Greyfriars in November.

13–30 May 1359: Marriages

Thirteen-year-old Princess Margaret married her close companion, twelve-year-old John Hastings, Earl of Pembroke at Reading Abbey on 13 May. Her attire was adorned with 2,000 pearls costing over £216.

Six days later, eighteen-year-old Prince John of Gaunt married the young and pretty seventeen-year-old Blanche, daughter of the Duke of Lancaster. The king's wedding gift to Blanche was a large eagle brooch with a huge diamond on its breast. To celebrate the wedding a three-day joust was first held in an adjacent meadow then moved to London where Lord Mayor John Lufkin challenged that he with his sheriffs and aldermen would 'keep the field for three days against all comers'.

The 'lords of the city' entered in rich armour, surcoats and shields with the city arms and their feats of arms thrilled the crowds. On the last day, to the joy and great pleasure of the citizens, the Lord Mayor revealed himself as King Edward, the two sheriffs as Princes Edward and Lionel while Princes John and Edmund with nineteen noblemen had pretended to be the aldermen.

28 October 1359–8 May 1360: God's Peace

Campaigning in France, the army in three divisions marched from Calais. Rain fell hard for weeks on end, turning roads into quagmires, and movement was slowed to a few miles a day. Originally the king had planned to be crowned in Reims but later changed his mind and decided on Paris. On Monday 13 April, the army made camp outside Chartres on an open plain. Under thunder and dark skies, rock-sized hailstones came down so fast that many soldiers and horses were killed. Others were struck by lightning and the temperature fell so 'bitterly cold that many men died on their horsebacks'. Taking it as a sign from God, on 8 May King Edward renounced his claim to the French throne in return for full sovereignty over Gascony, Calais, Guienne, Poitou and Ponthieu.

Christmas 1360: Woodbine

The royal family, inviting King John to stay with them, spent Christmas at Woodstock. King Edward wore a sleeveless black satin coat embroidered with the image of honeysuckle in gold and silk thread, with a motto in gold 'secure as the woodbine'.

23 March 1361: Death

Henry, Duke of Lancaster, aged fifty, died of plague at Leicester Castle. One of King Edward's most trusted friends and a companion of fifteen campaigns, he loved the song of the nightingale and the scent of roses, and enjoyed dancing (until gout prevented him), music, fine clothes and good wine. His favourite food was salmon.

3 July 1361: Marriage

At Woodstock, seventeen-year-old Princess Mary married John de Montfort, Duke of Brittany. Her wedding dress was a cloth-of-gold tunic and a very long mantle, trimmed with the fur of six hundred squirrels and forty ermines.

13 September 1361: Death

Princess Mary died today after developing a sleeping sickness from which no one could rouse her.

1 October 1361: Death

Princess Margaret died suddenly today of an unknown cause and will be buried with her sister in Abingdon Abbey. Of King Edward's five daughters there is only Isabella left, now aged twenty-nine and still in England, having refused to marry ten years earlier.

10 October 1361: Love Match

Shocking many, Prince Edward married thirty-three-year-old Joan, known as the Fair Maid of Kent, at Windsor Castle. She is the widow of Sir Thomas Holland, whom she married in 1340, but while he was on campaign in the same year she married William Montagu, Earl of Salisbury. The Pope ordered her to return to Thomas in 1349. The prince becomes stepfather to five children. The two will honeymoon at Berkhamsted.

19 July 1362: Prince of Aquitaine

King Edward has granted Aquitaine and Gascony, to be held as a principality, to Prince Edward, who is to give an ounce of gold each year for homage.

7 September 1362: Death

Queen Joan of Scotland died, aged forty-one, at Hertford Castle and will be buried in Greyfriars beside her mother.

13–14 November 1362: *Jubilee*

In Parliament to mark his fiftieth birthday, King Edward issued a general pardon to wrongdoers and decreed future pleas in court, still enrolled in Latin, are to be pleaded in English.

The king's sons were granted new titles: Lionel became Duke of Clarence, John of Gaunt the Duke of Lancaster and Edmund the Earl of Cambridge.

8 April 1364: *King John Dies*

King John of France died suddenly at Savoy Palace, barely forty-five years old. He had been in excellent health, spending winter 'cheerfully and sociably', visiting frequently with King Edward and his sons and enjoying several entertainments, dinners and suppers; he had travelled privately by boat to Westminster Palace frequently since his arrival in January. He bequeathed his bowels to St Paul's, his heart to Canterbury and his body to St Denis. The Dauphin will be crowned Charles V.

27 January 1365: *Firstborn*

Princess Joan was delivered of a son at Angouleme and he has been named Edward after his father.

6 January 1367: *Birth*

Princess Joan was delivered of a son about eight o'clock in the morning at Bordeaux. He has been named Richard.

15 April 1367: *Birth*

Blanche, Duchess of Lancaster gave birth at Bolingbroke Castle to a son and named him Henry. Duke John is away fighting with Prince Edward on behalf of King Pedro of Castile.

12 September 1368: *Death*

Blanche, Duchess of Lancaster died at Tutbury Castle, aged twenty-six. She will be buried at St Paul's. To commemorate her death, Geoffrey Chaucer wrote *Death of Blanche the Duchess*, recording that her speech and singing was sweet, that she was wonderfully kind, and that, so fair and bright, she was mourned grievously by her love, the black knight.

17 October 1368: *Death*

Only three months after Lionel, Duke of Clarence married thirteen-year-old Violante, daughter of Galeazzo Visconti, Lord of Milan in the presence of the poets Petrarch and Geoffrey Chaucer, he has succumbed to a mysterious fever and died. Tall and handsome, twenty-nine-year-old Lionel had been a widower since 1363.

3 June 1369: War
King Edward resumed his title as King of France after King Charles V, in May, summoned Prince Edward to Paris to pay homage for Aquitaine. Prince Edward said that he would come but assured him 'it will be with helmet on our head and sixty thousand men in our company'. The French king has declared the prince a disloyal vassal, voiding the treaty granting the English sovereignty over their continental lands. His troops are making raids on English-held towns and cities.

15 August 1369: Queen Philippa Dies
Her husband by her bedside, Queen Philippa died at Windsor Castle. When he first came, she had lifted her right hand off the red velvet tester and extended it to him to ask him three requests. Crying, he answered, 'Whatever you wish will be done.' She asked him to pay her debts, carry out her bequests and gifts, and lastly that when he died he would lie beside her. Since her fall from a horse while out hunting with the king in 1358, the queen has been in much pain and failing health; over the last few years she could only travel by barge or litter. After lying in state she will be buried in Westminster Abbey in the New Year.

24 August 1369: Marriage
Philippa, Countess of Ulster, the fourteen-year-old daughter and heir of the late Duke of Clarence, married seventeen-year-old Edmund Mortimer, 3rd Earl of March at Reading Abbey.

September 1370: Limoges
Even though he was so ill he had to be carried in a litter, Prince Edward besieged the city of Limoges, betrayed to the French by the Bishop of Limoges who had been godfather to the prince's eldest son. His brothers John and Edmund were with him, and though their army was small their sappers undermined the walls, which came crashing down on 19 September. The bishop was brought to the prince in chains and the city looted and burnt to the ground.

Returning to Bordeaux, Prince Edward found his son and heir, Edward, had died. Distraught and gravely ill, he made preparations to return to England with Joan and their son Richard, leaving his brother John in charge of the province and the funeral of his namesake.

21 September 1371: Marriage

At Roquefort, near Bordeaux, Prince John married Constanza, eldest daughter and heiress of King Pedro of Castile.

20 August–30 September 1372: Contrary Winds

Despite both being ill, King Edward and Prince Edward gathered a fleet of 400 ships to sail from Sandwich to France. On 30 August, the king embarked on his flagship the *Grace de Dieu* but from then on the fleet was either becalmed or beaten back by contrary winds. Now too late to save Thouars by the deadline of 30 September, the king ordered a return to England – and the winds changed.

27 June 1375: Truce of Bruges

A temporary peace for a year has been negotiated between England and France. England currently only holds Calais, Brest, Bordeaux and Bayonne.

28 April–8 June 1376: Dying

Although ill, King Edward attended the opening of Parliament at Westminster before returning to Havering. Prince Edward had himself carried from Berkhamsted to his London house on the Thames. Duke John attended to represent the king, despite hostile gossip saying he is openly and shamelessly committing adultery with his children's governess, Katherine Roet.

The first ever Speaker of the Commons, Sir Peter de la Mare, steward of Edmund Mortimer, Earl of March, after being elected immediately called for the 'coven' of evil counsellors around the king to be dismissed. He accused them of misrule, corruption extortion and embezzlement, particularly Lord William Latimer the chamberlain, John Neville the steward and Richard Lyons of the Royal Mint who were called into the chamber and impeached. The Earl of March was asked to oversee all royal business and appoint new councillors.

The king was also petitioned to have Alice Perrers removed from his side but on hearing she was married to William Windsor he begged for her to be dealt with gently. She has been forbidden to see him on pain of being exiled. An ordinance was also passed, resulting from her alleged activities, forbidding women to practise in courts of law.

King Edward, wishing to consult Prince Edward, arrived to find him bedridden, in pain and dying. His servants said he had scared them many times by falling into faints which resembled death. The king, having him carried to his chamber at the palace of Westminster, stayed by his bedside. On 7 June, the prince made his will in French, requesting burial in Canterbury Cathedral and for his shield, helmet, sword and surcoat to be placed above his grave. With his last words he asked his father to protect his son, Richard.

29 September 1376: Nation's Grief

Prince Edward was laid in a chariot drawn by twelve black horses led by his two chargers, one carrying his war armour and the other his tournament armour, followed by his warhorse. Around them were four sable banners with ostrich plumes. In deep mourning, the whole court followed his body through Charing, along the Strand, over London Bridge and onto the road to Canterbury. Passing through the town's West Gate, the cortege arrived at Canterbury Cathedral. Every way and every street was thronged with weeping mourners.

Buried in the Chapel of the Trinity near the Shrine of St Thomas, his armour, sword and scabbard, shield, jousting accoutrements, crimson velvet short-sleeved tabard covered with gold *fleurs-de-lis*, iron conical helm, velvet and ermine cap of estate and his leather-lined brass gauntlets ornamented with small lions riveted upon the knuckles were placed above his grave.

On the same day his son was buried, King Edward devised his own will, requesting to be buried in Westminster next to Philippa and confirming Richard of Bordeaux as his heir, bequeathing to him his best bed with all the hangings.

7 October 1376: Settlement

King Edward drew up his Settlement of Inheritance. After Richard, the next in line to the throne is John of Gaunt, Duke of Lancaster, then his son Henry as third in line. If neither survived then it should pass to Edmund and his sons, and lastly to Thomas and his sons.

27 January–2 March 1377: The Reverse Parliament

Duke John attended Parliament on behalf of King Edward, who had gone by barge to Windsor from Sheen, cheered by all the assembly as he passed. All the ordinances and impeachments made in the parliament of last April have been reversed and, because King Edward finds comfort in her presence and is ill, Alice Perrers has been allowed to be with him.

A poll tax was introduced as a new form of taxation, introduced and voted for by the Commons as a fairer tax than any before, which they assessed at the rate of 4*d* to be paid by every person over the age of fourteen.

23 April 1377: Knights of the Garter
At the ceremony of the Order of the Garter, King Edward nominated and knighted his grandsons Richard of Bordeaux and Henry of Lancaster. Also dubbed knights were his youngest son, twelve-year-old Thomas of Woodstock, along with Robert de Vere, John Mowbray, Henry, Thomas and Ralph Percy, Ralph Stafford and William Montagu and finally the thirteen-year-old John Southeray, his illegitimate son by Alice Perrers.

21 June 1377: Death of King Edward
Having lain prostrate for three days after a stroke and scarcely able to talk, King Edward, 'trusting the fond fables of Alice', believed he would recover and hawk and hunt again rather than thinking about the saving of his soul. As he lay dying at his manor of Sheen, Alice took the rings from his fingers and thanked him before bidding him adieu and withdrawing. In the early evening, he was left with only one priest. Trying to speak, his voice failed him. Scarcely saying the word 'Jesu', he died in his sixty-fifth year.

Richard II

1377–1399

With King Richard II believing powerfully in his God-given right to rule as he saw fit, it was inevitable he would clash with those of his magnates who believed theirs was the God-given right to hold key positions in government and 'advise him', which according to Richard amounted to them attempting to 'usurp his royal power'. Their manipulation of the king and his belief in strong kingship would eventually lead to his deposition. His strength of character first showed when he bravely faced down the rebel Wat Tyler in 1381 when he was fourteen years old. In 1388, his self-confidence and scorn for the nobles with whom he clashed led to the destruction of his small inner court and coterie of effective and trusted advisers at the hands of Parliament. Looking at the officials who were ousted or executed, King Richard appears to have created a body of hard-working, able and loyal ministers not picked from the nobility. During the 1390s he employed ministers of similar ilk, though this time they were considered proficient enough to continue working under the next king, Henry IV.

When the magnates curtailed his power and threatened him with deposition, perhaps it should not be wondered if he was left with a lingering sense of insecurity and felt the need to assert his royal dignity. He could be hot-tempered and abrupt in manner, and he flushed easily and stammered at times.

When his wife, Anne of Bohemia died in 1394, Richard seems to have lost some perspective for he loved her passionately. With her loss, he must have felt lonely, alone and vulnerable.

He empathised with his grandfather, Edward II. Like him, he had not forgiven his erstwhile antagonists and he struck back at those who had wronged and hurt him. Richard had been careful to whom he gave patronage, his rule had been peaceful and moderate, and taxes from 1389 had fallen sharply once the truce with France was completed. That was the crux of the conflict between Richard and the earls: they were bent on spending his revenue on expensive and futile wars and actively worked against him. Richard preferred peace, saying the war had gone on too long and too many brave men had been killed. He wished to make his court a centre of art and culture. To their discontent, he spent his revenue on illuminated manuscripts, jewellery, rich textiles and metalwork. Geoffrey Chaucer, while serving the king produced some of his best-known works; his friend John Gower was commissioned by the king to write *Confessio Amantis or Tales of the Seven Deadly Sins.*

It was Richard II who commissioned Westminster Hall's famous hammer-beam roof and decorated it with twenty-six angels with shields of the royal arms. Ironically, the first event to take place in his remodelled hall, decorated with his own image and white harts, was his own deposition. To Richard's misfortune his subjects felt he had little genuine care and regard for them and that he unfairly overtaxed them. In contrast, his cousin, Henry of Lancaster, was popular, a renowned crusader and jouster, spoke English and had four sons.

5 July 1377: Burial of Edward III

The torch-bearing procession escorting King Edward's corpse from the black cloth-covered chapel of Sheen Palace reached St Paul's Cathedral after three days. There, his body covered with white and red silk, he lay in state in his red silk-lined coffin. His face was left visible and thousands passed by to view him, murmuring how true the death mask was to his likeness. On 5 July he was carried to Westminster Abbey, through streets lit by crowds of mourning torch-bearers, and buried near his wife in the chapel of St Edward the Confessor.

15–16 July 1377: Coronation

After dinner, on the eve of his coronation, ten-year-old Richard watched the mayor and citizens assemble near the Tower of London, part of his procession to Westminster. Shortly after a bareheaded Richard rode through the richly adorned streets, his curling auburn hair ablaze against his all-white attire. Before him, his tutor Sir Simon Burley bore the sword of state. Joyful cheers and loud clapping emanated from the crowds lining the streets and those massed at every window and door.

A castle had been erected at the upper end of Cheap and inside a white-clothed maiden sat in each of its four towers. Blowing gold leaves and coins over him, they filled gold cups with wine and offered him and others to drink. At the top of the castle a gold angel held a crown and, bowing, offered it to him. Reaching his Great Hall, the new king drank a goblet of wine before retiring to sup and bathe in his chamber.

The next morning, after Mass, clothed in white with buskins on his feet, Richard sat patiently on his throne watching stewards arrange the procession. Taking his position on the carpet, he walked to the abbey under a canopy of purple silk, bells tinkling, while at the abbey gates Sir John Dymoke, in his best armour on his best steed, was discreetly told that his duty of King's Champion was called for *after* the ceremony and he withdrew as unobtrusively as he could. Richard's uncle, Duke John, bore Curtana, the duty taken over by his son, Henry, Earl of Derby after High Mass. Edmund, Earl of March bore the second sword and spurs while Thomas Beauchamp, Earl of Warwick bore the third sword. Richard FitzAlan, Earl of Arundel held the crown.

Reaching the high altar, King Richard lay prostrate while Simon Sudbury, Archbishop of Canterbury blessed him. Seated in the uplifted royal chair, he made his coronation oath. His clothes were cut open for his anointing. Once he was crowned and invested with sword, ring, sceptre and orb he was lifted onto his throne. At the end of the coronation ceremony Sir Simon Burley, contrary to custom, instead of taking the tired king to lay aside his regalia in the vestry, carried him on his shoulders from the abbey to his palace and en route the king lost his right shoe.

When all were seated at the banquet afterwards but before food was served, King Richard bestowed the following titles: Earl of Buckingham on his uncle Thomas of Woodstock, Earl of Northumberland on Henry Percy, and Earl of Nottingham on John de Mowbray. After partaking of a few dishes, the king went to his chamber while his knights and lords passed the rest of the day until suppertime in dancing and minstrelsy. In the palace courtyard a hollow marble pillar set on stops had on its top a large gold eagle and from under its feet flowed wine all day, free to all 'were he ever so poor or abject'.

25 July 1377: Council
'Certain lieges' are to arm and array all fit men between the ages of sixteen and sixty in response to Charles V sending troops to attack and destroy many coastal towns.

16 January 1378: Order
By order of the council, the sheriffs of London are to seize the goods of Alice Perrers forfeit into the king's hand and deliver them to the

keeper of the great wardrobe, namely a heavy, red silk bed canopy and coverlet, three curtains of red taffeta, an image of the Virgin in a tabernacle, two folding tables, one pair of tables in a case, three coffers bound with iron, one great coffer lined with linen cloth and one long table with trestles to the value of £20 17s 4d.

1 February 1378: Writ
King Richard granted to his nurse, Mundina Danos of Aquitaine, an annual pension of £30 for her life.

7 June 1380: Judicial Combat
Thomas Caterton, squire, accused Sir John Annesley of treason, and the crowds that thronged London's streets to see the judicial combat at Westminster lists were greater than those that came to the coronation. The herald called terms. They began with lances, then swords, and lastly daggers. The knight, disarming his adversary and intending to throw himself on top of him, was blinded by his perspiration and missed. The squire threw himself on top of the knight and Richard ordered a stop. While Sir John begged for the contest to be continued, the squire, unable to stand, was placed in a chair. An agreement was reached that the two could be placed as they were, with the esquire on top, but he then toppled from his seat and the battle was over. Though he was dead, Caterton was convicted and hanged at Tyburn to the great satisfaction of the people.

5 November 1380: Parliament
On a wet and miserable day at the Northampton parliament, Archbishop Simon told the assembly that not only had the Earl of Buckingham's military expedition in France drained the exchequer, but he had also been forced to pledge the king's jewels and to borrow on all sides. Asked to name a figure, he hesitated for a second before admitting the sum required was £160,000. After long debate, the Commons agreed a third poll tax, this time of one shilling per head on every adult, as being the least objectionable and fairest route of raising £100,000 if the clergy undertook to find the rest, adding a vague proviso that the wealthy assist the poor.

5 February 1381: Wedding
Defying Thomas of Woodstock, Joan FitzAlan, Countess of Hereford and widow of Humphrey de Bohun, married her ten-year-old daughter Mary to Henry, Earl of Derby at Rochford Hall. Thomas, married to

Mary's sister Eleanor and keen to retain sole inheritance by keeping Mary unwed, was then abroad. Mary will stay with her mother and Henry at the Savoy Palace for a time, her new husband being nominal head of the Lancaster household while Duke John is in Scotland. John sent Mary a diamond clasp and ruby and diamond rings, while Joan gave illuminated psalters to each of them. King Richard sent ten royal minstrels to play at the wedding.

12–15 June 1381: Riots

On 12 June, men from Essex, Suffolk, Norfolk and Hertfordshire poured into the environs of London and encamped at Highbury and Mile End, while 20,000 men of Kent, led by Wat Tyler, set up camp at Blackheath and Smithfield in military array, having learnt the craft in recent wars. Indignation and hostility abound in conversations and for the last fortnight there has been much unrest. Rioters have burnt rolls of taxation and released prisoners from gaols, and commons all over the counties say they can no longer bear such heavy taxes and subsidies as have been laid on them the last few years. Nor should tax collectors be allowed to act like a law unto themselves, demanding monies by force and lifting the skirts of underage girls to see if fathers speak true.

Having lodged the night at the Tower, on Thursday 13 June King Richard sailed from Tower Wharf to Rotherhithe meaning to meet with the rebels at Blackheath but so many people swarmed around the jetty it was unsafe for him to land. His barge was turned around, the mob following it along the bank, hooting and shouting. From the city, shrieks and cries tore the air as a mob ran amok killing officials and servants whom they pulled out of the homes of hated public figures, identified by London's poorest workers. Jewellery, gems, gold and silver vessels, tapestries and furniture looted from houses were burnt, smashed to pieces or thrown into sewers. Buildings were pulled down or burnt, including one of the fairest buildings in London, the Savoy Palace. Friar William Appleton, the Duke of Lancaster's physician, was killed and one of the duke's costly bejewelled jackets was stuck on a spear and used as an archery target to cheers of 'kill the duke'. King Richard and his cousin Henry, Earl of Derby watched the looting and burning from the Tower.

Friday, the king once again resolved to talk to the rebels. He rode to Mile End with William Walworth, Mayor of London. At his approach the rebels knelt. Asking what they wanted, he received the reply, 'The traitors.' He told them he would surrender to them any men convicted of treachery according to law. Believing the king meant they could bring all traitors to justice a mob left to go to the Tower. Leaving archers on the riverbank they broke open the gates. While the king was agreeing that serfs could have freedom and land would be rented annually at 4*d* per acre, men were kissing and manhandling his mother, frolicking on his bed and nearly killed Earl Henry, who was saved by a guard. In the chapel they found Treasurer Sir Robert Hales and Archbishop Simon and dragged them out to Tower Hill.

The archbishop, after forgiving his executioner, knelt and bent his neck for the blow and was struck clumsily by the axe. Touching his wound in reflex, the tips of his fingers were cut off. Still he was alive; it took eight blows before his head was put on a lance and set up on London Bridge, alongside Sir Robert's. In the city others were being beheaded in Cheap and Vintry, and Flemings dragged from churches and houses were massacred. Informed of the violence, King Richard rode to Blackfriars to spend the night at his great wardrobe.

About nine o'clock Saturday morning, after hearing Mass, King Richard rode to Smithfield to parley with Wat Tyler. As the two talked, Wat began to play with his dagger, then nonchalantly laid a hand on the bridle of the king's horse. Fearing treachery, the mayor stabbed a short sword into Wat's throat. As Tyler slumped in the saddle, his horse shied and archers drew their bows. King Richard galloped to their front line, shouting, 'Tyler was a traitor, come with me, I will be your leader' and led them into North Islington.

While Tyler was taken to the hospital by St Bartholomew's, the mayor called out the citizens to protect their king. A thousand armed men gathered in orderly array and marched to Islington, encircling the rebel host as if they were 'sheep being shut in a sheepfold'. Cudgels, choppers, axes, swords and bows and arrows were dropped as rebels fell to the ground to beg forgiveness. Though the king's knights begged to kill at least two hundred, King Richard stopped them, saying some would have joined the insurgents only out of fear and innocents could be killed. He ordered the rebels to return home and they began moving off.

22–28 June 1381: Revocation

While King Richard lodged at Waltham, a group of peasants from Billericay sent messengers to the king to ask if he intended to let them enjoy the freedom he had granted. The king replied that had they not been messengers they would have been hanged but they could give his message to those who sent them that they were 'detestable wretches' unworthy to live who sought 'equality with lords', that peasants they were and 'will always be ... for as long as we live we will strive to suppress you'.

18–23 January 1382: Royal Marriage

Through cheering crowds, Anne of Bohemia, petite daughter of the Holy Roman Emperor, with King Richard by her side, came to London, transformed into the 'City of Heaven' by pageants set up to welcome and delight her. She was fortunate to be safely ashore when she disembarked at Dover for a disturbance of the sea tossed all the ships in the harbour. The ship from which she had just alighted with Sir Simon Burley was in mere moments smashed to pieces.

On 20 January, Anne, eight months the king's senior, was married to Richard by the Bishop of London in Westminster Abbey and two days later she was crowned.

The first day of tournament was held the day after and fourteen-year-old Henry, the king's cousin, took part as possibly the youngest ever jouster. His tournament armour was decorated in silver spangles shaped like roses.

4 August 1382: Gifts

Romantically, King Richard has purchased a band for the queen's hair. It is decorated with a large ruby and two sapphires and three rings with four pearls set around a diamond.

6 August 1382: Tragedy

Tilting at the Windsor Castle tournament, William Montagu, 2nd Earl of Salisbury in a terrible accident killed his son and heir, William. Ironically, the earl's own father had died from injuries sustained while participating in a tournament at Windsor in 1344.

5–27 May 1384: 'Go to the devil'

About to discuss the Anglo-French peace treaty and Scottish raids in Parliament, Richard, Earl of Arundel rose. 'They would be aware', he said, that 'any kingdom in which prudent government is lacking stands in peril of destruction'; that England had lost its strength 'through bad government' and was almost in a 'state of decay', needing speedy remedy from the 'stormy whirlpool in which it is engulfed'. King Richard turned white with fury. Pointing a finger at the earl, he said that if he was blaming him for misgovernment, 'You lie in your teeth. You can go to the devil.' A complete hush fell until the king's uncle, Duke John, rose to try to calm them both.

Within the same parliamentary sitting, King Richard granted an audience to a Carmelite friar, who handed him a written accusation that his uncle John meant to dethrone and murder him. Raging, the king immediately ordered John's execution but the man himself fortuitously entered the room and intercepted an evil look from his nephew, who thrust the accusation at him. Once the king was convinced of his uncle's innocence, the friar was arrested. On the eve of his trial date, the friar was found dead in his cell. His body was dragged through the streets as a traitor at the horse's tail and men said the 'business was all huddled up', but the accusations proved false for Lord Zouche, also implicated, was so sick he was brought into council on a litter, acquitted and allowed to return home.

Christmas 1384: Love
The royal couple have spent their Christmas at Sheen and their New Year at Windsor Castle. Courtiers say King Richard is so much in love with Queen Anne he can scarce endure her out of his sight. Many wonder whether the queen might be pregnant.

24 February 1385: Plotting Murder
Duke John of Gaunt, who fled Westminster shortly after his return from France, donned armour and went to see his nephew at Sheen Palace. Leaving his large retinue some distance away, he entered the palace with a few of his knights. Privately conversing with Richard, John claimed to have proof that Richard had plotted to kill him and said he ought to be ashamed to dabble in private murder. When he suggested Richard should replace his councillors with some more honourable, the king assured him he was willing to listen to his advice. Duke John, asking leave to depart, told his nephew he had no wish to stay where people wished him dead.

20 July–17 August 1385: Rages
The French having sent an invasion force into Scotland to invade England, King Richard led an army to Durham. Before the campaign even began Lord John Holland killed Ralph Stafford, son and heir of the Earl of Stafford and a knight of the king's household, when he sought out Holland to apologise for one of his archers killing one of his esquires. Richard, raging in his grief, swore his half-brother would be treated as a 'common murderer'.

On the verge of entering Scotland, King Richard entitled his uncles Edmund and Thomas dukes of York and Gloucester, and his chancellor, Michael de la Pole, Earl of Suffolk. For loyal and willing service, Robert de Vere, Earl of Oxford was promoted to Marquis of Dublin.

Newly reconciled with the king, Duke John was commanded to lead the vanguard with his son, Henry, who led his own retinue. King Richard headed up the centre with the earls of Arundel and Warwick. Burning the abbeys at Dryburgh, Melrose and Newbattle, they reached Edinburgh on 11 August, pillaging and burning a large part of the city, but the Scots refused to fight, disappearing into the Highlands and living off the land. All provisions were taken with them, leaving nothing for the English to forage.

When Richard declined to pursue an enemy which melted away into the hills with starving soldiers and no supplies, Duke John argued they should continue to advance. Richard snapped that he could do so on his own. Then news came that Richard's mother had died. The withdrawal began on 17 August, the line of retreat guarded by Sir Henry 'Hotspur' Percy, nicknamed by the Scots for his speed in advance and attack.

7 August 1385: Death

Hearing Richard had sworn his half-brother would be submitted to the full 'rigour of law', Lady Joan immediately sent messengers from Wallingford to plead with him to 'not drench with tears his mother's face' and take pity on both. Told Richard was adamant, she took to her bed weeping, dying four or five days later. Her ladies say she had been weak and delicate for a long time and could 'hardly carry herself along because of her bulk'.

Wrapped in waxed linen, her body has been placed in a lead coffin awaiting the king's return from Scotland. She wrote her will on the day she died, asking to lie by the side of Thomas Holland, not the king's father, bequeathing to Richard her new bed of red velvet embroidered with silver ostrich feathers and gold leopard heads with boughs and leaves issuing out of their mouths.

20 October–6 December 1385: Conflict

In more scenes of disharmony in Parliament, the lords have insisted the king should have a commission of nine to reform his household, finance and government officers. They urged the king to employ suitable and wise councillors and, to temper his generosity to friends, take their advice before granting offices, lands or charters. Doing so would win him the hearts and love of his people; if not, the contrary would happen – to his great peril.

The eighteen-year-old king retorted that 'the king will do as he chooses and would change his ministers when it pleased him'. In the end, the Commons forced him to appoint a commission of four to reform his finances. The king had it proclaimed the Earl of March was heir presumptive to the crown.

2 January 1386: King Leo

Riding from Eltham one night, King Richard took King Leo into Westminster Abbey by candlelight to show him St Edward's shrine and his coronation regalia. The Armenian king, coming to ask for aid to drive the Turks from his land, was invited to spend Christmas and New Year at court.

24 June 1386: Shock Marriage

At Plymouth, pregnant Elizabeth of Lancaster was hastily married to Sir John Holland after Duke John managed to get her marriage to John Hastings, Earl of Pembroke annulled. No wonder that the charming Holland managed to seduce her for she was married to the earl in June 1380 when she was seventeen years old and her bridegroom only eight.

9 July 1386: Spanish Throne

In right of Constanza, John, Duke of Lancaster with his wife and daughters sailed from Plymouth for Spain to claim the throne of Castile. They had taken their leave of King Richard on Easter Day, when he gifted his uncle and aunt gold crowns and commanded the court to honour them as King and Queen of Spain.

1 October–28 November 1386: Threats

Members of Parliament entering Westminster Hall were greeted by the installation of new larger-than-life statues of kings, from Edward the Confessor to King Richard himself. In Chancellor Michael's opening address he requested a huge subsidy of £155,000, saying it was for a French campaign. The lords accused him of mismanagement and called for him to be instantly dismissed, along with the treasurer John, Bishop of Durham.

Furious, King Richard told them they had no right to command a king, that they were disloyal and treacherous, and that he would not 'dismiss the meanest servant from his kitchen if they asked'. He ordered Parliament dissolved and retired to his manor of Eltham. Ignoring him, Parliament stayed in session. While at Eltham, on 13 October, Richard promoted his close friend Robert de Vere to Duke of Ireland.

Asked for his presence at Westminster, the king told them to send a deputation to him. Rumour was he would have them ambushed and killed. To break the deadlock, the king's uncle Thomas, Duke of Gloucester with Thomas Arundel, Bishop of Ely visited him. They accused him of flouting the law and ignoring his nobles' advice. The bishop menaced that the law provided for the removal of kings guided by evil counsel, showing him the statute by which Edward II had been deposed.

Yielding, the king appeared at Westminster. The bishop was appointed chancellor in place of Earl Michael. And though immediately impeached, he ably defended himself against the charges brought against him. Near the session's end, and to his absolute fury and protests, King Richard had a commission of fourteen lords forced upon him, given full authority to supervise, investigate and reform his household and receive and disburse all crown income. It included Thomas, Duke of Gloucester; Richard FitzAlan, Earl of Arundel; Thomas Beauchamp, Earl of Warwick; Thomas Mowbray, 2nd Earl of Nottingham and his cousin Henry, Earl of Derby and Hereford.

August 1387: Ten Questions

The king while on his Midlands progress set up meetings with Sir Robert Tresilian, Chief Justice of the King's Bench and other senior justices. During those meetings they were asked ten questions. They confirmed he had the right to change or dismiss parliamentary ordinances and that the appointment of the commission was derogatory to his royal prerogative and in 'curbing the power of the king' they could be punished 'as traitors' though they were technically not guilty of treason. Other questions concerned his legal right to dissolve parliament and its authority to impeach royal ministers. All the answers were recorded in writing and sealed.

17 November 1387: Lords Appellant

Thomas, Duke of Gloucester and earls Richard of Arundel and Thomas of Warwick came to London with armed men. Entering Westminster Hall they personally presented to King Richard an Appeal of Treason against Robert de Vere, Michael de la Pole, Archbishop Alexander of York, Lord Chief Justice Robert Tresilian and Sir Nicholas Brembre, former Mayor of London, in which all were accused of exploiting the king's tender age, taking upon themselves royal power, manipulating him through their lies into loving them and making him hate his loyal lords who should be advising him.

20 December 1387: Escape
Robert de Vere, escaping London and the 'Lords Appellant', rode north and raised an army with Sir Thomas Molineux, Constable of Chester. Sir Nicholas Brembre, attempting similarly in London to protect the king, was caught and imprisoned, as was Simon Burley who was sent to Nottingham Castle. To blockade the army coming south, the Duke of Gloucester and the earls of Arundel and Warwick sent troops to block all the roads between the Midlands and London. When Oxford's army reached Pidnell Bridge he found it sabotaged and had to march to the next Thames crossing. In rising fog they reached Radcot Bridge and found it held by the earls of Derby and Nottingham. In disarray, some of Oxford's men refused to fight while others tried to cross the river and marshes but were killed or wounded by archers. Oxford dodged arrows and sought a ford but, finding none, slipped off his armour and swam away. Molineux was slain.

30 December 1387: Deposed?
Armed Lords Appellant, with 500 men-at-arms, marched into London. They demanded to see King Richard, who is at the Tower. Rumour says he will be deposed.

3 February–5 May 1388: Merciless Tyranny
Dressed in gold robes, the Lords Appellant entered the White Chamber, their arms linked. They advanced in a line slowly towards King Richard. In silence they looked at him, bowed and moved to take their places before declaring sentences of death on the earls of Suffolk and Oxford; both had already fled abroad, the former reaching Calais disguised as a poulterer.

Chief Justice Tresilian, who had taken sanctuary at Westminster Abbey, was forcibly removed to face Parliament on 5 February charged with deluding the king. Though found innocent, as soon as the king spoke up for him he was sentenced to hang at Tyburn alongside Sir Nicholas Brembre. Justices, along with dozens of royal clerks and secretaries, were charged and imprisoned or condemned and summarily executed, the king's chamber knights facing the latter fate.

Despite being defended by the Duke of York, Sir Simon Burley was accused by Gloucester and Arundel of exercising undue influence over the king. He was sentenced to death for forming a 'corrupt court'. The king, making a personal plea on Sir Simon's behalf, was told if he wished to retain his crown he should stop defending his friends.

Queen Anne fell on her knees in tears and pleaded for three hours for Sir Simon to be shown mercy. Gloucester commuted his sentence from hanging to beheading on 5 May on Tower Hill. Froissart mourned him for a 'wise and gentle knight'.

3 May–24 June 1389: 'Assume full rule'

On 3 May, King Richard told his council that being in his twenty-second year he would assume full rule for 'every person at age twenty-one is held capable of managing his own affairs' and he would not be 'deprived of a privilege given to the meanest subject of his realm'. No one opposed him when he dismissed all the chief officers of state and appointed his own. He then informed them he had had a twenty-four-day tournament proclaimed to be held at Smithfield and knights from Holland, Hainault and France were coming to participate.

On the first day of the tournament, twenty-four ladies on horseback led an equal number of Knights of the Garter by gold chains from the Tower, through the city to Smithfield. All wore the king's new livery: coats, armour, shields and trappings were decorated with white harts with crowns about their necks and chains of silver. At the banquets the king used a salt cellar in the shape of a hart. On the last day, jousts and feasts over, the king thanked all the strangers from overseas and gave them great gifts to carry home.

31 December 1389: Grief

At the New Year Tournament held at Woodstock, John Hastings, Earl of Pembroke, now seventeen years old, insisted on jousting against Sir John St John. As the two met, the earl's horse took fright and reared. Sir John's lance entered the earl's groin and flung him off his horse. His helm flew off and he was knocked senseless. He died at noon, without gaining consciousness. King Richard and Queen Anne are overcome with grief, the queen unable to stop crying. The earl will be buried at Hereford at the side of his father.

20–21 January 1390: Showing Faith

In Parliament, all the royal councillors surrendered their offices, begging King Richard to allow any who wished to complain about them be given the opportunity to do so. After the Commons praised them on the following day, King Richard, saying they need not take it as a precedent, solemnly restored everyone to their posts.

2 March 1390: *Aquitaine*

John, Duke of Lancaster returned to England after his unsuccessful expedition to Spain and sojourn in Aquitaine. He has been invested as Duke of Aquitaine for life by King Richard.

2–6 October 1390: *Smithfield Tournament*

Cheering crowds lined Cheapside to Smithfield, their cries competing with trumpeters and minstrels, to see the Feast of the Challenge, with sixty squires riding coursers out of the Tower at three o'clock in the afternoon. Then came sixty Ladies of the Garter, riding side-saddle on fair palfreys, each one leading by a gold chain a knight already dressed in jousting armour.

At Smithfield, the squires dismounted and the knights took their place, setting helms and rokettes – blunt-headed lances – to await all comers, native and stranger. Jousting continued until it was dark and all trooped in for supper, prize-giving and dancing, which continued until it was day. And so it continued for another three days and nights. On the last night, King Richard gave a supper for all the knights, whatever their nationality, and Queen Anne similarly for all their ladies and damsels.

21–22 August 1392: *Pardoned*

Riding from Sheen Palace, King Richard and Queen Anne were met at Wandsworth by kneeling citizens of London humbly craving his pardon. The warden presented him with the sword and keys of the city. Soon after the royal cavalcade was met by the Bishop of London, his clergy in procession singing the *Te Deum*. At London Bridge, the king was presented with two beautiful white steeds with silver saddles and trapped in red and white cloth-of-gold; the queen received a milk-white palfrey, saddled, bridled and covered in cloth-of gold. On each side of the street, citizens cried out, 'King Richard, King Richard!'

At Cheap Conduit, a little boy dressed like an angel offered them goblets of wine while maidens scattered gold coins. At the Standard, a stage had been erected and as if coming out of clouds an angel descended and placed a gold bejewelled crown on each royal head as they passed. When they reached the end of Cheap, the king was presented with a golden tablet with the Trinity; the queen received one of St Anne.

At St Paul's the king dismounted to make his offering and travelled on to Westminster along a route decorated with paintings, banners and cloth-of-gold draperies. In the abbey the king and queen were enthroned before being led into the palace. There they were presented with two silver basins filled with gold coins. Londoners prayed for his mercy, lordship and special grace that they might have his good love, liberties and franchises as they had before. Queen Anne fell on her knees and beseeched him to grant them. The king helped her to rise and said he granted all she asked.

24 March 1394: Death
Constanza, Duchess of Lancaster, Lady of the Garter died after a short illness at Leicester Castle. She was in her fiftieth year and is to be buried at the Church of the Annunciation of Our Lady of the Newarke in Leciester.

4 June 1394: Death
Mary de Bohun, Countess of Derby died at Peterborough Castle, having given birth to her sixth child and second daughter. The baby was named Philippa after the queen. Only twenty-four years old, Mary is to be buried in the Lady Chapel of Our Lady of the Newarke on 6 July.

7 June 1394: Death of Queen Anne
Queen Anne died today at the Palace of Sheen, a month past her twenty-eighth birthday. The king, ill with grief, has ordered the palace to be destroyed after the funeral as he cannot bear to face the memories of the happiness and love he shared with the queen.

3 August 1394: Funeral of Queen Anne
Richard FitzAlan, Earl of Arundel arrived late for the queen's funeral at Westminster Abbey and so angered the grieving King Richard that, in a rage, he snatched a wand and beat him around the head, knocking him to the ground. With his blood staining the pavement, the ceremony had to be delayed and the funeral went on into the night. The whole time the king kept breaking down in grief.

22 November 1395: 'Looked upon his face'
On the anniversary of the death of Robert de Vere, gored by a boar during a hunt and dying from his injuries in Louvain in 1392, King Richard had his embalmed body brought to England for reburial. When the coffin was opened, the king kissed his friend's hand and looked upon his face one last time.

13 January 1396: Marriage

Duke John married Katherine Swynford, his mistress of many years, as his third wife today at Lincoln Cathedral. They already have three sons and a daughter, all bearing the surname Beaufort.

Geoffrey Chaucer has become the duke's brother-in-law although Katherine's sister, Philippa de Roet, died in 1387.

27 October–4 November 1396: Royal Wedding

After months not recognising his wife or children and alternately believing he was St George or made of glass, Charles VI has recovered his wits and was able to sign the truce at Ardres. On 30 October, King Richard met his tearful fiancée. Three days short of her seventh birthday, Princess Isabelle was dressed in a blue velvet dress decorated with gold *fleurs-de-lis*. Telling her how she would be a 'great lady' and giving her a kiss, the bridegroom had the little girl smiling before she was whisked away by English ladies.

Packed in her trousseau are robes, one crimson velvet with gold birds perched on branches of pearls emeralds and a light blue velvet embroidered with pearl roses, two crowns (one valued at £1,740 and decorated with sapphires, rubies and clusters of pearls set around small diamonds), ornate chaplets, necklaces, brooches, jewels, gold and silver vessels for chamber and chapel and her dolls with miniature silver furnishings.

The French king's wedding gift to his son-in-law was a ship alms-dish poised on a bear's foot. A collared tiger stands in each forecastle, their two collars studded with three rubies and nine pearls.

The two were married in the Church of St Nicholas at Calais on 4 November. Afterwards, the couple went in procession to the castle, to be served with all manner of delicacies, meats and drinks, and all were made welcome in the great hall and the tents set up on the green outside the castle.

8 January 1397: Coronation Tragedy

As Isabelle of France made her entry into London, the Prior of Tiptree with eight other persons was crushed to death on London Bridge, so great was the press of people who had come to see her. The citizens of London presented her with a circlet of gold set with precious stones and pearls.

Today, they saw her crowned at Westminster Abbey.

2–12 February 1397: King Offended

After dining, King Richard summoned his lords from Parliament into his presence. He told them he was informed a bill had been presented criticising the number and cost of his household to his 'great grief and offence'. Three days after the bill, on 5 February, the king decreed anyone who proposed reform of his 'person, rule or regality' should be treated as a traitor.

The day after, by royal and papal decree, the Beauforts – John, Henry, Thomas and Joan – were legitimised as 'fully, freely and lawfully' as if they had been born in 'lawful wedlock' and John, the eldest, was created Earl of Somerset four days later.

Thomas Haxey, the clerk who had presented the bill which had offended the king, came before him on 7 February and was condemned to death. Thomas FitzAlan, Archbishop Arundel begged the king to pardon him and allow him to be put under his charge. To this the king consented.

10–11 July 1397: Arrests

For conspiring to depose him and spreading rumours he was not fit to wear the crown, King Richard personally arrested his uncle Thomas, Duke of Gloucester, rousing him from his sleep at Pleshey Castle. He gave custody of the duke to Thomas, Earl of Nottingham, who will take him to Calais Castle. The king, suspecting Richard, Earl of Arundel to also be involved, ordered him arrested and sent to Carisbrooke Castle on the Isle of Wight. Thomas, Earl of Warwick, invited to dine with the king, was arrested after the meal was over and sent to the Tower.

17–30 September 1397: Nemesis

While Westminster Hall is being remodelled, a temporary hall with a tiled roof supported on timber but open on all sides was constructed in the courtyard between the Clock Tower and the gate of the Great Hall. Crowds waiting to see the king arrive for Parliament were amazed when he came surrounded by hundreds of armed men wearing his white hart badge. While most surrounded the building, a bodyguard of archers entered the marquee with the king, bows bent and arrows nocked in their hands.

The opening address, given by the Bishop of Exeter, centred on the theme the king's subjects must be obedient to his laws or be punished. Sir John Bussy, speaker, entered and addressed the king and lords accusing Gloucester, Arundel and Warwick of treason. The charges included the executing of innocent persons in 1386.

On 21 September, John of Gaunt as Steward of England called for the Earl of Arundel to be brought in before him. The earl, wearing a robe with scarlet hood, was found guilty of treason by his peers. Sentenced to a traitor's death, commuted to beheading, his execution was carried out immediately on Tower Hill. A crowd of Londoners followed him on his last journey, mourning that he was to die, but his face 'never changed colour and he looked no paler than if he had been invited to a banquet'.

On the same day, Mowbray was given a writ to produce the Duke of Gloucester. Three days later Thomas entered Parliament to announce the duke had died in prison. He was posthumously convicted of treason, his lands and goods confiscated and his heirs barred from using the royal arms.

On 28 September, the Earl of Warwick was brought into Parliament. After the charges were read out, Warwick admitted his guilt and threw himself on the king's mercy, claiming he had been led astray by Duke Thomas and, sobbing, asked for everyone there to intercede with the king on his behalf.

'By St John the Baptist,' declared the king, 'this confession of yours, Thomas of Warwick, is worth more to me than the value of all the lands of the Duke of Gloucester and the Earl of Arundel.' Moved to tears, he exiled Warwick to the Isle of Man and granted him and his wife 500 marks for the terms of their lives.

In respect of the earls of Derby and Nottingham, King Richard said he accepted they were innocent of any wrongdoing, having 'loyally done their duty to the king', and had tried to use their influence to restrain the three Appellants. He created Henry as Duke of Hereford and Thomas as Duke of Norfolk. He also promoted his cousin Edward, Earl of Rutland, son of his uncle Edmund, to Duke of Aumale; Sir John Holland, Earl of Huntingdon became Duke of Exeter; Thomas Holland, Earl of Kent to Duke of Surrey and John, Earl of Somerset became Marquis of Dorset.

31 October 1397: Burial

Mystery surrounds the death of the Duke of Gloucester, who apparently did not die in prison. His body was released to his widow for burial at Westminster but today King Richard ordered it conveyed to Bermondsey Abbey. His weeping widow said there seemed to be no trace of violence on his corpse. Nevertheless, that he had met with foul play by order of the king was doubted by no one.

30–31 January 1398: 'Not to be trusted'

In dramatic proceedings in the Shrewsbury Parliament, Henry, Duke of Hereford made grave allegations against Thomas Mowbray, Duke of

Norfolk. He told the assembly that in December, conversing together as they rode between Brentford and London, Thomas suddenly said, 'We are about to be undone.'

When asked why, he replied, 'For our actions at Radcot Bridge.'

When Henry replied the king had said in Parliament 'we had been worthy and loyal to him', Thomas told him King Richard was not a man to be trusted and would do to them what he had already done to the others, 'for he wants to wipe that slate clean'. He claimed Henry, if not for fortunate intervention by others, would have been taken or slain at Windsor after the last parliament.

Hereford said he had no choice but to bring such allegations before Richard and Parliament. The duke then knelt before the king and begged his pardon for partaking in the past in any deeds contrary to Richard's majesty, which was granted.

16 September 1398: Trial by Battle

The dispute between the dukes of Hereford and Norfolk still raging, King Richard decreed a judicial duel to be held at Gosford Green near Coventry to settle their differences. To see the event, the king, his large bodyguard of archers, nobles and a huge crowd of ordinary people arrived early. At nine o'clock Duke Henry arrived and entered the field in Milanese armour with six mounted retainers. Announcing he had come to do his duty against the traitor Thomas of Norfolk, he crossed himself and rode to his pavilion set at one end of the lists. Duke Thomas entered and gave like declaration.

The two combatants rode to their ends. Henry called out 'God save the right' and spurred his horse forward but Mowbray remained still. The king rose from his throne and called loudly, 'Hold!' The dukes retired to the pavilions as the king withdrew. Two hours passed. Murmurs of speculation ran around the crowd. The Speaker of the Commons appeared: Hereford was to be banished from the realm for ten years; Mowbray was exiled for life. Loud calls of dismay resounded at the sentences.

15 March 1399: Funeral

John, Duke of Lancaster died at Leicester Castle on 3 February, aged fifty-eight years and was today buried by the side of his first wife, Blanche, in the choir of St Paul's Cathedral in the tomb he had built for £592, their two alabaster effigies holding hands. His eldest son, Henry, now inherits the dukedom of Lancaster with its vast territories and thirty castles. In his exile he is residing in Paris, where King Charles has given him a residence.

18 March 1399: Revocation
The king has told his uncle Edmund and cousin Edward and other nobles that, having given them without advice or due deliberation, he has revoked the letters patent in which he had assured the dukes of Norfolk and Hereford that exile would not bar them from any inheritances. He now decrees a banished man has no legal claim to his father's inheritance and, condemning Lancaster to 'perpetual exile', has shocked many by seizing his inheritance.

29 May 1399: Ireland
King Richard, with his court, many nobles and bishops in his train, sailed to Ireland leaving Edmund, Duke of York in charge of the kingdom. He has taken only a small force with him for this, his second expedition. There is a rumour that the king intends to make Thomas Holland King of Ireland in the Great Hall of Dublin Castle on 13 October.

28 June 1399: Rumours
Rumours say Henry, Duke of Lancaster will disobey the king and come into England. Duke Edmund has sent out letters to the shires to raise troops and muster at Ware, and ordered Chester Castle be put into a state of defence.

4–13 July 1399: Inheritance
Henry, Duke of Lancaster disembarked at Ravenspur on 4 July with 300 soldiers, accompanied by Thomas Arundel (archbishop-that-was) and the son and heir of Earl Richard of Arundel, who had recently escaped from Reigate Castle. First travelling to Bridlington, he swore on the church relics to the Earl of Northumberland and his son Hotspur that he had no intention of seizing the 'throne by violence' but only wished to claim his inheritance. Travelling via Pickering and Knaresborough, he lodged at his castle of Pontefract and found thousands waiting to flock to his banner.

10 July 1399: 'Pale with anger'
In Ireland, King Richard 'turned pale with anger' when he received the news of Henry's arrival in England and sent a small force with the Earl of Salisbury ahead of him with orders to raise a royal army in North Wales and Cheshire while he mustered ships to carry himself and his force to England.

24–29 July 1399: Movements
King Richard landed at Milford Haven on 24 July and marched to Carmarthen to meet up with the Earl of Salisbury.

Meanwhile, Duke Henry moved south from Doncaster to Leicester to Coventry and thence to Warwick where, at Berkeley on 27 July, he met with his uncle Edmund, Duke of York, who had been unsuccessful in raising men for Richard, no matter the amount offered. After the two privately conversed, Duke Edmund had declared Henry's cause as just. Anyone who disagreed were arrested.

Duke Edmund travelled on to Wallingford where Queen Isabelle is lodged after being moved from Windsor. Duke Henry marched to Bristol, where the Constable of Bristol Castle, faced with overwhelming numbers, surrendered. On 29 July, the king's innermost councillors, Scrope, Bushy and Green, who had travelled to Bristol to await the king, were summarily executed.

9 August 1399: Chester

Chester, the place that King Richard considered his heartland of support, surrendered to Duke Henry, who received news that King Richard is lodged at Conwy Castle.

5–23 August 1399: Conwy to Flint

Disguised as a poor priest, King Richard reached Conwy after fleeing Carmarthen, foiling a plot by his adoptive brother Edward, Duke of Aumale and Thomas Percy, Earl of Worcester to capture him and take him to Duke Henry on 5 August.

At Conwy he was given the devastating news that the Earl of Salisbury had raised an army but the men had 'slipped quietly away' and the Duke of York had defected. Convinced his only option was negotiation, King Richard sent the dukes of Exeter and Surrey to Duke Henry with his assent for the latter to enter his inheritance. They were arrested on arrival.

Henry sent the Earl of Northumberland to Conwy. Leaving the major part of his troops some distance away, the earl approached Conwy with just a small escort. On 14 August, King Richard agreed to leave Conwy to meet Henry at Flint Castle but when he saw Northumberland's troops he insisted on being allowed to return to Conwy; this was refused. When they stopped to dine at Rhuddlan, the king learned the castle, along with Flint Castle, was now held by Lancaster's men and he was therefore a prisoner. He told the few supporters still with him that Lancaster 'would be put to bitter death for this outrage he has done to us'.

They rode on to Flint. Arriving first, Richard went to hear Mass and then to dinner. Henry stood at the great hall door while the king ate, though he could 'swallow almost nothing'. When the two met there was no mention of the Lancastrian inheritance, only that the king had misgoverned England for twenty-two years and was offered assistance in correcting such a state of affairs. Reaching Chester on 23 September, the king was placed in the highest tower of the castle, guarded by the new earls of Gloucester and Arundel. In the king's name, Henry sent out a summons for a parliament to meet at the end of September. In the dark of the night, Richard attempted to escape by climbing down the outside of the tower but was spotted.

1 September 1399: Imprisoned

King Richard was a sorry figure as he was led through the streets of London on a 'pathetic nag'. On his journey he had neither been allowed to bathe nor change his clothing. He was lodged in the Tower of London.

30 September 1399: Deed of Renunciation

In the Great Hall at Westminster, the Archbishop of York and the Bishop of Hereford announced to the crowds filling it to the brim that King Richard II had renounced his throne the previous day in the presence of his lords spiritual and temporal, justices and other learned men. Their first visit to the Tower had been at nine o'clock and after dinner he was visited by the Duke of Lancaster and Thomas Arundel, restored as Archbishop of Canterbury. After much discussion, the fallen king said openly before everyone present that he would 'freely and gladly' renounce and leave off his dignity, signing the Deed of Renunciation with his own hand.

The parchment released all the king's subjects and their heirs from their oaths of fealty and homage and all bonds of allegiance. He resigned his kingly majesty, dignity and crown and swore on the evangelists that 'if it were in his power' Henry of Lancaster should be his successor and king after him, in token of which he removed his gold signet ring and placed it on the duke's finger. On hearing the account and seeing the signet ring, and upon the hearing and reading of the signed parchment, in Latin and in English, the estates with one assent held the renunciation 'firm and stable' owing to the crimes and evil governance of the realm, as acknowledged by King Richard, who said he 'were worthy to be deposed'. (The bruit is that King Richard in fact raged at the deputation who visited him, and declared in bitter anger that he would 'flay them alive'.)

Henry, Duke of Lancaster, dressed royally in cloth of gold, stood up. Making the sign of the cross on his forehead and breast, he announced in English that he 'Harry of Lancaster, claim the realm of England and the Crown', being descended 'by right of the blood'. Archbishop Arundel took King Henry IV by his right hand and led him to the throne but he stayed and prayed first, making a sign of the cross on the back and front of it. The archbishop pressed him to sit on his 'royal and kingly throne' to the jubilation of all those inside the hall, those without showing their joy and approval by clapping and throwing hoods. The coronation was scheduled for St Edward's Day.

Henry IV

1399–1413

Only a few months separated Henry and Richard in age but in worldly knowledge and personality the two were significantly different. Though Henry's mother died when he was a baby, he had an indulgent father who allowed him a measure of independence. When he and Mary de Bohun married, not only was their marriage loving but for much of the time they had a carefree life, enjoying hunting, reading, listening to and playing music. Family Christmases were spent at Hertford Castle. Their first child, Henry, was born at Monmouth in 1386 when Mary was sixteen years old and Henry was nineteen. In the autumn of the following year, Thomas was born, followed by John in June 1389. During that time, King Richard was tussling with the Lords Appellant.

Soon after, Henry went on the jousting circuit. In France, the renowned jouster Boucicaut was so impressed with Henry he asked him to go on crusade with him in Lithuania. Henry's preparations reveal a sweet tooth. He packed ginger sweets, sugar candy, lemon marmalade, aniseed sweets and barley sugar. He also took with him hunting gear, his falconer, six minstrels, trumpeters, pipers and a percussionist. People he met liked him and he received many gifts, including three bears, hawks, a wild bull and an elk.

When he returned to England he returned to jousting, buying new armour and eighteen lances. In October 1390 his son Humphrey was born. Just over a year later, Mary was pregnant again and when Henry attended Westminster for Parliament he sent Mary 100 apples and 150 pears.

Itching to go on crusade again, by the time he was ready to set off the Lithuanian crusade was over so Henry decided to go on pilgrimage to Jerusalem. Over seven months he travelled through Poland, Bohemia, Austria and Italy, sailing to Rhodes and Cyprus. From Jaffa he walked to Jerusalem. Returning, he stopped at Cyprus and was given a leopard which he brought home with him. He stayed a few weeks in Venice; his coat of arms was hung in St Mark's. In Milan, Lucia Visconti swooned when she met her jousting hero, saying at a later date she would have liked to have married Henry and would have waited for him forever, even if she died three days after the wedding.

By June 1393 he was back home. Mary soon fell pregnant again and they spent Christmas at Hertford. When Henry attended Parliament a month later, he sent her oysters, mussels and sprats. For himself, Henry bought a brooch with the motto 'think no evil'. The idyll ended when Mary, still only twenty-four years old, died on 4 June 1394 at Peterborough Castle in childbirth. The child survived and was named Philippa. On the anniversary of Mary's death, Henry sent twenty-four gowns to the chapel in which she was buried.

After Richard II exiled him, he was welcomed to Paris by Charles VI who gave him a house. One of the pursuits he enjoyed was to weigh theological arguments at the university. When his father died, the entire French royal family attended the Mass for his soul.

When, or even if, Henry decided to take the crown is unknowable but keeping it was harder than obtaining it. He weathered many plots to dethrone or kill him, the first of which ended in the death of Richard II. The roll entry for 20 March 1400 shows that Henry sent a clerk on 'secret affairs' to Pontefract Castle but whether this was to ascertain facts as to how Richard died or to tidy up after the event remains a mystery.

There were lighter events, such as the visit by the Emperor Emanuel II of Constantinople in 1400, with London citizens amazed by his priests who wore simple white gowns. In July 1409 a great joust was held at Smithfield, with many worthies coming from abroad and the king knighting skilful squires. Just before the event began, a seven-day play was put on at Skinners' Well beginning with the creation of the world. For the last few years of his short reign, bouts of ill health plagued him. His last Christmas was spent with his beloved second wife, Joan of Navarre, at Eltham Palace.

11–13 October 1399: Coronation

As Henry rode from Westminster to the Tower on 11 October, he was accompanied by forty-six squires he intended to knight. They supped, bathed and made vigil from sunset to sunrise in the Chapel of St John in the White Tower. After Mass the next day, the new Knights of the Bath received long straight-sleeved fur-lined green coats, a double knot of white silk and tassels on their left shoulders. The first three knighted were the king's sons: twelve-year-old Thomas, ten-year-old John and nine-year-old Humphrey, followed by the son and heir of the Earl of Warwick.

When they left the Tower after dinner, the cavalcade was 800–900 strong. The king, bareheaded, rode through the crowded and decorated streets on a pure white courser, dressed in a short cloth-of-gold jacket, blue garter clearly visible on his left leg. Nine fountains ran perpetually with white and red wines in Cheapside. When the liveried guilds joined the procession, it swelled to six thousand and cheering crowds were nearly hoarse by the time all had passed.

On St Edward's Day, walking in autumnal rain, slightly protected by the rich indigo-blue silk canopy over him, the king entered Westminster Abbey around nine in the morning, his lords following in long scarlet robes and ermine-trimmed mantles and hoods, dukes and earls with three bars of ermine on their left arm, the barons two. Four swords were carried before him: 'Lancaster Sword', his battle sword, carried by the Earl of Northumberland; wrapped in red and tied with gold bands, the Swords of Mercy were held by the earls of Somerset and Warwick; Curtana was held by the king's eldest son. Stepping onto the crimson-covered stage, Henry sat on the throne set in its centre while Archbishop Arundel from each corner asked the people if they wanted Henry to be king. The shouts of 'Aye' were loud and unanimous.

Descending to the high altar, Henry was stripped to his shirt. Laying on gold cloth he was anointed by the sacred oil of St Thomas from the chrism King Richard had discovered while searching the Tower for a necklace once worn by King John. A coif was placed on his head and shoes of crimson velvet on his feet, then the spurs. The archbishop blessed Curtana. The king slid it into the scabbard he wore. Then the Crown of St Edward was placed on his head. Henry swore to the archbishop that he would rule his people 'in mercy and in truth'.

At the banquet, Prince Henry served his father. There were three courses, and dishes served included venison in frumenty, an 'enarmed' boar's head, leche Lumbarde (a pork jelly), eggs in jelly, cygnets, capons, pheasant, herons, sturgeons, stuffed piglets, rashers of ham, curlews, pigeons, quails, snipes, rabbits, with various sauces, sweetmeats and subtleties.

When the feast was half over, a knight by name of Dymock, mounted and armoured as if for war, entered the hall holding aloft a black sword. Heralds proclaimed that the knight was ready to defy with his body any who dared say King Henry was not lawful sovereign. His horse's hooves thundered around the hall but no one spoke except the king who said, 'If need be, Sir Thomas, I will in mine own person ease thee of this office.'

3 October 1399: Death

Eleanor de Bohun, widow of Thomas, Duke of Gloucester, died at Barking Abbey.

14 October–10 November 1399: 'Murder will out'

On the first day of the new session, the first Act of Parliament declared King Richard's last parliament void. On the second day, Prince Henry was created Prince of Wales, Duke of Cornwall and Earl of Chester. The next event was the startling revelation that Thomas, Duke of Gloucester had been smothered under a 'featherbed' in the back room of the Princes' Inn at Calais by nine valets. On 18 October John Hall, a servant of the deceased Norfolk, who died of plague in September, confessed to the lords he had been present, ordered by King Richard, the Duke of Aumale and his ducal master. Aumale rose in denial. FitzWalter, shouting Aumale was 'midwife to the duke's murder' and he would prove it by battle, stood up and threw his hood into the middle of the hall. Aumale threw his own hood. Into the babble of voices, King Henry rose and called for order.

In the sudden silence, the king ordered the dukes of Aumale, Surrey and Exeter, the Marquis of Dorset and the earls of Salisbury and Gloucester to be arrested. John Hall was condemned and immediately taken out to be drawn and hanged, his bowels burnt while he still lived before he was beheaded and quartered. All those arrested vehemently denied any involvement in the duke's murder.

On 27 October, Lords and Commons stated unanimously that Richard should be 'kept under safe and close guard in some place where there was no coming and going of people' guarded by 'reliable and competent men' and his keeping 'done in the most secret manner possible'.

The day after at midnight, a prisoner was removed from the Tower of London and rowed along the Thames towards Gravesend and could be heard weeping and lamenting he had ever been born; the voice was that of King Richard.

On 3 November the king stripped the dukes of Aumale, Surrey and Exeter of their ducal titles but allowed them to retain their respective earldoms of Rutland, Kent and Huntingdon. The Earl of Somerset lost his marquisate and Thomas Depenser his earldom of Gloucester. Lands and goods received from King Richard since July 1397 were confiscated and they were told if any attempted to restore Richard to the throne they would be regarded as traitors.

Towards the end of this parliament it was revealed that, in response to his letter regarding the seizure of Wark Castle, King

Robert III refuses to acknowledge King Henry. As does Charles VI, who has refused Henry's ambassadors audience, forbidden trade with Englishmen, strengthened his border castles and embarked on preparations for a fleet at Harfleur. King Henry told his lords he would lead an army against the Scots and as for France, he would go further inland than his grandfather and uncle had ever done.

Christmastide 1399: Windsor
King Henry and his children enjoyed a family Christmas at Windsor Castle.

5 January 1400: Epiphany Miscarried
Partisans of King Richard met on 17 December at the Abbot of Westminster's lodgings to plot a rescue attempt. They included John Holland, Earl of Huntingdon and his nephew, Thomas, Earl of Kent; John Montagu, Earl of Salisbury; Thomas Despenser; Sir Thomas Blount; Sir Ralph Lumley; the newly ousted Archbishop Roger; and Richard Maudelyn, an esquire who bore an uncanny resemblance to the deposed king. Turning over ideas, John Holland suggested they could tell the king they would entertain him on Twelfth Day with a peaceful tournament, 'a mumming' between himself and a band of twenty against the Earl of Salisbury and a band of twenty, giving the perfect cover to bring in concealed weapons to kill King Henry, his sons and Archbishop Arundel during the revelling while their retainers mustered secretly at Kingston and Maudelyn, dressed in the king's armour, would gather Londoners to the royal banner.

Becoming aware of their purpose, the king's cousin Edward, Earl of Rutland forewarned the king on Twelfth Eve. Immediately, the king sent a messenger to warn Archbishop Arundel and left Windsor with his sons and rode swiftly to London, making a wide detour so as not to run into the conspirators as they made their way to Windsor. Some distance from London, the king met the Mayor of London who was on his way to Windsor to inform him that some six thousand armed men had assembled at Kingston. Carrying on to London, the king left his sons safely in the Tower while he quickly ordered closure of the ports and issued arrest warrants. He offered good silver to all Londoners who would ride with him. He also sent a trusted retainer north to kill Richard should there be an uprising. Within hours, he had an army of twenty thousand pitched on Hounslow Heath.

6–19 January 1400: Retribution

Seeing King Henry come safely into London, John Holland realised the plot had gone awry. Sending a message to his conspirators to flee, he sped to the coast. Thomas, Earl of Kent, Sir Ralph Lumley and John Montagu, Earl of Salisbury fled into hiding in Cirencester but they were spotted and captured. Their men, setting buildings on fire as a distraction to effect a rescue, merely persuaded enraged citizens to carry them out of town and behead them immediately. Their bodies were chopped up like carcases, salted and put in sacks which were carried to London on poles slung across men's shoulders.

A few days later, Thomas Despenser managed to reach Cardiff Castle and gathered enough jewels to pay his passage overseas but was overwhelmed by sailors who took his jewels and transported him to Bristol. He was beheaded at the market cross. Maudelyn had been immediately captured and hanged before having the opportunity to leave London. Many rebels were caught and brought before King Henry at Oxford Castle. Among those captured was Sir Thomas Blount, whom the king personally condemned to a traitor's death. He was executed in the Green Ditch near the city where he was hanged, cut down, his bowels cut out with a razor. Still alive, he watched his entrails being burnt and on being asked by one of his guards if he would like a drink, he politely demurred, saying he had 'taken away wherein to put it'.

John Holland was discovered hiding in a mill at the south-end of Prittlewell in Essex. Wind and storm had sent him back to shore. Thomas FitzAlan, Earl of Arundel was sent to fetch him. Once Huntingdon's ward, given his father's castles of Arundel and Reigate, Holland was hated by Thomas and on 10 January the latter arrived in London, trumpets sounding triumphantly, with his captive. A date of five days hence was set for his trial.

On the day appointed, Edward Courtenay, Earl of Devon (whose grandmother was Margaret de Bohun, great-aunt to Henry's deceased wife) was made Lord High Steward. The Constable of the Tower brought John, Earl of Huntingdon into Westminster Hall. His peers judged him guilty of treason. Responding to a written request by Joan FitzAlan, Countess of Hereford, the king sent him to be executed at Pleshey Castle.

Earl Thomas entered Pleshey Castle courtyard on 16 January, saluted his aunt and turned to his captive and said, 'Do you not repent of my father's death, the long holding of my land, the wicked government of myself till by very poverty I was obliged to depart England for I should have died of want? And you treated me as if I had been thy drudge. But now the hour has come when I will have vengeance upon thee.'

Tenants gathered to watch the execution were asked if any would undertake it. Into the silence, the countess cursed them as 'false villains, who are not brave enough to put a man to death'. One of her esquires offered and, axe in hand, he knelt before the earl to ask his pardon. Rising, he quailed and the countess told him, 'Do what you promised or lose your own head.' He swung up his axe and struck. He struck the breast and face of the earl, who said, 'For God's sake, deliver me quickly.' The esquire struck a further eight blows before landing one on the earl's neck. Still he lived. The esquire drew a knife and cut the earl's throat. Three days later the earl's head was placed on London Bridge along with those of the other conspirators after first ornamenting the battlements of Pleshey Castle.

17 February 1400: *King Richard Dead*
News has come to King Henry from his trusted friend, Thomas Swynford, that King Richard, on St Valentine's Day, was found dead lying in his bed at Pontefract Castle.

10–12 March 1400: *Funeral*
Escorted by a hundred men wearing black, the black-covered carriage drawn by four black horses came slowly into London, met by thirty Londoners all in white. All bore lit torches to accompany the body into St Paul's for Requiem Mass and vigil. Richard's head rested on a black cushion, face uncovered from the 'base of his forehead down to his throat', but his body was bound tight in waxed linen cloth, a red mantle over it.

Next day the corpse, face still uncovered, was carried into the Abbey of Westminster for the full funeral service. On both days, King Henry attended with many of his nobles; on the first day the king carried the funeral pall. From Westminster, the body was placed back into the carriage. Four esquires led the horses at a walking pace to Cheapside while the four knights walked at the corners, each bearing a banner, two of the arms of St George, two of the arms of St Edward. Halting for two hours, thousands of people passed by to view the king's face. The four knights then mounting their horses accompanied the body to King's Langley, arriving 'in the dead of night'. The abbot of St Albans conducted the last funeral rites before he was buried in the chapel. Afterwards there was no meal.

The accepted tale of the king's death is that in despair and grief at the death of his friends, King Richard refused to eat or drink, although a few say he was purposely starved to ensure he died as if from a natural death. Another rumour is that when an esquire mentioned the words 'King Henry' while he was eating dinner, Richard struck him with the knife he was using. Guards charged in and the king, pushing the table away, took a bill out of one man's hand and managed to slay four of them but one leapt onto the chair he had vacated and felled him with a stroke of his poleaxe.

March 1400: Apprentice Games
During Lent, London apprentices gathered together and chose kings among themselves and made war upon each other so fiercely that many died from blows or were trampled underfoot. The games only ceased when King Henry wrote to their parents and masters with grievous threats to prevent them.

July 1400: Love Match
During this month, Elizabeth, sister to the king and widow of John Holland, secretly married Sir John Cornwall. Sir John was arrested but King Henry has released him to fight in a 'feat of arms' before him at York, for he is famed for his prowess all over Europe. The king paid his sister £10 for a black bed and all its furniture which belonged to her late husband.

14 August–29 September 1400: Rebellions Subdued
Peace rebuffed by the Scots in May, King Henry mustered men for a Scottish campaign but at York, Scottish ambassadors came to him and said they would agree peace on the same terms as those agreed in 1328. Waiting for information on the 1328 terms, King Henry held jousts for his men. When the information came, he found out he had been insulted. Demanding Robert III pay homage to him at Edinburgh, he crossed the border into Scotland on 14 August but while he had been delayed the Scots had stripped their own fields and houses and deprived him of provisions. Lurking in thickets, caves and woods, they issued forth in lonely places, killing men or taking prisoners and doing more harm to his army than could be done to their guerrilla bands. He was forced to call the retreat.

As King Henry reached Leicester messengers told him that Owain Glyndwr, his erstwhile squire, who had studied law in London, had pronounced himself Prince of Wales on 16 September and immediately sent men to pillage and burn English towns, seize castles and drive out any English they had not slain, swearing he would kill the king and his eldest son.

King Henry marched towards Wales but, reaching Lichfield, news came that Sir Hugh Burnell, with a troop of men from Shropshire, Staffordshire and Warwickshire, had battled Glyndwr on 24 September, defeating him. Glyndwr was now a fugitive, having escaped from the battlefield by the River Severn not far from Welshpool. The king continued driving through North Wales along the coast road with knights, archers and cannon but the Welsh, like the Scots, faded away into the mountains and forests. Nonetheless, good news reached him: a Scottish host intending to destroy towns and massacre English inhabitants was soundly routed in Redesdale on 29 September by Sir Robert Umfraville and his troops.

November 1400: Poisoning Plot

Another assassination attempt was made on King Henry. Deadly poison was discovered smeared on the saddle of his horse, intended to kill him before he had ridden ten miles.

2 March 1401: Burning

William Sawtre, a Norfolk priest, was today burned at Smithfield for heresy. The king's writ ordered the mayor and sheriffs to 'burn him in a public and open place' and he was put in a barrel and set upon a fire in front of a very large crowd.

10 March 1401: Proclamations

Without licence, no person is to preach, teach or write anything contrary to the Catholic faith, nor encourage or maintain any such preachers, teachers or writers. Anyone possessing heretical works should deliver them up within forty days. Any heretic refusing to recant or relapsing afterwards will be publicly burnt.

Full-blooded Welshmen are forbidden to purchase lands in England and bear arms and in the border towns will not be allowed to hold office.

28 June 1401: 'Moved to pity'

Eleven-year-old widow Queen Isabella, released from house arrest, left London to begin the journey to her father Charles VI. Many were moved to pity seeing her clad in mourning, scarcely looking around her or speaking. It is reported in grief at losing her husband she 'estranged herself' from all 'pleasure or comfort'.

2 November 1401: Caernarfon

Owain Glyndwr made an unsuccessful attempt to seize Caernarfon Castle. His standard unfurled revealed a startlingly beautiful golden dragon against a white field.

6 July 1402: Marriage

Princess Blanche, accompanied by her uncle John Beaufort, was married at Cologne Cathedral to Louis, Elector Palatine, son and heir of King Rupert of Germany who, when he met his ten-year-old bride, said delightedly she had an 'angel's face'. Twelve ships guarded by a man-of-war transported her trousseau of furs, skins and cloth – wool and cloth of gold – along with saddles and horses along the Rhine to Dordrecht.

1 August 1402: Death

Edmund of Langley, Duke of York died in his sixty-second year at his birthplace and was buried there. His eldest son, Edward, inherits the dukedom.

27 August–14 September 1402: Campaigns

King Henry was furious when he heard Welsh women were cutting off dead Englishmen's genitals and stuffing them into the men's mouths during the latest rebellion in June. He has mustered three armies: one to leave from Chester under Prince Henry, one from Hereford under the Earl of Stafford, and one from Shrewsbury led by the king himself. The Welsh refused to battle and hid in the mountains while the king's armies battled torrential rain and violent gales. The king was almost killed when his tent was blown on top of him, prevented from injury by sleeping in his armour.

Unable to fight the weather, he terminated the campaign but good news came from Scotland: on 14 September, Henry, Earl of Northumberland with his son Henry 'Hotspur' Percy confronted an invading Scottish host and captured a hundred lords, knights and squires, some French too, and put the rest to flight. English grooms in the rear, mounting their masters' horses during the battle, shouted out, 'The Scots flee, The Scots flee.' Those in front, scared by the cries, in turning to look were killed 'by a storm of blows from maces about their ears and shoulders.'

13 December 1402: Defection

A written proclamation has been sent out by Sir Edmund Mortimer that his nephew, Edmund, 5th Earl of March, is rightful king, being the heir of King Richard. King Henry had long suspected that Sir Edmund, rather than fighting Glyndwr at Bryn Glas, had pretended to be captured in June. He had consistently refused to pay ransom or allow the Percy family to do so, despite Sir Edmund's sister being married to Hotspur. On 30 November, Sir Edmund married Owain's daughter Catrin.

7 February 1403: Royal Love Match

At Winchester Cathedral, King Henry married Joan of Navarre, widow of John, Duke of Brittany. The two have been corresponding for years since her husband's death in 1399 and it is believed to be a love match. In her thirties, she is beautiful and graceful in her bearing. Her coronation is set for 26 February.

Watching the ceremony were the king's younger sons, John and Humphrey, and Joan's younger daughters, Margaret and Blanche. Her sons – John, Arthur, Giles and Richard – have stayed in Brittany with the Duke of Burgundy acting as regent and guardian.

A lavish banquet, costing above £522, was provided with delicacies such as roast cygnets, capons, venison, pork loins, rabbits, bitterns, stuffed pullets, partridges, woodcock, plover, quail, snipe, fritters, cream of almonds and pears in syrup, each course divided by subtleties decorated by crowns and eagles. One cake was in the shape of crowned panthers, each panther having flames coming out of its mouths and ears.

10 May 1403: Death

Katherine Swynford, Duchess of Lancaster died in Lincoln in her fifty-third year and is to be buried in Lincoln Cathedral.

26 June–21 July 1403: Shrewsbury Field

Signing himself 'Your Mathathias', the Earl of Northumberland sent a letter to King Henry for urgent payment of £20,000 'for the safety of the kingdom'. The king was nonplussed for Mathathias' son was Judas Maccabeus, who led a revolt against King Antiochus. Recalling the angry confrontation of the previous year when Hotspur had demanded money, Henry wondered whether it was the safety of England or his own person that was threatened, for when the king had attempted to explain there was no money in the Exchequer as the Percy family themselves had tied his hands from collecting tax revenue, the argument had become heated. King Henry had punched Hotspur, who before storming out threatened, 'Not here, but in the field.'

After setting off north at the beginning of July, the king sent a letter on 10 July to his councillors from Higham Ferrers jubilantly informing them Prince Henry had successfully regained Harlech Castle and destroyed Glyndwr's manors. As the king reached Nottingham two days later, he was informed Hotspur had mustered Cheshire men. Four days later at Lichfield, he heard that Hotspur was publicly claiming, 'King Richard is alive' to gain support and intended to unite with Glyndwr and march on Prince Henry; further, his father the Earl of Northumberland was bringing a third army to unite with them both at Shrewsbury.

In the morning of 17 July, scouts came to Lichfield to tell Henry that Hotspur was at Sandiway. Both towns were roughly the same distance away from Shrewsbury. With no time to lose, King Henry immediately sent part of his army to augment his son's soldiers to hold the bridges and town and prevent Hotspur taking Shrewsbury. He took the rest to reach Shrewsbury from the east to trap Hotspur between himself, his son in the town and the river.

Two miles outside of Shrewsbury, in a pea field named Berwick, Hotspur made his stand, placing his archers, with their killing range of more than half a mile, at the top of a ridge where the king's vanguard would have to climb. The Earl of Stafford valiantly ascended it, trumpets and clarions sounding, into the thousands of arrows that turned the day as dark as if a thundercloud passed over, his men falling as fast as autumn leaves 'after the hoar frost'. He was killed in the arrow storm. Arrows depleted, out came swords and axes. Men and horses were killed as 'none spared his fellow [for] mercy had no place', fighting with an 'equality of bitterness'. It was 'horrible to hear the groans of the wounded, who ended their lives miserably beneath the hooves of the horses'. The vanguard began to give way and flee and the archers ripped arrows from bodies to shoot them in the back as they ran.

The king ordered the main body to advance and threw himself into the thick of the action while his son attacked the flank. The armies clashed at the foot of the slope. Hotspur, seeing the king, charged towards him but lost him in the general melee and was cut down. Prince Henry, raising his visor, was struck by an arrow just below his left eye. Two noble knights, wearing the king's armour to confuse 'any sniper', were killed. One was Sir Walter Blount, who loyally held his ground with the royal standard raised as long as he could. Afterwards, the Earl of Douglas, who had lost an eye, complained perplexedly, 'Have I not slain two King Henries with mine own hand? 'Tis an evil hour for us that a third yet lives to be our victor!'

Sir Thomas Percy, Earl of Worcester and Hotspur's uncle, was taken captive. When the king heard there was a murmuring that Harry Percy was still alive, he took the dead body from its grave and propped it against an axe stuck between two millstones in Shrewsbury's marketplace so that all men might see he was dead, ordering that the head should afterwards be displayed on Micklegate Bar in York. He allowed Sir Thomas to weep for the death of his nephew, as had the king himself when he viewed the body, and then had him beheaded for treason. He then ordered Hotspur's cousin Ralph Neville, Earl of Westmorland the Earl Marshal to search for and arrest the Earl of Northumberland.

20 October 1404: Author

John Serle, captured at York and sentenced on 26 July to be drawn through every city and borough, reached Guildhall in London today. From the Tower, he was drawn to Tyburn and hanged, beheaded and quartered. Letters supposedly sent by King Richard had in fact been authored and sent by him. He confessed he had taken Richard's privy seal, fled into Scotland and used it to seal letters to send to the king's friends, thereby proving the author of their deaths as well.

13 February 1405: Spirited Away

Their empty beds discovered, men were sent in pursuit and caught Constance of York, Lady Despenser, with Edmund and Roger Mortimer at Cheltenham. Brought back to Windsor, the children were returned to the nursery where Constance told King Henry that fourteen-year-old Edmund was rightful king and that she was taking them to Wales.

Since her husband's death in 1400 Constance has scandalised many by living in open adultery with Edmund Holland, Earl of Kent. The king ordered her to be imprisoned at Kenilworth Castle. Implicating her brother Duke Edward, the king had him arrested and sent to Pevensey Castle, though he protests his innocence.

23 May–12 July 1405: Bitter Actions

On 23 May, Prince John sent word that Richard le Scrope, Archbishop of York had sent out a manifesto proclaiming his father a murderer, perjurer and usurper and mustered an army with Thomas Mowbray, Earl of Norfolk. The king had been about to take an army into Wales to finally subdue Owain Glyndwr but instead he marched his army north. Five days later, the king received news that his son, with Ralph Neville, Earl of Westmorland, had confronted an army led by the Earl of Northumberland and Lord Bardolf and driven them into Berwick. Then they marched to confront Mowbray and Scrope at Topcliffe. They asked the earl and archbishop if they would parley; the two men agreed and were made welcome and offered wine. While they drank and talked, Westmorland secretly sent a knight to their army to tell them all were reconciled and they could leave for they were supping together that night.

As soon as the soldiers had dispersed Mowbray and Le Scrope were discreetly arrested and sent to Pontefract where the king collected them on his way to York. As he reached the city, citizens came out with halters about their necks and, 'lying naked to their drawers on the ground', sued for the king's pardon, which he granted. The archbishop asked to see the king but was refused and his crozier was taken from him.

Archbishop Arundel, hearing the king had taken him captive and fearing the worst, rode at breakneck speed. Late at night of 7 June, the fifty-one-year-old prelate rode into the castle courtyard and burst into the king's presence, pleading with Henry not to kill the archbishop and to think of Thomas Becket and Henry II. But as soon as Arundel retired to bed, the king called a court at which the archbishop and the Earl of Norfolk were found guilty of treason. About midday of the following day they were led out to a nearby field and beheaded. When the Archbishop of Canterbury heard, he collapsed.

Two days later, after riding in heavy gales and rain, the king took shelter at Green Hammerton Manor and became ill with fever. He complained that his skin was burning and his face was covered in red pustules. Many believed he was being punished by God. However, the king was taken to Ripon and as soon as he recovered his health he rode north to gain Northumberland's castles while the earl and Lord Bardolf fled into Scotland.

26 February 1406: Proclamation
During the sitting of Parliament a lighted lantern is to be hung every night outside each house in the high streets and lanes.

22 March 1406: Captured
Eleven-year-old James Stewart, son and heir of the King of Scotland, was captured in a boat off the coast at Flamborough Head after a storm drove it ashore. He had been sent away to safeguard him from the Duke of Albany who had murdered his elder brother. He will be lodged at Windsor Castle.

4 April 1406: Death
John Stewart, who ruled as King Robert III of Scotland, died at Rothesay Castle.

22–24 May 1406: *Checkmate*

In the first session of Parliament before Easter, King Henry was personally castigated for imprudent economy in his household and ill governance and defence of his realm by the speaker, Sir John Tiptoft. Opening of the second session was delayed while King Henry was unable even to travel by water through a severe illness in his leg, but he finally arrived on 22 May. The Commons forced him to agree that certain Breton and French aliens in his and his wife's household should 'leave for foreign parts'. On the same day he gave the Commons names of seventeen lords, headed by the Archbishop of Canterbury, as his councillors with his complete trust to bring about economical and effective government. However, the lords declined and asked for their refusal to be entered on the rolls. On 24 May, Sir John Tiptoft asked again whether the lords would take the said council upon themselves. The archbishop replied that they would 'if adequate revenue could be found with which to carry out good governance' and would do their utmost for 'the benefit of the king and kingdom', otherwise they would not. They won the skirmish.

26 October 1406: *Marriage*

Twelve-year-old Princess Philippa married King Eric of Denmark, Norway and Sweden at Lund Cathedral and was immediately crowned after the ceremony. She wore a white tunic and a white silken cloak bordered with squirrel fur and ermine. King Henry's wedding present to his daughter was a jewelled collar with the motto '*Soveignez*' and the letter 'S', ten amulets with nine pearls, twelve large diamonds, eight rubies, eight sapphires and a triangle clasp with a great ruby and four great pearls.

22 December 1406: *Third Session*

In the third session of Parliament, one of the longest held, Prince Henry, who has joined the king's council, was affirmed as heir apparent to the crown of England and praised for his good heart and stout courage. He then departed for Wales to subdue further rebellion. Sir John Tiptoft was made Treasurer of the Royal Household and charged to see if he could improve upon those whom he has been castigating, and the king agreed that after Christmas the royal household would retire to a quiet place for a thorough review of its finances. The Commons have asked him to agree a list of thirty-one articles whereby he will devote two days a week to public business, advised by his council. Ditto concerning grants, appointments and disputes – with regard to the latter in consultation with justices where necessary.

24 January 1407: Marriage

The Duke of Milan's sister, Lucia Visconti, arrived. King Henry, whom she had once adored, having fainted at meeting him at a tournament, gave her away at the church door of St Mary Overy in Southwark in marriage to Edmund, Earl of Kent.

24 October–10 December 1407: 'Honour to the king'

In the parliament held at Gloucester Abbey, Archbishop Arundel's opening speech was themed on 'honour to the king'. Thomas, son of Geoffrey Chaucer, was appointed Speaker of the Commons and immediately began requesting 'good governance' by the king, saying the previous grant was given in that expectation. He was stopped by the archbishop, who handed him a written schedule showing all income and outgoings and suggested the king should not continue being denigrated for the problems of the realm and that he and the lords had personally underwritten substantial loans for the common welfare and profit of the realm, believing they would receive agreement and gratitude. Seeing neither reward nor gratitude was forthcoming, they would resign their offices and so asked to be entirely discharged.

In response, Thomas complained about the king's purveyors and was told if any were breaking the law they should be reported like any other lawbreaker. The next complaint was that the king had failed to defend his seas and keep his people safe and, with regard to Welsh rebellion, they were neither obliged nor bound to support wars that should be funded by lords of the marches. Arundel responded by asking the Commons to elect a committee of twelve to meet with the lords to debate the best way to defend the realm and how to find the money to fund it. On the last day of this parliament, 2 December, the Commons granted the king the subsidy required.

News came that Louis, Duke of Orleans, brother of King Charles VI, had been killed by assassins on 23 November sent by John 'the Fearless', Duke of Burgundy, who is effectively ruler of France (as Louis had been when deputising for his brother during his bouts of illness and, said some, diverting royal revenue into his pocket and 'enjoying' the queen). On 7 December, French ambassadors agreed a truce between England and France regarding Gascony, ratified three days later.

The king will spend Christmas at Eltham.

January 1408: The Great Frost

It is the coldest winter in living memory. Men are calling it the 'great frost and ice', for not only has the Thames frozen over but even the sea.

19 February 1408: Bramham Moor
An army of Lowland Scots, led by Lord Bardolf and Henry, Earl of Northumberland marched towards York but told Sir Thomas Rokeby, High Sheriff, had gathered a force to resist them, they sought a strong position and awaited his arrival on Bramham Moor. Battle began as soon as Rokeby and his soldiers arrived in the field. Fighting was fierce in the early afternoon dusk. Fighting a rearguard action, the earl was slain. His army fled. Lord Bardolf was mortally wounded and died in the night. The Abbot of Hailes, in full armour, was executed but the Bishop of Bangor was spared as he was wearing his vestments. The grey-haired head of Northumberland and a quarter of Lord Bardolf will be sent for display on London Bridge.

17 March 1408: King's Cannon
Simon Flete, keeper of the private wardrobe in the Tower, showed off the cannon he had constructed which was devised by the king.

21 January 1409: Will
To the fright of all, King Henry, who has been on-and-off ill since last summer and had an attack so severe recently that he recalled his sons to be with him at Eltham for Christmas, today made his will in English. In it he requested the fees and wages of servants and officers be paid before any other and asks that his debts be paid 'in all haste possible'. All his lords and true people were thanked for their true service and all hope they will long be able to do so.

22 May 1409: Death
While pregnant with her second child, the king's seventeen-year-old daughter Blanche died of fever at Haugenau in Alsace. The letter from Louis to the king expressed his grief at losing his 'most loved and sweetest wife', whose death had taken away all the delight and joy of his life.

21 December 1409: Prince's Coup
Following many hot arguments in council between Prince Henry and the king's chancellor and treasurer, with the latter, Sir John Tiptoft, resigning on 11 December, Archbishop Arundel today resigned as Chancellor of England. Prince Henry now heads the royal council.

5 March 1410: Burning

At Smithfield, John Badby, tailor of Evesham, was placed in a barrel ready for burning for holding to his view that consecrated bread was not God's body. Counselled by Prince Harry to forsake his heresy, the prior of St Bartholomew brought the holy sacrament and asked him how he believed. John answered it was blessed bread but not God's body. With twelve lit torches the fire under the barrel was kindled and when he felt the fire he cried for mercy. The prince commanded the fire to be quenched and the barrel pulled away. But when asked by the prince if he forsook his heresy, he said he could not; the fire was relit and he in his barrel replaced on it and burnt.

16 March 1410: Death

John, Earl of Somerset, Constable of England and Captain of Calais, died in the Hospital of St Katharine-by-the-Tower aged thirty-nine years and will be buried in St Michael's Chapel in Canterbury Cathedral. He is succeeded by his son, Henry. Prince Henry was appointed Captain of Calais. Sorrowing, King Henry is staying with the archbishop at Lambeth.

23 April–9 May 1410: Prince's Parliament

During Parliament, on St George's Day, the Commons gave King Henry a list of eighteen articles. Going to respond to them three days later, he found notes appended showing Prince Henry and his council had dealt with two of them, signifying to the assembly Prince Henry has taken royal power to himself. Indeed, the Schedule of Councillors given to the Commons read as 'the preserve of the prince's friends'. Reluctantly, a subsidy was granted but smaller than requested split over three years. A bill was passed for six days' imprisonment for any servant or labourer playing ball games, with hand or foot, quoits, dice, skittles and other such useless games instead of practising their archery. Archers are required to be able to shoot a minimum of ten aimed arrows per minute.

August–September 1411: Civil War

Charles d'Orleans, son of murdered Louis, allied with Bernard, Count of Armagnac and the dukes of Berry, Bourbon and Brittany are fighting against the Duke of Burgundy. Civil war in France has brought King Henry and his son into argument. The king inclines to either remaining aloof or favours the Orleanists. The prince favours Burgundy and, wholly against his father's wishes, sent the Earl of Arundel, Reginald, Lord Cobham and others to help Burgundy regain Paris in September.

The bruit is Prince Henry asked King Henry to abdicate, telling him that his sickness meant he could no longer apply himself to the honour and profit of the realm. When the king refused, many wondered if the prince would openly rebel against his father.

30 November 1411: King's Coup

On 30 November in Parliament, King Henry publicly thanked the prince and his councillors for their labours on his behalf. As they knelt before him, he said they had discharged their duties in true and loyal fashion and now their responsibilities were at an end. Then they realised they had been graciously dismissed and the king had resumed control.

29 June 1412: Reconciliation

Desiring audience with his father, Prince Henry left his personal friends in the Great Hall at Westminster and ordered them to stir no further than the fire. The prince wore a strange gown of blue satin or damask with eyelets, and at every eyelet was a needle hanging by a thread of silk. About his arm he wore a dog's collar set with 'esses of gold'.

King Henry, unwell, had himself carried in a chair into his privy chamber and when his son asked entrance he was asked for what reason he came.

Entering, the prince knelt reverently at his father's feet and avowed he was innocent of any of the evil imputed to him, declaring, 'My life is not so desirous to me that I would live one day that I should be to your displeasure.' He gave his father his dagger and said he had made himself ready 'by confession and receiving of the sacrament. I beseech you, dear father, to ease your heart of all suspicions you have of me and despatch me here before your knees with this dagger. Thus ridding me out of life and yourself from all suspicion and before God, I faithfully protest clearly to forgive you.' The king threw away the dagger and tearfully embraced his son, vowing he would never give credence to any further reports.

9 July 1412: Ducal Creation

King Henry created his son, Thomas, now twenty-four years old, Duke of Clarence and is sending him to the aid of Charles, Duke of Orleans. At the end of last year, Thomas married Margaret Holland, Countess of Somerset and widow of his uncle John.

12 August 1412: False Collector

William Derman, labourer, was pilloried for walking about the city with a box bound of iron wherein he collected much money pretending to be a collector of alms for the hospital of Blessed Mary of Bedlam.

20 November 1412: Crusade

A great council was held at Whitefriars to discuss the king's decision to go on pilgrimage to Jerusalem and decided new galleys would need building and purveyance lists made for provisions.

20 March 1413: Death of King Henry IV

While praying at St Edward's Shrine, King Henry collapsed. Insensible, he was carried to a chamber in the abbot's lodging. When he came round, he asked where he was. He was answered, 'In the Jerusalem Chamber.' In an irony he had thought, he said, to die in Jerusalem. He was put on a pallet before the fire where he lay in great agony. Prince Henry came to his bedside. His father, as his end drew near, stretched out his hands and asked his son to kiss him and gave him his blessing. Soon after, between seven and eight in the morning, aged only forty-six years old, he died. The prince, in an agony of grief, retired to pray on his knees, in floods of tears, until night fell. In his will, the king had made his son, now King Henry V, his executor for the 'great trust that he held in him'.

Henry V

1413–1422

Hall, the Tudor chronicler, wrote of the warrior king Henry V that he was 'the blazing comet and apparent lantern in his days ... the flower of kings passed'. From a young age, Henry took delight in martial deeds and there are entries listing swords and scabbards being purchased for him. When his father was exiled, he was twelve years old. King Richard took him to Ireland, where he knighted him, saying, 'My fair cousin, henceforth be gallant and bold, for unless you conquer you will have little name for valour.' His valour was proved in Wales against Owain Glyndwr and, showing care for his troops, he pawned his own jewels and plate to pay them when his father could not.

In 1403, when sixteen, Henry fought alongside his father at Shrewsbury. Although wounded in the face by an arrow, he refused to be led away – 'If the prince flies, who will wait to end the battle? ... I may not say to my friends, "Go ye on first to the fight." Be it mine to say, "Follow me, my friends"' – and carried on fighting. The arrowhead, entering by his nose under his left eye, embedded itself into the back of his skull. The king's surgeon devised a small pair of hollow tongs the width of the arrowhead with a screw-like thread at the end of each arm and down the centre. To use it, he had to enlarge the wound by inserting well-dried 'pith of old elder' covered in linen and honey. Carefully extracting the arrowhead, he cleansed the wound with white wine and placed in it honeyed wads of flax, replaced every two days until after twenty days the wound was clean and the flesh regenerating.

Like his father he attended three Masses every day and during them would never conduct any kind of business. He worshipped in rapt devotion. John Streche, who knew the king well, wrote he spoke 'always in a low tone of voice', was moderate in food and drink, regular in fasting, liberal in giving alms and (especially in his war plans) was prudent and far-seeing. He enjoyed hunting, boating, walking, fishing and playing the harp (even on campaign in France he requested 'Thomas Walshe to procure workmen from London to make harps' for his amusement).

His sense of justice was strong – for all ranks of society. *The Brut* records one event which illustrates this. Retinues of two knights had fought, some being killed and others wounded. The knights, commanded to come to the king at Windsor, arrived as he was going to dinner. Stopping, he asked them whose men they were. They replied they were his 'liege men'.

'And what of your men?' he asked.

'They are your liege men,' came the reply.

'Then, by what authority or command had you to rise up my men to fight and slay each other in your quarrel? In this you are worthy to die.'

Into the silence he said they were either to come to accord by the time he had eaten his oysters or they would be hanged. Having savoured his oysters, the men were brought to him. When they said they had made peace, the king, speaking loudly, said that if they in the future 'or any other lords made insurrection or death of his subjects, without his command' no matter who they were, 'they should die according to the law'.

Other chroniclers said of him he was sparing with promises but true to his word once given, that he spoke always to the point and made sincere efforts to improve law and order. He had a genius for logistics and organisation and kept his army well supplied in the field all year round. His enemies spoke well of him. They said he was an honourable fighter, 'brave, loyal, upright, temperate in speech and above all unflinching in adversity'.

9 April 1413: Coronation

Passion Sunday, King Henry walked through falling snow to Westminster Abbey. Deeper drifts of snow had been cleared away and news from outside the city said men, beasts and even houses had been buried. It did not stop the streets being crowded with people to cheer and watch the procession. Among those made Knights of Bath were Edmund, Earl of March with his brother Roger, and Richard Despenser and John Holland, sons of the men executed thirteen years ago.

Candles and the packed mass of people warmed the abbey, watching as the king was led from his throne on the cloth-of-gold-draped stage to the high altar for his anointing and crowning.

Seated on a marble chair at his coronation feast in Westminster Hall, some murmured he looked like an angel. He is comely and gracious, with a handsome face which lights up with intelligence when he is speaking or deep in thought.

It being a festival, the king ate nothing at the banquet though for his delight Queen Joan had sent Brittany lampreys, a large pike and two Sussex does. There were three courses with delicacies of white meat in rice and almond milk, flampets of pork, figs boiled in small ale and fried cheese baked in a pastry coffin. Each course was preceded by subtleties made of sugar paste or jelly shaped as antelopes, eagles or swans holding mottos in their mouths, while the conduit in the palace courtyard ran with red Gascon and white Rhenish wines.

A Frenchman was overheard saying many thought the Earl of March should have been crowned and it was said that hint of murmur had made the king moody, but when Dymock cried his challenge no one rose to dispute with him.

20 May 1413: Copper Figure
King Henry has paid a London coppersmith the sum of £43 to make a figure of his mother to be placed on her grave at Leicester.

15 May–11 June 1413: First Parliament
Henry Beaufort, Chancellor and Bishop of Winchester, made the opening speech in the Painted Chamber and inevitably the Speaker's first request was 'good governance', truncated by King Henry's willing agreement to regulate household expenses, tackle his father's debts and expel aliens (reserving his right to exclude anyone it pleased him to stay). The Commons renewed the wool subsidy for four years and granted him a subsidy.

Edmund, Earl of March was acknowledged as being of full age and received his inheritance. The petition for knights and burgesses to reside in the places they were elected to represent, likewise for those who elected them, was granted. Parliament over on 9 June, the king proclaimed a general pardon. Two days later he gave the customary closing banquet at Westminster Hall, costing just over £151.

18 June 1413: Funeral
Today, Trinity Sunday, King Henry IV was buried at Canterbury Cathedral at the side of St Thomas' shrine. He had been embalmed

in myrrh, aloes, laurel and saffron and bound in linen strips and then dressed in a long robe with a crown placed on his head and his brown beard smoothed over his throat.

The corpse had journeyed by water from Westminster to Faversham, escorted by King Henry overland to the cathedral. Carried inside, the hearse was surrounded by a black cloth-covered barrier and around that ninety banners displaying the arms of all the kings of Christendom. Candles and wax torches burned day and night. On the eve of the burial, in honour of his father, Henry gave a feast which cost £127 7s 2d with £5 14s 8d extra spent on 1,320 gallons of wine.

7 July 1413: Devotional

At Canterbury, King Henry paid a devotional visit to the shrine of St Thomas and personally made an offering of two gold candlesticks and a gold head wrought with pearls and precious stones, which he had ordered at a cost of £160.

13 July 1413: Order

By order of Archbishop Arundel, all barber shops must close on Sundays; those that do not will be fined, in the belief that loss of money would have greater effect than excommunication.

1 August 1413: Windsor

Over the last two weeks, King Henry has 'rusticated' at a lodge in Windsor with his falcons and buckhounds, hunting and hawking for pleasure or watching wrestling matches in the forest. Today, he sent the monks at Westminster a huge stag which had just 'fallen to his crossbow'.

4 December 1413: Reburial

Exhuming the body of King Richard from Langley, King Henry had the body placed in a new elm coffin and placed on a black velvet-covered bier and brought to Westminster to be laid next to the body of his wife, Queen Anne. It came with 120 torches and banners borrowed from Canterbury. The king attended the funeral Mass and ordered four large tapers to burn continually at the tomb and alms to be given to the poor every week.

9 January 1414: Death Plot

Aiming to overthrow the king and reform the church, Sir John Oldcastle, a follower of Wycliffe who escaped from the Tower in

October after being imprisoned and convicted of heresy, arranged for fellow Lollards to rendezvous at Fickett's Field near Temple Bar. Warned, and saddened by the fact that one of his oldest friends plotted to kill him, King Henry with his officers waited for them to arrive and all were arrested except Oldcastle, who escaped and is outlawed.

January–February 1414: Peace?
After two months of negotiations, the truce between France and England was on 24 January extended for a further twelve months, with envoys being sent to arrange a match between King Henry and the French king's youngest daughter, twelve-year-old Katherine. Last August, Edward, Duke of York met the princess, who was prettily dressed in a silk gown interwoven with gold, and came back enthusing about her lovely figure, beauty and suitability; yet her own countrymen say she is 'like an owlet except for the feathers'.

Although the talk is all of peace, King Henry is accumulating stores of hauberks, helmets, shields, corselets, bucklers, lance-heads, gauntlets, swords, hammers, hoes, spades, caltrops and axes at Windsor and barrels of brimstone at Pountney's Inn. In the Tower he stocks bows, staves, strings, crossbows, arrows and quarrels. Tower forges are hot too, for blacksmiths sweat making guns and lances. In Bristol, siege engines and pontoons for bridging rivers are being made 'for secret reasons known to the king', and other places make and mend pavilions and tents.

12 February 1414: New Sheen
Yorkshire stone has been brought to the lovely spot on the Thames where once the manor of Sheen stood. King Henry has ordered 'a curious and costly building' to be built in among newly devised gardens.

19 February 1414: Kenilworth
At Kenilworth, King Henry has laid out a garden and is having a pretty timber 'pleasaunce' built for a banqueting house. He has cleared undergrowth and briars from the deep and large pool outside the west wall; now that it is filled with fish and fowl, he has requested a 'row-barge' be sent.

30 April–29 May 1414: Subpoena
Parliament was held in a building newly built for the purpose in the centre of Leicester, 120 feet by 40 feet, completed in twenty-four days,

roof and all. King Henry requested neither funds nor taxes, merely hoping when he needed them in future they would be forthcoming. The chancellor was given power to order the appearance of anyone by subpoena, a bid to remedy failures by sheriffs and justices in bringing criminals to book. On 16 May, the king created his brothers John and Humphrey dukes of Bedford and Gloucester respectively.

19 November–7 December 1414: 'Proper time'

Henry Beaufort opened Parliament with his text concerning how everything has its 'proper time': trees had their times for budding, blooming and bearing fruit, men had their times for peace and war, and for King Henry now was the time to recover his inheritance in France and so he would ask their advice, aid and money. Chaucer, Speaker again, suggested that although they would be happy to serve the king, he should resort first to peaceful means. A petition was granted forbidding anyone to appoint any justice of peace who resided outside the county he served. Henry Percy was granted his grandfather's title and was made Earl of Northumberland.

20 February 1415: The Holy Ghost

William Soper has made and painted many swans, antelopes and arms for the king's new great ship, called *The Holy Ghost* and lately built at Southampton.

8 June 1415: Ships

King Henry has purchased 700 ships from Holland and others from Brittany. Since April, ships found in any English haven have been impressed.

16 June 1415: Ready

Leaving London to join the fleet at Southampton, King Henry took a formal farewell of his stepmother, Queen Joan, and appointed Duke of Bedford regent. He left £200 to be distributed between his pages and boys.

20 June–6 July 1415: French Embassy

When King Henry reached Wolvesey Castle near Winchester on 20 June, he was informed ambassadors from Paris had arrived at Dover three days earlier and travelled on to Canterbury. Sending Sir John Wiltshire to escort Guillaume Boisratier, Archbishop of Bourges and his party to Winchester, they came into the hall to meet the king on 30 June. Bareheaded, he leant nonchalantly against a table, dressed head to foot in cloth of gold; his throne beside him was draped in the same. Bidding his visitors rise, he gave them a gracious welcome and after taking their letters, took wine and spice with them before going to Mass.

Their next interview was in the king's chamber. He sat on a throne beside his royal bed. The archbishop, saying Charles VI desired peace, gave his offer: if the king disbanded the army he had mustered, Charles would cede Aquitaine and provide 800,000 gold francs in dower for Princess Katherine. After the king commented he thought his cousin of France would also have discussed Normandy, the exchange turned heated. A day later the archbishop promised to throw in Limoges and Tulle and raise the dowry to 850,000 gold crowns.

On the last day appointed for a final reply, the French dined with King Henry after Mass. Bishop Beaufort asked for a fifty-year truce without prejudice to Henry's rights to the French crown and suggested 30 November as the date for bringing the princess, her jewels and dower to England. The French argued the time was much too short, even for coining the money.

King Henry, losing his temper, said he was the rightful King of France and meant to have the crown. The archbishop retorted he did not even have the right to the crown of England and they should be treating with the heirs of Richard. In a rage the king ordered the French to leave and stormed abruptly out of the room. Bishop Beaufort, staying behind, said it was obvious King Henry had to have recourse by means other than peace to regain Aquitaine, Normandy, Anjou, Touraine, Poitou, Maine and Ponthieu and, God willing, the crown of France. The archbishop, completely losing his self-control, shouted the French were unafraid; let Henry come on and he would be driven back, captured or killed.

5 August 1415: Southampton Plot

Richard of York, Earl of Cambridge and younger brother of Edward, Duke of York, was today beheaded. At the trial before his peers at Southampton Castle, it was revealed he had plotted to assassinate the king and his brothers and place the Earl of March on the throne. The latter himself revealed the plot to the king on 31 July. Co-conspirator Baron Scrope, particularly loved and trusted by the king, was dragged through the town on a hurdle before he was hanged and beheaded with the earl; Sir Thomas Grey was beheaded three days earlier.

11 August 1415: Sailed

King Henry embarked in his flagship *Trinity Royal*, at 540 tons one of the largest ships ever built, leading the fleet of fifteen hundred. Its mainsail, painted with the three lions of England and three *fleurs-de-lis* of France, billowed in the wind. The gold crown adorning the topcastle and the crowned leopard at the deck-head shone in the sun. Passing the Isle of Wight, the sailors were heartened by the good omen of swans swimming around the fleet, the swan being a personal device of the king. Making fair sail, the fleet set course for Harfleur.

22 September 1415: Surrender

After underground mines had shaken the walls, Harfleur citizens surrendered. Unclothed, they emerged with halters about their necks and asked for the king's protection. After they were divided into those allowed to stay and those asked to depart (with as much as they could carry), King Henry appointed the Earl of Dorset governor of the town. Meanwhile, many men have perished by a flux of the bowels including Michael de la Pole, Earl of Suffolk three days before the surrender and Richard Courtenay, Bishop of Norwich two days before that, the latter nursed by the king himself.

23 November 1415: Agincourt Celebrations

Riding into Blackheath from Eltham Palace, King Henry was met at ten o'clock by the Mayor of London and aldermen all dressed in 'orient-grained' scarlet, with 400 commoners in dark mulberry. Well mounted, they waited to escort him into London, crowds gathering to celebrate his return after the 'glorious field' of Agincourt on 25 October.

The king's face was grave, his demeanour quiet. Refusing to wear his armour or his dented helmet, he wore a simple gown of purple and had ordered there should be no ditties, only praise and thanks given to God, but it did not stop the people cheering and cheering their hero king.

At Agincourt, the king had received repeated blows upon his armour and helmet, at one point being beaten to his knees, while protecting his brother Humphrey who had fallen senseless at his feet. While the king protected his brother, he was in turn protected by his cousin Edward, Duke of York, who in so doing was killed by the Duke of Alencon. Edward's dukedom passes to Richard, the four-year-old son of the Earl of Cambridge, recently executed.

As King Henry and his small entourage, with the prisoners Charles, Duke of Orleans and Louis, Count of Vendome, entered onto London

Bridge, they were met by a giant porter taller than the walls; his gigantic wife bore the royal arms. Around them trumpets, clarions and horns harmonised to welcome them to the *Civitas Regis Justicie* (the City of the King of Justice). On each side of the drawbridge, two wooden pillars, covered with linen painted to look like white marble and jasper, bore the king's beasts: on the right the antelope holding a sceptre; on the left a lion holding a staff and royal standard unfurled. Further on, an armoured St George greeted them, on his head a laurel crown studded with gems. Behind him a tapestry depicted a multitude of glittering red-crossed shields. A choir of boys dressed as angels, wings glittering and sprigs of laurel in their hair, sang 'Our king went forth to Normandy' and thanked God for his victory. By the conduit on Cornhill a choir of Old Testament prophets, housed in a crimson pavilion, sang psalms. Dressed in gold coats and mantles, they released a great quantity of sparrows and to the king's surprise some of the birds descended onto his breast, some upon his shoulders while others circled around in 'twisted flight'. He was offered wine from the conduit and a dish of wafers of bread and silver leaves mimicking Melchizedek's reception of Abraham after his victory over the Four Kings.

So great were the crowds in Cheapside it was only with difficulty the retinue passed through, with all the windows in upper rooms packed with cheering people. The city wore 'its brightest aspect' and the happiness of the people was tangible but the king remained impassive.

At the Cross in Cheap a three-storeyed building with turrets and battlements spanned the street, built from planks and painted linen made to look like white marble threaded with green and crimson jasper. As the king halted, six citizens came through the gates and gave him two gold basins filled with gold. On a stage in front, a chorus of virgins sang and danced to drums and golden viols. By the conduit at the west end of Cheap, a tower erected there had a canopy painted with sky and clouds supported by four angel posts, and an archangel at the summit. Beneath the canopy a bright sun sat on a throne, while angels sang and played musical instruments. Pavilions round it held maidens who, using cups in their hands, blew forth golden leaves to drift around the king. At St Paul's the king dismounted and made offerings at the Holy Cross, the tomb of St Erkenwald and the high altar before leaving to dine at Westminster.

24 November 1415: Remembrance

A solemn Requiem Mass was held at St Paul's for all those – on both sides – who had been killed at Agincourt. Afterwards, the body of Edward, Duke of York was carried to Fotheringhay to be buried in the choir of the church of St Mary. The duke enjoyed quoting verses of Geoffrey Chaucer; when Henry was still a prince Edward had written a treatise in English on hunting called *The Master of Game* and dedicated it to him.

18 December 1415: Sudden Death

Dauphin Louis, one month short of his eighteenth birthday, died of dysentery, though he had not fought at Agincourt but stayed with his father at Rouen.

21–25 August 1416: Naval Victory

News reached England of a great naval victory won by John, Duke of Bedford on 21 August. King Henry, already on his way to Canterbury, gave great thanks at a solemn service in Canterbury Cathedral. Emperor Sigismund, on an extended visit from Germany, was present and his servants let fall along the streets some farewell lines in Latin telling England to rejoice in her glorious victory.

Two days later both monarchs arrived at Dover. The emperor set sail for Calais to lodge in the Prince's Inn in the Staple. King Henry rode to Sandwich where his fleet of forty vessels awaited him and at noon he embarked. Soon after sailing the wind dropped and sailors had to take to the oars but with the help of the tide made Calais in twelve hours.

Sigismund awaited the king on the beach. They embraced and walked through the town chatting and joking, Sigismund advising the king he should keep Calais and Dover as sure as his two eyes, it being an easy crossing. In Calais workmen had been busy making repairs to walls and buildings and tiling roofs. Provisions had been sent including spices. Tents and pavilions were set up, one as a chapel in front of the castle and another as a hall. A new stone house 70 feet by 23 feet had been built to house Henry's suite, although he and his inner court lodged in the castle.

9–13 October 1416: Truce

In Calais, the negotiations between France and England ended in a short truce until Candlemas that encompassed all the coastline to the entrance of the Mediterranean. As French envoys left the town frontier to the west, the Duke of Burgundy approached from the east. King Henry threw a great banquet for the duke in front of the castle before he left on 13 October. Rumour has it Duke John intends to support the king in his claim to the French crown and will render him formal homage as his sovereign when he gains it.

19 October–18 November 1416: Sixth Parliament

In his speech to open Parliament, Bishop Henry reminded all that King Henry in his first parliament had restored good government, in his second made good laws and in his third asked their support to recover his rights. In this sixth parliament he hoped to make war to gain peace and enable him to proclaim it in his seventh.

The anniversary of Agincourt was celebrated with a *Te Deum* in the royal chapel.

King Henry granted petitions ruling that employers will no longer be fined for paying wages higher than the scale fixed in 1388 and that shipowners must be compensated for the time their vessels are impressed in the king's service. On the parliament's last day the king granted his uncle Thomas Beaufort, Earl of Dorset the title of Duke of Exeter with £1,000 a year for himself and his heirs.

10 Feb 1417: Goose Feathers

By order of the king, sheriffs are to oversee that six wing feathers are plucked from every goose, except breeders, and packed and forwarded to London 'for winging arrows'.

14 March 1417: The Gracedieu

To Robert Berd, £500 for the king's great ship *The Gracedieu* newly built at Southampton.

29 June 1417: Channel Victory!

Patrolling the seas to protect vessels sailing to join the fleet growing at Southampton, at daybreak John, Earl of Huntingdon came across a fleet of twenty-six ships, commanded by a bastard son of Louis II, Duke of Bourbon. Nine Genoese carracks engaged to attack, packed with Biscayan, Spanish and Genoese crossbowmen. They at first inflicted grievous suffering on the sailors. Grappling at close quarters, English sailors turned the tide and after three hours of fierce fighting the English captured four of the carracks (which will be added to the fleet), the French commander Percival and the French crews' wages; the other ships dispersed and fled.

30 July 1417: Embarkation

At Portsmouth, King Henry embarked on board his flagship ready to lead his fleet numbering 1,500 vessels great and small, conveying 17,000 men-at-arms and archers, along with smiths, carpenters and miners. To the sound of trumpet and clarion, they sailed, bright with heraldic devices on sails, pennons and mastheads but their destination has been kept a secret.

10 August 1417: Tidings
A letter from King Henry to the Mayor of London arrived today to say the town of Touques and castle of Bonneville capitulated without a blow being struck. The road to Caen lies open.

September 1417: The Foul Raid
When Archbishop Bowet, old with sight failing, heard two large bodies of Scots had entered England, he led thousands of his tenants to fight the division led by the Earl of Douglas and forced them into ragged flight, leaving their baggage behind. The Scottish force led by the Duke of Albany attacked Berwick and was seen off by Robert Umfraville. Joined by men north of the Trent rushing to arms, the Scots are now harassed around Selkirk, Jedburgh, Lauderdale and Teviotdale.

19 September 1417: News
A letter has come from King Henry that the castle of Caen yielded on St Cuthbert's Day, 4 September, 'with right little death of our people'.

14 December 1417: 'Act like God'
After being captured in Powys, and despite being badly wounded while resisting arrest, John Oldcastle was brought before Parliament on 14 December and asked if he could show good cause why sentence of death should not be carried out on him. He defiantly declared that those who desired to be like God should act like God and be merciful. Pressed, he said he recognised no judge present while King Richard was alive in Scotland. He was immediately sent to St Giles Field where a gallows had been prepared for him. Saying he would rise again on the third day, he was suspended by an iron chain and burned, uttering no word or cry.

21 July 1418: Royal Letter
The list of towns taken by King Henry continues to grow: Bayeux, Lisieux, Louviers (where he hanged eight gunners who nearly killed him) and now Pont L'Arche. At his first coming to the town and seeing how well defended the bridge was, he blew the retreat and 'recoiled almost a mile backward' and made camp in a pleasant place by the riverside. 'During the night, with boats and barges, hogsheads and pipes', he conveyed a great part of his company over the broad river

and the next day they were able to assault the town on two sides. The road to Rouen lies open.

19–20 January 1419: Rouen
After a bitter six-month siege begun on the last day of July, Rouen has fallen. King Henry now controls the whole of Normandy. The day after the city surrendered, the king rode through the gates on a black horse, trapped in black damask with a gold breast-cloth. He insisted on no pipes, no clarions, nor ceremony. Alighting at the west door of the cathedral, he knelt in prayer at the high altar and when Mass was over rode to the castle. Only nine persons were excluded from his mercy and the populace welcomed him as their king.

30 May 1419: Negotiations
An area at Meulan on the River Seine was palisaded and sharp stakes driven into the river bed and trenches dug to create three zones: French, English and a neutral area for negotiations to take place. In 'England', King Henry's pavilion of blue and green velvet was embroidered with an antelope drawing a horse-mill on one side and on the other an antelope sitting on a high stage with an olive branch in its mouth and the motto 'After busy labour comes victorious rest'. At the summit was a great gold eagle 'whose eyes were orient diamonds that glistened and shone over the whole field'.

In 'France', King Charles' pavilion was blue velvet embroidered with *fleurs-de-lis* and a winged white hart at its summit made of silver with enamelled wings.

Between the two camps was a tent of purple velvet for the meeting, and on the appointed day King Henry with his brothers, uncles and other nobles entered the park and took his lodging; likewise into their pavilion went Queen Isabeau, her husband having fallen ill of his 'old disease', with the Duke of Burgundy and Princess Katherine. At a signal, all left their pavilions: at a designated spot, King Henry met and kissed the queen's hand; the Duke of Burgundy bowed his head and crooked his knee as the king embraced him and as King Henry kissed Katherine and took her hand, everyone noted the sweetness of her 'maiden blush' and how it charmed the king, who appeared captivated. In the central pavilion, two thrones had been erected about twelve feet apart.

September 1419: Accusation
Queen Joan, the king's stepmother, accused of plotting 'the death and destruction' of the king by vile witchcraft and sorcery, was arrested and imprisoned at Pevensey Castle.

10 September 1419: Montereau

Sixteen-year-old Dauphin Charles met with John, Duke of Burgundy under safe-conduct on the bridge at Montereau and had him murdered by one of his attendants.

20 September 1419: Alliance

Queen Isabeau has written to King Henry requesting a return to the negotiating table and urging his help in avenging the death of the Duke of Burgundy. Philip, the new Duke of Burgundy, vowing vengeance, also wishes to ally with the king.

17 January 1420: Disinherited

From Troyes, King Charles VI issued a proclamation declaring the Dauphin Charles unworthy to follow him on the throne of France after murdering the Duke of Burgundy, but over half of France is controlled by the Dauphin and his Armagnac supporters.

21 May 1420: Treaty of Troyes

Though unwell, King Charles VI signed the treaty in Troyes Cathedral along with his wife, Queen Isabeau, and Philip, Duke of Burgundy. The agreement stipulates that after King Charles dies the crown will pass to Henry V and his heirs. He is also to act as regent while the French king is ill, governing with a council of French nobles. He promised to maintain existing laws and customs, Parlement in its authority and all churches, colleges and universities in their privileges. The end clause confirms that when he becomes king each realm will retain its own laws, neither being subject to the other.

2 June 1420: Royal Marriage

A coach drawn by eight snow-white English hobbies – a gift from the bridegroom – brought Princess Katherine and her mother to Troyes Cathedral, preceded by numerous minstrels. The two were married according to French custom, performed by Henri, Archbishop of Sens and the royal couple offered three nobles each with their candles and the bridegroom put thirteen nobles on the book, with 200 more given to the church. The day ended with the 'wine-cup and the blessing of the bed'.

2 October 1420: Harps

King Henry has purchased harps from William Meuston for himself and Queen Katherine, at a cost of £8 13s 4d.

1 February 1421: Arrival

So eager were the barons of the Cinque Ports at King Henry and Queen Katherine's arrival at Dover, they rushed into the sea and carried them to land on their shoulders, to an equally enthusiastic welcome from vast crowds cheering them.

22–23 February 1421: Coronation

King Henry rushed to Eltham Palace so he and Queen Katherine could enter London together for her ride to the Tower. At Blackheath, the mayor and aldermen awaited them with a large number of craft-guilds dressed in white with red hoods. To the accompaniment of minstrels the royal couple met the giants guarding the gates, who bowed in reverence to her as she entered. Her journey was interrupted by castles manned with warriors, lions rolling their eyes and angels sitting on gleaming thrones. Singing from groups of virgins, angels and apostles filled the air, while the conduits ran with wine and the streets were hung with green branches and tapestries.

Next day Queen Katherine walked from Westminster Hall between two bishops under a rich canopy. She has a gracious manner and a beautiful oval face with large dark eyes. She is tall for a woman, standing about 5 foot 6 inches, with graceful arms and feet.

At the banquet afterwards the Archbishop of Canterbury and Bishop of Winchester sat upon her right hand and the King of Scots upon her left hand. The Duke of Gloucester was server and the Earl Marshal knelt at her right, holding the sceptre. The countesses of Kent and Marshal sat at her feet.

As it was Lent, delicacies comprised fish – fresh and salt – such as pike in herbs, trout, fried plaice, fresh salmon, crabs, fried minnows, sturgeon with whelks, prawns, roast porpoise and eels roasted with lampreys. Sweets included jelly with columbine flowers, a white blancmange decorated with hawthorn leaves and haws and marchpane decorated with angels. There were three subtleties for the queen dividing the three courses: the first showed a pelican sitting on her nest with her chicks and an image of St Catherine of Alexandria holding a book in one hand while disputing with doctors; the next was a panther with the queen's badge and St Catherine with her wheel; the third was a tiger looking in a mirror and an armoured knight sitting astride a horse holding in his arms a tiger cub.

6 April 1421: Clarence Killed

King Henry and Queen Katherine, on progress in the Midlands, received news today of the death on 22 March of Thomas, Duke of Clarence while acting in the king's absence as Governor of France.

Continuing his brother's fight, the duke had gone to Angers but found it better fortified than he had expected and had withdrawn to Beaufort-en-Valle. While at dinner, captive Scots were brought before him and revealed a troop of the Dauphin's soldiers were nearby at Bauge. Impetuously, the duke rose: 'Let us go against them, they are ours.' Ordering the Earl of Salisbury to follow with the main troop, the duke set out with only a few men-at-arms, his bodyguard, the earls of Somerset and Huntingdon, and Edmund Beaufort. When Huntingdon and Gilbert Umfraville advised him he was being too rash and had too few men, he told them, 'If thou be afeared, go home thy way and keep the churchyard.'

The little party was spotted by French scouts, who raised the alarm as they raced back into town. The English followed hard on their heels but their horses refused to carry on into the storm of Scottish arrows so they dismounted. Clarence, wearing a golden coronet glittering with jewels on his helm, took the lead. After the parties charged at each other and engaged in desperate hand-to-hand fighting, the English were overwhelmed, being outnumbered at least three-to-one. The king's brother was the first to fall, along with Lord Roos and Gilbert Umfraville. The earls of Huntingdon and Somerset, Edmund Beaufort and Lord FitzWalter were taken prisoner. Those English who survived scattered in various directions, chased hotly until darkness fell and they could elude their pursuers in the woods and relay the news of what had happened.

In a bid to trap the Earl of Salisbury the French blocked all the roads to Normandy. The moment day broke the earl took his men straight through wooded country, collecting doors from houses in villages as they passed. He made for La Fleche, where he used the doors as a bridge to cross the river to get to Le Mans and safety.

10 June 1421: France

King Henry sailed today after his magnates agreed he needed to return to France fast, with a powerful force.

4 September 1421: Campaign Harp

King Henry has sent to John Bore of London for a new harp for himself with a case and twelve dozen strings.

6 December 1421: Royal Birth

At Windsor, Queen Katherine bore a son at four o'clock in the afternoon who has been named Henry after his father.

22 May 1422: Overseas

Recovered from childbirth, Queen Katherine wanted to be with her husband. Leaving his brother Humphrey as *Custos* of England, John, Duke of Bedford accompanied her and they sailed to Harfleur with a large fleet of ships full of men-at-arms and archers. From Rouen, Queen Katherine was set to travel to Meaux, which the king had been besieging on four sides since October; it surrendered on 10 May but not before young John of Cornwall, only seventeen, had his head blown off while standing next to his father, and many soldiers had died of dysentery and smallpox as well as their wounds. During the siege the king had set up markets to enable his soldiers to buy provisions.

The defenders had first asked to treat at the end of April but the king was in truculent mood for some men had taken an ass onto the ramparts, beat it till it brayed and called to the English to come and rescue their king. Many think it was more to do with his suspicion some of his own soldiers enjoyed the jibe at his expense.

30 May 1422: Pentecost

To celebrate Pentecost, King Henry joined his wife and her parents at Bois-de-Vincennes before they travelled to Paris, the English couple to the Louvre and King Charles and Queen Isabeau to their Palace of St Pol. Sitting in estate for dinner, King Henry and Queen Katherine sat in rich robes, with gold diadems decorated with precious stones and jewels, and the people of Paris murmured the king looked more like an emperor than a king. After the feast the king intends to go to the aid of the Duke of Burgundy at Cosne.

13 July 1422: Release

Lest it should be 'charge unto his conscience', King Henry has ordered Queen Joan to be freed and her goods and dower returned with full restitution. She has his full permission to employ any officer she likes so long as they are good and his liege men. With the return of all her goods she is to additionally have five or six gowns of cloth and colour of her choice to be made such as she used to wear together with horses for eleven chariots so she may remove whither she pleases.

10 August 1422: Vincennes

King Henry, when he reached Senlis, was forced to admit he was too ill to mount or ride a horse and was carried by litter to the royal castle at Bois-de Vincennes, east of Paris, for its coolness in the hot weather. Nevertheless, his sickness worsens.

31 August 1422: Death of Henry V

Realising King Henry was dying, John and Humphrey raced to his bedside along with his closest friends the earls of Salisbury and Warwick. They embraced him and wept when they saw the extent of his agony. He, with neither sad countenance nor sorrow, comforted them, telling them his last wishes. Tears rolling down their faces, they promised to observe all he said. He recited the seven psalms, received the sacrament and died as if he was merely going to sleep. He was a fortnight short of his thirty-sixth birthday.

Henry VI

1422–1461

John Blackman, a chaplain to King Henry, wrote a memorial in which he praised his king for being a 'simple and upright' man who, fearing God, would 'rather pray than practise vain sports and pursuits … [he was] continually occupied in prayer or reading scriptures or chronicles … counselling the young to leave vice and follow virtue and admonishing his elders'. At times he acted like a monk, 'rising quickly at table, observing silence and giving thanks to God'. In church or chapel, he never sat but knelt all service with bared head, eyes and hands upturned whispering with the priest the prayers and gospels; when engaged in such devotion he went always bareheaded, even when riding, 'so that many times he would let his royal cap drop to the ground even from his horse's back unless it were quickly caught by his servants'. He would suffer neither hawks nor blades to be brought into church, he never walked to and fro as some did, and in his crown he had crosses set rather than flowers or leaves.

Henry VI was chaste and pure, and so modest he utterly avoided any unguarded sight of naked women 'so as not to be snared by unlawful desire'. One Christmas a great lord thought to entertain him with young ladies dancing bare-bosomed but he averted his eyes and angrily left the room. Another time, riding near the warm baths at Bath, the king saw naked men bathing and found such nudity offensive and displeasing. He safeguarded the chastity of his own servants, keeping careful watch through hidden windows lest any of his men should fall, and his half-brothers were put under care of priests during boyhood. The only oath he uttered was 'forsooth', and he bitterly rebuked anyone who swore.

Not coveting wealth, he was bountiful in giving. In fact, he gave away more royal land than any of his predecessors, leading to spiralling debt, and many believed all his household stole from him.

But continuing with John Blackman: he showed humility even in the clothes he wore, which from youth was a long gown with a rolled hood like a townsman and full coat reaching below his knees, with black, round-toed shoes or boots like a farmer.

At principal feasts of the year, he would wear his crown and a rough hair shirt beneath his robes to restrain his body from excess. On high days and Sundays he devoted himself wholly to hearing divine office and praying. He avoided banquets, vain talk and 'used but very brief speech' and then usually only to enlighten others. Sir Richard Tunstall said that once while in his chamber at Eltham reading his holy books there was a knock at the door from a mighty duke of the realm and the king said, 'They do so interrupt me that by day or night I can hardly snatch a moment to be refreshed by reading of any holy teaching without disturbance.'

When asked how he dealt with the troubles that pressed upon him, the king replied, 'The kingdom of heaven, unto which I have devoted myself always from a child, do I call and cry for. For this kingdom which is transitory and of the earth I do not greatly care.' Many of his contemporaries regarded King Henry as saintly, but the chronicler Hall wrote of him that he was governed by those 'he should have ruled and bridled' and 'studied only the health of his soul'.

6–7 November 1422: Funeral of Henry V

Two rings of mourners, with 200 noble torchbearers around them, kept vigil all night around the hearse of King Henry V in St Paul's Cathedral.

The next day, eight chamber knights carried the king's coffin from St Paul's to the open funeral carriage. Four knights carried a gold silk canopy above the life-sized crowned figure made from leather, dressed in regal robes, laid on top of the coffin covered with gold-embroidered vermilion silk. Six horses drew the carriage towards Westminster Abbey through black-draped streets of silent and mourning citizens, a torchbearer standing outside every house. Knights and pages carrying his hatchments followed the coffin. Around the chariot rode 500 men-at-arms all in black armour, lances held pointing downwards, their horses with sable trappings. Around them a great company clothed in white, all bearing lit torches, was followed by the king's household, officers of state and the royal family in black. At the west door the clergy met the bier and the coffin was taken from the chariot and borne up the nave to the high altar, the king's three chargers behind it ridden by armoured men bearing the arms of England and France. After the Requiem Mass, the body with sceptre and rod was laid to rest between the shrine of St Edward and the Chapel of the Virgin; his shield, helm and blue-velvet covered saddle were placed above.

5 December 1422: Protector
All Parliament agreed Henry's uncle, John, Duke of Bedford should be appointed protector and defender of the realm, but with Charles VI dying on 21 October he has assumed the regency of France. He therefore decreed the title of protector fall to his brother Humphrey, Duke of Gloucester while he is absent overseas.

13 May 1423: Marriage
In a rumoured love match, Duke John married Anne of Burgundy, daughter of Duke John the Fearless, in Troyes Cathedral.

17 November 1423: Baby Tales
Today, sitting on his mother's lap, a lively and happy Henry was brought from Windsor, through London to Westminster and into the Painted Chamber. It is a different story to three days ago, when, crying and screaming, he refused to travel further. In a few days Henry goes to Waltham Cross, thereafter to Hertford.

21 February 1424: Governess
Lady Alice Butler, appointed Henry's governess by the council, was granted licence to 'reasonably chastise' him from time to time as might be required without 'afterwards being molested or injured on account of such correction'.

18 October 1424: Burgundy
Embarking today for Hainault, Humphrey, Duke of Gloucester since marrying Jacqueline, Countess of Hainault and Holland has been brought into his wife's dispute with the Duke of Burgundy over her lands. Duke John is displeased for their actions run counter to England's foreign policy.

19 January 1425: Death
Edmund Mortimer, Earl of March died of plague at Trim Castle in Ireland. Leaving no issue, his estate and titles descend to Richard, 3rd Duke of York and son of his sister Anne.

28 April 1425: Royal Steps
Having been brought from Windsor, three-year-old Henry was carried to the west door of St Paul's Cathedral where, between his uncles the dukes of Gloucester and Exeter, he walked to the steps of the choir before being carried to the high altar. People who saw him, whether in

the streets or in the cathedral, said he was the very image of his father and had his lovely countenance.

1 March 1426: Bigamy
Jacqueline, Duchess of Gloucester has been told by the Pope she is still married to the Duke of Brabant and her marriage to Humphrey is invalid.

19 May 1426: Henry Knighted
On Whitsunday at Leicester, where Parliament remains sitting, the Duke of Bedford knighted Henry. Forthwith he knighted thirty-four others including Richard, Duke of York, John Mowbray, son and heir of the Duke of Norfolk, and the sons of the earls of Ormond, Oxford, Westmorland and Northumberland.

Enmity between Lord Humphrey and Cardinal Henry Beaufort has led the ordinary people to call the Leicester assembly the 'Parliament of Bats'. Having flared into violence, their servants were ordered to leave knives and swords behind; instead they took bats and staves. Duke John rebuked the lords generally – though his criticism was truly aimed at the two culprits – for allowing 'private malice and inward grudge' to encourage people to fight during a time of war.

31 December 1426: Death
Thomas Beaufort, Duke of Exeter and Earl of Dorset, died at Greenwich aged forty-nine. He is to be buried at the abbey of Bury St Edmunds. A widower without issue, his titles now become extinct.

9 January 1428: Disruption
Respectably attired women today disrupted Parliament and presented letters reproaching Duke Humphrey for not helping his wife, Jacqueline, imprisoned by the Duke of Burgundy. They complain his love is cold, shown by his publicly living in adultery with Dame Eleanor Cobham. Remarriage coming under debate, the lords decided no man could marry a Queen of England without special licence and royal assent, to be given after a king reaches the age of discretion.

3 November 1428: Siege of Orleans
After a stray cannon ball carried away most of his face on 27 October, Thomas Montagu, Earl of Salisbury died today at Orleans and will be brought home for burial at Bisham Abbey. He had no issue by his second wife, Alice Chaucer. By his first wife, Eleanor Holland, he leaves one

daughter, Alice, who is married to Richard Neville, son of Earl Ralph of Westmorland, who by right of his wife becomes 5th Earl of Salisbury.

8 November 1428: Lucky Escape
In the early evening, the Duke of Norfolk boarded his barge at St Mary Overy to go to Greenwich, having to pass through London Bridge. By misguidance of the steersmen, the barge knocked into one of the bridge's piles and overturned. Nearly all were drowned except the duke and a few others who managed to leap upon the piles, after which they were drawn up on ropes by people above and saved.

17 July 1429: False King
Dauphin Charles was crowned as Charles VII at Reims Cathedral after a young maid, called *La Pucelle*, brought new heart to the French at the siege of Orleans in April. The English say she dresses as a man, guiding and leading companies of men-of-war under a standard bearing the arms of France: field azure, a sword point upward in pale silver between two *fleurs-de-lis* with a crown of gold.

5–6 November 1429: Coronation
A month short of his ninth birthday, Henry rode from Kingston over London Bridge where, conducted by the mayor and aldermen in scarlet hoods, he was met by a tower of angels. Reaching the Tower in time for dinner, he emerged again after noon, wearing cloth-of-gold robes, to ride to Westminster through streets thronged with joyous people, his newly made Knights of the Bath all in blue preceding him.

Next morning dawned fair and clear for his walk to the abbey, his prelates before him, each bearing a relic except the Abbot of Westminster who carried the king's sceptre. Watched proudly by his mother, the boy was led to his throne on the high scaffold. At the congregation assenting to his coronation, Henry moved to the high altar where he humbly lay down. After praying, he was stripped to his shirt and anointed. Wearing St Edward's spurs, he was dressed in a scarlet gown with a pane of ermine. To show that virtue and the power of the crown came from the Holy Church, Curtana was laid on the high altar and blessed before he received it. St Edward's crown was placed on his head, a bishop either side helping him bear its weight. While he knelt, during Mass the Bishop of London served him wine from St Edward's chalice. At the saint's shrine his regalia was removed and he changed into rich cloth of gold and wore the crown which King Richard had made for himself.

Sitting in estate in Westminster Hall, he was served a pleasant wine and a banquet of three courses. The first included an embattled boar's head, boiled beef and mutton, stewed capons, roasted herons and cygnets, venison frumenty, a great pike and a red jelly ornamented with crowned lions. Next came chickens, bitterns, rabbits, roasted cranes, feathered peacock (feathers replaced after cooking), gilded suckling pig, a great bream, a fritter shaped like a sun with *fleurs-de-lis* and another like a leopard's head, white blancmange decorated with bars of gold and a white leche with a crowned antelope shining like gold. The third course comprised roast venison, egrets, curlew, partridges, plover, quails, snipes, larks, carp, crab, fritter crisps and a 'cold bakemeat' made like a shield quartered red and white decorated with gilt lozenges and borage flowers.

Each course was closed with a subtlety made of sugar and pastry: the first was of saints Edward and Louis blessing King Henry standing in his coat armour; the second had the king kneeling before Emperor Sigismund and his father; third was Mary, with Jesus on her lap. She held a crown while saints George and Denis knelt on either side presenting King Henry to her.

22–23 April 1430: Calais

Having spent Easter at Canterbury, King Henry rode to Dover. As the wind was fair during the night, he embarked and sailed to Calais, landing at seven o'clock in the morning. With him sailed Duke Richard of York. Duke Humphrey has been appointed regent during the king's absence.

23 May 1430: La Pucelle *Taken*

News has come from the Duke of Burgundy that Sir John of Luxembourg has taken 'the witch' called *La Pucelle d'Orleans* at the siege of Compiegne, leaving French soldiers in great despair.

28 January 1431: Order

Roger Johnson, smith of London, is ordered to press as many smiths as necessary to complete the ironwork of the tomb of King Henry V in Westminster Abbey.

30 May 1431: Joan of Arc Burned

King Henry wrote to the Duke of Burgundy to inform him that nineteen-year-old Joan, the Maid of Orleans, was burnt in the old market within the city of Rouen.

When first captured, Joan was delivered to 'the bishop of the diocese where she was taken. He, with the vicar and inquisitor of errors and heresies', called doctors and masters to interrogate her. 'She declared she was sent from God' and 'had communication personally and visible' with saints Michael, Catherine and Margaret. After confessing to her errors, she had been sentenced to 'do open penance'.

'Then the fire of her pride burst out' and she abjured her previous statements, 'obstinate in her trespasses', and was delivered to the secular authorities. Just before she burned, she said that 'the spirits which to her often did appear were evil and false, and apparent liars; and that their promise which they had made to deliver her out of captivity was false and untrue'. Tied to a tall pillar, she asked if she might hold a cross. An English soldier constructed a small cross for her which she put in the front of her dress, while two French priests held a crucifix before her while she burned.

2 December 1431: Paris Pageants

As the king approached the silver ship at the gate of St Denis, three red hearts were suddenly hung over its side by cheering people. The hearts were opened and white doves flew out, revealing a script welcoming him with all their hearts. Six bareheaded men dressed in blue with garlanded hoods came forward to hold a cloth-of-gold canopy over him. At the conduit, three mermaids swam while wildmen raced around. Next was a *tableau vivant* of Mary and the birth of Jesus, so still they looked like painted images. After the pageant of the Life of St Denis, a green hedge had been created around the Fountain of St Innocent, out of which ran harts and hounds. King Henry was presented with a hart trapped in the arms of Paris. Because of the great frost, the streets had been strewn with straw to stop the horses sliding. Riding to Notre Dame, King Henry made his offering before riding to his lodgings at the House of Tournelles. Tomorrow, he will meet his grandmother Queen Isabeau and they will ride to Bois de Vincennes to remain together until the eve of his coronation.

16 December 1431: Coronation

Accompanied by lords both from England and France, King Henry walked from the Palais de Paris to Notre-Dame where he was anointed and crowned King of France by Cardinal Beaufort. As French custom, the king offered bread and wine during the ritual. After the ceremony he departed to the palace wearing one crown and holding a sceptre; his other crown and sceptre were borne before him. Afterwards was a host of 'dainty dishes, pleasant conceits, costly wines, musical instruments and sweet harmony' at the banquet to be followed by jousts and tourneys. The king will spend Christmas at Rouen.

21 February 1432: Welcome Home

Conducted from Blackheath by the mayor and aldermen in scarlet and crafts all in white, King Henry was welcomed home at London Bridge by a mighty giant holding a drawn sword. At the drawbridge tower, Ladies Nature, Grace and Fortune presented him with the gifts of science, wisdom, prosperity and riches. Either side of the tower, seven white-dressed maidens stood singing a roundel of welcome. On the right they wore sapphire-blue baldrics and released doves denoting gifts of the Holy Ghost. Those on the left, their gowns speckled with golden stars, gave him the Gifts of Grace: the crown of glory, sceptre of clemency and pity, sword of right and victory, shield of faith, mantle of prudence, helm of health and a girdle of love and perfect peace. A tabernacle to the sciences was set up at Cornhill and at the conduit a circular pageant with a pretty child dressed like a king and around him Dame Clemency and Ladies Mercy and Truth.

After the speech the king 'rode on a quicker pace' until he came to Cheap conduit where awaited the Wells of Mercy, Grace and Pity. There goblets of water were offered, turned into wine for any who asked. Around them was an orchard of trees called Paradise. All bore leaves and fruit such as oranges, almonds, pomegranates, olives, lemons, dates, pippins, quinces, peaches and more commonly pears, apples and plums. A celestial throne awaited the king at the conduit near the gate of St Paul's with a personification of the Trinity with angels singing and playing instruments.

At the churchyard, the archbishop and bishops awaited to conduct him into the church where he made his oblations. Taking his horse at the west door of St Paul's, he rode to Westminster where the abbot and convent received him to conduct him to St Edward's shrine. The *Te Deum* finished, he left for his palace.

22 April 1433: Marriage

John, Duke of Bedford, after losing his beloved Anne to plague in Paris last November, has remarried at Therouanne, taking as his second wife Jacquetta of Luxembourg.

1–5 February 1435: Frost Fair

The winter has been so cold and severe the Thames has frozen over. Small sheep are being roasted on the ice – a view costs 6*d*; a slice of roasted meat 12*d*. Several stalls have been set up selling beer, toys and foodstuffs with everything labelled, 'Bought on the Thames'. Anyone wishing to enter the Frost Fair must pay the watermen a toll of 2*d* or 3*d*.

14 September 1435: Death

John, Duke of Bedford died, aged forty-six years, at his castle of 'Joyeux Repos' in Rouen and will be buried in the cathedral. Leaving no issue, his titles become extinct. Duke Humphrey becomes heir apparent to King Henry.

9 December 1435: Appointment

With the defection of Duke Philip of Burgundy to King Charles VII, Parliament has elected Richard, Duke of York to serve as Governor of France in place of the Duke of Bedford. With him go the earls of Salisbury and Suffolk and 8,000 men.

13 April 1436: Paris

Fighting almost to the gates of Paris, Duke Richard was unable to prevent the city falling to Charles VII. Having received neither assistance nor funds from England, he has used his own money to feed his soldiers and reinforce all the garrisons in Normandy.

27 July 1436: Calais

Duke Philip began a siege of Calais on 9 July but fled as soon as he received news of the imminent arrival of a fleet with an army commanded by Duke Humphrey, mustered at Sandwich five days ago. All those taking part have free licence to retain all they take from the Flemings.

8–9 February 1437: Funeral

Queen Katherine, who died at Bermondsey Abbey on 2 or 3 January aged thirty-six, was conveyed by water to the Church of St Katharine-by-the-Tower. A funeral service was performed before she was carried to St Paul's, and the next day she was interred in the Lady Chapel at Westminster Abbey. News has trickled out that she was secretly married to Owen Tudor and bore him children, including Edmund and Jasper. Outraged councillors have arrested Owen for violating the law and sent Edmund and Jasper to live with Katherine de la Pole, Abbess of Barking. Although rumour has it the queen died in childbirth, she had retired to Bermondsey because of illness and her will states she had suffered 'a long and grievous malady'.

10 June 1437: Death
Queen Joan, who has lived quietly for years at Nottingham Castle, died peacefully at Havering-atte-Bower, aged sixty-nine. She will be buried at Canterbury next to her husband King Henry IV.

24 October 1437: Pardon
Richard Wydeville and Jacquetta, Duchess of Bedford have been granted forgiveness by the king for marrying without his licence, albeit with a fine of £1,000. The couple are very much in love.

30 April 1439: Death
The Earl of Warwick, once the king's tutor and Lieutenant of France and Normandy since the Duke of York's commission ended, died at Rouen. Fourteen-year-old Henry, by his second wife Isabel le Despenser, succeeds to the earldom.

12 November–21 December 1439: Discord
Discord occurred in Parliament when Duke Humphrey, after criticising Cardinal Beaufort's foreign policy and involvement in war finance, accused him of taking upon himself royal estate and turning King Henry against him. The Archbishop of Canterbury and Richard, Duke of York asked for the cardinal's dismissal for inducing the king to give up his right and title to the crown of France, ignoring that King Henry had assumed personal control. However, an infectious sickness called the pestilence is killing so many that Parliament was prorogued. Those who normally kiss the king in homage asked to omit it for his health and welfare. The University of Oxford also asked the king to give Duke Humphrey thanks for his generous gift of a thousand pounds' worth of precious books.

2 July 1440: Second Appointment
Richard, Duke of York was appointed the king's governor and lieutenant general in Normandy and France for five years and goes 'over the sea with a royal power'. He will ship out from Portsmouth.

12 September–11 October 1440: Colleges
Purchasing various lands and properties, King Henry intends to found a college of priests at Eton and a college at Cambridge for a rector and twelve poor scholars.

28 October 1440: Liberated
Charles, Duke of Orleans, prisoner since a few days before his twenty-first birthday after being discovered trapped under a pile of corpses at

Agincourt, was formally given his freedom at Westminster Abbey. He is well-loved for his witty love poems, written in French and English.

6–18 November 1441: Witchcraft

Found guilty of witchcraft and treason for consorting with fortune-tellers who predicted King Henry's death from illness in July, Eleanor, Duchess of Gloucester was divorced from her husband by the Archbishop of Canterbury and sentenced to perpetual imprisonment after her penance. This was to walk from Westminster on three market days in bare feet, bareheaded, dressed in black carrying a two-pound burning taper to present on Monday at St Paul's, on Wednesday at Christchurch and on Friday at St Michael in Cornhill. So meek was she in bearing penance that many felt pity for her.

Lady Eleanor had denied the accusations made against her by fellow accused Roger Bolingbroke and Thomas Southwell. All she wanted to know, she said, was whether she would bear her husband a child; she claims the potions she bought from Margery Jourdemayn were to help her conceive.

Roger was brought into Guildhall on 18 November. He was found guilty of necromancy, sorcery and treason. At Tyburn he was hanged and quickly cut down. Viewing the burning of his bowels, he kept saying he died guiltless, had never trespassed against his king, nor ever imagined or devised an image of wax to destroy him. Thomas Southwell, before he could be arraigned, died in the Tower on 25 October. Margery, surnamed the Witch of Eye, was burnt at Smithfield.

September 1442: Pressing

Boldly rebuked by a woman of Kent for his ungodly treatment of Duchess Eleanor, and told he should allow her to be with her husband, King Henry angrily ordered her arrest. Appearing before the justices of the King's Bench and reproved for her foolhardy speaking, she answered nothing except to ask for the king's mercy. On the second day, saying only the same thing, she was sentenced to stand in a cart to travel through London to Blackheath and back again, with a paper saying she had used lewd language to the king, then to be pressed by iron on her body until she died.

30 May 1444: Death

John Beaufort, made Duke of Somerset last August, died at Wimborne aged forty. He had fallen ill on campaign but some say it was not illness that killed him, rather he took his own life out of shame that his actions had lost Guienne. He fought in the French campaigns in 1419 and he and his brother, captured by the French, had been imprisoned for seventeen years. He leaves one daughter, baby Margaret, made a ward of William de la Pole, Earl of Suffolk, famous for being knighted by his French captor for his bravery when captured in 1429.

1 February 1445: Storm

Wind, hail, snow, rain, thunder and lightning reigned for four hours this afternoon. Lightning set St Paul's great steeple alight and the people quenched it with vinegar. Much harm has been done to the lead and timber.

3–22 April 1445: Smallpox Bride

On 3 April, fifteen-year-old Margarete, niece of Charles VII, embarked for England from Harfleur. The *Cock John of Cherbourg*, captained by Collin Freon, was specially sent to transport her in comfort. Sailing between Portsmouth and Southampton, the royal fleet was serenaded by seven trumpeters aboard two Genoese galleys. For reward the queen gave them 23s 4d.

Arriving at Portchester on 10 April and having been seasick and poorly, Margarete was carried ashore by William de la Pole, newly made Marquis of Suffolk, through a tremendous storm of thunder and lightning. Crowds had gathered, braving deluge and darkness, to see the girl whose portrait has ensnared the king. Finding Margarete had contracted smallpox, her physician prescribed aromatic confections for her costing 69s 2d and King Henry removed himself to Southwick to go hunting. On 22 April, Margarete married twenty-three-year-old King Henry at Titchfield Abbey. Her wedding ring was made from the coronation ring King Henry wore in Paris, remade with a fair ruby. She gave him a lion as a wedding gift which has been sent to the Tower of London. People sighed at her beauty, relieved her face remains unmarked.

8 May 1445: Inspection

With the expectation of huge crowds turning out to watch Queen Margarete ride through London, an inspection of roofs and balconies was ordered to ensure the safety of spectators using them for vantage points and of those standing below.

28–30 May 1445: Coronation

Mayor and aldermen, dressed in blue gowns and red hoods, met Margarete at Blackheath to conduct her to the Tower. A Pageant of Peace and Plenty was set up at London Bridge entrance and a Noah's Ark on the bridge. At Leadenhall, Lady Grace awaited her, at Cornhill St Margaret, and at the Cross in Cheap was a Garden of Paradise. The queen was also charmed by the many men who wore a daisy in their bonnets.

The following afternoon the queen, all in white, set out from the Tower of London to journey to Westminster in a horse-bier with two steeds trapped in gold-powdered white damask much like the pillows she sat upon. The queen's fair hair was combed down about her shoulders and she wore a gold coronal with pearls and jewels. Through the crowded streets she was followed by seventeen chariots of ladies and all the lords on horseback. To watch her go by, King Henry stayed in the house of the goldsmith, William Flour, giving him by way of reward £13 6s 8d.

Crafts of the city lined all the way to St Paul's while around them maidens sang like angels. At the cathedral the queen climbed from her litter and walked to the high altar, where she made an offering, and then back to her bier for the journey to Westminster.

On 30 May, Margarete left the palace to walk to the abbey to be crowned by John Stafford, Archbishop of Canterbury. She wore the king's gift of a gold collar decorated with four rubies, four great sapphires and thirty-two great pearls and other pearls and the two brooches in gold decorated with rubies, pearls and diamonds which cost 2,000 marks.

Her father, Rene d'Anjou, King of Sicily and Jerusalem, sent five minstrels for the day. Two more minstrels came from the Duke of Milan, to record the event and for the three days of jousting which will ensue.

22 December 1445: Peace
In the interests of peace, King Henry has written confidentially to King Charles that he would cede Maine and Anjou to the queen's father.

9 April 1446: Decisions
In Parliament, the announcement was made that King Henry has agreed to meet personally with King Charles VII in October. The Lords said they wanted it made clear all decisions on foreign affairs now laid with the king, who is determined to have peace.

10 February–3 March 1447: Died of Grief
Parliament was summoned by King Henry to meet at Bury St Edmunds on 10 February and all knights ordered to come armed. Eight days later arrived Duke Humphrey, hoping to gain a pardon for his wife who has been transferred to the Isle of Man, but when he was half a

mile away a king's messenger arrived to advise him that he should go to his lodgings and take his meal. While he was eating, John, Viscount Beaumont entered and arrested him for high treason, put him under house arrest and took away his officers.

The shock caused the duke, in his fifty-seventh year, to be overcome by illness, deeply aggrieved that the king could believe he would conspire to kill him. He died suddenly at three in the afternoon on 23 February, although people whisper that he was murdered. The next day, lords and knights came to view his dead body. Towards nightfall he was disembowelled, rolled in cerecloth and chested in lead. Two days later, with twenty torches, he was carried to Greyfriars for the dirge and Mass before being removed for burial at the Abbey of St Albans.

On 3 March an Act was passed created to debar Lady Eleanor from claiming any dower from her husband's estate as if she was legally dead. It also became clear that before he had even died some of the duke's estates had already been granted to the queen, nobles and the king's colleges.

11 April 1447: Bed Bequest
Cardinal Henry Beaufort died aged seventy-three years at Winchester. In his will, most bequests were for charity but to Queen Margarete, whom he esteemed, he left the bed of Damascus cloth and arras hangings of the chamber in which she slept when she visited him at Waltham and which he kept solely for her use. He also left the king £2,000 which Henry refused to take, saying, 'He was always a good uncle to me whilst he lived. God reward him!' He nonetheless agreed it could be bestowed on his two colleges at Eton and Cambridge.

31 March 1448: Creation
Edmund Beaufort was created Duke of Somerset, the title his brother held, and has been appointed to replace the Duke of York as commander in France.

15 April 1448: Queen's College
Queen Margarete, emulating her husband's piety, has resolved to establish a college near her husband's at Cambridge and laid the first stone today.

23 July 1449: Warwick
After the death of Henry, Earl of Warwick's infant daughter, the earldom passed to his sister Anne, and by right of his wife Richard Neville becomes Earl of Warwick.

29 October 1449: Rouen Lost
The Duke of Somerset, caving in to pressure from the citizens – and principally his wife – surrendered Rouen to King Charles VII.

Public Outcry

The people of England were sorely unhappy with the loss of lands in France, first manifested by the murder of Adam, Bishop of Chichester at Portsmouth on 9 January 1450, held responsible as a member of the government which delayed sending help to Normandy. In Parliament the Commons accused William de la Pole, Duke of Suffolk of losing Maine and Anjou owing to his negotiations for the king's marriage. Although he had robustly defended himself, King Henry, to appease the Commons, ordered him to the Tower, consenting to banish him for five years from 1 May.

On 4 May, shocking news came that on May Day William had boarded his ship at Dover and been intercepted in the Channel by *Nicolas of the Tower*. Asking to speak with the duke, the captain sent a boat across to fetch him. As he boarded, the captain called him a traitor and pushed him back into the boat. He was beheaded with a rusty sword after half a dozen strokes. Taking his russet gown and velvet doublet, sailors laid his body on the sands at Dover, placing his head on a pole alongside.

Exposed to French attacks, the people of the southern coast organised themselves into a militant band under a leader calling himself John Mortimer who in a document of 'points, cause and mischiefs' made accusations that as the king swears to keep the law so he cannot make and break it as he pleases; that the king should understand his false council has lost his law, the sea and France, and in taking his revenue has made it so he is unable to pay for his meat or drink; and that they accused not all lords, only those found guilty by just and true enquiry. It also requested that those who labelled the 'Good Duke' a traitor be punished. The document being signed by a man named Mortimer, King Henry blamed the Duke of York for it, especially as it contained a request for the king to have about his noble person the dukes of York, Exeter, Buckingham and Norfolk as the true blood of his realm.

Shopkeepers, craftsmen, landowners and peasants assembled at Blackheath on 11 June. As if in war they made a field, diked it and staked it, and kept military order. A day later, King Henry rode out fully armed and asked them to name the persons they would charge at law; they offered his Lord High Treasurer James Fiennes, Lord Saye and his confessor, William Ayscough, Bishop of Salisbury. In front of them, the king ordered Lord Saye taken to the Tower. Lodging at Greenwich that night, the king received news the Bishop of Salisbury had been murdered in Wiltshire. Fearing for his own life, King Henry decided to leave London and take refuge at Kenilworth.

Aware the king had left London, on 3 July the rebels decided to move into Southwark where Mortimer set up his headquarters at the White Hart Inn. The next day, cutting the ropes of the drawbridge, he crossed into London and struck London Stone with his sword, declaring himself Lord Mayor. At the Guildhall he ordered Lord Saye to be brought before him. Declaring the lord guilty of corruption and treason, he sent him to be beheaded at Cheapside with his son-in-law, William Crowmer, Sheriff of Kent. Their heads were placed on pikes and paraded through the streets, made to look like they were kissing, before being set on London Bridge.

When rebels began looting the city, any sympathy they might have won was lost. That night, as they returned to Southwark, the bridge was closed and barricaded. The next day many were wounded and killed trying to keep rebels from crossing. Attempting to find a way to end the bloodshed, Archbishop John Kemp issued pardons to all rebels who would return home and they were snapped up. King Henry revoked them a few days later – not that it mattered to John Mortimer, for his name was Jack Cade, thereby making his pardon void. On 12 July, he was discovered hiding in a garden. Wounded while resisting arrest, he died before he reached London but the king insisted on putting him on trial and beheading the dead body at Newgate.

On 12 August, to add to general discontent, Edmund, Duke of Somerset lost Cherbourg and England had now 'not a foot of land in Normandy'. Public opinion was that Charles VII would turn his attention to Aquitaine. To add further to public censure, King Henry appointed Duke Edmund Constable of England on 21 September.

Richard, Duke of York and Lieutenant General of Ireland, left Dublin to attend Parliament and reached London on 27 September. He went directly to see the king at Westminster Palace where he complained about the lack of assistance sent to him in Ireland, the slanders said about him in court and the attempt to arrest him when he landed. Insisting he was a loyal subject, he urged the king to arrest those who *were* corrupt, offering his aid. The king thanked him, saying he intended to make the duke a member of his council and that he had already sent out the Duke of Somerset with a commission of oyer and terminer in Kent to investigate miscarriages of justice, extortions, trespasses and oppressions. After the Commons in Parliament put forward petitions of corruption and removal of certain persons from government, King Henry countered he only had virtuous persons about him and knew 'no cause sufficient why they should be removed'. On 1 December, had not the Earl of Devon smuggled him to safety, the Duke of Somerset would have been abducted from his lodgings at Blackfriars.

2 February 1451: Harvest of Heads

At Canterbury, King Henry and the Duke of Somerset, together with many lords and justices, held sessions for four days. There were so many beheadings the men of Kent called it the 'harvest of heads'.

16 February–1 March 1452: Brent Heath

Duke Richard, having gathered a force in the marches, moved towards London but was denied access through London. Crossing over Kingston Bridge, he made camp at Brent Heath. King Henry, with the Duke of Somerset, gathered a force which followed him and camped at Blackheath. Sending the bishops of Winchester and Ely and the earls of Salisbury and Warwick to mediate with him, Duke Richard told them he had no quarrel with the king but accused Duke Edmund of turning the king against him, of misconduct in France and of grievously oppressing the commonalty.

After they returned, King Henry sent Duke Richard a message that he had committed Somerset to ward to answer his charges in Parliament. Disbanding his army, the Duke of York went to the king's tent. Contrary to the royal promise, the Duke of Somerset was attending the king and Duke Richard was sent to the Tower.

23 November 1452: Honours

Today, King Henry honoured his two half-brothers by creating Edmund Earl of Richmond and Jasper Earl of Pembroke.

12 May 1453: Lost Honour

Richard, Duke of York was replaced by James, Earl of Wiltshire and Ormond in the lieutenancy of Ireland.

2 July 1453: Replaced

Edmund, Duke of Somerset was given the Duke of York's position as justice of the forests south of the Trent.

17 July 1453: Castillon

Sixty-six-year-old war veteran and hero John Talbot, Earl of Shrewsbury was killed today. He had gone to the aid of Bordeaux last October, heeding the city's request for help to be freed of French rule. In a short while he had taken back control of the city and most of western Gascony and the wine fleet was once again sailing to England.

On 8 July, the French king retaliated by besieging Castillon with an army and 300 new guns. Responding to pleas for help, the earl set off ahead of his main army with a troop of 500 men-at-arms and 800 archers. Seeing the French apparently retreating and without waiting for the larger part of his army, the earl ordered his men to battle to pursue them. They ran full tilt into the French guns and were decimated, each gun killing six at once. The earl had his horse killed from underneath him and while he was pinned down a French soldier dispatched him with an axe. As the rest of the army caught up, they were mown down along with the earl's son, Viscount Lisle. The battle lasted just over an hour. Only Calais now remains to England.

13 October 1453: Royal Birth

Queen Margarete gave birth to a prince at Westminster to great rejoicing, naming him Edward. The Duke of Somerset has been asked to be his godfather (which set tongues wagging that he is the father). The Duchess of Buckingham has been asked to be godmother. His christening mantle, to wrap him after his immersion, is embroidered with pearls and lined with fine white linen and cost a massive £554 16s 8d.

27 March 1454: Protector

In light of the shock revelation of how severely ill the king is after a deputation visited him at Windsor on 25 March to inform him of the death of the Archbishop of Canterbury, the council appointed Richard, Duke of York protector, defender and chief councillor of the realm, to last either until the king recovers or his son, Prince Edward, created Prince of Wales, reaches his years of discretion. The Commons petitioned for removal of the Duke of Somerset from office.

It has been revealed openly that King Henry has been in a catatonic state since at least mid-July last, that he is unable to speak, walk or eat, having to be spoon fed and taken care of as if he was a little child. Duke Richard has appointed three physicians and two surgeons to watch over him.

25–31 December 1454: Recovery

On Christmas Day at Greenwich, King Henry started to recover his wits. On 31 December, Queen Margarete brought the prince to her husband, telling him she had named him Edward. He held up his hand and thanked God, saying he 'never knew him till that time, nor knew what was said to him, nor where he had been while he had been sick'.

5 February 1455: Released

Without Parliament's assent, Queen Margarete ordered the release of Edmund, Duke of Somerset from the Tower. Nobles and commons murmur that the queen and duke govern as they did before.

22–23 May 1455: First Blood

With rumours swirling that the dukes of Somerset and Exeter are persuading King Henry to destroy the three Richards – Duke of York, Earl of Salisbury and the latter's son the Earl of Warwick – and the king summoning a great council to meet at Leicester in May, those allied to the latter began raising troops. In response the king raised his own force.

Duke and earls marched to intercept the king at St Alban's. On 22 May, the king sent a herald to Duke Richard to keep the peace. His reply was he would dismiss his troops if King Henry delivered up Duke Edmund and submitted him to the law. The king replied he would rather die than give up a lord faithful to him. Suddenly, houses and fences demolished, the Earl of Warwick's men rushed into St Peter's Street, slaying all who resisted them. Reaching the abbey where the king's banner was displayed, the lords around him were picked off by archers, felling Duke Edmund; Henry, son of Hotspur and Earl of Northumberland; Humphrey, Earl of Stafford, son of the Duke of Buckingham; and John, Lord Clifford. The king, left standing under his banner, was nicked in the neck by an arrow.

Next morning, while showing great deference, Duke Richard escorted the king from the abbey to London, Warwick riding ahead bearing the king's sword of state. They lodged him in the Bishop of London's palace and called a Parliament to be held at Westminster in July to discuss the rule and funding of the royal household, the defence of Calais and payment of its soldiers.

18–31 July 1455: Undone

In Parliament it was affirmed 'all thing done' at St Alban's 'well done, and nothing done there never after this time to be spoken of'.

Humphrey, Duke of Gloucester was exonerated and declared the king's 'true liegeman until his death'.

23 October 1455: Murder Most Foul

Thomas, son of the Earl of Devonshire, went with sixty men-at-arms to Nicholas Radford's place and, setting the gatehouse on fire to get the gates opened, rode in to loot the house and take the horses. Abducting the old and infirm man, they made him walk until he fell and then cut his throat where he lay. At two after midnight a messenger was sent with the news to the Duke of York; it is 'afeared' the king at Hertford is sick again.

12–19 November 1455: Protector Again

Richard, Duke of York, sitting in proxy for the king, was asked if he would once again take on the role of protector and defender of the kingdom either until he is discharged by Parliament or Prince Edward comes of age. The duke asked them to appoint a council of reason, wisdom and impartiality to assist him. They appealed, bearing in mind his previous well-ordered governance, that he would prevent the 'outrages, rebellions, murders and riots' committed daily which the king in his present infirmity cannot address.

25 February 1456: Discharged

Queen Margarete influenced King Henry to attend Parliament, where he declared himself fully 'restored to health'. The Duke of York was discharged of the 'responsibility, charge and name of protector and defender of England'.

14 September 1456: Coventry

Having a special love of Coventry since his first visit five years ago to see the new spire of St Michael's church, King Henry has been living quietly in the city. Arriving to join her husband, Queen Margarete, with two-year-old Prince Edward, was welcomed with many pageants including Joshua promising to fight as her knight, David eulogising her many virtues and at the conduit St Margaret fighting and slaying a fire-breathing dragon.

28 January 1457: Birth

Margaret Beaufort, widow of Edmund Tudor, Earl of Richmond, today gave birth to a baby boy at Pembroke Castle, three months after his father's death. The young mother has called her baby Henry after the king.

26 January–5 April 1458: Perfect Love

Summoned to London by King Henry, Richard, Earl of Salisbury entered with a small force as did the Duke of York on 26 January with just 140 horse. A few days later, Henry, Duke of Somerset, Henry, Earl of Northumberland and Lord Egremont, sons of those slain at St Alban's, arrived with great retinues. The Mayor of London, Sir Geoffrey Boleyn, uneasy with the situation, has detailed officers to ride about the city and suburbs to keep the peace. Two thousand men-at-arms keep the night watch until seven in the morning when the day watch take over.

On 14 February, the wind having been against him, the Earl of Warwick arrived from Calais with his men dressed in red jackets embroidered with white ragged staffs. Finally, King Henry and Queen Margarete arrived and lodged at the Bishop of London's palace.

After much mediation, on 5 April the king ordered a public thanksgiving to show the perfect love between his lords. Preceding the crowned king in his royal robe, watched by crowds lining the streets, walking hand-in-hand came the Duke of Somerset with the Earl of Salisbury, John Holland, Duke of Exeter with Richard, Earl of Warwick and after the king, the Duke of York holding hands with Queen Margarete.

23 September 1459: Blore Heath

At Coventry, Queen Margarete recruited armed supporters, giving an emblem of a silver swan to any she enlisted personally. Aware the queen is intent on their destruction, the Earl of Salisbury at Middleham and his son at Warwick were no less active, intending to link forces with the Duke of York and his seventeen-year-old son Edward, Earl of March at Ludlow.

Lord Audley, ordered to intercept Salisbury before he reaches Ludlow, chose farmland at Blore Heath, close to the aptly named town of Loggerheads, to set up an ambush behind a 'great hedge'. Spotting banners sticking up above the hedge, Salisbury's scouts warned him of the enemy force and mentioned that it was double the size of his own. He swiftly ordered his troops into battle order before emerging from woodland. Just out of bowshot, the two armies could clearly see each other across the heathland with a wide, fast-flowing brook between them. Salisbury, realising crossing the brook could only lead to the slaughter of his men, withdrew far enough to make Audley's men believe he was retreating. Audley then launched a cavalry charge, and once they were committed Salisbury ordered his men back and 'shortly encountered Lord Audley and his chief captains, ere the residue of his army could pass the water. The fight was sore and dreadful.' Lord

Audley was killed. Some of the Lancastrian soldiers joined their enemy and began attacking their own side. Once the rout was complete, Salisbury employed a local friar to remain on the heath all night periodically discharging a cannon while he went on to Ludlow.

At the same time, the Earl of Warwick had managed to avoid the forces sent by the queen to intercept him, led by the Duke of Somerset.

12–13 October 1459: Ludford Bridge

Making camp near Ludford, the Yorkist army excavated a defensive ditch near the bridge and set up cannon among a barricade of carts and stakes. Morale was low for not only was the force blocking their way double their own, the Royal Standard could be seen flying in the Lancastrian camp, showing King Henry was present and in full armour, for although Queen Margarete had tried to persuade the king to abdicate and place the prince on the throne, he had refused.

Seeing the standard and sure their troops would not fight against the king, the Duke of York and the two earls told their men they were retiring to Ludlow for the night but instead fled into Wales, collapsing the bridges after them.

Next morning, the leaderless Yorkist troops knelt in submission before King Henry, who pardoned them. At Ludlow market cross, the duke's wife, Cecily Neville, and their two younger sons, ten-year-old George and seven-year-old Richard, awaited King Henry who sent them into the care of her sister Anne, Duchess of Buckingham.

The king's 'gallants at Ludlow, when they had drunk enough wine' from taverns or plundered from other places, 'robbed the town, spoiled to the bare walls and bore away bedding, clothes and other stuff and defiled many women'.

20 November 1459: Attainder

Richard, Duke of York was accused of plotting with John Cade; bringing out of Ireland a great force to Westminster arrayed for war and there breaking down screens and walls in the king's chamber; allying himself with the earls of Warwick and Salisbury, who showing diabolical inhumanity slew James Lord Audley and others; forcing the king to his detriment to camp in bare fields in the cold season; and at Ludford firing guns upon him before stealing away at midnight. He, the earls, their supporters and Alice, wife of the Earl of Salisbury, were attainted of treason and they and their heirs disinherited forever of all estates, honours and dignities. Those who threw themselves on the king's mercy were left only their lives.

Two Kings

The following summer, the earls of Warwick, Salisbury and March landed at Sandwich and found people flocking to join them. In anticipation of their arrival, King Henry had mustered an army which, on 10 July, was encamped in the grounds of Delapre Abbey. To their rear was the River Nene and on three sides a staked, water-filled trench was made. The Duke of Buckingham, refusing to listen to negotiations, told the messenger that if the Earl of Warwick arrived he would die. Warwick responded that he would speak with the king at two o'clock.

Hard rain blowing in their faces, the column of Yorkists advanced at two o'clock. Lord Grey of Ruthin on the Lancastrian left flank ordered his men to lay down their weapons and let the Yorkists pass. Rain swelling the river, there was no room to manoeuvre inside the fortifications. The fighting lasted only thirty minutes, during which time the Duke of Buckingham was killed. King Henry was found in a tent patiently awaiting the outcome. With deference, he was escorted first to the abbey and then to Northampton. Queen Margarete and her son, with the Duke of Somerset, fled into Yorkshire.

Trumpet and clarion announcing his arrival into London, on 10 October Richard, Duke of York, in livery of white and blue embroidered with fetterlocks, entered the Painted Chamber, a sword borne upright before him. Standing beneath the cloth of estate, he announced to the lords that he 'purposed not to lay down his sword but to challenge his right' to the throne. In the Commons, the crown that hung in the middle of the refectory fell to the ground.

While King Henry hunted at Eltham and Greenwich, the lords in debate reached a decision that King Henry should remain king until he died or abdicated and the Duke of York was named his heir; anyone plotting to kill him or his heirs would be deemed traitors. On 9 November the agreement was proclaimed and Queen Margarete gathered forces in northern England under command of the dukes of Somerset and Exeter.

Aware the Duke of York and Earl of Salisbury were spending Christmas at Sandal Castle near Wakefield, Margarete placed an army in front of the castle and set ambush troops either side of Wakefield Green, one force commanded by Lord Clifford and the other by the Earl of Wiltshire. On 30 December, York issued forth to engage her forces and those waiting in ambush fell upon his rear, throwing his forces into disarray. Lord Clifford slew the duke and then, despite the pleas of the boy's tutor, butchered the duke's young son Edmund, Earl of Rutland as he fled over Wakefield Bridge. Cutting off both their heads, Clifford sent them to the queen, who ordered them placed on Micklegate Bar at York, with a paper crown to adorn the duke's head. The Earl of Salisbury escaped the battlefield but was captured during the night and taken to Pontefract Castle, where he was immediately beheaded.

Edward, now Duke of York, vowed vengeance. Spies telling him Queen Margarete was headed towards London, he raced to reach the city before her. She sent Jasper, Earl of Pembroke and James Butler, Earl of Ormond and Wiltshire to stop him. On 2 February at Mortimer's Cross, after ferocious fighting in dazzling sunshine, Edward routed the Lancastrians. Jasper Tudor managed to escape but every captured Lancastrian was executed, including the king's elderly stepfather, Owen Tudor. He was beheaded at Hereford market cross, his head placed on its highest step, where a mad woman washed his face, combed his hair and set down lighted candles.

The queen, hearing of the defeat, was even more determined to reach the city to release her husband. Her army had been given allowance to plunder houses and churches along the way and had left a path of destruction in villages and the towns of Grantham, Stamford, Peterborough, Huntingdon and Royston. On 17 February, aware of the devastation left in her army's wake, a force came from London, led by the dukes of Norfolk and Suffolk with the earls of Warwick and Arundel who brought with them King Henry. Her troops were forced to retreat from the marketplace of St Albans to the west end of town.

The two armies met in a place named No Man's Land. The fighting and killing continued as night drew on. The Earl of Warwick fled. The king, heard singing and laughing during the battle, was found by the queen in Warwick's tent. Embracing and kissing his wife and son, he was taken to the abbey where the abbot petitioned him to protect the abbey and town from the queen's soldiers, which he did – in vain, for they declared the queen had promised them all the spoils. The king also kindly visited John Grey, Lord Ferrers, who was married to Elizabeth, daughter of Richard Wydville, Earl Rivers who lay dying in the village of Colney. He knighted him on his deathbed.

While the soldiers pillaged, the advance on the city was stymied.

On 28 February, Edward of York slipped through the gates of London and was rapturously received by the people. In St John's

Fields, ringed by a crowd of people, the Earl of Warwick read out the agreement reached between king and duke at the last parliament and asked the crowd whether they assented to Edward as their sovereign, which set up a large shout of consent and cheers. On 4 March 1461, at Westminster, Edward was proclaimed King Edward IV.

Edward IV

1461–1483

In direct contrast to the passive Henry VI, Edward IV was a vital, larger-than-life figure, standing six foot three, broad-chested and 'of visage lovely'. Women were charmed by him, and his affability and easy disposition made him popular with men. Though he dented his esteem slightly after he married the commoner Elizabeth Wydville in 1464. Edward's queen never truly gained acceptance inside or outside of court, mainly because the noblest families were dismayed to see Edward heaping honours and wealth upon every member of the large Wydville family. Her father Richard, seen as a social upstart, became Treasurer of England and Lord High Constable and Earl Rivers in 1466. Five of her sisters married into aristocracy, wedding the Duke of Buckingham (scornful of marrying an esquire's daughter), the earls of Arundel and Kent, the heir of the Earl of Essex and Lord Herbert, who became Earl of Pembroke. Her brother Anthony became Lord Scales by marriage to Elizabeth, the orphaned daughter of Thomas, Baron Scales, and her nineteen-year-old brother John was married to the dowager Duchess of Norfolk, Katherine Neville, this match being named 'the diabolical marriage' because the bride was sixty-nine years old. Elizabeth's eldest son was created Marquis of Dorset and married Anne, the king's niece and heiress of the Duke of Exeter.

Edward was no political statesman but on the battlefield his decision-making was rapid and masterful; no one could doubt his astuteness, skill and strength. He understood the value of early information, stationing a single horseman every 20 miles and thereby initiating the 'post-haste', meaning news from Scotland was only ever two days away. However, he was adrift when it came to courtly deceit or the machinations of European rulers. He might have had clearer vision if he had viewed diplomacy like a battlefield and revised his strategies accordingly.

He may have been dynamic enough to gain the throne on two occasions, but with success came self-indulgence. As his subjects grew more prosperous, Edward was enriched through trading ventures and friendships with the merchants of London. With money came leisure to purchase land, beautiful relics and fine clothes made by his Italian tailor. His splendid court was considered an asset to the nation and all the brothers had a company of minstrels. He also ate hard and drank hard, and a ballad mentioned how his summer pastime was always the hunt. He boasted that he had three concubines: 'one the merriest, the other the wiliest and the third the holiest harlot in the realm'.

Although he died young, Edward left one legacy that is still admired today: in 1473 he began rebuilding the chapel of St George at Windsor from the foundation upwards, collecting relics with which to adorn it. In 1478 he paid £50 for an image of St George to be made and gold to gild it, and the next year he ordered seven copes of white silk damask embroidered with angels. On 6 December 1479 a charter of incorporation was granted to the deans and canon. By the time he died, the building was nearly complete, merely awaiting a roof for the west end of the chapel.

29 March 1461: 'Unnatural conflict'

At nine o'clock on Palm Sunday, twenty-five days after Edward proclaimed himself king, Lancastrians and Yorkists came face to face in a plain field between Towton and Saxton. To cries of 'No quarter!', both sides advanced. Almost at that instant, huge snowflakes blinded the eyes of the Lancastrian soldiers. Using the blizzard and wind to his advantage, the Yorkist Lord Fauconberg ordered every archer to shoot one flight then stand stock still. Henry's soldiers shot back in the direction the arrow-storm had come, but their arrows fell short in the wind. Yorkist archers moved forward and gathered their enemy's arrows, firing them back.

Battle raged, ebbing and flowing around Edward, who comforted his men, helping the wounded and the weary. Dead and wounded of both sides coloured the snow red. Flowing into streams and through villages, blood stained the fields for miles around. The ailing Duke of Norfolk had passed command to his cousin Lord John Howard, and although his troops arrived late they were also fresh, wading into the battle about noon, attacking the Lancastrian flank and crushing their courage. Henry's soldiers were hunted down through the evening, night and almost all the next day. The dukes of Somerset and Exeter had escaped but the earls of Northumberland and Westmorland were slain along with many others. People called the battle an unnatural conflict for 'son fought against son, brother against brother, tenant against his lord' and too many Englishmen died. Gaining the victory, Edward rode to York, where his first order was for the heads of his father, brother and friends to be removed from Micklegate Bar and buried with their bodies; his second was for the beheading of the Earl of Devonshire. His last order was to find King Henry, but his prey had already fled into Scotland.

1 May 1461: Monk Beheaded

James Butler, Earl of Wiltshire and Ormond, was beheaded at Newcastle. He was reputed as the handsomest man of England and, being 'frightened of losing his beauty', fought 'mainly with the heels'. Leaving Towton field, he had left his armour in a ditch and disguised himself as a monk. He left no issue, so his title goes to his brother John.

26 June–1 July 1461: Coronation

On 26 June the mayor and aldermen in scarlet and 400 citizens dressed in green rode with King Edward as he entered London en route to the Tower. Next afternoon, riding to Westminster, the king was preceded by the newly created Knights of the Bath, among them his brothers Richard and George.

Sunday morning, 29 June, Edward was crowned with all due solemnity with the confessor's crown by Archbishop Thomas Bourchier. As he stands head and shoulders above everyone, the ceremony was clearly seen and his face under its mop of brown hair was all geniality.

Swans, peacocks, pheasants and other dainties were served at the banquet, and at the end of the feasting the mayor offered to 'the king's mouth' spiced wine in a covered gold cup, with a water-filled golden ewer to temper it. London citizens, as of ancient custom, helped the Chief Butler of England serve at table in the hall.

The following day, the king wore his crown in Westminster Abbey. Later that day in the Bishop of London's palace he named his brother George as Duke of Clarence. Tuesday, again wearing his crown, King Edward went to St Paul's where an angel 'came down and censed' him and the crowds were as great as they had been the previous days. Lord Henry Bourchier, married to the king's aunt Elizabeth and brother of the Archbishop of Canterbury, was created Earl of Essex; the king's uncle Lord Fauconberg was made Earl of Kent, while John Neville, brother to Richard, Earl of Warwick, was made Lord Montagu.

30 September 1461: Pembroke

The siege of Pembroke Castle was broken by Lord Herbert. Inside they found the four-year-old Henry Tudor, who is to stay in the care of Lord Herbert. All Welsh castles, apart from Harlech, have surrendered.

1 November 1461: Dukedom

A month after his ninth birthday, Prince Richard, the king's youngest brother, was created Duke of Gloucester and Earl of Richmond.

6 November 1461: Death

John Mowbray, 3rd Duke of Norfolk and Earl Marshal, died aged forty-six and will be buried at Thetford Priory. He is succeeded by his only son, John, who is married to Elizabeth Talbot, daughter of the Earl of Shrewsbury and younger sister of Eleanor, wife of Sir Thomas Butler.

3–21 December 1461: Parliament

For his actions against King Edward and his father, the lords adjudged the erstwhile king Henry guilty of high treason. Edward offered Henry's attainted supporters a one-time grace period if they would submit to him before Twelfth Day. Acts made by Lancastrian kings have been determined as legitimate as those made by rightful kings, excepting those which deprived Richard II of his throne.

2–26 February 1462: Conspiracy Unveiled

On 26 February, John, Earl of Oxford was led on foot from Westminster to Tower Hill and beheaded. He was buried at Blackfriars. His second son, John, is his heir as his eldest son, Aubrey de Vere, was beheaded on Tower Hill six days earlier. They were arrested on 2 February and imprisoned in the Tower for plotting, it is said, with the Duke of Somerset to land an army on the Essex coast. Elizabeth Howard, Countess of Oxford is under house arrest.

3 November 1462: Sunk

Unfurling her standard in England, Queen Margarete, with a force of Frenchmen and Scotsmen, seized the castles of Bamburgh, Dunstan and Alnwick, 'stuffing them' with soldiers. Although she held the most part of Northumberland, on news of King Edward approaching with a greater host she broke her field and fled by sea. Such a storm broke that her caravel sunk and only by chance was she rescued by a fishing boat. At Edinburgh she was reunited with her son and husband.

15 May 1464: Hexham Field

John Neville, Lord Montagu marched by night to surprise Henry's soldiers in their trenches. He reported that the king-that-was, Henry of Windsor, was 'the best horseman of his company for he fled so fast no one could overtake him'. His three henchmen, on horses trapped in blue velvet, were not so lucky. One wore Henry's helmet, decorated with two rich crowns and pearls, which was sent to King Edward at York. The Duke of Somerset was captured as he fled the battlefield and was beheaded; the Earl of Kent was taken at Redesdale and beheaded at Newcastle. The Percy family being attainted, the earldom of Northumberland was given to Lord Montagu and Lord Herbert was created Earl of Pembroke in place of the fugitive Jasper Tudor.

29 September 1464: Secret Marriage

Revealed as Queen of England, twenty-six-year-old Elizabeth, daughter of Richard Wydville, Baron Rivers, was escorted by the Duke of Clarence and the Earl of Warwick into the chapel at Reading Abbey. A jewelled crown on her head, she wore a dress of richest blue bordered with ermine set off purely by a simple pearl necklace.

Telling the court he was off hunting, King Edward secretly married her on May Day at Grafton Manor, witnessed by her mother. Rumourmongers say she had at first refused his amorous intentions, holding his own dagger against her throat. His horrified privy council told him 'Elizabeth was not the wife' for him; his mother said the marriage was impolitic and injurious. Warwick, only just returned from the French court to negotiate Edward's marriage, was furious and humiliated, especially when Edward said Burgundy and Brittany make better allies for English trade. Both nobles and commoners murmur at the marriage, for despite her mother being a duchess the bride is a commoner, a widow of a Lancastrian knight and mother of two children, Thomas and Richard Grey.

April 1465: Challenge

Chester Herald was sent by King Edward to the renowned champion Antoine, Comte de la Roche, called the Bastard of Burgundy, to challenge him to break a lance in England. While Anthony, Lord Scales knelt before his sister at Sheen, the queen's ladies tied a garter of pearls holding a flower around his thigh and dropped a little roll of parchment tied with golden thread into his bonnet as it lay on the floor. In the king's chamber, King Edward broke the thread to find the ladies had requested a two-day tournament, lances and swords on one day, axes and daggers on the second.

25–27 May 1465: Coronation

Preceded by Knights of the Bath created for her coronation, Elizabeth Wydville was conveyed by a beribboned horse-litter drawn by bay and white coursers through the gaily decorated streets of London to Westminster on Saturday 25 May. Five of the knights were aldermen, proudly cheered by their fellow citizens.

On Whitsunday, she was crowned at Westminster Abbey by the archbishop. On the following day a tournament took place at which Count James of St Pol of the House of Luxembourg took part. He brought with him a hundred knights. Lord Stanley won the prize of a ring set with a ruby.

24 July 1465: Captured!

Henry of Windsor was spotted at Waddington Hall eating dinner. He fled, but on 13 July he was captured in Clitherwood in Lancashire and brought into London, feet bound to the stirrups of his horse. On the way to the Tower he was pelted with rubbish. King Edward has ordered he is to be treated with respect and kindness. He has granted the king-that-was an allowance of five marks a week for his expenses and appointed a chaplain to perform divine service daily.

11 February 1466: Firstborn

At Westminster, Queen Elizabeth gave birth to the king's first child, a daughter named Elysabeth. Her godfather is to be the Earl of Warwick and her duchess grandmothers, Cecily and Jacquetta, godmothers. It is said Master Dominic, the king's physician, so sure the child would be a boy, stayed outside so as to be the first to tell the king. When he heard the child cry, he knocked softly to enquire and was told by one of her ladies, 'Whatsoever the queen's grace has here within, sure it is that a fool stands there without.'

March 1466: Churching

At Queen Elizabeth's churching in Westminster Abbey, the Queen of Bohemia's brother Leo was invited to attend and one Master Tetzel of Nuremberg was a member of the party. He said the procession began with clergymen carrying sacred relics, then scholars singing and bearing lighted candles. Trumpeters, pipers and players of stringed instruments led the heralds and sixty lords and knights, followed by the queen under a canopy, flanked by the dukes of Clarence and Gloucester, followed by her mother and sixty ladies.

At dinner afterwards, there were so many guests they filled four large halls. The queen sat alone on a golden stool while her mother and the king's sister knelt down before her, holding their position for all three hours of the feast. Master Tetzel said he was surprised by the grandeur and hauteur of the queen when compared to the king's affable manners. When the meal was over, minstrels entered and Margaret, the king's sister, danced with her ducal brothers before the queen.

28 May–24 June 1467: Great Tournament

After Garter King-of-Arms welcomed the Bastard of Burgundy at Gravesend, on 29 May his four caravels, with bright, colourful pennons and banners flying in the breeze, sailed to Blackwell where barges belonging to lords, ladies and London citizens sailed with him to St Katherine's. He has been assigned lodgings, set up with beds and arras, at the Bishop of Salisbury's house in Fleet Street.

Arranged to start on 10 June, beautiful pavilions and stands were erected at Smithfield. On the day appointed, King Edward, dressed all in purple, entered the royal stand and sat, councillors surrounding him. Opposite, a lower stand was erected for the mayor, aldermen and prominent citizens. At each corner of the field, ninety by eighty yards, stood a king-of-arms.

Preceded by George, Duke of Clarence and the Earl of Arundel bearing helmets, and his weapons carried by the Duke of Buckingham, Earl of Kent and Lords Herbert and Stafford, Lord Scales entered. He declared he wished to perform deeds of arms and retired to his blue satin pavilion. Likewise rode in the Bastard. The weapons were inspected and approved by the Earl Marshal.

Combat ended almost as soon as it began. At the first rush, the Bastard's horse hit its head against a sharp point of Lord Scales' saddle, reared and fell dead, dragging its rider to the ground. The king was incensed, thinking there had been foul play, but the Earl Marshal confirmed there was nothing unlawful about the saddle. Nonetheless, a halt was called for the day. The second day the fighting was on foot with axes and daggers and the combat was fierce and waxed hot. The point of Scales' axe got caught in the Bastard's helm and the king once again stopped the event. The Bastard asked to use the poleaxe, but after consultation with the masters of the lists the judgement was that if they fought again the axe had be fixed as it was when the tournament was stopped, whereupon the Bastard was content to relinquish his challenge. 'Joustings, tiltings and feastings' continued until the Bastard received word Duke Philip of Burgundy had died on the evening of 15 June. He perforce took a sorrowful leave to attend his father's funeral.

11 August 1467: Birth
At Windsor, Queen Elizabeth gave birth to a second daughter, Mary.

3 July 1468: Marriage
Between five and six in the morning, twenty-one-year-old Princess Margaret married Charles, Duke of Burgundy at Damme. Afterwards, a crown on top of her flowing hair, her white cloth-of-gold and ermine gown bright against the crimson-covered litter, she made her entry into Bruges, welcomed with ten pageants despite the fine drizzle and grey skies. Combatants of the joust of peace were dressed in colourful cloth-of-gold, silk and silver with goldsmiths' work with prizes going to the Prince of Orange and Sir John Wydville. Sir John Paston imagined King Arthur's court would be very much like the duke's. Hot on the heels of the marriage came news that the French king, intent on war, was within four or five days' journey of Bruges and the bridegroom prepared to ride out.

20 March 1469: Birth
Queen Elizabeth gave birth to a daughter, named Cecily after her paternal grandmother.

26 April 1469: Insurgency
John Neville, Earl of Northumberland scattered the latest rising in the north.

June 1469: Progress
On summer progress in East Anglia, King Edward, with his brother Richard and the queen's father and brothers Anthony and John, visited Bury St Edmunds, Norwich, then Our Lady at Walsingham. At Croyland the king was so delighted by the peace of the abbey and the village he decided to stay the night and enchanted everyone by walking around praising houses and the stone bridge. The next morning he boarded a boat to sail to Fotheringhay where Queen Elizabeth awaited his arrival; there he stayed a week awaiting troops to go north and

assist the Earl of Northumberland while his wife and daughters prepared their own journey into Norfolk.

11–13 July 1469: Defiance

In a clear act of defiance, George, Duke of Clarence married Isabel Neville, daughter of the Earl of Warwick on 11 July at Notre Dame church in Calais, despite his brother forbidding the marriage. The ceremony was performed by the earl's brother, George, Archbishop of York. Two days later, duke, archbishop and earl arrived at Sandwich. At Canterbury they issued a proclamation, almost the duplicate of one issued by rebels in the north, who, moving south, veered to the west of the king who was marching northwards. They accuse King Edward of allowing his realm to be misruled by covetous persons and the queen's mother of witchcraft.

18 July 1469: Norwich

Entering Norwich by Westwick Gate, Queen Elizabeth and her daughters were cheered and welcomed by two crowned giants (made of wood and leather and stuffed with hay) standing on a red-and-green-covered stage with angels, two patriarchs, twelve apostles and sixteen virgins.

At the gates of the Friars Preachers was set up a staircase and a stage covered with tapestry. A great chair was brought from St Luke's Guild so the queen could sit comfortably and watch the entertainment put on by 'Fakke and his boys'. But the show was rudely interrupted by a huge downpour of rain and, while the queen hurried to her lodgings, ruined decorations and stage clothes were being rushed into the Guildhall and various houses.

26 July 1469: Edgecote Moor

A third army, intending to join the king, marched across England led by the earls of Pembroke and Devonshire but the two quarrelled and Devonshire flounced off in temper, taking his contingent of archers with him. Soon after, Pembroke was confronted by northern rebels marching south to join Warwick. Led by Robin of Redesdale, the battle took place in a plain beyond Banbury and many Welshmen were slain, as were Sir Henry Neville, son and heir to the mad George, Lord Latimer, and the son and heir of Thomas Wake. Pembroke fought bravely despite having no archers. Then came the cry 'A Warwick, A Warwick' and men wearing the white bear and ragged staff entered the battle. Under the weight of so many, the earl and his brother Sir Richard Herbert were taken and beheaded at Northampton.

14 August 1469: Anguish

Grievous news reached the queen at Norwich: King Edward was captured in dead of night from Olney or Honiley at the end of July by Archbishop George, and taken without ceremony to the Duke of Clarence and the Earl of Warwick. They forced her husband to watch the executions at Kenilworth of her father and brother, taken captive at Chepstow. The queen's mother, seized by Thomas Wake, was accused of crafting leaden images to make the king marry her daughter and to kill the Earl of Warwick. Taken into London, Duchess Jacquetta feistily asked for protection from the mayor and aldermen.

7 October 1469: Reconciliation

Although out of his way, King Edward rode through Cheap to ensure as many London citizens as possible saw him. With him rode the dukes of Gloucester and Suffolk, earls of Arundel, Northumberland and Essex and other lords to a thousand horse and more.

King Edward, taken from Warwick to Middleham, escaped to York after Archbishop George had allowed him to go out hunting; his friends, seeing the opportunity to free him, brought troops.

In the council the king held at York on 22 September, his policy was reconciliation. Sir John Paston noted 'the king has good language of the Lords Clarence and Warwick, saying they be his best friends, but it is not what his household says'. The archbishop was escorted to his house of The Moor to await the king's pleasure. Anthony Wydville, now Earl Rivers, has emerged from hiding and returned to court'.

The Bishop of Ely was appointed treasurer in place of the queen's father. Robert Stillington, Bishop of Bath and Wells remains chancellor.

27 October 1469: Elevations

Hoping to appease the north, King Edward accepted Henry Percy's oath of fidelity, released him from the Tower and restored to him the earldom of Northumberland. John Neville, very much loved by the king and instrumental in helping him stay secure on the throne, was elevated to Marquis of Montagu and to compensate for the loss of Percy estates was granted the lands of the executed Earl of Devonshire. The new marquis was dejected, complaining he had been granted 'a magpie's nest' insufficient to maintain his new estate. John's four-year-old son George was created Duke of Bedford and it is rumoured he is to marry the king's daughter Elysabeth.

4–16 March 1470: Lincolnshire Rebellion

When one of his household knights was attacked by Lord Welles and Sir Thomas Dymock, King Edward summoned the two to court for an explanation. While they travelled, the son of Lord Welles riled up people in Lincolnshire by telling them King Edward was coming with a 'great power' and the king's judges would 'draw and hang' a great number of them. He summoned men to muster at Ranby Howe to resist the king coming to destroy the people.

Artillery and troops ready on Sunday 4 March, King Edward delayed his departure after his brother George said he would like to see him. Two days later, the two said their goodbyes, Edward leaving for Waltham Abbey and George saying he was looking forward to seeing his wife in the West Country.

Next day, a letter came from George. He had changed his mind. He, with the Earl of Warwick, would come to assist Edward if he sent commissions for them to raise extra forces in Worcestershire and Warwickshire. Meanwhile, Lord Welles and Sir Thomas Dymock had by now reached London and Edward ordered them to be brought to him wherever he was lodging.

The king reached Stamford on 12 March and rested his troops. Letters came from George and Warwick that they were at Coventry, ready to move to Leicester. Spies told the king the Lincolnshire rebels had passed Grantham on the road to Leicester but Sir Robert Welles, realising he had passed the king, wheeled his company about and marched them to Empingham. Informed Welles was now only four miles away from him and readying for battle, Edward had Lord Welles and Dymock executed under the Royal Standard before, marching his men in battle array, they attacked the moment they saw the enemy force. Artillery threw Lincolnshire commons into confusion and they broke up and fled, casting away their coats in haste to escape. The rout of 'Losecoat Field' was not pursued rigorously; the king said the commons were but 'dupes and pawns in the hands of far greater traitors' for, to his great sorrow, the rebels had shouted, 'A Warwick! A Clarence!'

On 16 March, after hearing their confessions, Edward had Sir Robert Welles and Richard Warren beheaded at Doncaster in the presence of the entire army. Before they died they confirmed they had acted at the bidding of Clarence and Warwick who had hoped to depose the king and put twenty-year-old Clarence on the throne in his place, and that Clarence had gone to London to delay the king so he could be caught between the two forces led by Welles and Warwick.

14–17 April 1470: *Thwarted*

News came to King Edward while he was at Exeter that Warwick and Clarence after embarking at Dartmouth had attempted to seize Warwick's ship *Trinity* in Southampton harbour but were thwarted by Earl Rivers. Making for Calais, Lord Wenlock fired on Warwick's ship and though his daughter Isabel was giving birth no one was permitted to land, although some wine was sent out to comfort her.

7 August–13 September 1470: *Warnings Ignored*

Strengthening the Tower with ordnance and leaving his pregnant wife and daughters there for safety, King Edward marched north but by the time he reached York on 7 August the latest rebellion was over. The Duke of Burgundy, patrolling the Channel, warned Edward he had been lured north and should return south post-haste for Warwick's daughter, Anne had been betrothed to the son of Henry and Margarete. Ignoring his brother-in-law, Edward stayed at York but a storm dispersed Burgundy's ships. Clarence and Warwick, with Jasper Tudor, John Courtney and John de Vere, exiled late earls of Pembroke, Devon and Oxford, took the opportunity to sail across and land in England on 13 September. Their goal had changed: they sought to rescue King Henry VI from his rebel and enemy Edward, usurer, oppressor and destroyer.

29 September 1470: *King Escaped*

Hurrying south, King Edward ordered forces to join him at Doncaster where he would unite with the host being brought by the Marquis of Montagu. On 29 September, Alexander, sergeant of the minstrels, woke Edward saying enemies were near at hand to seize him. Lazily the king said they were but Montagu's men. Alexander said not so; some of the marquis' men had sent warning Montagu had turned against him. Flying cross-country to King's Lynn, Edward boarded as much of his force as possible to travel by sea. The king took leave of those forced to remain behind, saying they should make terms and await a better day. Then the king, with his brother Richard, sailed into Holland with no bag nor baggage. To pay for their passage, King Edward gave his rich gown and promises.

3–6 October 1470: *King Released*

The Bishop of Winchester, by order of the Duke of Clarence and Earl of Warwick, entered the Tower of London to remove King Henry who was not 'worshipfully arrayed as a prince and not so cleanly kept as should seem such a prince'. They dressed him in clean robes and with great reverence brought him to Westminster and put the crown on his head before lodging him at the Bishop of London's palace.

Wheel of Fortune

Once again Warwick had a king in his power, even lodging with him. In November, Jasper Tudor brought his nephew, thirteen-year-old Henry, removed from the care of William Herbert's widow, to meet King Henry. Jasper regained his title of Earl of Pembroke and returned to Wales with his nephew on 14 November. At Parliament on 26 November the crown was settled on Henry and his male heirs, failing which it would descend to George, Duke of Clarence, son and heir of Richard, Duke of York. His two brothers were attainted and declared traitors.

A general pardon was issued in December and those in sanctuary were left in peace, including Elizabeth Wydville in Westminster, who was granted half a beef and two muttons a week from a London butcher. With her confinement near, Henry's council allowed Lady Scrope to wait upon her.

Overseas, Queen Margarete and the Countess of Warwick watched their children marry at Amboise on 13 December. They left Paris for Rouen and sent word they were ready to come to England. King Henry paid out £2,000 for ships and men to bring them home but the weather was so stormy no passage was possible. That was still the case when the Earl of Warwick fruitlessly awaited their arrival at Dover on 27 February.

In March commissions were sent out to raise troops to defend the country against Edward, who on 14 March 1471 landed at Ravenspur. His fleet, carrying 900 Englishmen and 300 Flemings with handguns, was scattered by a storm. Richard made land four miles away, Earl Rivers fourteen miles away, and a ship of horses was lost completely. Edward's arrival was ignored. York shut its gates against him, but he told officials he came merely to claim his inheritance, the duchy of York, so they allowed him to enter and refresh himself and his men. Travelling south, he passed Wakefield and Sandal. At Pontefract the Marquis of Montagu ignored his passing. Armed men began joining him, and at Nottingham Edward found well-arrayed troops awaiting his arrival. Suddenly he had an army, and once more he proclaimed himself King of England.

Scouts came and told him that the Duke of Exeter and Earl of Oxford had four thousand men gathered at Newark but Edward decided to march to meet the Earl of Warwick, who, having left London, was gathering forces around Coventry. Sir John Paston assured his mother the world was 'right queasy'.

Near Banbury, Clarence, with a great deal of men, came towards Edward. When he was half a mile away, Edward set his soldiers in array with banners displayed. Taking Richard and Lords Rivers and Hastings, the king met him. In between the two hosts, the three brothers exchanged affectionate greetings.

13–14 April 1471: Barnet Field

Attempting to raise troops for his brother, Archbishop George paraded King Henry through the city while the recorder and aldermen directed everyone to go home. One citizen remarked the sight had been as 'pleasing as a fire painted on a wall warmed the old woman'. Around dinnertime, King Edward slipped into the city and offered at St Paul's before being rowed to Westminster to see and kiss his wife and new son, Edward, born on 2 November.

When he left a little later, King Henry accompanied him. A thick fog fell that evening, and outside Barnet, knowing Warwick's men were close, King Edward made camp with his seven thousand men roughly half a mile away, ordering them to stay silent and armed. During the night, knowing Edward must be near, Warwick's men shot guns in hopes that a response would reveal his position.

At four in the morning, thick fog still coating the world so that neither side could perfectly see the other, the fighting began. In the rage of battle, liveries were mistaken and the Earl of Warwick's men shot accidentally into the Earl of Oxford's men who cried 'Treason' and fled from the field. With Oxford fled, Warwick leapt upon a horse but as he reached woodland he was spotted and killed by a soldier who stripped him naked. The Duke of Exeter had been left for dead, stripped naked on the field, but his physician found him alive and had him carried to sanctuary at Westminster.

After the battle was over, the king commanded the bodies of the Earl of Warwick and the Marquis of Montagu to be put in a cart and taken to be displayed at St Paul's so every man might see them. Henry, kept safe during the battle, was returned to the Tower.

16–23 April 1471: Shadows

News came that Queen Margarete and seventeen-year-old Prince Edward had arrived at Weymouth on the day of Barnet Field. Continuing the fight under the prince's banner, Edmund, Duke of

Somerset began gathering men in Devon and Cornwall, while Jasper Tudor went to recruit soldiers in Wales. Spies shadowing Margarete as she moved from Exeter to Bath via Glastonbury, King Edward surmised she was making for Gloucester and sent word for Tudor's forces to be blocked at Gloucester, forcing her to move towards Tewkesbury.

3–4 May 1471: Tewkesbury

Margarete's soldiers arrived outside Tewkesbury about four in the afternoon on 3 May. Weary after travelling between woods and heathland in hot weather without refreshment, they made camp. The Duke of Somerset ordered the men to build entrenchments on three sides, with the River Severn behind them. King Edward's force had shadowed the queen's army and, hearing they were camped, made camp within three miles of them, making sure to take meat and drink.

Next morning the king's men marched, armed and ordered into three battles with spearmen sent into the woods. With banners fluttering and trumpets blowing, Richard was directed by his brother to attack first. Somerset sent his men forward ordering them to outflank him, but Richard wheeled his division around to keep facing one flank while spearmen came out of the woods to attack the other. Realising not all his troops had advanced, Somerset rode back to Lord Wenlock and angrily knocked out his brains with his battle-axe. Gaps opening in the lines, Edward and Clarence entered, slaying Lancastrians caught in their own entrenchments. All was panic, confusion and blood. Many retreated but drowned in the river. Others ran towards town, church and abbey. The hand-to-hand fighting was fierce. Prince Edward, attempting to reach the town, was slain in the field.

21–23 May 1471: Triumphant

On 21 May, King Edward triumphantly entered London. Richard, Duke of Gloucester, arriving in his brother's train, left that day for Kent to deal with Lord Fauconberg and Kentish rebels who had attacked London but been repelled.

On the afternoon of 23 May, the body of King Henry was brought into St Paul's in a wooden coffin, blood dripping on the paving stones. The bruit is he died of grief at the death of his son but no one doubts the probable occurrence. Costs of clergy, embalming spices, torches for his journey to St Paul's and Blackfriars Stairs to be carried by boat for interment in Our Lady Chapel at Chertsey Abbey came to just above £15.

6 January 1472: Honour
London was honoured by King Edward inviting the mayor, aldermen and prominent citizens to dinner in the White Hall on Twelfth Day.

25 March 1472: Found
Pressured by King Edward, George, Duke of Clarence gave his consent for Richard to marry his sister-in-law Anne. George had imprisoned her but Richard, after rescuing her, has placed her in sanctuary at St Martin's in London. George told Edward he had moved Anne to safety to prevent Richard marrying Anne by force. By right of his wife, George is claiming the earldoms of Warwick and Salisbury, disallowing Anne her share of her father's inheritance. Richard has agreed for the inheritance to be settled by arbitration so long as he retains Penrith, Sheriff Hutton and Middleham.

10 April 1472: Birth
Queen Elizabeth gave birth to her fourth daughter, named Margaret.

12 July 1472: Marriage
Richard, Duke of Gloucester, now nineteen years of age, married his sixteen-year-old childhood sweetheart, Anne Neville, at St Stephen's Chapel at Westminster in the presence of the king and court.

Summer 1472: Pestilence
Summer had been 'great hot for man and beast', and many died. During harvest time men fell down suddenly with fevers all over England, as they had done last summer.

September–October 1472: Baths
At his coming to Calais, Louis de Bruges, Lord of La Gruthuyse, who had supported King Edward in his exile, was feasted for two or three days before he crossed to Dover. At Canterbury he was gifted with wine, capons, pheasants, partridges and other luxuries. Allowed to rest in London for a few days, he travelled to Windsor Castle. In a chamber richly hung with cloth of arras, King Edward and Queen Elizabeth waited to welcome him and take him to supper. Afterwards he was led into the queen's chamber, where the ladies were playing board games and musical instruments.

Next morning, between Mass and breakfast, Louis was given a gold cup with pearls and a piece of unicorn horn, its cover decorated by a huge sapphire. After he had eaten he was presented to Prince Edward. Hunting in the park later, the king gave him his own hobby, royal crossbow (with silk string and velvet case) and gilt-headed quarrels. Dining at the lodge, they continued hunting until dusk when the king showed off his garden and 'vineyard of pleasure'. Supper was taken in the queen's chamber. Louis and his son sat at the royal table.

There was dancing until nine o'clock when the king and queen, with all her ladies, took Lord Louis and his son to 'three chambers of pleasance', all carpeted and hung with white silk and linen. In the first was a bed of down with sheets of finest linen and a counterpane of cloth-of-gold furred with ermine, curtains of white sarcenet and soft pillows; the second likewise held an all-white bed of estate hung with a netting tent. In the third chamber, baths had been prepared with tents of white cloth. There Louis and his son were left alone to bathe, served with green ginger, comfits and Hippocras to sweeten their dreams before retiring.

The next day the court moved to Westminster, and on 13 October Lord Louis, for his constancy in time of trouble, was created Earl of Winchester, granted £200 annual revenue and the right to add a square of the arms of England to his escutcheon.

11 December 1472: Death
Baby Princess Margaret died and has been buried in Westminster Abbey in a grey marble tomb at the altar end of St Edward's Shrine.

17 August 1473: Second Prince
Today at Shrewsbury, Queen Elizabeth gave her husband a second son, who is named Richard after his uncle.

29 September 1473: Instructions
Earl Rivers has been appointed Prince Edward's governor and tutor at the prince's separate household at Ludlow Castle. King Edward instructs that the prince shall rise every morning according to his age and only the earl, chaplains and chamberlains may enter his chamber. Breakfast can be taken immediately after Mass and appropriate lessons given until dinner, at which time he will listen to noble stories at the earl's discretion. In his presence only virtue, honour, science, wisdom and deeds of worship are to be discussed. After meat there is more learning along with convenient games, sports and exercises. After evensong and supper at four, the curtains around his bed are to be drawn at 8 p.m. Only his attendants, who must make him merry and joyous towards his bed, are to be allowed in his chamber during the night.

28 May 1475: Creation
Prince Richard, second son of the king, was created Duke of York.

4 July 1475: France
Following his army of 15,000 soldiers, who had already crossed over to Calais in flat-bottomed boats, King Edward today sailed into Calais. Awaiting the 2,000 archers from Brittany, the plan is for France to be attacked on two flanks, Edward coming from Brittany and Duke Charles from Burgundy. Prince Edward has been appointed *Custos* of England in the king's absence.

29 August 1475: Bridge of Picquigny
Discovering Duke Charles's army had been decimated at Neuss, the kings of England and France mutually agreed to come to terms. On the bridge at Picquigny near Amiens a strong wooden lattice cage with a wooden barrier in the middle was erected, the bars only wide enough to admit one arm. On each side of the barrier there was room only for ten to twelve men and both kings took impersonators to befuddle would-be assassins.

The Duke of Gloucester, who thinks the treaty dishonourable, was conspicuously absent. The Duke of Clarence attended his brother. At the barriers, the two kings raised their hats and bowed low to each other. King Edward's cap was of black velvet, adorned with a *fleur-de-lis* in precious stones, and the chronicler Commines was heard to remark as Edward bowed to within a foot of the ground that he was 'inclining to corpulence ... but still handsome', with no detriment to his notorious womanising.

The peace treaty was signed with five thousand crowns for the troops to leave, an annual pension of fifty thousand gold coins for the king, with marriage agreed between Princess Elysabeth and the Dauphin.

2 November 1475: Birth
The king and queen have a fifth daughter who has been named Anne.

14–15 January 1476: Death
John Mowbray, Duke of Norfolk died suddenly in the night. Aged only thirty-two, his death is a mystery as he was in good health the day before. His widow, Elizabeth Talbot, is heavily pregnant and his heir for the moment is his daughter Anne.

25 April 1476: Pilloried
Agnes Deyntee, found guilty of selling rancid dishes of butter that appeared good outside but corrupt and unwholesome inside, was condemned to stand under the pillory with her dishes about her neck for half an hour, then to quit the city.

24–30 July 1476: Reinterment
Richard Plantagenet's body, exhumed at Pontefract on 24 July, was 'garbed in an ermine-furred mantle and cap, covered with cloth of gold', laying in state under a hearse blazing with candles, guarded by a silver angel bearing a gold crown to signify the duke had been a king. The body of Edmund, Earl of Rutland was placed in a coffin covered in cloth of gold and black velvet.

The day after, the cortege began its journey to Fotheringhay. Richard, Duke of Gloucester was chief mourner, following his father's funeral chariot drawn by six horses trapped in black. Every person who honoured the dead at the stopping places received 1*d*, every woman with child 2*d*.

Arriving on 29 May, King Edward, dressed in blue gown and cap of mourning and with tears streaming down his face, 'made obeisance to the body and kissed it crying all the time' as it proceeded through the churchyard into the church to the choir, where a hearse was set up for the duke; there was another for Edmund in the Lady Chapel. The king retired to his closet and officers, lords and nobles and ambassadors from France, Denmark and Portugal stationed themselves around the hearses to keep vigil while Masses were sung. The next day, after three Masses, the duke's hatchments were offered. Lord Ferrers rode a courser in full armour holding an axe reversed while the king, queen and princesses Elysabeth and Mary offered the Mass penny. When the funerals were over, five thousand people came to receive alms and four times that number partook of the dinner, served partly in the castle and partly in tents and pavilions. Capons, cygnets, herons, rabbits and sweet delicacies were served at a cost above £300.

22 December 1476: Death
Isabel, Duchess of Clarence has died. Sick with consumption, she never recovered after giving birth to a son, named Richard, on 5 October at Tewkesbury. Margaret and Edward will be sent to live with their aunt Anne.

5 January 1477: Death
Duke Charles, besieging Rene, Duke of Lorraine in his capital of Nancy, was killed in a battle fought outside its walls. He leaves a

sole daughter by his first wife, Mary. He and Margaret had no issue. The king has forbidden his brother Richard from sending troops to Burgundy to defend their sister from French attacks and has forbidden his brother George from marrying Mary.

12–15 April 1477: Clarence's Law

Early in the afternoon of Saturday 12 April, Ankarette Twynho, a widow, was abducted from her manor home at Cayford in Somerset by more than twenty men, roughly manhandled for the next two days and thrown into prison at Warwick. Her family and servants were threatened with violence whenever they tried to attend her. On Tuesday, Ankarette was forcibly brought before the king's justices where George, Duke of Clarence accused his wife's lady-in-waiting of giving her poisoned ale at Warwick on 10 October which killed her on 22 December. Violently threatening the jurors, they pronounced her guilty. She was immediately drawn to the gallows at Myton with tearful jurors begging her forgiveness all the way. She was hanged until she was dead alongside Thursby, accused by the duke of poisoning his newborn son, who died on New Year's Day and was buried with his mother at Tewkesbury Abbey.

19–20 May 1477: King's Law

All the nobles came to attend the trial on 19 May of three retainers of the Duke of Clarence: Oxford astronomer Stacy, Burdett and Chaplain Blake. When racked they confessed they had used magic arts and necromancy in an attempt to bring about the deaths of King Edward and his sons. Found guilty of treason, they were returned to the Tower to repose their souls before being hanged the next day at Tyburn where, upon the gallows, they protested their innocence. At the 'eleventh hour', the Bishop of Norwich secured a pardon for Blake.

22–23 May 1477: Innocent

The Duke of Clarence pushed his way into the council chamber at Westminster and had declarations of innocence by Burdett and Stacy read out. King Edward, racing back to London from Windsor, summoned his brother to Westminster Palace the following day. Before the mayor and aldermen, Edward personally accused Clarence of violating the laws of England and threatening the security of judges and jurors. He ordered him arrested and lodged in the Bowyer Tower of the Tower of London.

18 November 1477: Printing Press

A great many citizens wended their way to the Almonry at Westminster where William Caxton has set up his wondrous printing press. Today, the first book off his press was *Dictes and Sayings of the Philosophers*, translated from the French into English by Earl Rivers, who is presenting this first copy to the king.

15–22 January 1478: Marriage

King Edward's son Richard, Duke of York and Earl of Nottingham married six-year-old Anne, sole heiress of John Mowbray, Duke of Norfolk in the presence of the king, queen and all their children. Earl Rivers and the Earl of Lincoln supported the bride as she walked into the king's great chamber from the queen's chamber, through the White Hall and into the royal chapel hung with azure carpets decorated with gold *fleurs-de-lis*. In right of his wife, Richard receives the title of Duke of Norfolk.

After the wedding Mass, while spices and wines were drunk, Richard, Duke of Gloucester dipped his hands into gold basins filled with gold and silver coins and threw them over everyone before leading the bride to her wedding banquet, prepared in the great chamber, where the press was so great it was hard to see who was there.

Jousts were held afterwards, with runs in harness and tourneys with swords. Earl Rivers began the event, dressed as a white hermit on a horse trapped in tawny satin with trees of gold. After a bell tolled, behind him was brought in a black velvet pavilion made to look like a hermitage with windows, sporting a cross of St Anthony. Throwing off his habit, he revealed his suit was blue and tawny embroidered with flames.

The new Duchess of York distributed the prizes: a gold 'A' with diamond to Thomas Fiennes, Lord Dacre's son as best jouster, who was ordered after dinner to take a lady by the hand and begin the dancing; a gold 'E' with a ruby to Richard Haute as best runner; and to Robert Clifford, best with swords, a gold 'M' with emerald.

8 February 1478: Sentenced

George, Duke of Clarence was found guilty of high treason, despite avowals of innocence, at his trial before Henry Stafford, Duke of Buckingham, who was appointed High Steward. King Edward declared he had forgiven his brother many times for his past 'commotions' but now he had conspired new plots against him, such treason being 'heinous, unnatural and loathly' contrived and imagined as it was by his own brother. Afterwards, the sentence on Ankarette Twynho was reversed.

18 February 1478: Executed
It is reported that George, Duke of Clarence died last night in the Tower and 'justice was executed upon him'. He is to be buried beside his wife at Tewkesbury Abbey. His son, Edward, has been allowed to retain the earldom of Warwick; his earldom of Salisbury has been granted to Richard's son, Edward.

12 November 1478: Conduit
A wax chandler of Fleet Street, who had pierced a conduit pipe to bring water into his house, was made to ride throughout the city with a vessel styled like a conduit on his head, with pipes running water all over him, refilled whenever the water emptied. He was returned to prison afterwards.

March 1478: Birth
A third son was born to Queen Elizabeth, named George after his deceased uncle.

14 August 1479: Birth
Princess Catherine, a sixth daughter, was born to the king and queen today at Eltham Palace.

12 May 1480: Commission
Richard, Duke of Gloucester was given command of an army to repel any invasion by the Scots although King James denies giving authority for any acts of hostility occurring across the border.

22 June 1480: Negotiations
A treaty of marriage is being negotiated for Prince Edward to marry Anne, eldest daughter of the Duke of Brittany.

July–September 1480: Visit
The king's sister Margaret came on a visit to England from Burgundy, lodged in Coldharbour House in Thames Street. He sent his own ship *The Falcon* to bring her from Calais with an escort all dressed in new jackets of purple and blue velvet, led by Sir Edward Wydville. From Gravesend she was conducted to Greenwich on the royal barge, the oarsmen also in new jackets of purple and blue garnished with roses. The duchess stayed until 13 September, setting out from London riding a new pillion of blue and purple cloth of gold fringed with Venice

Gold, a gift from her brother, along with ten hobbies and palfreys and a licence to import oxen, sheep and rams.

10 November 1480: Birth
Queen Elizabeth gave birth today to a seventh daughter who has been called Bridget.

23 May 1482: Death
Princess Mary died. Her health had been declining for some time and the proposals for her to marry the King of Denmark had already been broken off.

15–18 July 1482: Scotland
On 15 July Richard, Duke of Gloucester with the Earl of Northumberland marched forward expecting to meet a Scottish army but was instead met with a deputation of Scottish barons. The duke, who has already taken the town of Berwick, asked them in good faith to surrender Berwick Castle. Refused, he continued the siege while he marched on to Edinburgh, burning towns and villages but ordering his troops not to molest the citizens or steal any goods. Two days later, in the city the provost and community of Edinburgh undertook that their king would keep his promise and marry Princess Cecily, and if the king wished to revoke the arrangement they would refund the dowry already advanced. The duke awaits instructions from the king while he continues to besiege Berwick.

July–August 1482: Summer Entertaining
King Edward rode out hunting into the forest of Waltham with the Lord Mayor of London, aldermen and prominent citizens and, causing game to be hounded before them course after course, they slew many red and fallow deer. Afterwards, led to a lodge made out of green boughs, they partook of many dainty dishes and drank white, red and claret wine. Journeying home, the king gave the company plenty of venison to take with them.

The following month, King Edward sent two harts and six bucks with a tun of wine to the mayoress and 'her sisters' the aldermen's wives for a feast at the Drapers' Hall.

24 August 1482: Berwick
Berwick, castle and town, belongs once more to England. King Edward wrote to the Pope of his jubilation at his brother's success.

25 August 1482: Death

Margarete, once Queen of England, died in poverty at the castle of Dampierre-sur-Loire near Anjou aged fifty-two.

Christmas 1482: Gaiety

King Edward kept crowned estate the whole feast-tide at Eltham, remaining in his chamber while Queen Elizabeth stayed in hers. Every day more than 2,000 persons were served, the king appearing in a great variety of costly robes with shoulder rolls and sleeves full and hanging, lined with furs.

20 January–18 February 1483: Parliament

After the death of Prince Richard's wife, Anne Mowbray, Duchess of York on 19 November, King Edward passed an Act giving the Mowbray estates, which should have passed to John, Lord Howard and William, Viscount Berkeley, to his own son and his heirs, even though a widower has no interest in his wife's lands unless there are children.

9 April 1483: Death of King Edward

King Edward died on 9 April after falling seriously ill at the end of March, some say from a cold he caught while on a fishing trip. Whatever the cause, he was in constant agony and when calling his lords to his bedside had to be raised up with pillows to talk to them and add codicils to his will.

His corpse was laid upon a board, covered from the navel to the knees, and for ten or twelve hours he was viewed by all the lords, the mayor and aldermen then cered and taken to the chapel where the next morning three solemn Masses will be sung and for the next eight nights vigil will be kept by his nobles and household officers.

Edward V

April–June 1483

Edward spent most of his childhood in his separate household at Ludlow Castle with occasional visits to court, his maternal family in turn visiting him at Ludlow. His uncle Anthony, Lord Rivers remained his governor and tutor, with the appointment set to end when he reached the age of fourteen, which was only nineteen months away when his father passed.

Just over a month before King Edward died on 9 April 1483, he had sent a new instruction allowing his son to go to bed at nine o'clock instead of eight.

16–19 April: Funeral

From its lying-in-state in St Stephen's Chapel, King Edward's body was placed upon a blue canopied bier, a large black cloth of gold with a white cross over it, and carried into Westminster Abbey by fifteen knights who laid it in a hearse with a crowned effigy of the king placed on top.

After the funeral service the next morning, Edward's body was placed in a chariot hung with black velvet and drawn by six coursers trapped in black. The cortege began its journey to Windsor, Lord John Howard riding in front holding the king's banner. At Charing Cross, after the chariot was censed, everyone mounted and they rode to Sion Nunnery where they rested overnight.

Through the gates of Windsor Castle next day, the cortege was met by the Archbishop of York and bishops. The body was carried into the beautiful but not quite finished Chapel of St George to the hearse beside the marble tomb King Edward had commissioned only a few months previously, and which broke the crane when it was lifted into place. That night a great watch was kept by lords, knights and others. Next morning the final rites were performed. At the offering, the king's shield was offered along with the rich sword sent from the Pope, his helmet, his crimson velvet coat of arms with pearls and rubies. Then Sir William Parr, bare headed, in full armour and holding an axe 'pole downward', rode up to the choir door, dismounted and made his offering as 'the man of arms'. After he was lowered into his tomb, the king's officers threw their staffs into the grave and the heralds their coats of arms. The funeral cost £1,496 17s 11d, and despite this expense Edward was probably the first English king to die without debt.

24 April: Setting Out

After celebrating St George's Day at Ludlow, King Edward and Lord Rivers set off for London on 24 April, with an armed retinue of two thousand horse.

29–30 April: Meeting

Arriving at Northampton with six hundred horse, Richard, Duke of Gloucester awaited to meet King Edward as had been arranged but instead Anthony, Earl Rivers and Richard Grey arrived, informing him that they had sent the king and his household fourteen miles further south to lodge at Stony Stratford. The duke invited them to supper and the early evening was passed in pleasant conversation.

Late in the evening, Henry, Duke of Buckingham arrived with three hundred horse. The dukes conversed into the night after everyone else had retired to their lodgings. At dawn, the dukes were ready to ride and roused the earl's party. They set off, but along the way Buckingham accused Rivers and Lord Grey of intending to 'set distance between the king and them' and had them arrested.

Arriving at Stony Stratford, they found King Edward already organised to ride on to London. The dukes, with their retinues, uncovered their heads and bent the knee, showing the king due reverence. The king was then informed that Rivers, Grey and Thomas Grey, Marquis of Dorset desired to 'seize government' and kill the 'noble blood of the realm' and that the latter had taken the king's arms and treasure from the Tower and sent men to sea.

King Edward said he could not answer for his brother Dorset but his uncle and brother were innocent of any evil. He was told certain matters had been kept from his knowledge. Like Rivers and Grey,

Sir Thomas Vaughan and Sir Richard Haute were arrested and sent under guard 'into northern parts'. With the elder styled protector, Richard and Edward continued the journey to London.

2 May: Tidings

News of the arrests reached Queen Elizabeth just before midnight. Immediately, she took Richard Duke of York and her daughters into sanctuary at Westminster Abbey, lodging in the abbot's house.

4 May: Entry

King Edward, arriving in London, was received by the mayor, aldermen and sheriffs in scarlet, with 500 commoners dressed in dark purple to conduct him to the Bishop of London's Palace near St Paul's while Duke Richard lodged at Baynard's Castle with his mother.

13 May: Writs

Writs were sent out to summon a parliament for 25 June.

14 May: Orders

Richard, Duke of Gloucester, Protector of the Realm by royal appointment, ordered Edward Brampton and John Welles to take ships to sea to capture Sir Edward Wydville, patrolling the Channel in royal ships. Commissions of peace have been sent into several counties; it was noted previous commissions of a fortnight earlier were sent in the names of the Marquis of Dorset, Earl Rivers and Lord Hastings.

2 June: Great Seal

At council the Great Seal was taken from the Archbishop of York, Dr Rotherham, after it was revealed he had given it to the queen when he found he found her sobbing on the floor of her lodgings. Although he had since retrieved it, he was sent to the Tower. The seal was given to Dr John Russell, Bishop of Lincoln, considered by all a wise man.

5 June: Knights

Anne, Duchess of Gloucester has journeyed from Middleham to join her husband at Crosby Place. By advice of his uncle, 'protector of our realm during our young age', King Edward sent letters to fifty men informing them they should be at the Tower on 18 June as he intended to make them Knights of the Bath in readiness for his coronation set for 22 June.

9 June: Westminster

According to Simon Stallworth, all the lords including the dukes 'were at Westminster in the Council Chamber from ten in the morning until two in the afternoon'.

11–15 June: Request

Sir Richard Ratcliffe has been sent to York with a letter requesting of the city as many men as 'you can defensibly array to aid and assist us against the queen, her blood, adherents and affinity which have intended and daily doth intend to murder and utterly destroy us and our cousin Duke of Buckingham', asking that they muster at Pontefract and march to London under the leadership of the Earl of Northumberland and Lord Neville. York council agreed to send 200 men, with 100 men from Ainsty, at pay of 12*d* a day and harness, though the men will have to pay for their own jackets.

13 June: Traitors

In London, pageants were being made day and night and animals killed ready for the feasting while the royal council met at the White Tower to discuss the order for the coronation. The Lord Protector entered about nine o'clock and apologised for oversleeping and asked if John Morton, Bishop of Ely would allow him to have a dish of strawberries from out of his garden in Holborn. At the bishop's assent he withdrew to his chamber but between ten and eleven he returned, looking pensive. Sitting silently for a while, he finally asked, 'What should happen to those that imagine the destruction of me, being so near of blood to the king and protector of his realm?'

Lord Hastings replied that 'they were worthy to be punished as heinous traitors'.

Richard rose up and opened the chamber door to admit soldiers who came in and arrested Lords Hastings and Stanley and John Morton, Bishop of Ely. Around noon, after making confession, Lord Hastings was taken out to Tower Green and beheaded. Duke Richard granted his last wish by sending his body entire for burial in St George's Chapel at Windsor.

15 June: Brothers United

Cardinal Bourchier, Archbishop of Canterbury persuaded Queen Elizabeth to allow Prince Richard, Duke of York to join his brother in the Tower, the council thinking it a shame the king was alone, having moved into the royal apartments in the Tower a month ago.

When the prince was brought into the Star Chamber, the Lord Protector took him into his arms and kissed him: 'Welcome lord, with all my very heart.'

The prince, departing with the chancellor, looked happy to be reunited with his brother.

17 June: Parliament Cancelled

From Westminster, Edward appointed John Countes, William Colles and Thomas Huntley to provide victuals for his household. Writs of supersedeas were sent cancelling the coming parliament.

22 June: Sermon

A sermon delivered at St Paul's Cross proclaimed the Lord Protector, Richard Plantagenet, the only true inheritor of the throne. It was further offered that King Edward had bigamously married Dame Elizabeth Grey while contracted to Lady Eleanor Butler, making the two princes bastards. The bruit is the information came from Robert Stillington, Bishop of Bath and Wells.

24 June: A-buzzing

The Duke of Buckingham spoke at Guildhall to the mayor, aldermen and a great multitude of citizens, enlarging upon the royal title of the Duke of Gloucester, exciting the people who whispered amongst themselves 'like a swarm of bees'.

24–25 June: Pontefract

All those arrested by Richard were brought to trial at Pontefract before Henry, Earl of Northumberland. Found guilty, Lord Rivers, Richard Grey and Sir Thomas Vaughan were beheaded, the executions superintended by Sir Richard Ratcliffe. The night before Earl Rivers wrote, 'Somewhat musing and more mourning in remembering, the unsteadfastness this world being...' and made Richard an executor of his will.

26 June: King

At Baynard's Castle, a delegation came to Richard and petitioned him to take the crown of England. After a moment's reflection he assented. A great shout of 'King Richard' went up through the streets of London. Riding in state to Westminster Hall, he was led to the royal throne, the Duke of Suffolk on his right and Lord Howard on his left. Standing, he gave a speech in which he promised to observe 'fairness and equity in justice' for all his subjects. Parliament gave unanimous consent to his title to the throne and he was proclaimed King Richard III. Many welcome his coronation as he is an able administrator and soldier, though others say the matter be 'kings' games – as it were stage plays – in which poor men be but lookers-on' and that 'they that wise be meddle not' lest they 'disorder the play and do themselves no good'.

Leaving Westminster, King Richard rode to St Paul's through cheering crowds and was welcomed with procession into the cathedral, receiving the acclamation of all there assembled.

Richard III

1483–1485

Loyaulte me lie was Richard's motto. 'Loyalty binds me.' Betrayal cut him to the quick, perhaps a consequence of the betrayal by Warwick, his childhood tutor. Richard inspired great loyalty in those who knew him. He lived up to his motto until the death of Edward IV, completely loyal to his king and brother.

Aha, comes the cry, why did that much-vaunted loyalty not extend to his son? Consider, perhaps, if Edward IV had actually married bigamously. Under canon law the children would be illegitimate, which would have debarred them from the throne. The council of lords who debated the issue all knew of his brother's womanising ways. What to make of Elizabeth Wydville's silence? Why did the council accept the boys' bastardy? But of course the council was terrorised by Richard's soldiers, those soldiers who arrived days after he had accepted the crown; the council must have been quaking in their boots. And as king, he was still bound by loyalty – to his realm.

No one ever called Richard dishonest. His military skill was undisputed and his enemies called him a gallant knight. He was intelligent: the Archbishop of St Andrews said that within his frame was a great mind of 'such remarkable powers'. He genuinely believed in impartial justice, even punishing one of his own retainers. John Rous said that while he was king he 'ruled his subjects punishing offenders especially extortioners and oppressors of his commons'. This reputation clearly survived: in 1525, when Cardinal Wolsey berated London citizens for refusing to pay an extortionate tax by quoting a statute made by a 'usurping and murderous Richard', they replied, 'Yet in his time were many good acts made.'

In his short parliament of 1484, Richard reformed specific legal issues: all land sales were published and it became punishable to conceal from a purchaser land that belonged to someone else; every Justice of the Peace had authority to grant bail to those suspected of felony and their goods were prevented from being seized before they were found guilty; jurors had to be of good name and reputation, living in the county where they were elected, and anyone who elected a juror contrary to this was fined 40s per person. He arranged for all laws and statutes to be translated from French into English and instituted a court, which later became the Court of Requests, to which poor people who could not afford legal representation could apply for their grievances to be heard. In the north he had made himself personally accessible.

His lasting legacy is the creation of the College of Arms, by which heralds had access to the mansion of Coldharbour, where they could lodge, live and commune together with a place to keep their writings and rolls.

As for the 'princes in the Tower', it is anyone's guess, but many who knew Richard adamantly believed they had been 'conveyed secretly away'. The Tower being on the River Thames, a party could easily have slipped into the night sailing from Tower Wharf to Gravesend and thence to Flanders. Both Richard and John, Duke of Norfolk owned ships.

Richard had an extensive library that seemed to reflect a fascination with history and chivalry. He owned Monmouth's history of English kings, Chaucer's tales, Lydgate's Siege of Troy, the Chronicles of St Denis and Wycliffe's New Testament. A younger Richard enjoyed reading romance and moral tales. In his Latin book of hours he added prayers of his own; there is one he added after he was king, perhaps after the death of his beloved wife and son, wherein he asked Jesus to deign to 'free your servant King Richard, from every tribulation, sorrow and trouble in which I am placed'.

28 June 1483: Creations

Lord John Howard was created Duke of Norfolk and Earl Marshal and Lord Admiral of England. His son, Thomas, was granted the earldom of Surrey. William, Lord Berkeley was created Earl of Nottingham and Francis Lovell made Viscount Lovell and the king's chamberlain.

28 June 1483: Indenture

In the order for clothes and banners to be ready by 3 July that King Richard ordered from Piers Curteys, he included for one of Edward's daughters, Lady Bridget, use of two long pillows of fustian stuffed with down and two pillows of Holland cloth; for the queen sheets of Brussels-cloth and two folding chairs, and to have of especial gift of the king four yards of purple cloth-of-gold, 20 yards of purple cloth-of-gold with garters and seven yards of purple velvet. With it was a list of apparel for Lord Edward, son of the late King Edward IV: five long gowns, one of crimson lined with green damask, two of purple velvet lined with russet satin, two blue velvet lined with black satin and a demi-gown of the same; two short gowns, one crimson lined with black velvet and the other in purple velvet lined with green damask; two black satin doublets, a black stomacher and a bonnet of purple velvet; nine blue velvet harnesses, one of purple and blue silk; stirrup leathers covered in black velvet; hats, gloves, sheets, spurs, seven pairs of Spanish leather shoes; and, for each of his seven henchmen, green gowns, black damask doublets and hoods, bonnets, hats, hose and points, shoes, slips, boots and spurs.

4–6 July 1483: Coronation

King Richard and Queen Anne came to the Tower by water where that night on 4 July the king created seventeen Knights of the Bath, among them Edmund de la Pole, the Duke of Suffolk's son; George Grey, the Earl of Kent's son; William, the Lord Zouche's son; and Thomas, son of Sir William Boleyn.

Leaving the Tower for Westminster the next day and riding through great crowds, the king wore a blue cloth-of-gold doublet decorated with nets and pineapples with a long riding gown of ermined purple velvet. He resembles his father in face and height, with brown hair and blue eyes. 'Slight of build', he has 'uneven shoulders', the left slightly lower than the right.

The Duke of Buckingham followed, his blue velvet trapper embroidered with golden burning carts, carried by footmen to stop it sweeping the ground; then came the dukes of Norfolk and Suffolk, earls, lords and knights.

The queen, a month past her twenty-seventh birthday, travelled in a white damask litter with gold silk ribbons lifting into the breeze. Her kirtle was white decorated with silver rings under a white mantle with white silk lace, gold ribbons and buttons. Her gentlemen ushers rode before her in crimson damask, and her ladies after in crimson, riding or in chariots.

Trumpets sounded as the king and queen entered the Great Hall. Heralds, the cross and clergy began the procession for the coronation. The Earl of Huntingdon bore the gilt spurs, the Earl of Bedford St Edward's staff. The Earl of Northumberland, bareheaded, bore

Curtana, while Thomas, Lord Stanley bore the mace. The sceptre was carried by the Duke of Suffolk, and his son, the king's nephew John, Earl of Lincoln, carried the ball and cross. The sword of estate was held by the Earl of Surrey while his father, the Duke of Norfolk, carried the crown between his hands.

Walking barefoot on the red carpet from the King's Bench to St Edward's Shrine under a royal canopy with tinkling silver bells, King Richard in robes of purple velvet entered the abbey, the bishops of Bath and Durham walking on each side of him, his train carried by the Duke of Buckingham.

Then came Queen Anne under her own canopy, preceded by earls and barons. Like the king, her robe, surcoat and kirtle made of purple velvet, the kirtle decorated with annulets of silver, and a long-trained mantle with a lace of silk and gold with buttons and tassels was carried by Margaret Beaufort, Countess of Richmond, now married to Lord Stanley. Then followed noble ladies and gentlewomen. The royal pair came to their seats of estate.

After Masses, they both moved to the high altar where they were divested of their robes and anointed by Cardinal Archbishop Bourchier. Ascending to their thrones, they were crowned and given their sceptres, then the orb was given to the king and the rod and dove to the queen. Afterwards, they descended to the high altar where one host was divided between them. They offered at the shrine of St Edward, where King Richard left St Edward's crown and put on his own, before they returned to Westminster Hall and their own chambers while the Duke of Norfolk came into the hall, his horse trapped to the ground in cloth of gold, and, as high marshal, emptied the room.

About four in the afternoon the king and queen entered the hall, dressed in fresh robes of crimson velvet embroidered with gold. For the banquet, the queen was served on silver dishes and the king on gold, and among the dainty delicacies were his favourites peacock and swan. Other dishes included carp, pike, and wildfowl.

12 July 1483: Gifts
Twenty-four citizens of York rode to Middleham Castle to present ten-year-old Prince Edward with a gift of pain-main, two barrels of wine (one red, one white), six cygnets, six herons and two dozen rabbits.

29 July 1483: Oxford
Just before leaving Minster Lovell, news came to King Richard that about fifty Londoners had attempted to abduct Lords Edward and

Richard from the Tower. The enterprise being unsupported, the ringleaders were soon rounded up; four of them faced execution. Since leaving Windsor on progress the king had left John, Duke of Norfolk and Cardinal Bourchier in charge.

The two boys have been seen several times shooting and playing in the Tower Garden, but for now they are ordered 'withdrawn into the inner apartments of the Tower proper' with specially appointed custodians.

At Oxford University, the king was welcomed by Bishop Waynflete and conducted around the colleges where he listened to learned disputations and gave gifts to scholars who excelled.

August 1483: Summer Progress

Taking leave of the Duke of Buckingham at Gloucester intent on his own affairs, King Richard arrived at Tewkesbury on 4 August, and then travelled via Worcester to Warwick, arriving on 8 August. There Queen Anne joined him, travelling from Windsor and bringing with her the Spanish ambassador. Queen Isabella, in her letter to the king, wrote that the king's brother had been most unkind in his 'refusing of her and taking to wife a widow of England' but now Edward was dead and Louis had broken his treaty she was desirous of an alliance with England, and so proposed a marriage between Prince Edward and one of her daughters.

Moving via Coventry and Leicester, they reached Nottingham on 20 August and, travelling through Doncaster, reached Pontefract on 23 August where Prince Edward awaited them, having come from Middleham to enjoy 'family time' for a few days before going to York. They gave the prince a black satin-covered primer, a psalter and a bridle bit.

In every place the king and queen are received with pageants, and the king has sat with his lords and judges at every place to determine 'complaints of poor people with due punishment of offenders against his laws'.

29 August–21 September 1483: York Celebration

At Breckles Mills, the Mayor of York and his aldermen in scarlet and bridgemasters in red waited on horseback to welcome King Richard and Queen Anne. The crafts in blue waited on foot to give their own welcome at St James' Church without Micklegate Bar. The royal party travelled through crowded streets hung with arras and tapestries sufficient to impress southern lords. Riding with the king were seven of his henchmen dressed in green and crimson, captained by Sir James Tyrell, master of horse.

King Richard, within three days, sent to his wardrober to bring him his purple and tawny doublets with matching stomachers; two short green velvet-lined crimson cloth-of-gold gowns, one with tassels, the other with nets; a violet cloak and cape lined with black velvet; and a gown of green velvet lined with tawny satin.

On 7 September, Richard and Anne were entertained to the York 'Creed Play' staged by citizens in the Common Hall. The following day, as promised by King Richard, the city was honoured with a wondrous sight: the clergy, all richly vested, walked in procession around the city. After them walked King Richard and Queen Anne in royal robes, both crowned and holding sceptres; on the queen's left, Prince Edward, with a demi-crown, was holding his mother's hand. They entered York Minster to the sound of cheers without and within. Hundreds of pennons were set up, forty trumpeters were present and five heralds carried the banners of Our Lady, the Trinity and saints George, Edward and Cuthbert.

Prince Edward, first knighted by his father, was given the golden wand, wreath and kiss that created him Prince of Wales. King Richard also knighted his bastard son, twelve-year-old John, George's son Edward of Warwick and the Spanish ambassador, Galfridus de Sasiola, keen to tell all that King Richard had personally placed a gold collar about his neck and struck him thrice with a sword on the shoulder.

Thomas Langton, Bishop of St David's, disclosed that Richard contented the people wherever he went, for he had relieved and helped many a poor man during his progress; he had, he said, never liked a prince so well, and God had sent him 'to us for the weal of us all'.

8–31 October 1483: Rebellion

An uprising was fostered in Kent with the stated aim of marching on London and reinstating Edward V under their leader the Duke of Buckingham. John, Duke of Norfolk moved swiftly by blocking the Thames Estuary. London secured, he began to contain the rising. Richard received news of events at Lincoln on 12 October and that day he wrote to Chancellor Russell saying he was sorry to hear he was ill but could he be sent the Great Seal, adding in his own hand, 'We would most gladly you came yourself', and calling the Duke of Buckingham 'the most untrue creature living'.

As details were revealed it transpired that separate forces were to have assembled on 18 October at Maidstone, Rochester, Gravesend and Guildford under Sir John Guildford, Sir Giles Daubeney and

Sir John Cheyne; at Newbury and Salisbury men were to muster under Lionel Wydville, Bishop of Salisbury, while Peter Courtenay, Bishop of Exeter, with his brother Edward, would raise men in Devon. Henry Tudor was to land with 3,500 Breton soldiers and join forces with Buckingham, who was bringing his tenants from Wales and was busy circulating rumours that the sons of King Edward had died 'a violent death but it was uncertain how'.

On 17 October a storm of unusual violence broke over the whole of the west of England. Heavy rains swelled rivers, which overflowed, sweeping away houses, corn and cattle. Two hundred people were drowned in or about Bristol, shipping was damaged and children in cradles were seen floating in the fields in 'the Great Water'. The same storm drove off most of Henry's vessels. He approached near Poole the next day with two ships but found the coast well guarded. He then stood off Plymouth. People in arms lined the shore but something made him suspect they were Richard's and not Buckingham's men, and so he hoisted sail.

The Duke of Buckingham had hoped to cross the Severn at Gloucester, but with the bridges broken by Humphrey Stafford it was impossible to cross the swelling river. Richard moved rapidly westward at the head of a considerable army. The duke's reluctant forces melted away and he disguised himself and escaped.

2 November 1483: Beheading

At Salisbury, the Duke of Buckingham was beheaded in the marketplace near the Bull's Head Inn. He had been found hiding in the cottage of a poor man. His presence was revealed by the greater quantity of provisions carried there. King Richard refused to see him, especially after he saw a copy of the letter the duke had written in September to Henry to come with a great fleet and destroy him. Margaret Beaufort has been stripped of all her titles and estates for committing high treason and left under house arrest in charge of her husband.

16 December 1483: York Council

John Key, cordwainer, was accused before the Mayor of York of being a horse thief during his journey with King Richard to Salisbury. His fellow soldiers say he took the steed honestly, for it belonged to the traitor John Cheyne, meaning the horse was equally a traitor.

1 March 1484: Promise

At the request of Elizabeth Wydville, King Richard personally promised in front of the mayor and aldermen and all his lords that he would pay an annual pension of 700 marks to her for her natural life and he would give dowries in lands and tenements to the annual value of 200 marks for her daughters and find them fitting husbands as his kinswomen.

9 April 1484: Death
Prince Edward died suddenly. The news was brought to Nottingham Castle and 'you might have seen his father and mother in a state almost bordering on madness, by reason of their sudden grief'.

8 June 1484: Order
An order for crimson, blue and tawny pieces of cloth of gold, crimson and blue velvet, crimson and black satin cloth was sent from Pontefract by King Richard for new clothes for Edward of Warwick and his sister Margaret, along with Lady Katherine, his fourteen-year-old natural daughter, who is soon to marry William Herbert, Earl of Huntingdon.

1 July 1484: Truce
King Richard and Francis, Duke of Brittany have come to accord; a truce has been granted until 24 April.

23 July 1484: Ordnance
The council of the north, now part of the royal council, is headed by Lords Lincoln, Warwick and Morley. Ordnances by the king are, firstly, hours of God's service; diet; going to bed and rising; and shutting of gates at reasonable times and hours convenient. Secondly, Lords Lincoln and Morley are to be at one breakfast; the children together at one breakfast; such as be present of the council at one breakfast; also that the household go to dinner at farthest by 11 a.m. on flesh day. Thirdly, the treasurer is to pay Lord Lincoln's costs when he rides to council sessions or meetings; other ridings, hunts and sports are at his own cost and charge. Measures of bread, wine and ale must be measurable and convenient. All letters and judgements to resolve land disputes and punish lawbreakers should be issued on the king's behalf, in his name.

12 August 1484: Reinterment
The body of Henry VI was, by King Richard's order, removed from Chertsey Abbey and interred, with the greatest solemnity, in St George's Chapel at Windsor on the south side of the high altar

opposite Edward IV. The vault was richly decorated with the arms of England and France, badges and royal beasts.

18 September 1484: Treaty

At Nottingham, a treaty of peace between England and Scotland was signed, to be ratified by the marriage of Anne de la Pole, the king's niece, with Prince James, eldest son of the Scots king.

1 December 1484: Traitors

After it was revealed that William Collingbourne had corresponded with Henry Tudor to encourage him to land at Poole with as many men as he could raise, suggesting also that Henry send an envoy to the French king to tell him Richard intended to war on him, he was found guilty of high treason and hanged on Tower Hill. Collingbourne was the author of the disparaging – but catchy – lampoon posted on the doors of St Paul's last July: 'The Cat, the Rat and Lovell our Dog, Rule all England under a Hog.'

News has come that since mid-October Henry Tudor escaped Brittany and now lodges in France and, backed by Charles VIII, has begun signing his documents as *Henricus Rex* and claiming he is rightful King of England.

16 March 1485: Death

Queen Anne died today during the solar eclipse. She has been ill for some weeks, some say of consumption. She fell ill shortly after Christmas and much has been made of Queen Anne and Lady Elysabeth appearing in similarly coloured dresses while they themselves look alike. The queen was 'seemly, amiable and beauteous' and 'full gracious'. The king's physicians forbade him to visit her while she was ill in case he caught the same illness.

22 March 1485: Envoys

Envoys have been sent by King Richard to Portugal to negotiate a marriage between Elysabeth of York and Prince Manuel. Now the king is a widower, they have been additionally instructed to negotiate a marriage for himself with Princess Joanna.

25 March 1485: Funeral

Queen Anne was buried at Westminster Abbey on the south side of the high altar. The grief-stricken king wept openly during the ceremony.

30 March 1485: Declaration
Obviously sorrowing and angry, King Richard publicly declared today at the Hospital of St John that he was grieving for his wife, Anne, and neither in thought nor mind intended marrying Elysabeth; that he was sorry and heavy of heart as any could man could be for the loss of his wife, and that anyone who continued to repeat slander about him and Elysabeth would be arrested. His niece has been sent to Sheriff Hutton. King Richard intends to stay with his mother at Berkhamsted.

9 June 1485: Headquarters
Arriving today, King Richard has decided to make Nottingham his headquarters for its central location, which facilitates easy movement.

11 August 1485: Landing
News arrived today at Nottingham that Henry Tudor and his thousand mercenaries came in seven ships and landed at Milford Haven four days ago and are being joined by the Welsh. The Tudor is flying the red dragon of Cadwaladr. The king has sent out a muster for troops to come to Nottingham by 18 August.

16 August 1485: Pestilence
At the York council only three aldermen were present to hear the muster. Since spring and all through summer, a plague has broken out in the city and killed many; in London there has been 'a great death' called the 'sweating sickness'.

22 August 1485: Bosworth Field
At daybreak the two forces faced each other, and the fighting began. Henry's knights made straight for King Richard. The Earl of Oxford, commanding Henry's army, drew up his forces opposite John, Duke of Norfolk who began to push them back for a while, but when Norfolk was killed King Richard risked all on a gamble, charging at Henry in a bid to personally kill his rival. He led a mounted force, riding his white warhorse, White Surrey, directly towards Henry Tudor, unhorsing champion jouster Sir John Cheyne and killing Henry's standard bearer, the giant Sir William Brandon. Then he was a few yards away, then a sword's stroke away when Sir William Stanley poured in his troops to overpower Richard's bodyguard while his brother, Henry's stepfather, watched. Richard was unhorsed. Refusing a horse and declining to retreat, he said he would win the battle as king or die as one.

Before he could strike Henry, Stanley's soldiers reached Richard and he fought on in the thickest press of his enemies. He received a cut to his lower jaw. Multiple blows to his head brought him to his knees, a halberd cut into his skull and a sword sliced into the back of his head. The king was killed in his first ever military defeat.

His corpse was stripped and mutilated, 'nothing left about him, not so much as a cloth to cover his privy members'. His pursuivant of arms, Blanc Sanglier (White Boar), placed his naked body on a horse, 'head and arms hanging on one side, legs on the other side, all besprinkled with mire and blood' and he was transported thus to Greyfriars in Leicester and buried with neither ceremony nor reverence, lacking clothes, shroud or coffin.

23 August 1485: Epitaph

John Sponer brought back the sorrowful tidings. York council recorded that King Richard, 'late mercifully reigning upon us was through great treason … piteously slain and murdered to the great heaviness of this city'.

Bibliography

Abrahams, B. L., *The Expulsion of the Jews from England in 1290* (Oxford: B. H. Blackwell, 1895)

Appleby, John T., *John King of England* (New York: Alfred A Knopf, 1959)

Archer, T. A., *The Crusade of Richard I 1189–1192* (London: David Nutt, 1900)

Ashley, W. J., *Edward III and His Wars 1327–1360* (London: David Nutt, 1887)

Barker, Juliet, *Agincourt: Henry V and the Battle that Made England* (New York: Little, Brown and Company, 2006)

Bateson, Mary, *Medieval England* (New York: G P Putnam's Sons, 1851)

Beames, John, *A Translation of Glanville* (Washington: John Byrne & Co, 1900)

Beltz, George Frederick, *Memorials of the Most Noble Order of the Garter* (London: William Pickering, 1841)

Blaauw, William Henry, *The Barons' War* (London: Bell & Daldy, 1871)

Bohn, Henry G., *Chronicles of the Crusades being Contemporary Narratives of the Crusade of Richard Coeur de Lion by Richard of Devizes and Geoffrey de Vinsauf and of the Crusade of St Louis by Lord John de Joinville* (London: Henry G Bohn, 1848)

Brayley, Edward Wedlake and John Britton, *The History of the Ancient Palace and late Houses of Parliament at Westminster* (London: John Weale, 1836)

Breverton, Terry, *Richard III: The King in the Car Park* (Stroud: Amberley Publishing, 2015)

Brie, Friedrich W. D., *The Brut or The Chronicles of England* (London: Kegan Paul, Trench, Trubner & Co Ltd., 1906 & 1908)

British Museum, *A Chronicle of London from 1089 to 1483 from MSS in the British Museum* (London: Longman, Rees, Orme, Brown and Green, 1827)

Brookes, John, *Manners and Customs of the English Nation* (London: James Blackwood, 1800)

Buckledee, John, *http://medievaldunstable.org.uk/tournaments.html* (accessed 25 April 2021)

Carson, Annette, *Richard III: The Maligned King* (Stroud: The History Press, 2009)

Chambers, R., *The Book of Days* (London & Edinburgh: W & R Chambers, 1864)

Chaplais, Pierre, *Piers Gaveston: Edward II's Adoptive Brother* (Oxford: University Press, 1994)

Clayton, Joseph, *St Hugh of Lincoln* (London: Burns Oates & Washbourne Ltd, 1931)

Cleaveland, E., *A genealogical History of the Noble and Illustrious Family of Courtenay* (Edward Farley, 1735)

Clephan, R. Coltman, *The Tournament: Its Periods and Phases* (London: Methuen & Co. Ltd., 1910)

Cockerill, Sara, *Eleanor of Castile: The Shadow Queen* (Stroud: Amberley Publishing, 2016)

Cowper, Marcus, *Henry V* (Oxford: Osprey Publishing, 2010)

Creighton, Charles, *A History of Epidemics in Britain* (Cambridge: University Press, 1891)

Cunningham, Sean, *Richard III: A royal enigma* (London: The National Archives, 2003)

Davies, Rev. John Silvester (ed), *An English Chronicle of the Reigns of Richard II, Henry IV, Henry V and Henry VI written before the year 1471* (London: Camden Society, 1856)

Davies, Robert, *Extracts from the Municipal Records of the City of York* (London: J. B. Nichols and Son, 1843)

Devon, Frederick, *Issues of the Exchequer* (London: John Murray, 1837)

Dodd, Gwilym and Anthony Musson (ed), *The Reign of Edward II: New Perspectives* (York: York Medieval Press, 2006)

Dodge, Walter Philps, *Piers Gaveston* (London: T. Fisher Unwin, 1899)

Duncan, Jonathan, *The Dukes of Normandy* (London: Joseph Rickerby, 1839)

Eyton, Rev. R.W., Court, *Household and Itinerary of King Henry II* (London: Taylor & Co, 1878)

Fabyan's *Chronicle* (London: William Rastell, 1533)

Fenn, John, *Original Letters Written During the Reigns of Henry VI Edward IV and Richard III* (London: 1787)

Forester, Thomas (ed), *The Chronicle of Henry of Huntingdon* (London: Henry G. Bohn, 1853)

Forester, Thomas (ed), *The Chronicle of Florence of Worcester* (London: Henry G. Bohn, 1854)

Forester, Thomas (ed), *The Ecclesiastical History of England and Normandy by Ordericus Vitalis, Vol III* (London: Henry G. Bohn, 1854)

Froude, James Anthony, *Life and Times of Thomas Becket* (New York: Scribner, Armstrong & Co, 1878)

Gairdner, James, *History of the Life and Reign of Richard the Third* (Cambridge: University Press, 1898)

Gairdner, James (ed), *The Paston Letters* (London: Chatto & Windus, 1904)

Given-Wilson, Paul Brand, Seymour Phillips, Mark Ormrod, Geoffrey Martin, Anne Curry and Rosemary Horrox (eds), *Parliament Rolls of Medieval* England (Woodbridge, 2005) (accessed at British History Online, www.british-history.ac.uk)

Giles, J. A., (ed), *The Chronicle of Richard of Devizes* (London: James Bohn, 1841)

Giles, J. A., *The Life and Letters of Thomas à Becket* (London: Whittaker & Co, 1846)

Giles, J. A., *William of Malmesbury's Chronicle* (London: Henry G. Bohn, 1847)

Giles, J. A., (ed), *Roger of Wendover's Flowers of History in two Volumes* (London: Henry G Bohn, 1849)

Giles, J. A., *Matthew Paris's English History from the year 1235 to 1273 Volumes I-III* (London: Henry G Bohn, 1852–1854)

Giles, J. A., (ed), *The Anglo-Saxon Chronicle* (London: G Bel & Sons Ltd, 1914)

Gordon, Donna Mildred, *A translation of the Letters and Charters of Eleanor of Aquitaine* (USA: University of Alberta, 1970)

Green, Mary Anne Everett, *Lives of the Princesses of England Vol II* (London: Henry Colburn, 1850)

Halliwell, James Orchard, (ed), *A Chronicle of the First Thirteen Years of the Reign of King Edward the Fourth by John Warkworth* (London: Camden Society, 1839)

Halliwell, James Orchard, (ed), *Letters of the Kings of England* (London: Henry Colbourn, 1846)

Halstead, Caroline A., *Richard III as Duke of Gloucester and King of England* (Philadelphia: Carey and Hart, 1844)

Hamilton, J. S., *The Plantagenets: History of a Dynasty* (London: Continuum, 2010)

Hardy, Thomas Duffus, *A Description of the Close Rolls in the Tower of London* (London: Privately Printed, 1833)

Hardy, Thomas Duffus, *A Description of the Patent Rolls in the Tower of London* (London: The Commissioners on the Public Records of the Kingdom, 1835)

Hardy, Thomas Duffus, *Rymer's Foedera 1066–1377* (London: Longmans, Green & Co, 1869)

Hardy, Thomas Duffus, *Rotuli Litterarum Patentium* Vol I (London: The Commissioners of the Public Records of the Kingdom, 1835)

Hardy, Sir William and Edward L.C.P. Hardy, *A Collection of the Chronicles and Ancient Histories of Great Britain, now Called England by John de Wavrin 1399 to 1422* (London: HMSO, 1887)

Harrod, Henry, *Queen Elizabeth Woodville's Visit to Norwich in 1469 in Norfolk Archaeology Volume 5* (Norwich: Cundall, Miller & Leavis, 1859)

Hereford, George B., *Battles of English History* (London: Methuen & Co, 1896)

Holbach, Maude M, *In the Footsteps of Richard Coeur de Lion* (Boston: Little, Brown & Co, 1912)

Hookham, Mary Anne, *The Life and Times of Margaret of Anjou* (London: Tinsley Brothers, 1872)

Horrox, Rosemary and P W Hammond (ed) *British Library Harleian Manuscript 433* (Gloucester: Alan Sutton Publishing Ltd for Richard III Society, 1979–1982)

Hurry, Jamieson B., *The Trial by Combat of Henry de Essex and Robert de Montfort at Reading Abbey* (London: Elliot Stock, 1919)

Hutton, William Holden, *Philip Augustus* (London: Macmillan & Co Ltd, 1896)

Hutton, Rev. W. H., *Simon de Montfort and his cause 1251–1266* (London: David Nutt, 1888)

Hutton, Rev. W. H., *St. Thomas of Canterbury. An account of his life and fame from the Contemporary Biographers and other Chroniclers* (London: David Nutt, 1899)

James, M. R., *Henry the Sixth: A Repint of John Blacman's Memoir* (Cambridge: University Press, 1919)

Jarman, Thomas Leckie, *William Marshal First Earl of Pembroke* (Oxford: Basil Blackwell, 1930)

Johnes, Thomas, *Chronicles of England, France, Spain and the Adjoining Countries by Sir John Froissart in Two Volumes* (London: Henry G. Bohn, 1849; George Routledge & Sons, 1868)

Lane-Poole, Stanley, *Saladin* (London and New York: G P Putnam's Sons, 1898)

Lewis, Suzanne, *The Art of Matthew Paris in the Chronica Majora* (USA: University of California Press, 1987)

Magnusson, Eirikr, (ed), *A Life of Archbishop Thomas Becket, Vol II* (London: Longmans & Co, 1883)

McGlynn, Sean, *Blood Cries Afar* (Spellmount/The History Press, 2013)

Morris, John E., *Bannockburn* (Cambridge: University Press, 1914)

Morris, Marc, *A Great and Terrible King: Edward I* (London: Windmill Books, 2009)

Mortimer, Ian, *The Fears of Henry IV: The Life of England's Self-made King* (London: Vintage, 2008)

Mortimer, Ian, *The Perfect King: the Life of Edward III, Father of the English Nation* (London: Vintage Books, 2008)

Murray Smith, Mrs A., *The Roll-Call of Westminster Abbey* (London: Smith, Elder & Co, 1903)

Nichols, J., *A Collection of all the Wills now known to be Extant of the Kings and Queens of England* (London: 1780)

Nichols, J. B., *London Pageants* (London: 1837)

Norgate, Kate, *England under the Angevin Kings* (London: Macmillan & Co, 1887)

Olson Clair C. and Martin M. Crow (eds), *Chaucer's World compiled by Edith Rickert* (New York: Columbia University Press, 1948)

Pegge, Samuel, *The Forme of Cury, A Roll of Ancient English Cookery* (London: J. Nichols, 1780)

Pirie-Gordon, C.H.C., *Innocent the Great: An Essay on his Life and Times* (London: Longmans, Green and Co., 1907)

Preest, David, *The Chronica Majora of Thomas Walsingham 1376–1422* (Woodbridge: Boydell Press, 2005)

Radford, Lewis B., *Thomas of London before his Consecration* (Cambridge University Press, 1894)

Ramsay, Sir James H., *The Angevin Empire or the Three Reigns of Henry II, Richard I and John* (Oxford: Humphrey Milford, 1903)

Ridgeway, Rev. James, *Westminster Abbey, its History, Pageants, and Royal Memorials* (London: Bell and Daldy, 1865)

Riley, Henry T., *The Annals of Roger de Hoveden* (London: H G Bohn, 1853)

Riley, Henry Thomas (ed), *Memorials of London and London Life 1276–1419* (London: Longmans, Green & Co, 1868)

Salzmann L. F., *Medieval Byways* (London: Constable & Co Ltd, 1913)

Scofield, Cora L., *The Life and Reign of Edward the Fourth* (London: Longmans, Green & Co, 1923)

Sharp, Reginald R., (ed) *Calendar of Letter-Books of the City of London* (London: Corporation of London, 1912)

Shirley, Rev. Walter Waddington, *Royal and other Historical Letters Illustrative of the Reign of Henry III 1216 to 1235* (London: Longman, Green, Longman and Roberts, 1862)

Shirley, Rev. Walter Waddington, *Royal and other Historical Letters Illustrative of the Reign of Henry III 1236 to 1272* (London: Longmans, Green, Reader and Dyer, 1866)

Short, Ian, *King John: a Flemish Perspective by the Anonyme de Bethune*, 2019 (translated from Michel, Francisque, *Histoire des ducs de Normandie et des Rois d'Angleterre (Anonyme de Bethune*, Paris: 1840), sourced on www.anglo-norman-texts.net on 18 March 2021

Sinclair, William MacDonald, *Memorials of St Paul's Cathedral* (London: Chapman & Hall Ltd, 1913)

Stanley, Arthur P., *Historical Memorials of Canterbury* (London: John Murray, 1869)

Stevenson, Rev. Joseph, *The Church Historians of England Vol III – Part I containing the History of the Kings of England and of his own times by William of Malmesbury* (London: Seeleys, 1854)

Stevenson, Rev. Joseph, *The Church Historians of England Vol IV part I containing The Chronicles of John and Richard of Hexham; The Chronicle of Holyrood; The Chronicle of Melrose etc. and part II containing the History of William of Newburgh and the Chronicles of Robert de Monte* (London: Seeleys, 1856)

Stevenson, Rev. Joseph, *The Church Historians of England Vol 5 part I containing History of King Henry the First; the Acts of Stephen etc.; Giraldus Cambrensis concerning the Instruction of Princes; Richard of Devizes; The History of the Archbishops of Canterbury by Gervase, Monk of Canterbury; Robert of Gloucester's Chronicle; The Chronicle of the Isle of Man* (London: Seeleys, 1858)

Sutton, Anne, F and Livia Visser-Fuchs with Hannes Kleineke *The Children in the Care of Richard III: New References. A Lawsuit between Peter Courteys, Keeper of Richard III's Great Wardrobe and Thomas Lynom, Solicitor of Richard III, 1495–1501* from the Ricardian, Volume XXIV (2014)

Taylor, Edgar, (ed), *Master Wace His Chronicle of the Norman Conquest from the Roman de Rou* (London: William Pickering, 1837)

The Society of Antiquaries of London, *Archaeologia: or, Miscellaneous Tracts relating to Antiquity, The Third Edition* (London: 1804)

The Antiquarian Repertory: *A Miscellany Volume II* (London: 1779)

The Chronicles of The White Rose of York: A series of Historical Fragments relating to the reign of King Edward the Fourth (London: James Bohn, 1845)

Thompson, Sir Edward Maunde (Trans), *Chronicon Adae de Usk 1377–1421* (London: Henry Frowde, 1904)

Thoms, William J., *The Book of the Court* (London: Richard Bentley, 1838)

Vincent, N., *King John's Diary & Itinerary* (The Magna Carta Project, http://magnacarta.cmp.uea.ac.uk)

Wallerstein, Ruth, *King John in Fact and Fiction* (USA: University of Pennsylvania, 1905)

Warner, Kathryn, http://edwardthesecond.blogspot.com/2019/02/the-belongings-of-madame-yzabel-of.html (accessed 26 March 2021)

White, Robert, *A History of the Battle of Bannockburn* (Edinburgh: Edmonston and Douglas, 1871)

Wickham, Leopold G., *English Coronation Records* (Westminster: Archibald Constable & Co Ltd, 1901)

Williams, Par Benjamin, *Chronicque de la Traison et Mort de Richart Deux Roy D'Engleterre* (London: 1846)

Woolley, Reginald Maxwell, *St Hugh of Lincoln* (London: Macmillan, 1927)

Wylie, James Hamilton, *The Reign of Henry the Fifth Volume I* (Cambridge: University Press, 1914)

Wylie, James Hamilton and William Templeton Waugh, *The Reign of Henry the Fifth* Volume III (Cambridge: University Press, 1929)

Yonge, C. D., *The Flowers of History* (London: Henry G. Bohn, 1853)

Ziepel C., *The Reign of Richard II and Comments upon an alliterative poem on the deposition of that monarch* (Berlin: J. Draeger, 1874)